STUDY GUIDE WITH SOLUTIONS
FOR USE WITH

FUNDAMENTAL
ACCOUNTING
PRINCIPLES

SIXTH CANADIAN EDITION

KERMIT D. LARSON
THE UNIVERSITY OF TEXAS AT AUSTIN

MICHAEL ZIN
UNIVERSITY OF WINDSOR

MORTON NELSON
WILFRID LAURIER UNIVERSITY

IRWIN
HOMEWOOD, IL 60430
BOSTON, MA 02116

Printed in the United States of America

ISBN 0–256–08305–3

3 4 5 6 7 8 9 0 VK 7 6 5 4 3 2 1

TO THE STUDENT

This booklet is designed to help you review the material covered in *Fundamental Accounting Principles,* 6th Canadian edition. You should understand that the booklet is not intended to substitute for your review of *Fundamental Accounting Principles.* Instead, the objectives of this booklet are as follows:

1. To remind you of important information that is explained in the text. For example, the topical outline of each chapter reminds you of important topics in the chapter. In reading the outline, you should ask yourself whether or not you understand sufficiently the listed topics. If not, you should return to the appropriate chapter in *Fundamental Accounting Principles* and read carefully the portions that explain the topics about which you are unclear.

2. To provide you with a quick means of testing your knowledge of the chapter. If you are unable to correctly answer the problems that follow the chapter outline, you should again return to the appropriate chapter in *Fundamental Accounting Principles* and review the sections about which you are unclear.

   Your best approach to the use of this booklet is as follows:

First, read the learning objectives and ask whether your understanding of the chapter seems adequate for you to accomplish the objectives.

Second, review the topical outline, taking time to think through (describing to yourself) the explanations that would be required to expand the outline. Return to *Fundamental Accounting Principles* to cover areas of weakness.

Third, answer the requirements of the problems that follow the topical outline. Then check your answers against the solutions that are provided after the problems.

Fourth, return to *Fundamental Accounting Principles* for further study of the portions of the chapter about which you made errors.

CONTENTS

1 Accounting, an Introduction to Its Concepts

After studying Chapter 1, you should be able to:

1. Describe the function of accounting and the nature and purpose of the information it provides.

2. List the main fields of accounting employment and the kinds of work carried on in each field.

3. Describe the information contained in the financial statements of a business and be able to prepare simple financial statements.

4. Briefly explain the accounting concepts and principles introduced in the chapter and describe the process by which generally accepted accounting principles are established.

5. Briefly explain the differences between a single proprietorship, a partnership, and a corporation, comparing the differing responsibilities of their owners for the debts of the business.

6. Recognize and be able to indicate the effects of transactions on the elements of an accounting equation.

7. Define or explain the words and phrases listed in the chapter Glossary.

Topical Outline

I. Accounting as a profession

   A. Accounting is a service activity. Its function is to provide quantitative information about economic entities.

   B. Provinces license public accountants.

II. The work of an accountant typically includes:

   A. Public accounting; the services of public accountants involve:

      1. Auditing—critical examination of an entity's accounting records and statements that is made for the purpose of determining whether the statements fairly reflect the entity's financial position and operating results, in accordance with generally accepted accounting principles.

      2. Management advisory services—the design, installation, and improvement of a client's accounting system, plus advice on financial planning, budgeting, forecasting, and inventory control.

      3. Tax services—the preparation of tax returns, with advice as to how transactions may be completed in such a way as to incur the smallest tax liability.

   B. Private accounting; the work of accountants employed by a single enterprise involves:

      1. General accounting—the recording of transactions, processing of the recorded data, and preparation of financial statements.

      2. Cost accounting—the determination and control of costs, and assessing the performance of managers who are responsible for costs.

      3. Budgeting—the process of developing formal plans for future business activities, which then serve as bases for evaluating actual accomplishments.

      4. Internal auditing—checking records and operating procedures for the purpose of making sure that established accounting procedures and management directives are being followed. Also includes evaluation of operating efficiency.

   C. Governmental accounting; a variety of accounting positions in governmental agencies.

III. Important accounting statements include:

   A. The income statement, which indicates whether a business earned a net income (a profit) by showing the:

      1. Revenues earned—an inflow of assets received in exchange for goods or services provided to customers as part of the major or central operations of the business.

      2. Expenses incurred—outflows or the using up of assets as a result of the major or central operations of a business.

      3. Net income (excess of revenues over expenses) or net loss (excess of expenses over revenues).

   B. The balance sheet—shows the financial position of a business on a specific date by listing the:

      1. Assets—probable future economic benefits obtained or controlled by a particular entity as a result of past transactions or events.

      2. Liabilities—probable future sacrifices of economic benefits arising from present obligations of a particular entity to transfer assets or to provide services to other entities in the future as a result of past transactions or events.

      3. Equity—the residual interest in the assets of an entity that remains after deducting its liabilities. Also called net assets.

   C. Statement of changes in owner's equity—discloses all changes in owner's equity during the period, including investments by the owner, withdrawals by the owner, and net income or net loss.

D. Statement of cash flows—discloses the inflows and outflows of cash during the period, classified in terms of cash flows from operations, cash flows from investing activities, and cash flows from financing activities.

IV. Generally accepted accounting principles—broad rules adopted by the accounting profession as guides in measuring, recording, and reporting the financial affairs and activities of a business.

    A. Sources of accounting principles

        1. The Accounting Standards Committee of the CICA.
        2. Financial Accounting Standards Board (FASB).
        3. International Accounting Standards Committee (IASC).
        4. Securities and Exchange Commission (SEC)—the dominant authority in the U.S. in establishing accounting principles.

    B. Important accounting principles and concepts

        1. Business entity concept—a business is a separate entity that is distinct from its owner or owners and from every other business.
        2. Cost principle—assets and services plus any resulting liabilities are to be recorded in the accounting records at cost, which is the cash or cash-equivalent amount of the consideration given in exchange for the purchased assets and services.
        3. Objectivity principle—the amounts used in recording transactions are to be based on verifiable evidence such as business transactions between independent parties.
        4. Continuing-concern concept—the assumption that a business will continue to operate and that the assets held for use in the business will not be sold.
        5. Stable-dollar concept—the idea that the purchasing power of the unit of measure used in accounting, the dollar, does not change.
        6. Realization principle—the inflow of assets associated with a revenue does not have to be in the form of cash; a revenue should be recorded as a revenue at the time, but not before, it is earned; and the amount of a revenue should be measured in terms of the cash plus cash-equivalent amount of other assets received.

V. Business organizations include three general types:

    A. Single proprietorship—a business owned by one individual. There are no legal requirements to be met in starting a single proprietorship business. They are the most numerous of all business concerns.
    B. Partnership—a business that is owned by two or more people but is not organized as a separate legal entity. A partner is personally responsible for all the debts of the partnership.
    C. Corporation—a business that is established under the laws of a province or the federal government as a separate entity. The owners of a corporation are called shareholders because their ownership of the corporation's equity is divided into units that are called shares of stock.

VI. Recording transactions

    A. Accounting equation (or balance sheet equation)

    Assets = Liabilities + Owner's Equity

    B. Double-entry system—every transaction recorded affects two or more items in the accounting equation, so that the equation remains in balance.

Problem I

The following statements are either true or false. Place a (T) in the parentheses before each true statement and an (F) before each false statement.

1. ( ) The phase of accounting that has to do with determining and controlling costs, and assessing the performance of managers who are responsible for costs is called auditing.

2. ( ) The dollar is used in recording and reporting accounting information because it is a stable unit of measure.

3. ( ) Land appraised at $40,000 and worth that much to its purchaser should be recorded at its worth ($40,000), even though it was purchased through hard bargaining for $35,000.

4. ( ) If a business is to be liquidated and its assets sold, the losses incurred in converting assets into cash must exceed the equity of the owner or owners before the creditors will incur any losses.

5. ( ) Net income + Owner's investments − Owner's withdrawals = The increase in owner's equity during the year.

Problem II

You are given several words, phrases or numbers to choose from in completing each of the following statements or in answering the following questions. In each case select the one that best completes the statement or answers the question and place its letter in the answer space provided.

_____ 1. Financial statement information about Company B is as follows:

December 31, 1989:
Assets $42,000
Liabilities 17,000
December 31, 1990:
Assets 47,000
Liabilities 14,800
During 1990:
Net income 18,000
Owner's investments .... ?
Owner's withdrawals 10,800
The amount of owner investments during 1990 is:

a. $ 7,200.
b. $14,400.
c. $25,000.
d. $ −0−.
e. Some other amount.

_____ 2. The term "management advisory services" describes:
a. the phase of public accounting dealing with the critical examination of an entity's accounting records and statements.
b. the phase of public accounting dealing with the design, installation, and improvement of a client's accounting system.
c. the phase of accounting dealing with the development of formal plans for future business activities, which serve as bases for evaluating actual accomplishments.
d. the phase of public accounting dealing with the preparation of tax returns and advice as to how transactions may be completed in such a way as to incur the smallest tax liability.
e. the phase of accounting dealing primarily with recording tansactions and preparing financial statements.

4

_____ 3. The cost principle:
   a. states that the inflow of assets associated with a revenue does not have to be in the form of cash; a revenue should be recorded as a revenue at the time, but not before, it is earned; and the amount of a revenue should be measured in terms of the cash plus cash-equivalent amount of other assets received.
   b. requires that wherever possible the amounts used in recording transactions be based on verifiable evidence such as business transactions between independent parties.
   c. states that all expenses incurred in earning a revenue be deducted from the revenue in determining net income.
   d. requires assets and services plus any resulting liabilities to be recorded in the accounting records at cost.
   e. is another name for the recognition principle.

_____ 4. The Accounting Standards Committee is a:
   a. professional association of accountants.
   b. committee of the Canadian Institute of Chartered Accountants responsible for formulating CICA Handbook recommendations.
   c. agency of the federal government that was established to administer the provisions of various securities and exchange laws.
   d. organization of persons interested in accounting; generally identified as the professional association of academic accountants.
   e. certification of an individual's professional level of competence in the field of internal auditing.

_____ 5. If on January 16, 1990, Mary Kay Company rendered services for a customer in exchange for $175 cash, what would be the effects on the accounting equation?
   a. Assets, $175 increase; Liabilities, no effect; Owner's Equity, $175 increase.
   b. Assets, no effect; Liabilities, $175 decrease; Owner's Equity, $175 increase.
   c. Assets, $175 increase; Liabilities, $175 increase; Owner's Equity, no effect.
   d. Assets, $175 increase; Liabilities, $175 decrease; Owner's Equity, $350 increase.
   e. There is no effect on the accounting equation because Mary Kay Company is a single proprietorship.

Problem III

Many of the important ideas and concepts discussed in Chapter 1 are reflected in the following list of key terms. Test your understanding of these terms by matching the appropriate definitions with the terms. Record the number identifying the most appropriate definition in the blank space next to each term.

_____ AAA	_____ Audit
_____ Accounting	_____ Balance sheet
_____ Accounting concept	_____ Balance sheet equation
_____ Accounting equation	_____ Bookkeeping
_____ Accounting Standards Committee	_____ Budgeting
_____ Accounts payable	_____ Business entity concept
_____ Accounts receivable	_____ Business transaction
_____ AICPA	_____ CA
_____ APB	_____ CGA
_____ Assets	_____ CMA

_____ Continuing-concern concept

_____ Controller

_____ Corporation

_____ Cost accounting

_____ Cost principle

_____ CPA

_____ Creditor

_____ Debtor

_____ Equity

_____ Expense

_____ FASB

_____ GAAP

_____ General accounting

_____ Generally accepted accounting principles

_____ Going-concern concept

_____ IASC

_____ Income statement

_____ Internal auditing

_____ Liabilities

_____ Management advisory services

_____ Net assets

_____ Net income

_____ Net loss

_____ Objectivity principle

_____ Partnership

_____ Realization principle

_____ Recognition principle

_____ Revenue

_____ SEC

_____ Shareholder

_____ Single proprietorship

_____ Stable-dollar concept

_____ Statement of cash flows

_____ Statement of changes in owner's equity

_____ Statement of financial position

_____ Stock

_____ Stockholders

_____ Tax services

1. A financial report showing the assets, liabilities, and equity of an enterprise on a specific date. Also called a statement of financial position.

2. The accounting rule that wherever possible the amounts used in recording transactions be based on verifiable evidence such as business transactions between independent parties.

3. American Institute of Certified Public Accountants, the professional association of certified public accountants in the United States.

4. A service activity that provides quantitative information about economic entities; the information is primarily financial in nature and is intended to be useful in making economic decisions.

5. The phase of public accounting dealing with the preparation of tax returns and with advice as to how transactions may be completed in such a way as to incur the smallest tax liability.

6. An inflow of assets (or decrease in liabilities) received in exchange for goods or services provided to customers as part of the major or central operations of the business.

7. A financial statement showing revenues earned by a business, the expenses incurred in earning the revenues, and the resulting net income or net loss.

8. Another name for the balance sheet equation.

9. A business that is established under the laws of a province or the federal government as a separate entity.

10. The accounting rule that requires assets and services plus any resulting liabilities to be recorded in the accounting records at cost, which is the cash or cash-equivalent amount of the consideration given in exchange for the purchased assets and services.

11. The residual interest in the assets of an entity that remains after deducting its liabilities.

12. Financial Accounting Standards Board, the seven-member board that currently has the authority to issue pronouncements of generally accepted accounting principles.

13. A business that is owned by two or more people and that is not organized as a separate legal entity.

14. Another name for the balance sheet.

15. Another name for the realization principle.

16. The use of a business's own accounting employees to check records and operating procedures for the purpose of making sure that established accounting procedures and management directives are being followed.

17. The excess of revenues over expenses.

18. The process of developing formal plans for future business activities, which then serve as bases for evaluating actual accomplishments.

19. The phase of accounting that has to do with determining and controlling costs, and assessing the performance of managers who are responsible for costs.

20. Another name for the continuing-concern concept.

21. The excess of expenses over revenues.

22. A person or organization that is obligated to pay a liability.

23. Outflows or the using up of assets (or incurrance of liabilities) as a result of the major or central operations of a business.

24. The owners of a corporation.

25. The idea that accounting reports should be based on the assumption that the purchasing power of the unit of measure used in accounting (the dollar) does not change.

26. The chief accounting officer of a large business.

27. Amounts owed to a business by its customers for goods or services sold to them on credit.

28. The accounting rule which states that the inflow of assets associated with a revenue does not have to be in the form of cash; a revenue should be recorded as a revenue at the time, but not before, it is earned; and the amount of a revenue should be measured in terms of the cash plus cash-equivalent amount of other assets received.

29. A completed exchange of economic consideration, for example, goods, services, money, or the right to collect money, between two or more parties.

30. Equity of a corporation that is divided into units or shares.

31. Broad rules adopted by the accounting profession as guides in measuring, recording, and reporting the financial affairs and activities of a business.

32. A critical examination of an entity's accounting records and statements that is made for the purpose of determining whether the statements fairly reflect the entity's financial position and operating results in accordance with generally accepted accounting principles.

33. A financial statement that discloses all changes in owner's equity during the period, including investments by the owner, withdrawals by the owner and net income or net loss.

34. The phase of public accounting dealing with the design, installation, and improvement of a

client's accounting system, plus advice on financial planning, budgeting, forecasting, and inventory control.

35. Securities and Exchange Commission, an agency of the U.S. federal government that was established to administer the provisions of various securities and exchange laws.

36. An individual or organization to whom a debt is owed.

37. Probable future sacrifices of economic benefits arising from present obligations of a particular entity to transfer assets or to provide services to other entities in the future as a result of past transactions or events.

38. The record-making phase of accounting.

39. The American Accounting Association, an organization of persons interested in accounting; generally identified as the professional association of academic accountants.

40. The assumption that a business will continue to operate and that the assets held for use in the business will not be sold.

41. Liabilities resulting from the credit purchase of goods or services.

42. Probable future economic benefits obtained or controlled by a particular entity as a result of past transactions or events.

43. The idea that a business is a separate entity that is distinct from its owner or owners and from every other business.

44. An expression in dollar amounts of the equivalency of the assets, liabilities, and equity of an enterprise, usually stated as Assets = Liabilities + Owner's Equity.

45. Chartered Accountant—appellation granted by provincial Institutes of Chartered Accountants upon successful completion of study and practical experience.

46. A business owned by one individual.

47. Accounting Principles Board, a committee of the AICPA that was responsible for formulating generally accepted accounting principles prior to the FASB.

48. Certified public accountant, an accountant who has met legal requirements as to age, education, experience, residence, and moral character and is licensed to practice public accounting in the U.S.

49. Another name for a stockholder.

50. That phase of accounting dealing primarily with recording transactions, processing the recorded data, and preparing financial statements.

51. Generally accepted accounting principles.

52. Committee of the Canadian Institute of Chartered Accountants charged with issuing recommendations (CICA Handbook) with regard to accounting practice in Canada.

53. A financial statement that discloses the inflows and outflows of cash during the period, classified in terms of cash flows from operations, cash flows from investing activities, and cash flows from financing activities.

54. An abstract idea that serves as an important assumption underlying generally accepted accounting principles and procedures.

55. Certified Management Accountant—appellation granted by provincial societies of the Society of Management Accountants.

56. Certified General Accountant—appellation granted by provincial associations of the Certified General Accountants' Association of Canada upon successful completion of the prescribed course of study and practical experience.

57. Another name for equity, or the residual interest in the assets of an entity that remains after deducting its liabilities.

58. International Accounting Standards Committee.

Problem IV

Complete the following by filling in the blanks.

1. The _____ principle of accounting requires that assets and services be recorded at cost. Assets and services are recorded at cost because normally costs are based on verifiable evidence and thus meet the requirements of the _____ principle, the accounting principle which requires that transaction amounts be objectively established. It is important that transaction amounts be objectively established because if accounting information is to be fully useful, it must be based on _____ data and information.

2. The _____ is a form of business organization that requires the organizers to obtain articles of incorporation or a charter from one of the provinces or the federal government.

3. Under the _____ concept, for accounting purposes, every business is conceived to be a separate entity, separate and distinct from its _____ or _____ and from every other _____.

4. Does a balance sheet show current market values for the assets listed on it? _____ (Yes or No) If the dollar amounts do not represent current market values, what do they represent?

_____.

5. Equity on a balance sheet is the _____ of the owner in the net assets of the business.

6. The statement of changes in owner's equity discloses all changes in owner's equity during the period, including _____ by the owner, _____ by the owner, and

_____

_____.

7. The balance sheet equation is _____ equal _____ plus _____. It is also called the _____ equation.

8. Probable future sacrifices of economic benefits arising from present obligations of a business to transfer assets or to provide services to other entities as a result of past transactions are _____.

9. Accounting is a service activity, the function of which is _____

_____

_____.

10. The assets of a business are the _____

_____

owned by the business.

11. Bookkeeping is the _____-making part of accounting, and bookkeeping and accounting _____ (are, are not) the same thing.

12. There are several kinds of accounting work done by employees of business firms. These include (a) _____, (b) _____, (c) _____, and (d) _____.

13. An income statement prepared for a business shows whether or not the business earned a _____ or suffered a _____.

14. Revenues are inflows of _____ or other _____ received in exchange for goods or services provided to customers.

15. A balance sheet prepared for a business shows its financial position on a specific _____. Financial position is shown by listing the _____ of the business, its _____, and the _____ of the owner or owners in the business.

16. Expenses are goods and services _____ in operating a business or other economic unit.

17. The accounting equation for a single proprietorship is _____ _____.

Problem V

The assets, liabilities, and owner's equity of Susan Thompson's law practice are shown on the first line in the equation on the next page; and following the equation are eight transactions completed by Ms. Thompson. Show by additions and subtractions in the spaces provided the effects of each transaction on the items of the equation. Show new totals after each transaction as in Illustration 1-8 in the text.

		ASSETS			=	LIABILITIES	+	OWNER'S EQUITY
Cash	+ Accounts Receivable	+ Prepaid Rent	+ Law Library	+ Office Equipment =		Accounts Payable	+	S. Thompson, Capital
$4,000			$8,000	$7,250				$19,250
1.								
2.								
3.								
4.								
5.								
6.								
7.								
8.								

1. Paid the rent for three months in advance on the law office, $3,000.

2. Purchased a new typewriter for the office, paying cash, $900.

3. Completed legal work for Ray Holland, a client, and immediately collected $2,500 in cash in full payment therefor.

4. Purchased on credit from Legal Book Publishers law books costing $700.

5. Completed on credit $1,500 of legal work for Julie Landon and immediately entered in the accounting records both the right to collect and the revenue earned.

6. Paid Legal Book Publishers for the books purchased in Transaction 4.

7. Received $1,500 from Julie Landon for the legal work of Transaction 5.

8. Paid the weekly salary of the office secretary, $575.

Refer to your completed work above and fill in the blanks.

a. Did each transaction affect two items of the equation?

_____. (Yes or No)

11

b. Did the equation remain in balance after the effect or effects of each transaction were entered? _____.
    (Yes or No)

c. If the equation had not remained in balance after the effect or effects of each transaction were entered, this
    would have indicated that _____
    _____.

d. Ms. Thompson earned $2,500 of revenue upon the completion of Transaction 3 and the asset that flowed into
    her practice as a result of this transaction was in the form of _____.

e. Ms. Thompson earned $1,500 of revenue upon the completion of Transaction 5, and the asset that flowed into
    the law practice upon the completion of this transaction was _____
    _____.

f. The right to collect $1,500 from Julie Landon was converted into _____
    in Transaction 7. Nevertheless, although the $1,500 was not received in cash until Transaction 7, the revenue
    was earned upon the completion of the _____ in Transaction 5.

g. The $1,500 collected in Transaction 7 was recognized as revenue in Transaction 5 because of the requirements
    of the _____ principle, which (1) defines a revenue as an inflow of assets, not
    necessarily _____ in exchange for goods or services; (2) requires that the
    revenue be recognized at the time, but not before, it is _____, which generally
    is at the time title to goods sold is _____ or services are _____;
    (3) requires that the amount of revenue recognized be measured by the cash received plus the cash
    equivalent of any other _____ received.

Problem I

1. F
2. F
3. F
4. T
5. T

Problem II

1. D
2. B
3. D
4. B
5. A

Problem III

AAA	39
Accounting	4
Accounting concept	54
Accounting Standards Committee	52
Accounting equation	8 or 44
Accounts payable	41
Accounts receivable	27
AICPA	3
APB	47
Assets	42
Audit	32
Balance sheet	1
Balance sheet equation	44
Bookkeeping	38
Budgeting	18
Business entity concept	43
Business transaction	29
CA	45
CGA	56
CMA	55
Continuing-concern concept	40
Controller	26
Corporation	9
Cost accounting	19
Cost principle	10
CPA	48
Creditor	36
Debtor	22
Equity	11
Expense	23
FASB	12

GAAP	51 or 31
General accounting	50
Generally accepted accounting principles	31
Going-concern concept	20 or 40
IASC	58
Income statement	7
Internal auditing	16
Liabilities	37
Management advisory services	34
Net assets	57 or 11
Net income	17
Net loss	21
Objectivity principle	2
Partnership	13
Realization principle	28
Recognition principle	15 or 28
Revenue	6
SEC	35
Shareholder	49 or 24
Single proprietorship	46
Stable-dollar concept	25
Statement of cash flows	53
Statement of changes in owner's equity	33
Statement of financial position	14 or 1
Stock	30
Stockholders	24
Tax services	5

Problem IV

1. cost, objectivity, objective

2. corporation

3. business entity, owner, owners, business

4. No. Costs or costs less accumulated depreciation. (The phrase "accumulated depreciation" will be explained further in Chapter 3.)

5. interest or ownership right

6. investments, withdrawals, net income or net loss

7. Assets, Liabilities, Owner's Equity, accounting

8. liabilities

9. to provide quantitative information, primarily financial in nature, about economic entities

10. property or property rights

11. record, are not

12. (a) general accounting
    (b) cost accounting
    (c) budgeting
    (d) internal auditing

13. net income, net loss

14. cash, assets (properties)

15. date, assets, liabilities, equity

16. used up (consumed)

17. Assets = Liabilities + Owner's Equity

    or

    Assets − Liabilities = Owner's Equity

Problem V

	Cash	+	Accounts Receivable	+	Prepaid Rent	+	Law Library	+	Office Equipment	=	Accounts Payable	+	S. Thompson, Capital
	$4,000						$8,000		$7,250				$19,250
1.	−3,000				+3,000								
	$1,000				$3,000		$8,000		$7,250				$19,250
2.	− 900								+ 900				
	$ 100				$3,000		$8,000		$8,150				$19,250
3.	+2,500												+2,500
	$2,600				$3,000		$8,000		$8,150				$21,750
4.							+ 700				+ 700		
	$2,600				$3,000		$8,700		$8,150		$ 700		$21,750
5.			+1,500										+1,500
	$2,600		$1,500		$3,000		$8,700		$8,150		$ 700		$23,250
6.	− 700										− 700		
	$1,900		$1,500		$3,000		$8,700		$8,150		$ 0		$23,250
7.	+1,500		−1,500										
	$3,400		$ 0		$3,000		$8,700		$8,150		$ 0		$23,250
8.	− 575												− 575
	$2,825		$ 0		$3,000		$8,700		$8,150		$ 0		$22,675

a. Yes

b. Yes

c. an error had been made

d. cash

e. the right to collect $1,500 from Julie Landon, an account receivable

f. cash, legal work

g. realization (or recognition), cash, earned, transferred, rendered, asset or assets

2

Recording Transactions

After studying Chapter 2, you should be able to:

1. State the names of several commonly used accounts and the nature of the items recorded in those accounts.

2. Explain the mechanics of double-entry accounting and tell why transactions are recorded with equal debits and credits.

3. Describe the rules of debit and credit and apply the rules in recording transactions.

4. Tell the normal balance of any asset, liability, or owner's equity account.

5. Record transactions in a General Journal, post to the ledger accounts, and prepare a trial balance to test the accuracy of the recording and posting.

6. Define or explain the words and phrases listed in the chapter Glossary.

Topical Outline

I. Steps in the accounting process include:

   A. Analyzing the economic events of an entity and recording the effects of those events.

   B. Classifying and summarizing the recorded effects in reports or financial statements that individuals find useful in making economic decisions about the entity.

II. Accounting records include:

   A. Business papers—printed documents (sales slips, invoices, cheques) that businesses use in the process of completing business transactions and that provide evidence of the transactions.

   B. Journal—a book of original entry in which transactions are first recorded and from which transaction amounts are posted to the ledger accounts.

   C. Ledger—a group of accounts used by a business in recording its transactions.

III. Accounts are separate locations in an accounting system, one of which is used in recording and summarizing the increases and decreases in each type of revenue, expense, asset, liability, or owner's equity item.

   A. Types of accounts include:

      1. Assets accounts (Cash, Notes Receivable, Accounts Receivable, Prepaid Expenses, Supplies, Equipment, Buildings, Land, etc.)

      2. Liability accounts (Accounts Payable, Notes Payable, Unearned Revenues, Other Short-Term Payables, etc.)

      3. Owner's equity accounts (Capital account, Withdrawals account, Revenue and Expense accounts)

   B. T-account—a simple form of account that illustrates the debits and credits required in recording a transaction.

   C. Balance-column account—an account that has debit and credit columns for entering changes in the account and a column for entering the new account balance after each debit or credit is posted to the account.

IV. The mechanics of double-entry accounting—Assets = Liabilities + Owner's Equity. Every transaction is recorded in two or more accounts with equal debits and credits.

   A. Debit—the left-hand side of a T-account.

   B. Credit—the right-hand side of a T-account.

   C. Asset accounts are debited for increases and credited for decreases.

   D. Liability and owner's equity accounts are debited for decreases and credited for increases.

   E. Owner's equity is increased by owner's investments and by revenues; owner's equity is decreased by expenses and by withdrawals.

      1. Investments by the owner are credited to the owner's capital account.

      2. Withdrawals of assets are debited to the owner's withdrawals account.

      3. Revenues are credited to a revenue account.

      4. Expenses are debited to an expense account.

V. Journalizing—the process of recording transactions in a journal. The transaction date, the names of the accounts involved, the amount of each debit and credit, and an explanation of the transaction are recorded for each transaction.

VI. Posting—the process of copying information from a journal to a ledger.

VII. Trial balance—a list of the accounts that have balances in the ledger, the debit or credit balance of each account, the total of the debit balances, and the total of the credit balances.

A trial balance tests the equality of the debit and credit balances to provide evidence of accuracy in the accounts.

VIII.   Bookkeeping techniques—locate and correct errors by checking journalizing and posting procedures.

Problem I

The following statements are either true or false. Place a (T) in the parentheses before each true statement and an (F) before each false statement.

1. ( ) Debits are used to record increases in assets, withdrawals, and expenses.

2. ( ) To credit a liability account means to increase it.

3. ( ) The journal record makes it possible to trace the debits and credits into the accounts for the purpose of locating errors.

4. ( ) An unearned revenue is an owner's equity account that will be satisfied by delivering the product or service paid for in advance.

5. ( ) The cost of renting an office during the current period is an expense; however, the cost of renting an office six periods in advance is an asset.

Problem II

You are given several words, phrases or numbers to choose from in completing each of the following statements or in answering the following questions. In each case select the one that best completes the statement or answers the question and place its letter in the answer space provided.

_____ 1. Hal Hammer, the owner of Hal Company, had a capital balance of $12,300 on June 30 and $23,800 on July 31. Net income for the month of July was $14,000. What were the owner's withdrawals during July?

    a. $22,100.
    b. $25,500.
    c. $ 2,500.
    d. $11,500.
    e. $ –0–.

_____ 2. Which of the following transactions does not affect the owner's equity in a proprietorship?

    a. investments by the owner.
    b. withdrawals of cash or other assets by the owner.
    c. cash receipts for revenues.
    d. cash receipts for unearned revenues.
    e. cash payments for expenses.

_____ 3. A ledger is a(n):

    a. book of original entry in which a complete record of transactions are first recorded.
    b. group of accounts used by a business in recording its transactions.
    c. book of original entry in which any type of transaction can be recorded.
    d. book of special journals.
    e. accountant's book of rules and principles.

_____ 4. The following transactions occurred during the month of October:
    1) Paid $1,500 cash for store equipment.
    2) Paid $1,000 in partial payment for supplies purchased 30 days previously.
    3) Paid October's utility bill of $600.
    4) Paid $1,200 to owner of the business for his personal use.
    5) Paid $1,400 salary of office employee for October.

    What was the total amount of expenses during October?

    a. $3,000.
    b. $4,500.

20

c. $2,000.
d. $3,500.
e. $5,700.

_____ 5. The journal entry for the completion of legal work for a client on credit and billing the client $1,700 for the services rendered would be:

a. Accounts Receivable 1,700
    Legal Fees Earned 1,700
b. Legal Fees Earned 1,700
    Accounts Receivable 1,700
c. Accounts Payable 1,700
    Legal Fees Earned 1,700
d. Legal Fees Earned 1,700
    Revenues 1,700
e. Accounts Receivable 1,700
    Unearned Revenues 1,700

Problem III

Jon Wheeler has just begun a new small repairs business he calls Wheeler's Repair Shop, and the first ten transactions completed by the business follow:

a. Mr. Wheeler sold a personal investment in Southern Cable stock for $1,921.50 and began his business by depositing $1,800 of the proceeds in a bank account opened in the name of the business.

b. Paid three months' rent in advance on the shop space, $675.

c. Purchased repair equipment for cash, $700.

d. Completed repair work for customers and collected cash therefore, $505.50.

e. Purchased additional repair equipment on credit from Comet Company, $415.50.

f. Completed repair work on credit for Fred Baca, $175.

g. Paid Comet Company $290.50 of the amount owed to it.

h. Paid the local radio station $75.00 for an announcement of the shop opening.

i. Fred Baca paid for the work of Transaction (f).

j. Mr. Wheeler withdrew $350 cash from the business to pay personal expenses.

Required:

1. Record the transactions directly in the T-accounts provided on the next page. Use the transaction letters to identify the amounts in the accounts.

2. Prepare a trial balance on the form provided on the next page.

Cash

Accounts Payable

Jon Wheeler, Capital

Accounts Receivable

Jon Wheeler, Withdrawals

Prepaid Rent

Revenue from Repairs

Repair Equipment

Advertising Expense

WHEELER'S REPAIR SHOP
Trial Balance
——————————————, 19—

Problem IV

Journalize the following transactions and post to the accounts following.

  a. On November 5 of the current year, Sherry Dale invested $1,500 in cash and office equipment having a fair value of $950 in a real estate agency.

  b. On November 6, she purchased for cash office equipment costing $425.

GENERAL JOURNAL   Page 1

DATE	ACCOUNT TITLES AND EXPLANATION	P.R.	DEBIT	CREDIT

GENERAL LEDGER

Cash   Account No. 1

DATE	EXPLANATION	P.R.	DEBIT	CREDIT	BALANCE

Office Equipment   Account No. 8

DATE	EXPLANATION	P.R.	DEBIT	CREDIT	BALANCE

Sherry Dale, Capital   Account No. 15

DATE	EXPLANATION	P.R.	DEBIT	CREDIT	BALANCE

Problem V

Many of the important ideas and concepts discussed in Chapter 2 are reflected in the following list of key terms. Test your understanding of these terms by matching the appropriate definition with the terms. Record the number identifying the most appropriate definition in the blank space next to each term.

_____ Accounts   _____ Chart of accounts

_____ Account balance   _____ Compound journal entry

_____ Account number   _____ Credit

_____ Balance column account   _____ Debit

_____ Book of final entry   _____ Double-entry accounting

_____ Book of original entry   _____ Drawing account

_____ Business papers   _____ Folio column

_____ Capital account   _____ General Journal

_____ Internal transactions   _____ Prepaid expenses

_____ Journal   _____ Promissory note

_____ Journal page number   _____ Source documents

_____ Ledger   _____ T-account

_____ Personal account   _____ Trial balance

_____ Posting   _____ Unearned revenue

_____ Posting Reference column   _____ Withdrawals account

1. Liabilities created by the receipt of cash from customers in payment for products or services that have not yet been delivered to the customers; the liabilities will be satisfied by delivering the product or service.

2. A list of the accounts that have balances in the ledger, the debit or credit balance of each account, the total of the debit balances, and the total of the credit balances.

3. An account that has debit and credit columns for entering changes in the account and a column for entering the new account balance after each debit or credit is posted to the account.

4. Another name for business papers.

5. A book of original entry in which transactions are first recorded and from which transaction amounts are posted to the ledger accounts.

6. A unique number that is assigned to an account as a means of identifying that account.

7. A simple form of account that is widely used in accounting education to illustrate the debits and credits required in recording a transaction.

8. A posting reference number entered in the Posting Reference column of each account to which an amount is posted and which shows the page of the journal from which the amount was posted.

9. Another name for the withdrawals account.

10. An account used to record the owner's investments in the business plus any more or less permanent changes in the owner's equity.

11. The left-hand side of a T-account, or entries that increase assets, or decrease liabilities, or decrease owner's equity.

12. Assets created by payments for economic benefits that do not expire until some later time; then, as the benefits expire or are used up, the assets become expenses.

13. The difference between the increases and decreases recorded in an account.

14. The account used to record the transfers of assets from a business to its owner.

15. Another name for the Posting Reference column.

16. A list of all the accounts used by a company, showing the identifying number assigned to each account.

17. A journal entry that has more than one debit or more than one credit.

18. A book of original entry that is designed so flexibly that it can be used to record any type of transaction.

19. A journal in which transactions are first recorded.

20. A ledger to which amounts are posted.

21. The right-hand side of a T-account, or entries that decrease assets, or increase liabilities, or increase owner's equity.

22. A formal written promise to pay a definite sum of money on demand or at a fixed or determinable future date.

23. A group of accounts used by a business in recording its transactions.

24. Transcribing the debit and credit amounts from a journal to the ledger accounts.

25. A name sometimes given to economic events that have an effect on an entity's accounting equation but that do not involve transactions with outside parties.

26. A system of accounting in which each transaction affects and is recorded in two or more accounts with equal debits and credits.

27. A column in a journal and in each account that is used for cross-referencing amounts that have been posted from a journal to the account.

28. Separate locations in an accounting system, one of which is used in recording and summarizing the increases and decreases in each type of revenue, expense, asset, liability, or owner's equity item.

29. Printed documents that businesses use in the process of completing business transactions and that provide evidence of the transactions.

Problem VI

Complete the following by filling in the blanks.

1. A group of accounts used by a business in recording its transactions is called _____
_____.

2. Transactions are first recorded in a _____ and are then posted to the ledger accounts.

3. The balance of an account is _____
_____.

4. A journal entry linking together the debits and credits of a transaction makes it possible to _____
_____ into the accounts and to see that they are equal and were properly recorded.

5. A T-account has a left side and a right side; and in entering increases and decreases in a T-account, the

_____ are placed in one side of the account and the _____ are placed on the other side. This placement makes it possible to add the increases, add the decreases, and subtract the sum of the decreases from the sum of the increases to learn the amount of the item recorded in the account that the business has, owns, or owes.

6. The last step in posting an amount is _____
_____

_____.

7. Accounts are a device used by a business in recording and summarizing the _____

and _____ in each asset, liability, and owner's equity item appearing on its balance sheet and each revenue and expense on its income statement.

8. The steps in preparing a trial balance are: _____

    _____

    _____

    _____

    _____

    _____

    _____

    _____.

9. Revenues increase owner's equity and are _____ to revenue accounts. Expenses decrease owner's equity and are _____ to expense accounts.

10. a. The normal balance of an asset account, such as Cash is _____.
    b. The normal balance of a liability account is _____.
    c. The normal balance of the owner's capital account is _____.
    d. The normal balance of the owner's withdrawals account is _____.
    e. The normal balance of a revenue account is _____.
    f. The normal balance of an expense account is _____.

11. Increases in assets are recorded as _____ (debits, credits) and decreases are recorded as _____. Likewise, increases in liability and owner's equity items are recorded as _____ and decreases are recorded as _____.

12. When an account has an opposite from normal kind of balance, this opposite from normal kind of balance is indicated by _____

    _____

    _____

    _____.

13. Debits to accounts _____ (are, are not) always increases.

14. A trial balance that fails to balance is proof that _____
    _____ either in recording transactions, in posting, or in preparing the trial balance.

15. A trial balance that balances is not absolute proof that there were no errors in recording, posting, and preparing the trial balance because _____

    _____

    _____.

Problem VII, Uno Computer Services

(This is a serial problem that is continued in chapters 3, 4, and 5.)

On October 1, 1990, John Conard started a computer service company named Uno Computer Services. Uno is organized as a single proprietorship, with John doing consulting services, computer system installations, and computer program development to meet specific customer needs. John expects to prepare financial statements for the first time on December 31, 1990. To begin accounting for the business, John opened the following general ledger accounts.

Accounts	Number
Cash	111
Accounts Receivable	114
Prepaid Insurance	115
Prepaid Rent	116
Computer Supplies	117
Office Equipment	131
Computer	133
Accounts Payable	211
John Conard, Capital	311
John Conard, Withdrawals	312
Computer Services Revenue	411
Advertising Expense	611
Auto Expense	612
Computer Repair Expense	614
Electric Expense	616
Miscellaneous Expense	619
Telephone Expense	623
Wages Expense	625

Journalize and post the following transactions completed by Uno Computer Services during October and November.

Oct. 1 John Conard invested $5,000 personal cash into the business, along with a $3,000 computer and $340 of office equipment.

2 Rented office space in the Town Hall Shopping Center for $225 per month and paid four months' rent in advance.

3 Purchased computer supplies on credit for $50 from Ajax Supply Company.

4 Paid one year's premium on a fire/theft and liability insurance policy, $195.

5 Billed Ball Company $500 for work this week installing a new computer.

8 Paid for the computer supplies purchased from Ajax Supply.

10 Hired an assistant, Ann White, for $70 a day, as needed. She will start on October 15 and will be paid every other Friday.

12 Withdrew $600 for personal expenses.

12 Worked this week again at Ball Company and billed them for $750.

15 Received $500 from Ball Company for work performed the first week of October.

17 Purchased $25 of parts to repair Uno's computer, which was damaged in the move to the new office.

18 Billed AB Company for computer services performed this week, $1,000.

19 Paid $15 for an advertisement in the Shopper Newspaper announcing Uno's grand opening.

22 Received the $750 billed to Ball Company on 10/12.

23 Received $250 cash from Dog Enterprise for computer services.

24 Completed work for Ear Hearing and billed them $425.

25 Paid Ann White for six days' work.

25 Purchased on credit from Ajax Supply additional computer supplies for $55.

28 Billed Call Company for computer services, $725.

30 Paid the hydro bill for the month, $47; and the telephone bill, $115.

30 Paid $600 to John for personal use.

Nov. 1 Reimbursed Ann's business car mileage, 150 km., at $0.24 per km.
1 Reimbursed John's business car mileage, 450 km., at $0.24 per km.
4 Received $425 from Ear Hearing for work done on October 24.
5 Received $300 cash from Dog Enterprise for computer services.
6 Received $1,000 from AB Company, billed on October 18.
7 Purchased an additional $45 of computer supplies from Ajax Supply. Paid for both this purchase and the one on October 25.
8 Billed Farm Research for services, $895.
8 Paid Ann White for five days' work.
11 Notified by AB Company that Uno's bid of $1,500 was accepted and began work this day.
13 Received a notice from Republic Bank that a $4 service charge had been deducted from Uno's chequing account.
15 Paid John $600 as a withdrawal.
18 Paid John's home water bill, $35.
20 Received $500 from Call Company against the bill dated October 28.
22 Gave a $10 donation to the Canadian Cancer Society on behalf of Uno.
22 Paid Ann White for six days' work.
25 Completed work begun on November 11 for AB Company and billed them for the amount due.
27 Sent another bill to Call Company for the past due amount of $225 related to billings on October 28 and November 20.
28 Paid the hydro bill for the month, $49; and the telephone bill, $118.
28 Paid $650 to John as a withdrawal.
29 Reimbursed Ann's business car mileage, 200 km., at $0.24 per km.
29 Reimbursed John's business car mileage, 500 km., at $0.24 per km.

DATE	ACCOUNT TITLES AND EXPLANATION	P.R.	DEBIT	CREDIT

DATE	ACCOUNT TITLES AND EXPLANATION	P.R.	DEBIT	CREDIT

DATE	ACCOUNT TITLES AND EXPLANATION	P.R.	DEBIT	CREDIT

DATE	ACCOUNT TITLES AND EXPLANATION	P.R.	DEBIT	CREDIT

DATE		ACCOUNT TITLES AND EXPLANATION	P.R.	DEBIT	CREDIT

Cash   Account No. 111

DATE		EXPLANATION	P.R.	DEBIT	CREDIT	BALANCE

Accounts Receivable — Account No. 114

DATE		EXPLANATION	P.R.	DEBIT	CREDIT	BALANCE

Prepaid Insurance — Account No. 115

DATE		EXPLANATION	P.R.	DEBIT	CREDIT	BALANCE

Prepaid Rent — Account No. 116

DATE		EXPLANATION	P.R.	DEBIT	CREDIT	BALANCE

Computer Supplies — Account No. 117

DATE		EXPLANATION	P.R.	DEBIT	CREDIT	BALANCE

Office Equipment   Account No. 131

DATE		EXPLANATION	P.R.	DEBIT	CREDIT	BALANCE

Computer   Account No. 133

DATE		EXPLANATION	P.R.	DEBIT	CREDIT	BALANCE

Accounts Payable   Account No. 211

DATE		EXPLANATION	P.R.	DEBIT	CREDIT	BALANCE

John Conard, Capital   Account No. 311

DATE		EXPLANATION	P.R.	DEBIT	CREDIT	BALANCE

John Conard, Withdrawals   Account No. 312

DATE		EXPLANATION	P.R.	DEBIT	CREDIT	BALANCE

Computer Services Revenue   Account No. 411

DATE		EXPLANATION	P.R.	DEBIT	CREDIT	BALANCE

Advertising Expense   Account No. 611

DATE		EXPLANATION	P.R.	DEBIT	CREDIT	BALANCE

Auto Expense   Account No. 612

DATE		EXPLANATION	P.R.	DEBIT	CREDIT	BALANCE

Computer Repair Expense   Account No. 614

DATE		EXPLANATION	P.R.	DEBIT	CREDIT	BALANCE

Hydro Expense

Account No. 616

DATE		EXPLANATION	P.R.	DEBIT	CREDIT	BALANCE

Miscellaneous Expense

Account No. 619

DATE		EXPLANATION	P.R.	DEBIT	CREDIT	BALANCE

Telephone Expense

Account No. 623

DATE		EXPLANATION	P.R.	DEBIT	CREDIT	BALANCE

Wages Expense

Account No. 625

DATE		EXPLANATION	P.R.	DEBIT	CREDIT	BALANCE

Solutions for Chapter 2

Problem I

1. T
2. T
3. T
4. F
5. T

Problem II

1. C
2. D
3. B
4. C
5. A

Problem III

Cash			
(a)	1,800.00	(b)	675.00
(d)	505.50	(c)	700.00
(i)	175.00	(g)	290.50
		(h)	75.00
		(j)	350.00

Repair Equipment		
(c)	700.00	
(e)	415.50	

Jon Wheeler, Withdrawals	
(j)	350.00

Accounts Receivable			
(f)	175.00	(i)	175.00

Accounts Payable			
(g)	290.50	(e)	415.50

Revenue from Repairs		
	(d)	505.50
	(f)	175.00

Prepaid Rent	
(b)	675.00

Jon Wheeler, Capital		
	(a)	1,800.00

Advertising Expense	
(h)	75.00

WHEELER'S REPAIR SHOP
Trial Balance, Current Date

Cash	$ 390.00	
Prepaid rent	675.00	
Repair equipment	1,115.50	
Accounts payable		$ 125.00
Jon Wheeler, capital		1,800.00
Jon Wheeler, withdrawals	350.00	
Revenue from repairs		680.50
Advertising expense	75.00	
Totals	$2,605.50	$2,605.50

40

DATE		ACCOUNT TITLES AND EXPLANATION	P.R.	DEBIT	CREDIT
19— Nov.	5	Cash	1	1 500 00	
		Office Equipment	8	9 50 00	
		Sherry Dale, Capital	15		2 450 00
		Invested in a real estate agency.			
	6	Office Equipment	8	4 25 00	
		Cash	1		4 25 00
		Puchased office equipment.			

GENERAL LEDGER

Cash   Account No. 1

DATE		EXPLANATION	P.R.	DEBIT	CREDIT	BALANCE
19— Nov.	5		G–1	1 500 00		1 500 00
	6		G–1		4 25 00	1 075 00

Office Equipment   Account No. 8

DATE		EXPLANATION	P.R.	DEBIT	CREDIT	BALANCE
19— Nov.	5		G–1	9 50 00		9 50 00
	6		G–1	4 25 00		1 375 00

Sherry Dale, Capital   Account No. 15

DATE		EXPLANATION	P.R.	DEBIT	CREDIT	BALANCE
19— Nov.	5		G–1		2 450 00	2 450 00

Problem V

Problem VI

1. a ledger

2. journal

3. the difference between the debits and credits entered in it

4. trace the debits and credits

5. increases, decreases

6. to enter in the journal the ledger account number to which the amount was posted

7. increases, decreases

8. (a) Determine the balance of each account; (b) List in their ledger order the accounts having balances, with the debit balances in one column and the credit balances in another; (c) Add the debit balances; (d) Add the credit balances; (e) Compare the two totals for equality.

9. credited, debited

10. (a) debit (b) credit (c) credit (d) debit (e) credit (f) debit

11. debits, credits. credits, debits

12. entering the balance in the account in red or entering it in black and circling it

13. are not

14. one or more errors have been made

15. some types of errors do not cause debits to be unequal to credits

Problem VII, Uno Computer Services

GENERAL JOURNAL

Date		Account	Ref	Debit	Credit
Oct.	1	Cash	111	5,000.00	
		Computer	133	3,000.00	
		Office Equipment	131	340.00	
		John Conard, Capital	311		8,340.00
		To record owner's investment.			
	2	Prepaid Rent	116	900.00	
		Cash	111		900.00
		Paid four months' rent in advance.			
	3	Computer Supplies	117	50.00	
		Accounts Payable	211		50.00
		Purchased computer supplies on credit.			
	4	Prepaid Insurance	115	195.00	
		Cash	111		195.00
		Paid one-year insurance premium.			
	5	Accounts Receivable	114	500.00	
		Computer Services Revenue	411		500.00
		Installed computer for Ball Company.			
	8	Accounts Payable	211	50.00	
		Cash	111		50.00
		Paid for Oct. 3 purchase of supplies.			
	10	No entry required.			
	12	John Conard, Withdrawals	312	600.00	
		Cash	111		600.00
		Owner withdrew cash for personal use.			
	12	Accounts Receivable	114	750.00	
		Computer Services Revenue	411		750.00
		Completed work for Ball Company.			
	15	Cash	111	500.00	
		Accounts Receivable	114		500.00
		Received payment from Ball Co. for work done on Oct. 5.			
	17	Computer Repair Expense	614	25.00	
		Cash	111		25.00
		Purchased parts to repair computer.			
	18	Accounts Receivable	114	1,000.00	
		Computer Services Revenue	411		1,000.00
		Completed work for AB Company.			
	19	Advertising Expense	611	15.00	
		Cash	111		15.00
		Paid for newspaper advertisement.			
	22	Cash	111	750.00	
		Accounts Receivable	114		750.00
		Received payment from Ball Co. for work completed on Oct. 12.			
	23	Cash	111	250.00	
		Computer Services Revenue	411		250.00
		Completed work for Dog Enterprise.			

Oct.	24	Accounts Receivable	114	425.00	
		Computer Services Revenue	411		425.00
		Completed work for Ear Hearing.			
	25	Wages Expense	625	420.00	
		Cash	111		420.00
		Paid Ann White for six days' work.			
	25	Computer Supplies	117	55.00	
		Accounts Payable	211		55.00
		Purchased supplies from Ajax Supply.			
	28	Accounts Receivable	114	725.00	
		Computer Services Revenue	411		725.00
		Completed work for Call Company.			
	30	Hydro Expense	616	47.00	
		Telephone Expense	623	115.00	
		Cash	111		162.00
		Paid Oct. hydro and telephone bills.			
	30	John Conard, Withdrawals	312	600.00	
		Cash	111		600.00
		Owner withdrew cash for personal use.			
Nov.	1	Auto Expense	612	36.00	
		Cash	111		36.00
		Reimbursed Ann White for mileage.			
	1	Auto Expense	612	108.00	
		Cash	111		108.00
		Reimbursed owner for business mileage.			
	4	Cash	111	425.00	
		Accounts Receivable	114		425.00
		Received payment from Ear Hearing for work completed on Oct. 24.			
	5	Cash	111	300.00	
		Computer Services Revenue	411		300.00
		Completed work for Dog Enterprise.			
	6	Cash	111	1,000.00	
		Accounts Receivable	114		1,000.00
		Received payment from AB Company for Oct. 18 work.			
	7	Computer Supplies	117	45.00	
		Accounts Payable	211	55.00	
		Cash	111		100.00
		Paid Ajax Company for 25/10 and 7/11 supplies purchases.			
	8	Accounts Receivable	114	895.00	
		Computer Services Revenue	411		895.00
		Completed work for Farm Research.			
	8	Wages Expense	625	350.00	
		Cash	111		350.00
		Paid Ann White for five days' work.			
	11	No entry required.			
	13	Miscellaneous Expense	619	4.00	
		Cash	111		4.00
		To record bank service charge.			

Nov.	15	John Conard, Withdrawals	312	600.00	
		Cash	111		600.00
		Owner withdrew cash for personal use.			
	18	John Conard, Withdrawals	312	35.00	
		Cash	111		35.00
		Paid owner's home water bill.			
	20	Cash	111	500.00	
		Accounts Receivable	114		500.00
		Received a partial payment from Call Company for Oct. 28 work.			
	22	Miscellaneous Expense	619	10.00	
		Cash	111		10.00
		Made donation in name of Uno to Canadian Cancer Society.			
	22	Wages Expense	625	420.00	
		Cash	111		420.00
		Paid Ann White for six days' work.			
	25	Accounts Receivable	114	1,500.00	
		Computer Services Revenue	411		1,500.00
		Completed work of 11/11 for AB Company.			
	27	No entry required.			
	28	Hydro Expense	616	49.00	
		Telephone Expense	623	118.00	
		Cash	111		167.00
		Paid Nov. hydro and telephone bills.			
	28	John Conard, Withdrawals	312	650.00	
		Cash	111		650.00
		Owner withdrew cash for personal use.			
	29	Auto Expense	612	48.00	
		Cash	111		48.00
		Reimbursed Ann White's mileage.			
	29	Auto Expense	612	120.00	
		Cash	111		120.00
		Reimbursed owner for business mileage.			

GENERAL LEDGER

Cash — No. 111

Date	Debit	Credit	Balance
1990			
Oct. 1	5,000.00		5,000.00
2		900.00	4,100.00
4		195.00	3,905.00
8		50.00	3,855.00
12		600.00	3,255.00
15	500.00		3,755.00
17		25.00	3,730.00
19		15.00	3,715.00
22	750.00		4,465.00
23	250.00		4,715.00
25		420.00	4,295.00
30		162.00	4,133.00
30		600.00	3,533.00
Nov. 1		36.00	3,497.00
1		108.00	3,389.00
4	425.00		3,814.00
5	300.00		4,114.00
6	1,000.00		5,114.00
7		100.00	5,014.00
8		350.00	4,664.00
13		4.00	4,660.00
15		600.00	4,060.00
18		35.00	4,025.00
20	500.00		4,525.00
22		10.00	4,515.00
22		420.00	4,095.00
28		167.00	3,928.00
28		650.00	3,278.00
29		48.00	3,230.00
29		120.00	3,110.00

Prepaid Insurance — No. 115

Date	Debit	Credit	Balance
1990			
Oct. 4	195.00		195.00

Prepaid Rent — No. 116

Date	Debit	Credit	Balance
1990			
Oct. 2	900.00		900.00

Computer Supplies — No. 117

Date	Debit	Credit	Balance
1990			
Oct. 3	50.00		50.00
25	55.00		105.00
Nov. 7	45.00		150.00

Office Equipment — No. 131

Date	Debit	Credit	Balance
1990			
Oct. 1	340.00		340.00

Computer — No. 133

Date	Debit	Credit	Balance
1990			
Oct. 1	3,000.00		3,000.00

Accounts Receivable — No. 114

Date	Debit	Credit	Balance
1990			
Oct. 5	500.00		500.00
12	750.00		1,250.00
15		500.00	750.00
18	1,000.00		1,750.00
22		750.00	1,000.00
24	425.00		1,425.00
28	725.00		2,150.00
Nov. 4		425.00	1,725.00
6		1,000.00	725.00
8	895.00		1,620.00
20		500.00	1,120.00
25	1,500.00		2,620.00

Accounts Payable — No. 211

Date	Debit	Credit	Balance
1990			
Oct. 3		50.00	50.00
8	50.00		—0—
25		55.00	55.00
Nov. 7	55.00		—0—

John Conard, Capital — No. 311

Date	Debit	Credit	Balance
1990			
Oct. 1		8,340.00	8,340.00

John Conard, Withdrawals   No. 312

Date	Debit	Credit	Balance
1990			
Oct. 12	600.00		600.00
30	600.00		1,200.00
Nov. 15	600.00		1,800.00
18	35.00		1,835.00
28	650.00		2,485.00

Computer Services Revenue No. 411

Date	Debit	Credit	Balance
1990			
Oct. 5		500.00	500.00
12		750.00	1,250.00
18		1,000.00	2,250.00
23		250.00	2,500.00
24		425.00	2,925.00
28		725.00	3,650.00
Nov. 5		300.00	3,950.00
8		895.00	4,845.00
25		1,500.00	6,345.00

Advertising Expense   No. 611

Date	Debit	Credit	Balance
1990			
Oct. 19	15.00		15.00

Auto Expense   No. 612

Date	Debit	Credit	Balance
1990			
Nov. 1	36.00		36.00
1	108.00		144.00
29	48.00		192.00
29	120.00		312.00

Computer Repair Expense   No. 614

Date	Debit	Credit	Balance
1990			
Oct. 17	25.00		25.00

Hydro Expense   No. 616

Date	Debit	Credit	Balance
1990			
Oct. 30	47.00		47.00
Nov. 28	49.00		96.00

Miscellaneous Expense   No. 619

Date	Debit	Credit	Balance
1990			
Nov. 13	4.00		4.00
22	10.00		14.00

Telephone Expense   No. 623

Date	Debit	Credit	Balance
1990			
Oct. 30	115.00		115.00
Nov. 28	118.00		233.00

Wages Expense   No. 625

Date	Debit	Credit	Balance
1990			
Oct. 25	420.00		420.00
Nov. 8	350.00		770.00
22	420.00		1,190.00

3

Adjusting the Accounts and Preparing the Statements

After studying Chapter 3, you should be able to:

1. Explain why the life of a business is divided into accounting periods of equal length and why the accounts of a business must be adjusted at the end of each accounting period.

2. Prepare adjusting entries for prepaid expenses, accrued expenses, unearned revenues, accrued revenues, and depreciation.

3. Explain the difference between the cash and accrual bases of accounting.

4. Prepare entries to record cash receipts and cash disbursements of items that were recorded at the end of the previous period as accrued revenues and accrued expenses.

5. Define each asset and liability classification appearing on a balance sheet, classify balance sheet items, and prepare a classified balance sheet.

6. Define or explain the words and phrases listed in the chapter Glossary.

After studying the appendix to Chapter 3 (Appendix A), you should be able to:

7. Explain why some companies record prepaid and unearned items in income statement accounts and prepare adjusting entries when this procedure is used.

Topical Outline

I. Adjusting the accounting records at the end of an accounting period

   A. Time-period concept—the idea that the life of a business is divisible into time periods of equal length for the purpose of preparing periodic financial reports for the business. The specific period a business adopts is its:

      1. Fiscal year—a period of any 12 consecutive months used by a business as its annual accounting period. This annual accounting period may be the:

         a. Calendar year—January 1 to December 31.
         b. Natural business year—the 12-month period that ends when the activities of a business are at their lowest point.

   B. Accounts that require adjustments are:

      1. Prepaid expenses—expenses that have been paid for in advance of use. These expenses remain assets until they are consumed in the operation of the business.
      2. Depreciation—expiration of the usefulness of plant and equipment and allocation of the cost of such assets to expense of the periods during which the assets are used.
      3. Accrued expenses—expenses that are incurred during an accounting period but that, prior to end-of-period adjustments, remain unrecorded because payment is not due.
      4. Unearned revenues—liabilities created by the receipt of cash from customers in payment for products or services that have not yet been delivered to the customers.
      5. Accrued revenues—revenues that are earned during an accounting period but that, prior to end-of-period adjustments, remain unrecorded because payment has not been received.

   C. The adjustment process—recording appropriate adjusting entries and assigning to each accounting period that portion of a transaction's effect applicable to the period, based on:

      1. The realization principle—requires that revenue be assigned to the accounting period in which it is earned.
      2. The matching principle—requires that expenses be reported in the same period as the revenues earned as a result of the expenses.

   D. Bases of accounting are the:

      1. Cash basis—revenues and expenses are reported in the income statement when cash is received or paid; no adjustments are made for prepaid, unearned, and accrued items.
      2. Accrual basis—the adjustment process is used to assign revenues to the periods in which they are earned and to match expenses with revenues.

II. Preparing financial statements

   A. The adjusted trial balance—prepared after end-of-period adjustments to the accounts have been made.
   B. Classification of balance sheet items

      1. Current assets—cash, temporary investments, notes receivable, accounts receivable, merchandise inventory, prepaid expenses, office supplies
      2. Investments—long-term assets such as stocks, bonds, promissory notes, and land held for future expansion
      3. Plant and equipment—equipment, buildings, land
      4. Intangible assets—goodwill, patents, trademarks, franchises, copyrights
      5. Current liabilities—short-term notes payable, accounts payable, wages payable,

current portions of long-term liabilities, unearned revenues, interest payable, taxes payable

     6.   Long-term liabilities—notes payable, bonds payable

     7.   Owner's equity—single proprietorship, partnership, corporation

  C. Balance sheet format

     1.   Account form—assets are listed on the left and liability and owner's equity items are listed on the right.

     2.   Report form—vertical format, shows the assets above the liabilities and the liabilities above the owner's equity.

III. Appendix A

  A. If prepayments of expenses are debited to expense accounts—

     1.   End-of-period adjusting entries must be designed to transfer unused or unexpired amounts to prepaid expense accounts.

     2.   Beginning-of-period balances in prepaid expense accounts must be considered when you prepare adjusting entries.

  B. If cash receipts of unearned revenues are credited to revenue accounts—

     1.   End-of-period adjusting entries must be designed to transfer remaining unearned amounts to liability accounts.

     2.   Beginning-of-period balances in unearned revenue accounts must be considered when you prepare adjusting entries.

Problem I

The following statements are either true or false. Place a (T) in the parentheses before each true statement and an (F) before each false statement.

1. ( ) The effect of a debit to an unearned revenue account and a corresponding credit to a revenue account is to transfer the earned portion of the fee from the liability account to the revenue account.

2. ( ) If the accountant failed to make the end-of-period adjustment to remove from the Unearned Fees account the amount of fees earned, the omission would cause an overstatement of assets.

3. ( ) The economic effect of a revenue generally occurs when it is earned, not when cash is received.

4. ( ) The equity section of a balance sheet is the same for a single proprietorship, a partnership, or a corporation.

5. ( ) Under the cash basis of accounting, revenues are recognized when they are earned and expenses are matched with revenues.

Problem II

You are given several words, phrases or numbers to choose from in completing each of the following statements or in answering the following questions. In each case select the one that best completes the statement or answers the question and place its letter in the answer space provided.

_____ 1. The average time a business takes to invest cash in merchandise or raw materials that are manufactured into finished products, sell the products, and convert the receivables (if sales are on credit) back into cash is the:

   a. accounting period of a business.
   b. fiscal year.
   c. time-period concept.
   d. operating cycle of a business.
   e. natural business year.

_____ 2. Depreciation is:

   a. expenses that are incurred during an accounting period but that, prior to end-of-period adjustments, remain unrecorded because payment is not due.
   b. the expiration of the usefulness of plant and equipment, and the related process of allocating the cost of such assets to expense of the periods during which the assets are used.
   c. an account the balance of which is subtracted from the balance of an associated account to show a more proper amount for the item recorded in the associated account.
   d. a distribution, generally of assets, made by a corporation to its shareholders.
   e. economic benefits or resources without physical substance, the value of which stems from the privileges or rights that accrue to their owner.

_____ 3. X Company has four employees who are each paid $40 per day for a five-day work week. The employees are paid every Friday. If the accounting period ends on Wednesday, X Company should make the following entry to accrue wages:

   a. Salary Expense 800
        Salaries Payable 800
   b. Salary Expense 800
        Cash 800

52

c. Salary Expense 480
   Salaries Payable 480
d. Salary Expense 320
   Salaries Payable 320
e. No entry should be made until the salaries are actually paid.

_____ 4. Lori Teach owns a sole proprietorship. During April of 1990 Lori's business received $250 cash in advance for future services. The following entry should be made when the money is received:

a. Cash 250
   Services Owed 250
b. Accounts Receivable 250
   Unearned Revenue 250
c. Cash 250
   Unearned Revenue 250
d. Unearned Revenue 250
   Earned Revenue 250
e. No entry should be made until services are actually rendered.

_____ 5. B & B Corporation had $175,000 of common stock issued and outstanding during all of 1990. It began the year with $50,000 of retained earnings, and it declared and paid $10,000 of cash dividends to its shareholders. B & B earned a $15,000 net income in 1990 and invested $5,000 in G. I. Jane common stock. What is the retained earnings balance at the end of 1990?

a. $230,000.
b. $ 45,000.
c. $ 40,000.
d. $ 50,000.
e. $ 55,000.

_____ 6. The Epicure Restaurant prepares monthly financial statements. On January 31, the balance in the Supplies account was $1,600. During February, $2,960 of supplies were purchased and debited to Supplies Expense. What is the adjusting entry on February 28 to account for the supplies assuming a February 28 inventory showed that $1,300 of supplies were on hand?

a. Supplies Expense 300
   Supplies 300
b. Supplies 300
   Supplies Expense 300
c. Supplies 3,260
   Cash 3,260
d. Supplies Expense 3,260
   Supplies 3,260
e. Some other entry.

_____ 7. Calculate the missing item in the following case:

The Owner, capital, January 1, 1990 .... $57,000
Total revenues during 1990 .... ?
Total expenses during 1990 27,900
Withdrawals during the year 15,750
The Owner, capital, December 31, 1990 63,300

a. $29,100.
b. $49,950.
c. $47,550.
d. $46,350.
e. $18,450.

Problem III

Many of the important ideas and concepts discussed in Chapter 3 are reflected in the following list of key terms. Test your understanding of these terms by matching the appropriate definitions with the terms. Record the number identifying the most appropriate definition in the blank space next to each term.

_____ Account form balance sheet	_____ Dividends
_____ Accounting period	_____ Fiscal year
_____ Accrual basis of accounting	_____ Intangible assets
_____ Accrued expenses	_____ Interim financial reports
_____ Accrued revenues	_____ Long-term liabilities
_____ Accumulated depreciation	_____ Matching principle
_____ Adjusted trial balance	_____ Natural business year
_____ Adjusting entry	_____ Operating cycle of a business
_____ Cash basis of accounting	_____ Paid-in capital
_____ Classified balance sheet	_____ Plant and equipment
_____ Common stock	_____ Report form balance sheet
_____ Contra account	_____ Retained earnings
_____ Contributed capital	_____ Time-period concept
_____ Current assets	_____ Unadjusted trial balance
_____ Current liabilities	_____ Unclassified balance sheet
_____ Depreciation	

1. Expenses that are incurred during an accounting period but that, prior to end-of-period adjustments, remain unrecorded because payment is not due.

2. The portion of a corporation's equity that represents investments in the corporation by its shareholders.

3. Obligations that are not due to be paid within one year or the current operating cycle of the business.

4. A trial balance that shows the account balances after they have been revised to reflect the effects of end-of-period adjustments.

5. Revenues that are earned during an accounting period but that, prior to end-of-period adjustments, remain unrecorded because payment has not been received.

6. A trial balance that is prepared before any adjustments have been recorded.

7. The idea that the life of a business is divisible into time periods of equal length for the purpose of preparing periodic financial reports of the business.

8. The portion of a corporation's equity that represents its cumulative net incomes, less net losses and dividends.

9. A period of any 12 consecutive months used by a business as its annual accounting period.

10. The expiration of the usefulness of plant and equipment, and the related process of allocating the cost of such assets to expense of the periods during which the assets are used.

11. Tangible, long-lived assets that are held for use in the production or sale of other assets or services.

12. A journal entry made at the end of an accounting period for the purpose of assigning revenues to the period in which they are earned, assigning expenses to the period in which the expiration of benefit is incurred, and to correct related liability and asset accounts.

13. The accounting requirement that expenses be reported in the same accounting period as are the revenues that were earned as a result of the expenses.

14. The 12-month period that ends when the activities of a business are at their lowest point.

15. The total amount of depreciation recorded against an asset or group of assets during the entire period of time the asset or assets have been owned.

16. A balance sheet prepared with a vertical format that shows the assets above the liabilities and the liabilities above the owner's equity.

17. The accounting system in which revenues are reported in the income statement when cash is received and expenses are reported when cash is paid; no adjustments are made for prepaid, unearned, and accrued items.

18. Another name for contributed capital.

19. Cash or other assets that are reasonably expected to be realized in cash or be sold or consumed within one year or one operating cycle of the business, whichever is longer.

20. The name given to a corporation's stock when it issues only one kind or class of stock.

21. A balance sheet that presents a single list of assets and a single list of liabilities with no attempt to divide them into classes.

22. Economic benefits or resources without physical substance, the value of which stems from the privileges or rights that accrue to their owner.

23. A system of accounting in which the adjustment process is used to assign revenues to the periods in which they are earned and to match expenses with revenues.

24. The average time a business takes to invest cash in merchandise or raw materials that are manufactured into finished products, sell the products, and convert the receivables (if sales are on credit) back into cash.

25. An account the balance of which is subtracted from the balance of an associated account to show a more proper amount for the item recorded in the associated account.

26. The length of time into which the life of a business is divided for the purpose of preparing periodic financial statements.

27. A balance sheet that is arranged so that the assets are listed on the left and the liabilities and owner's equity items are listed on the right.

28. A balance sheet that shows assets and liabilities grouped in meaningful subclasses.

29. A distribution, generally of assets, made by a corporation to its shareholders.

30. Obligations that are due to be paid or liquidated within one year or one operating cycle, whichever is longer.

31. Financial reports of a business that are based on one-month or three-month accounting periods.

Problem IV

On October 1 of the current year, Harold Lloyd began business as a public stenographer. During the month he completed the following transactions:

Oct. 1 Invested $3,000 in the business.
1 Paid three months' rent in advance on the office space, $1,245.
1 Purchased office equipment for cash, $925.50.
2 Purchased on credit office equipment, $700, and office supplies, $75.50.
31 Completed stenographic work during the month and collected cash, $1,725. (Combined into one entry to conserve space.)
31 Withdrew $725 for personal living expenses.

After the foregoing entries were recorded in the journal and posted, the accounts of Harold Lloyd appeared as follows:

Cash   Account No. 1

DATE		EXPLANATION	P.R.	DEBIT	CREDIT	BALANCE
Oct.	1		G–1	3000 00		3000 00
	1		G–1		1245 00	1755 00
	1		G–1		925 50	829 50
	31		G–2	1725 00		2554 50
	31		G–2		725 00	1829 50

Prepaid Rent   Account No. 2

DATE		EXPLANATION	P.R.	DEBIT	CREDIT	BALANCE
Oct.	1		G–1	1245 00		1245 00

Office Supplies   Account No. 3

DATE		EXPLANATION	P.R.	DEBIT	CREDIT	BALANCE
Oct.	2		G–1	75 50		75 50

Office Equipment   Account No. 4

DATE		EXPLANATION	P.R.	DEBIT	CREDIT	BALANCE
Oct.	1		G–1	925 50		925 50
	2		G–1	700 00		1625 50

Accumulated Depreciation, Office Equipment   Account No. 5

DATE		EXPLANATION	P.R.	DEBIT	CREDIT	BALANCE

Accounts Payable   Account No. 6

DATE		EXPLANATION	P.R.	DEBIT	CREDIT	BALANCE
Oct.	2		G–1		775 50	775 50

Harold Lloyd, Capital   Account No. 7

DATE		EXPLANATION	P.R.	DEBIT	CREDIT	BALANCE
Oct.	1		G–1		3000 00	3000 00

Harold Lloyd, Withdrawals   Account No. 8

DATE		EXPLANATION	P.R.	DEBIT	CREDIT	BALANCE
Oct.	31		G–2	725 00		725 00

Stenographic Revenue   Account No. 9

DATE		EXPLANATION	P.R.	DEBIT	CREDIT	BALANCE
Oct.	31		G–2		1725 00	1725 00

Rent Expense   Account No. 10

DATE		EXPLANATION	P.R.	DEBIT	CREDIT	BALANCE

Office Supplies Expense   Account No. 11

DATE		EXPLANATION	P.R.	DEBIT	CREDIT	BALANCE

Depreciation Expense, Office Equipment   Account No. 12

DATE	EXPLANATION	P.R.	DEBIT	CREDIT	BALANCE

On October 31, Harold Lloyd decided to adjust his accounts and prepare a balance sheet and an income statement. His adjustments were:

a. One month's rent had expired.

b. An inventory of office supplies showed $40 of unused office supplies.

c. The office equipment had depreciated $35 during October.

Required:

1. Prepare and post general journal entries to record the adjustments.

2. After posting the adjusting entries, complete the adjusted trial balance.

3. From the adjusted trial balance complete the income statement, statement of changes in owner's equity, and balance sheet.

GENERAL JOURNAL   Page 2

DATE	ACCOUNT TITLES AND EXPLANATION	P.R.	DEBIT	CREDIT

HAROLD LLOYD

Adjusted Trial Balance

October 31, 19—

Cash			
Prepaid rent			
Office supplies			
Office equipment			
Accumulated depreciation, office equipment			
Accounts payable			
Harold Lloyd, capital			
Harold Lloyd, withdrawals			
Stenographic revenue			
Rent expense			
Office supplies expense			
Depreciation expense, office equipment			
Totals			

HAROLD LLOYD

Income Statement

For Month Ended October 31, 19—

Revenue:			
Stenographic revenue			
Operating expenses:			
Rent expense			
Office supplies expense			
Depreciation expense, office equipment			
Total operating expenses			
Net income			

HAROLD LLOYD

Statement of Changes in Owner's Equity

For Month Ended October 31, 19—

Harold Lloyd, capital, October 1, 19—			
October net income			
Less withdrawals			
Excess of income over withdrawals			
Harold Lloyd, capital, October 31, 19—			

HAROLD LLOYD

Balance Sheet

October 31, 19—

Assets										
Current Assets:										
Cash										
Prepaid rent										
Office supplies										
Total current assets										
Plant and Equipment:										
Office equipment										
Less accumulated depreciation										
Total plant and equipment										
Total assets										
Liabilities										
Current Liabilities:										
Accounts payable										
Total liabilities										
Owner's Equity										
Harold Lloyd, capital, October 31, 19—										
Total liabilities and owner's equity										

Problem V

a. Blade Company has one employee who earns $72.50 per day. The company operates with monthly accounting periods, and the employee is paid each Friday night for a workweek that begins on Monday. Assume the calendar for October appears as shown below and enter the four $362.50 weekly wage payments directly in the T-accounts below. Then enter the adjustment for the wages earned but unpaid on October 31.

OCTOBER						
S	M	T	W	T	F	S
	1	2	3	4	5	6
7	8	9	10	11	12	13
14	15	16	17	18	19	20
21	22	23	24	25	26	27
28	29	30	31			

Cash	Wages Payable	Wages Expense

b. Blade Company's October income statement should show $_____

of wages expense, and its October 31 balance sheet should show a $_____
liability for wages payable. The wages earned by its employee but unpaid on October 31 are an example of

an _____ expense.

c. In the space that follows give the general journal entry to record payment of a full week's wages to the Blade Company employee on November 2.

DATE	ACCOUNT TITLES AND EXPLANATION	P.R.	DEBIT	CREDIT

61

Problem VI

Riverview Properties operates an apartment building. On December 31, at the end of an annual accounting period, its Revenue from Rents account had a $335,500 credit balance, and the Unearned Rents account had a $3,600 credit balance. The following information was available for the year-end adjustments: (a) the credit balance in the Unearned Rents account resulted from a tenant paying his rent for six months in advance beginning on November 1; (b) also, a tenant in temporary financial difficulties had not paid his rent for the month of December. The amount due was $475.

Required: Enter the necessary adjustments directly in the T-accounts below.

Rents Receivable	Unearned Rents	Revenue from Rents
	Nov. 1 3,600	Bal. 335,500

After the foregoing adjustments are entered in the accounts, the company's Revenue from Rents account has a

$_____ balance which should appear on its income statement as revenue earned

during the year. Its Unearned Rents account has a $_____ balance, and this should

appear on the company's balance sheet as a _____. Likewise, the company's Rents

Receivable account has a $_____ balance, and this should appear on its balance

sheet as a _____.

Problem VII

1. Under the cash basis of accounting, revenues are reported as being earned in the accounting period in which

    _____; expenses are charged to the period in which _____;

    and net income for the period is the difference between _____ and

    _____. Under the accrual basis of accounting, revenues are credited to the

    period in which_____, expenses are_____with
    revenues, and no consideration is given as to when cash is received or disbursed.

2. Current assets consist of cash and assets that are expected to be realized in cash or (complete definition)

    _____

    _____

    _____

    _____

Problem VIII (This problem applies to Appendix A.)

The following statements are either true or false. Place a (T) in the parentheses before each true statement and an (F) before each false statement.

1. ( ) If a business follows the practice of debiting prepayments of expenses to expense accounts, the adjusting entries for prepaid expenses require debits to prepaid expense accounts.

2. ( ) If a business records receipts of unearned revenues with debits to cash and credits to revenue accounts, no adjusting entries are required at the end of the period.

Problem IX (This problem applies to Appendix A.)

You are given several words, phrases, or numbers to choose from in completing each of the following statements or in answering the following questions. In each case select the one that best completes the statement or answers the question and place its letter in the answer space provided.

_____ 1. Hanover Company prepares monthly financial statements and follows the procedure of crediting revenue accounts when it records cash receipts of unearned revenues. During April, the business received $4,800 for services to be rendered during April and May. On April 30, $2,000 of the amounts received had been earned. What is the adjusting journal entry on April 30 for service fees?

   a. Service Fees Earned 2,000
      Unearned Service Fees   2,000
   b. Unearned Service Fees 2,800
      Service Fees Earned   2,800
   c. Cash 2,000
      Service Fees Earned   2,000
   d. Unearned Service Fees 2,000
      Service Fees Earned   2,000
   e. Service Fees Earned 2,800
      Unearned Service Fees   2,800

_____ 2. Xanadu Company prepares monthly financial statements. On August 31, the balance in the Office Supplies account was $300. During July, $500 of supplies were purchased and debited to Office Supplies Expense. What is the adjusting journal entry on September 30 to account for the supplies assuming a September inventory of supplies showed that $250 were on hand.

   a. Office Supplies 350
      Office Supplies Expense   350
   b. Office Supplies Expense 250
      Office Supplies   250
   c. Office Supplies Expense 50
      Office Supplies   50
   d. Office Supplies Expense 350
      Office Supplies   350
   e. Office Supplies 250
      Office Supplies Expense   250

Problem X, Uno Computer Services

(This problem is a serial problem that started in Chapter 2 and is continued in Chapters 4 and 5. If you did not complete the solution in Chapter 2, you can begin the problem at this point. However, as you continue, you may need to review some of the facts presented in the Chapter 2 segment of the problem.)

Uno Computer Services has had a successful two months of business since it started on October 1, 1990. At the request of John Conard, the owner, you already recorded the transactions that occurred during October and November. (This was done in Chapter 2.) Now, before making the December entries, several additional accounts have been added to the general ledger, as follows:

Accounts	Number
Accumulated Depreciation, Office Equipment	132
Accumulated Depreciation, Computer	134
Unearned Computer Fees	213
Wages Payable	215
Insurance Expense	615
Computer Supplies Expense	617
Rent Expense	621
Depreciation Expense, Office Equipment	622
Depreciation Expense, Computer	624

Journalize and post the following December transactions and end-of-period adjusting entries:

Dec. 2 Paid $300 to the Town Hall Shopping Centre for your share of advertising that benefited all businesses in the centre.

3 Paid $76 to repair the company's computer.

5 Received total amount due from AB Company as a result of the transaction on November 11.

6 Paid Ann White for four days' work at her regular daily rate of $70.

9 Received notice from AB Company that our bid of $1,850 for computer services was accepted. An advance of $450 was received.

11 Purchased on credit from Ajax Supply additional computer supplies, $85.

12 Sent a second bill to Farm Research for Services originally recorded on November 8.

13 Received notice that Republic Bank had deducted a $4 service charge from the chequing account.

16 Paid Shopper Newspaper $15 for newspaper advertisement.

18 Completed work for Dog Enterprise and received $495.

20 Paid John $675 for personal use.

20 Ann White did not work during the last two weeks.

22–26 Took the week off for Christmas holiday.

29 Received a $450 payment from Farm Research on their outstanding account balance that resulted from a November 8 transaction.

30 Paid hydro bill of $51 and telephone bill of $110.

31 Reimbursed Ann's business car mileage, 50 km., at $0.24 per km.

31 Reimbursed John's business car mileage, 300 km., at $0.24 per km.

31 In anticipation of preparing financial statements for the three month period since the business started, gathered the following information to make adjusting entries.

   a) Computer Supplies ending inventory, $17.

   b) Three months' insurance has expired.

   c) December 31 falls on Wednesday, and Ann has worked three days, but will not be paid until Friday, January 2.

   d) The computer is expected to have a three-year useful life with no salvage value.

   e) The office equipment is expected to have a four-year useful life with no salvage value.

   f) Recalled that four month's rent had been paid in advance early in October.

After you have journalized and posted the above transactions and adjusting entries, prepare an adjusted trial balance, an income statement for the last three months of 1990, a statement of changes in owner's equity for the last three months of 1990, and a December 31, 1990, balance sheet.

DATE	ACCOUNT TITLES AND EXPLANATION	P.R.	DEBIT	CREDIT

DATE	ACCOUNT TITLES AND EXPLANATION	P.R.	DEBIT	CREDIT

Cash   Account No. 111

DATE		EXPLANATION	P.R.	DEBIT	CREDIT	BALANCE
1990 Nov.	30	Balance				3 1 1 0 00

Accounts Receivable   Account No. 114

DATE		EXPLANATION	P.R.	DEBIT	CREDIT	BALANCE
1990 Nov.	30	Balance				2 6 2 0 00

Prepaid Insurance   Account No. 115

DATE		EXPLANATION	P.R.	DEBIT	CREDIT	BALANCE
1990 Nov.	30	Balance				1 9 5 00

Prepaid Rent   Account No. 116

DATE		EXPLANATION	P.R.	DEBIT	CREDIT	BALANCE
1990 Nov.	30	Balance				9 0 0 00

Computer Supplies   Account No. 117

DATE		EXPLANATION	P.R.	DEBIT	CREDIT	BALANCE
1990 Nov.	30	Balance				1 5 0 00

Office Equipment   Account No. 131

DATE		EXPLANATION	P.R.	DEBIT	CREDIT	BALANCE
1990 Nov.	30	Balance				3 4 0 00

Accumulated Depreciation, Office Equipment   Account No. 132

DATE		EXPLANATION	P.R.	DEBIT	CREDIT	BALANCE

Computer   Account No. 133

DATE		EXPLANATION	P.R.	DEBIT	CREDIT	BALANCE
1990 Nov.	30	Balance				3 0 0 0 00

Accumulated Depreciation, Computer   Account No. 134

DATE		EXPLANATION	P.R.	DEBIT	CREDIT	BALANCE

Accounts Payable — Account No. 211

DATE		EXPLANATION	P.R.	DEBIT	CREDIT	BALANCE
1990 Nov.	30	Balance				– 0 –

Unearned Computer Fees — Account No. 213

DATE	EXPLANATION	P.R.	DEBIT	CREDIT	BALANCE

Wages Payable — Account No. 215

DATE	EXPLANATION	P.R.	DEBIT	CREDIT	BALANCE

John Conard, Capital — Account No. 311

DATE		EXPLANATION	P.R.	DEBIT	CREDIT	BALANCE
1990 Nov.	30	Balance				8 3 4 0 00

John Conard, Withdrawals — Account No. 312

DATE		EXPLANATION	P.R.	DEBIT	CREDIT	BALANCE
1990 Nov.	30	Balance				2 4 8 5 00

Computer Services Revenue — Account No. 411

DATE		EXPLANATION	P.R.	DEBIT	CREDIT	BALANCE
1990 Nov.	30	Balance				6 3 4 5 00

Advertising Expense   Account No. 611

DATE		EXPLANATION	P.R.	DEBIT	CREDIT	BALANCE
1990 Nov.	30	Balance				1 5 00

Auto Expense   Account No. 612

DATE		EXPLANATION	P.R.	DEBIT	CREDIT	BALANCE
1990 Nov.	30	Balance				3 1 2 00

Computer Repair Expense   Account No. 614

DATE		EXPLANATION	P.R.	DEBIT	CREDIT	BALANCE
1990 Nov.	30	Balance				2 5 00

Insurance Expense   Account No. 615

DATE		EXPLANATION	P.R.	DEBIT	CREDIT	BALANCE

Hydro Expense   Account No. 616

DATE		EXPLANATION	P.R.	DEBIT	CREDIT	BALANCE
1990 Nov.	30	Balance				9 6 00

Computer Supplies Expense   Account No. 617

DATE		EXPLANATION	P.R.	DEBIT	CREDIT	BALANCE

Miscellaneous Expense   Account No. 619

DATE		EXPLANATION	P.R.	DEBIT	CREDIT	BALANCE
1990 Nov.	30	Balance				1 4 00

Rent Expense   Account No. 621

DATE		EXPLANATION	P.R.	DEBIT	CREDIT	BALANCE

Depreciation Expense, Office Equipment   Account No. 622

DATE		EXPLANATION	P.R.	DEBIT	CREDIT	BALANCE

Telephone Expense   Account No. 623

DATE		EXPLANATION	P.R.	DEBIT	CREDIT	BALANCE
1990 Nov.	30	Balance				2 3 3 00

Depreciation Expense, Computer   Account No. 624

DATE		EXPLANATION	P.R.	DEBIT	CREDIT	BALANCE

| | Wages Expense | | | | | Account No. 625 |

DATE		EXPLANATION	P.R.	DEBIT	CREDIT	BALANCE
1990 Nov.	30	Balance				1 1 9 0 00

UNO COMPUTER SERVICES
Adjusted Trial Balance
December 31, 1990

UNO COMPUTER SERVICES

Income Statement

For Quarter Ended December 31, 1990

UNO COMPUTER SERVICES

Statement of Changes in Owner's Equity

For Quarter Ended December 31, 1990

Solutions for Chapter 3

Problem I

1. T
2. F
3. T
4. F
5. F

Problem II

1. D
2. B
3. C
4. C
5. E
6. A
7. B

Problem III

Account form balance sheet 27

Accounting period 26

Accrual basis of accounting 23

Accrued expenses 1

Accrued revenues 5

Accumulated depreciation 15

Adjusted trial balance 4

Adjusting entry 12

Cash basis of accounting 17

Classified balance sheet 28

Common stock 20

Contra account 25

Contributed capital 2

Current assets 19

Current liabilities 30

Depreciation 10

Dividends 29

Fiscal year 9

Intangible assets 22

Interim financial reports 31

Long-term liabilities 3

Matching principle 13

Natural business year 14

Operating cycle of a business 24

Paid-in capital .... 18 or 2

Plant and equipment 11

Report form balance sheet 16

Retained earnings 8

Time-period concept 7

Unadjusted trial balance 6

Unclassified balance sheet 21

Problem IV

Oct. 31 Rent Expense	415.00	
Prepaid Rent		415.00
31 Office Supplies Expense	35.50	
Office Supplies		35.50
31 Depreciation Expense, Office Equipment	35.00	
Accumulated Depreciation, Office Equipment		35.00

Cash

Date	Debit	Credit	Balance
Oct. 1	3,000.00		3,000.00
1		1,245.00	1,755.00
1		925.50	829.50
31	1,725.00		2,554.50
31		725.00	1,829.50

Accounts Payable

Date	Debit	Credit	Balance
Oct. 2		775.50	775.50

Harold Lloyd, Capital

	Debit	Credit	Balance
Oct. 1		3,000.00	3,000.00

Prepaid Rent

Oct. 1	1,245.00		1,245.00
31		415.00	830.00

Office Supplies

Oct. 2	75.50		75.50
31		35.50	40.00

Office Equipment

Oct. 1	925.50		925.50
2	700.00		1,625.50

Accumulated Depr., Office Equipment

Oct. 31		35.00	35.00

Harold Lloyd, Withdrawals

Oct. 31	725.00		725.00

Stenographic Revenue

Oct. 31		1,725.00	1,725.00

Rent Expense

Oct. 31	415.00		415.00

Office Supplies Expense

Oct. 31	35.50		35.50

Depr. Expense, Office Equipment

Oct. 31	35.00		35.00

HAROLD LLOYD
Adjusted Trial Balance
October 31, 19—

Cash	$1,829.50	
Prepaid rent	830.00	
Office supplies	40.00	
Office equipment	1,625.50	
Accumulated depreciation, office equipment		$ 35.00
Accounts payable		775.50
Harold Lloyd, capital		3,000.00
Harold Lloyd, withdrawals	725.00	
Stenographic revenue		1,725.00
Rent expense	415.00	
Office supplies expense	35.50	
Depreciation expense, office equipment	35.00	
Totals	$5,535.50	$5,535.50

HAROLD LLOYD
Income Statement
For Month Ended October 31, 19—

Revenue:		
Stenographic revenue		$1,725.00
Operating expenses:		
Rent expense	$ 415.00	
Office supplies expense	35.50	
Depreciation expense, office equipment	35.00	
Total operating expense		485.50
Net income		$1,239.50

HAROLD LLOYD
Statement of Changes in Owner's Equity
For Month Ended October 31, 19—

Harold Lloyd, capital, October 1, 19—		$3,000.00
October net income	$1,239.50	
Less withdrawals	725.00	
Excess of income over withdrawals		514.50
Harold Lloyd, capital, October 31, 19—		$3,514.50

HAROLD LLOYD
Balance Sheet
October 31, 19—

Assets

Current Assets:		
Cash	$1,829.50	
Prepaid rent	830.00	
Office supplies	40.00	
Total current assets		$2,699.50
Plant and Equipment:		
Office equipment	$1,625.50	
Less accumulated depreciation	35.00	
Total plant and equipment		1,590.50
Total assets		$4,290.00

Liabilities

Current Liabilities:		
Accounts payable		$ 775.50
Total liabilities		$ 775.50

Owner's Equity

Harold Lloyd, capital, October 31, 19—		3,514.50
Total liabilities and owner's equity		$4,290.00

Problem V

a.

Cash			Wages Expense			Wages Payable		
Oct. 5	362.50		Oct. 5	362.50			Oct. 31	217.50
12	362.50		12	362.50				
19	362.50		19	362.50				
26	362.50		26	362.50				
			31	217.50				

b. $1,667.50; $217.50; accrued

c.	Nov. 2	Wages Expense	145.00	
		Wages Payable	217.50	
		Cash		362.50

77

Problem VI

Rents Receivable		Unearned Rents			Revenue from Rents	
Dec. 31 475		Dec. 31 1,200	Nov. 1 3,600			Bal. 335,500
						Dec. 31 1,200
						31 475

Revenue from Rents, $337,175
Unearned Rents, $2,400, current liability
Rents Receivable, $475, current asset

Problem VII

1. they are received in cash, they are paid, revenue receipts, expense disbursements, earned, matched

2. be sold or consumed within one year or within one operating cycle of the business, whichever is longer

Problem VIII

1. T
2. F

Problem IX

1. E
2. C

Problem X, Uno Computer Services

GENERAL JOURNAL

Date		Account	Ref.	Debit	Credit
Dec.	2	Advertising Expense	611	300.00	
		Cash	111		300.00
		Paid for advertising.			
	3	Computer Repair Expense	614	76.00	
		Cash	111		76.00
		Repairs to computer.			
	5	Cash	111	1,500.00	
		Accounts Receivable	114		1,500.00
		Received payment from AB Company for work completed Nov. 25.			
	6	Wages Expense	625	280.00	
		Cash	111		280.00
		Paid Ann White for four days' work.			
	9	Cash	111	450.00	
		Unearned Computer Fees	213		450.00
		Received advance payment from AB Company for future services.			
	11	Computer Supplies	117	85.00	
		Accounts Payable	211		85.00
		Purchased supplies from Ajax Supply.			
	12	No entry required.			
	13	Miscellaneous Expense	619	4.00	
		Cash	111		4.00
		Chequing account service charge.			

Dec. 16	Advertising Expense	611	15.00	
	Cash	111		15.00
	Paid for newspaper advertisement.			
18	Cash	111	495.00	
	Computer Services Revenue	411		495.00
	Completed work for Dog Enterprise.			
20	John Conard, Withdrawals	312	675.00	
	Cash	111		675.00
	Owner withdrew cash for personal use.			
20	No entry required.			
22	No entry required.			
29	Cash	111	450.00	
	Accounts Receivable	114		450.00
	Received Farm Research's payment on account.			
30	Hydro Expense	616	51.00	
	Telephone Expense	623	110.00	
	Cash	111		161.00
	Paid December hydro and telephone bills.			
31	Auto Expense	612	12.00	
	Cash	111		12.00
	Reimbursed Ann White for mileage.			
31	Auto Expense	612	72.00	
	Cash	111		72.00
	Reimbursed owner for business mileage.			

Adjusting entries:

31	Computer Supplies Expense	617	218.00	
	Computer Supplies	117		218.00
31	Insurance Expense	615	48.75	
	Prepaid Insurance	115		48.75
31	Wages Expense	625	210.00	
	Wages Payable	215		210.00
31	Depreciation Expense, Computer	624	250.00	
	Accumulated Depr., Computer	134		250.00
31	Depreciation Expense, Office Equipment	622	21.25	
	Accum. Depr., Office Equipment	132		21.25
31	Rent Expense	621	675.00	
	Prepaid Rent	116		675.00

(The following accounts include the October and November postings made in the Chapter 2 segment of this problem.)

GENERAL LEDGER

| | Cash | | No. 111 |
Date	Debit	Credit	Balance
1990			
Oct. 1	5,000.00		5,000.00
2		900.00	4,100.00
4		195.00	3,905.00
8		50.00	3,855.00
12		600.00	3,255.00
15	500.00		3,755.00
17		25.00	3,730.00
19		15.00	3,715.00
22	750.00		4,465.00
23	250.00		4,715.00
25		420.00	4,295.00
30		162.00	4,133.00
30		600.00	3,533.00
Nov. 1		36.00	3,497.00
1		108.00	3,389.00
4	425.00		3,814.00
5	300.00		4,114.00
6	1,000.00		5,114.00
7		100.00	5,014.00
8		350.00	4,664.00
13		4.00	4,660.00
15		600.00	4,060.00
18		35.00	4,025.00
20	500.00		4,525.00
22		10.00	4,515.00
22		420.00	4,095.00
28		167.00	3,928.00
28		650.00	3,278.00
29		48.00	3,230.00
29		120.00	3,110.00
Dec. 2		300.00	2,810.00
3		76.00	2,734.00
5	1,500.00		4,234.00
6		280.00	3,954.00
9	450.00		4,404.00
13		4.00	4,400.00
16		15.00	4,385.00
18	495.00		4,880.00
20		675.00	4,205.00
29	450.00		4,655.00
30		161.00	4,494.00
31		12.00	4,482.00
31		72.00	4,410.00

| | Accounts Receivable | | No. 114 |
Date	Debit	Credit	Balance
1990			
Oct. 5	500.00		500.00
12	750.00		1,250.00
15		500.00	750.00
18	1,000.00		1,750.00
22		750.00	1,000.00
24	425.00		1,425.00
28	725.00		2,150.00
Nov. 4		425.00	1,725.00
6		1,000.00	725.00
8	895.00		1,620.00
20		500.00	1,120.00
25	1,500.00		2,620.00
Dec. 5		1,500.00	1,120.00
29		450.00	670.00

| | Prepaid Insurance | | No. 115 |
Date	Debit	Credit	Balance
1990			
Oct. 4	195.00		195.00
Dec. 31		48.75	146.25

| | Prepaid Rent | | No. 116 |
Date	Debit	Credit	Balance
1990			
Oct. 2	900.00		900.00
Dec. 31		675.00	225.00

| | Computer Supplies | | No. 117 |
Date	Debit	Credit	Balance
1990			
Oct. 3	50.00		50.00
25	55.00		105.00
Nov. 7	45.00		150.00
Dec. 11	85.00		235.00
31		218.00	17.00

| | Office Equipment | | No. 131 |
Date	Debit	Credit	Balance
1990			
Oct. 1	340.00		340.00

Accum. Depr., Office Equip.   No. 132

Date	Debit	Credit	Balance
1990 Dec. 31		21.25	21.25

Computer   No. 133

Date	Debit	Credit	Balance
1990 Oct. 1	3,000.00		3,000.00

Accum. Depr., Computer   No. 134

Date	Debit	Credit	Balance
1990 Dec. 31		250.00	250.00

Accounts Payable   No. 211

Date	Debit	Credit	Balance
1990 Oct. 3		50.00	50.00
8	50.00		—0—
25		55.00	55.00
Nov. 7	55.00		—0—
Dec. 11		85.00	85.00

Unearned Computer Fees   No. 213

Date	Debit	Credit	Balance
1990 Dec. 9		450.00	450.00

Wages Payable   No. 215

Date	Debit	Credit	Balance
1990 Dec. 31		210.00	210.00

John Conard, Capital   No. 311

Date	Debit	Credit	Balance
1990 Oct. 1		8,340.00	8,340.00

John Conard, Withdrawals   No. 312

Date	Debit	Credit	Balance
1990 Oct. 12	600.00		600.00
30	600.00		1,200.00
Nov. 15	600.00		1,800.00
18	35.00		1,835.00
28	650.00		2,485.00
Dec. 20	675.00		3,160.00

Computer Services Revenue No. 411

Date	Debit	Credit	Balance
1990 Oct. 5		500.00	500.00
12		750.00	1,250.00
18		1,000.00	2,250.00
23		250.00	2,500.00
24		425.00	2,925.00
28		725.00	3,650.00
Nov. 5		300.00	3,950.00
8		895.00	4,845.00
25		1,500.00	6,345.00
Dec. 18		495.00	6,840.00

Advertising Expense   No. 611

Date	Debit	Credit	Balance
1990 Oct. 19	15.00		15.00
Dec. 2	300.00		315.00
16	15.00		330.00

Auto Expense   No. 612

Date	Debit	Credit	Balance
1990 Nov. 1	36.00		36.00
1	108.00		144.00
29	48.00		192.00
29	120.00		312.00
Dec. 31	12.00		324.00
31	72.00		396.00

Computer Repair Expense   No. 614

Date	Debit	Credit	Balance
1990 Oct. 17	25.00		25.00
Dec. 3	76.00		101.00

Insurance Expense No. 615

Date	Debit	Credit	Balance
1990 Dec. 31	48.75		48.75

Depr. Exp., Office Equip. No. 622

Date	Debit	Credit	Balance
1990 Dec. 31	21.25		21.25

Hydro Expense No. 616

Date	Debit	Credit	Balance
1990 Oct. 30	47.00		47.00
Nov. 28	49.00		96.00
Dec. 30	51.00		147.00

Telephone Expense No. 623

Date	Debit	Credit	Balance
1990 Oct. 30	115.00		115.00
Nov. 28	118.00		233.00
Dec. 30	110.00		343.00

Computer Supplies Expense No. 617

Date	Debit	Credit	Balance
1990 Dec. 31	218.00		218.00

Depr. Expense, Computer No. 624

Date	Debit	Credit	Balance
1990 Dec. 31	250.00		250.00

Miscellaneous Expense No. 619

Date	Debit	Credit	Balance
1990 Nov. 13	4.00		4.00
22	10.00		14.00
Dec. 13	4.00		18.00

Wages Expense No. 625

Date	Debit	Credit	Balance
1990 Oct. 25	420.00		420.00
Nov. 8	350.00		770.00
22	420.00		1,190.00
Dec. 6	280.00		1,470.00
31	210.00		1,680.00

Rent Expense No. 621

Date	Debit	Credit	Balance
1990 Dec. 31	675.00		675.00

UNO COMPUTER SERVICES
Adjusted Trial Balance
December 31, 1990

Cash	$ 4,410.00	
Accounts receivable	670.00	
Prepaid insurance	146.25	
Prepaid rent	225.00	
Computer supplies	17.00	
Office equipment	340.00	
Accumulated depr., office equipment		$ 21.25
Computer	3,000.00	
Accumulated depreciation, computer		250.00
Accounts payable		85.00
Unearned computer fees		450.00
Wages payable		210.00
John Conard, capital		8,340.00
John Conard, withdrawals	3,160.00	
Computer services revenue		6,840.00
Advertising expense	330.00	
Auto expense	396.00	
Computer repair expense	101.00	
Insurance expense	48.75	
Hydro expense	147.00	
Computer supplies expense	218.00	
Miscellaneous expense	18.00	
Rent expense	675.00	
Depr. expense, office equipment	21.25	
Telephone expense	343.00	
Depreciation expense, computer	250.00	
Wages expense	1,680.00	
Totals	$16,196.25	$16,196.25

UNO COMPUTER SERVICES
Income Statement
For Quarter Ended December 31, 1990

Revenue:		
Computer services revenue		$ 6,840.00
Operating expenses:		
Advertising expense	$ 330.00	
Auto expense	396.00	
Computer repair expense	101.00	
Insurance expense	48.75	
Hydro expense	147.00	
Computer supplies expense	218.00	
Miscellaneous expense	18.00	
Rent expense	675.00	
Depreciation expense, office equipment	21.25	
Telephone expense	343.00	
Depreciation expense, computer	250.00	
Wages expense	1,680.00	
Total operating expenses		4,228.00
Net income		$ 2,612.00

UNO COMPUTER SERVICES
Statement of Changes in Owner's Equity
For Quarter Ended December 31, 1990

John Conard, capital, October 1, 1990	$ –0–
Plus:	
Owner's investment	8,340.00
Net income	2,612.00
Total	$10,952.00
Less withdrawals by owner	3,160.00
John Conard, capital, December 31, 1990	$ 7,792.00

UNO COMPUTER SERVICES
Balance Sheet
December 31, 1990

Assets

Current assets:			
Cash		$ 4,410.00	
Accounts receivable		670.00	
Prepaid insurance		146.25	
Prepaid rent		225.00	
Computer suplies		17.00	
Total current assets			$ 5,468.25
Plant and equipment:			
Office equipment	$ 340.00		
Less accumulated depreciation	21.25	$ 318.75	
Computer	$3,000.00		
Less accumulated depreciation	250.00	2,750.00	
Total plant and equipment			3,068.75
Total assets			$ 8,537.00

Liabilities

Current liabilities:		
Accounts payable	$ 85.00	
Unearned computer fees	450.00	
Wages payable	210.00	
Total liabilities		$ 745.00

Owner's Equity

John Conard, capital, December 31, 1990	7,792.00
Total liabilities and owner's equity	$ 8,537.00

4

The Work Sheet and Closing the Accounts of Proprietorships, Partnerships, and Corporations

After studying Chapter 4, you should be able to:

1. Explain why a work sheet is prepared and be able to prepare a work sheet for a service-type business.

2. Prepare closing entries for a service business and explain why it is necessary to close the temporary accounts at the end of each accounting period.

3. Prepare a post-closing trial balance and explain its purpose.

4. Explain the nature of a corporation's retained earnings and its relationship to the declaration of dividends.

5. Prepare entries to record the declaration and payment of a dividend and to close the temporary accounts of a corporation.

6. List the steps in the accounting cycle in the order in which they are completed and perform each step.

7. Define or explain the words and phrases listed in the chapter Glossary.

After studying the appendix to Chapter 4 (Appendix B), you should be able to:

8. Prepare reversing entries and explain when and why they are used.

Topical Outline

I. The work sheet and adjusting entries

    A. A work sheet is prepared at the end of each accounting period to:

        1. Reflect the effects of adjustments before adjusting entries are made.
        2. Provide the information used in preparing financial statements by sorting adjusted account balances into appropriate income statement and statement of changes in owner's equity or balance sheet columns.
        3. Calculate and prove the mathematical accuracy of net income.

    B. To prepare a work sheet:

        1. List all accounts contained in the unadjusted trial balance.
        2. Make adjusting entries in appropriate columns.
        3. Combine amounts in Unadjusted Trial Balance columns and Adjustment columns and carry these amounts to Adjusted Trial Balance columns.
        4. Add Adjusted Trial Balance columns to prove their equality.
        5. Sort amounts into Statement of Changes in Owner's Equity and Balance Sheet or Income Statement columns.
        6. Determine net income (or loss) by taking the difference between debit and credit totals of Income Statement columns, and balance the Balance Sheet columns by adding net income (or loss).

    C. Journalize and post adjusting entries.

II. Closing entries

    A. Closing entries are made to:

        1. Transfer the effects of revenues, expenses, and withdrawals to the capital account.
        2. Bring the temporary (revenue, expense, withdrawal, and Income Summary) account balances to zero, so that revenues, expenses, and withdrawals in the next accounting period can be properly recorded and closed.

    B. Closing the accounts

        1. Revenue accounts, which have credit balances, are closed by debiting the accounts and crediting Income Summary.
        2. Expense accounts, which have debit balances, are closed by crediting the accounts and debiting Income Summary.
        3. The balance of the Income Summary account is transferred to the proprietor's capital account.
        4. The withdrawals account is closed to the proprietor's capital account.

    C. Accounts that appear in the balance sheet are called real or permanent accounts. Those that are closed at the end of each period are called nominal or temporary accounts.

III. Accounting for partnerships and corporations

    A. Partnership accounting is like accounting for a single proprietorship, except:

        1. Separate withdrawals and capital accounts are kept for each partner.
        2. The Income Summary account is closed with a compound journal entry to allocate each partner's share of income (or loss).

    B. Corporation accounting is also like accounting for a single proprietorship, except:

        1. There are two kinds of shareholders' equity accounts:

            a. Contributed capital accounts (such as Common Stock)
            b. Retained Earnings account

2. The Income Summary account is closed to the Retained Earnings account.
3. Dividend declarations are recorded in Dividends Declared, which is closed to the Retained Earnings account.

IV. The accounting cycle—the sequence of accounting procedures followed each accounting period:

A. Journalizing
B. Posting
C. Preparing an unadjusted trial balance
D. Completing the work sheet
E. Preparing the statements
F. Adjusting the ledger accounts
G. Closing the temporary accounts
H. Preparing a post-closing trial balance

V. Appendix B

A. Reversing entries are optional entries prepared after closing entries and dated the first day of the new period.
B. Reversing entries are usually applied to asset and liability account balances that arose from the accrual of revenues and expenses.
C. The accrued asset and liability account balances are transferred to related revenue and expense accounts.
D. When reversing entries are used, subsequent cash receipts (and payments) are recorded in revenue (and expense) accounts.

Problem I

The following statements are either true or false. Place a (T) in the parentheses before each true statement and an (F) before each false statement.

1. ( ) If the Income Statement columns of a work sheet are equal after transferring from the Adjusted Trial Balance columns, then it can be concluded that there is no net income (or loss).

2. ( ) The only reason why the Statement of Changes in Owner's Equity or Balance Sheet columns of a work sheet might be out of balance would be if an error had been made in sorting revenue and expense data from the Adjusted Trial Balance columns of the work sheet.

3. ( ) After all closing entries are posted at the end of an accounting period, the Income Summary account balance is zero.

4. ( ) Throughout the current period, one could refer to the balance of the Income Summary account to determine the amount of net income or loss that was earned in the prior accounting period.

5. ( ) On a work sheet, net income would be understated if a liability was extended into the Income Statement—Credit column.

Problem II

You are given several words, phrases, or numbers to choose from completing each of the following statements or in answering the following questions. In each case select the one that best completes the statement or answers the question and place its letter in the answer space provided.

_____ 1. Equipment, Wages Expense, and The Owner, Capital would be sorted to which respective columns in completing a work sheet?

  a. Statement of Changes in Owner's Equity or Balance Sheet—Debit; Income Statement—Debit; and Statement of Changes in Owner's Equity or Balance Sheet—Debit.
  b. Statement of Changes in Owner's Equity or Balance Sheet—Debit; Income Statement—Debit; and Statement of Changes in Owner's Equity or Balance Sheet—Credit.
  c. Statement of Changes in Owner's Equity or Balance Sheet—Debit; Income Statement—Credit; and Statement of Changes in Owner's Equity or Balance Sheet—Debit.
  d. Statement of Changes in Owner's Equity or Balance Sheet—Debit; Income Statement—Credit; and Statement of Changes in Owner's Equity or Balance Sheet—Credit.
  e. Statement of Changes in Owner's Equity or Balance Sheet—Credit; Income Statement—Credit; and Statement of Changes in Owner's Equity or Balance Sheet—Credit.

_____ 2. Based on the following T-accounts and their end-of-period balances, what will be the balance of the Joe Cool, Capital account after the closing entries are posted?

Joe Cool, Capital		Joe Cool, Withdrawals		Income Summary
Dec. 31 7,000	Dec. 31 9,600		

Revenue		Rent Expense		Salaries Expense
Dec. 31 29,700	Dec. 31 3,600		Dec. 31 7,200	

88

Insurance Expense		Depr. Expense, Equipment		Accum. Depr., Equipment	
Dec. 31	920	Dec. 31	500	Dec. 31	500

    a. $12,880 Debit.
    b. $12,880 Credit.
    c. $24,480 Credit.
    d. $14,880 Credit.
    e. $10,480 Debit.

———— 3. The following items appeared on a December 31 work sheet. Based on the following information, what are the totals in the Statement of Changes in Owner's Equity or Balance Sheet columns?

	Unadjusted Trial Balance		Adjustments	
	Debit	Credit	Debit	Credit
Cash	975			
Prepaid insurance	3,600			150
Supplies	180			70
Equipment	10,320			
Accounts payable		1,140		
Unearned fees		4,500	375	
The Owner, capital		9,180		
The Owner, withdrawals	1,650			
Fees earned		5,850		375
				300
Rent expense	1,500			
Salaries expense	2,100		315	
Utilities expense	345			
	20,670	20,670		
Insurance expense			150	
Supplies expense			70	
Depreciation expense, equipment			190	
Accumulated depreciation, equipment				190
Salaries payable				315
Accounts receivable			300	
			1,400	1,400

    a. $16,805.
    b. $16,505.
    c. $14,950.
    d. $14,820.
    e. Some other amount.

———— 4. In what order are the following steps in the accounting cycle performed?
    1) Preparing an unadjusted trial balance
    2) Journalizing and posting closing entries
    3) Journalizing transactions
    4) Preparing a post-closing trial balance
    5) Preparing the financial statements
    6) Completing the work sheet
    7) Journalizing and posting adjusting entries
    8) Posting the entries to record transactions

a. (1), (3), (8), (7), (6), (2), (4), (5)
b. (3), (8), (1), (6), (5), (7), (2), (4)
c. (1), (3), (8), (6), (7), (2), (5), (4)
d. (3), (1), (8), (7), (6), (5), (4), (2)
e. (3), (8), (1), (7), (6), (2), (4), (5)

_____ 5. Real accounts are:

a. accounts that are closed at the end of each accounting period; therefore, the revenue, expense, Income Summary, and withdrawals accounts.
b. accounts used to record the owner's investment in the business plus any more or less permanent changes in the owner's equity.
c. accounts the balance of which is subtracted from the balance of an associated account to show a more proper amount for the item recorded in the associated account.
d. also called temporary accounts.
e. also called permanent accounts.

Problem III

Many of the important ideas and concepts discussed in Chapter 4 are reflected in the following list of key terms. Test your understanding of these terms by matching the appropriate definitions with the terms. Record the number identifying the most appropriate definition in the blank space next to each term.

_____ Accounting cycle

_____ Closing entries

_____ Date of declaration

_____ Date of payment

_____ Date of record

_____ Deficit

_____ Dividends Declared

_____ Income Summary

_____ Nominal accounts

_____ Permanent accounts

_____ Post-closing trial balance

_____ Real accounts

_____ Reversing entries

_____ Shareholders of record

_____ Temporary accounts

_____ Working papers

_____ Work sheet

1. The shareholders of a corporation as reflected in the records of the corporation.

2. A trial balance prepared after all adjusting and closing entries have been posted.

3. The recurring accounting steps that are performed each accounting period and that begin with the recording of transactions and proceed through posting the recorded amounts, preparing a trial balance and completing a work sheet, preparing the financial statements, preparing and posting adjusting and closing entries, and preparing a post-closing trial balance.

4. A temporary account that serves the same function for a corporation as does a withdrawals account for a proprietorship, and which is closed to Retained Earnings at the end of each accounting period.

5. Accounts that are closed at the end of each accounting period; therefore, the revenue, expense, Income Summary, and withdrawals accounts.

6. A negative amount (debit balance) of retained earnings.

7. The date on which a dividend liability of a corporation is satisfied by mailing cheques to the shareholders.

8. Another name for permanent accounts.

9. The date on which a dividend is declared by a corporation's board of directors.

10. Entries made at the end of each accounting period to establish zero balances in the temporary accounts and to transfer the temporary account balances to a capital account or accounts or to the Retained Earnings account.

11. The account used in the closing process to summarize the amounts of revenues and expenses, and from which the amount of the net income or loss is transferred to the owner's capital account in a single proprietorship, the partners' capital accounts in a partnership, or the Retained Earnings account in a corporation.

12. A working paper on which the accountant shows the unadjusted trial balance, shows the effects of the adjustments on the account balances, calculates the net income or loss, and sorts the adjusted amounts according to the financial statements on which the amounts will appear.

13. The date on which the shareholders who are listed in a corporation's records are determined to be those who will receive a dividend.

14. The memoranda, analyses, and other informal papers prepared by accountants in the process of organizing the data that goes into the formal financial reports given to managers and other interested parties.

15. Accounts that remain open as long as the asset, liability, or owner's equity items recorded in the accounts continue in existence; therefore, accounts that appear in the balance sheet.

16. Optional entries that transfer the balances in balance sheet accounts which arose as a result of certain adjusting entries (usually accruals) to income statement accounts.

17. Another name for temporary accounts.

Problem IV

Complete the following by filling in the blanks.

1. A work sheet is prepared after all transactions are recorded but before _____

_____

_____.

2. Revenue accounts have credit balances; consequently, to close a revenue account and make it show a zero balance, the revenue account is _____ and the Income Summary account is _____ for the amount of the balance.

3. In sorting the amounts in the Adjusted Trial Balance columns of a work sheet to the proper Income Statement or Statement of Changes in Owner's Equity and Balance Sheet columns, two decisions are involved. The decisions are:

(a) _____ and

(b) _____.

4. Expense accounts have debit balances; therefore, expense accounts are _____ and the Income Summary account is _____ in closing the expense accounts.

5. In preparing a work sheet for a concern, its unadjusted ledger account balances are entered in the _____ _____ of the work sheet form, after which the _____ _____ are entered in the second pair of money columns. Next, the unadjusted trial balance amounts and the amounts in the Adjustments columns are combined to secure a _____ in the third pair of money columns.

6. Only balance sheet accounts should have balances appearing on the post-closing trial balance because the balances of all temporary accounts are reduced to _____ in the closing procedure.

7. A work sheet is a tool of the accountant, that is used to:

   (a) _____,

   (b) _____,

   (c) _____.

8. A corporation has two kinds of shareholders' equity accounts, called _____ _____ and _____.

9. Closing entries are necessary because if at the end of an accounting period the revenue and expense accounts are to show only one period's revenues and expenses, they must begin the period with _____ balances, and closing entries cause the revenue and expense accounts to begin a new period with _____ balances.

10. Closing entries accomplish two purposes: (1) they cause all _____ accounts to begin the new accounting period with zero balances, and (2) they transfer the net effect of the past period's _____, _____, and withdrawal transactions to the owner's capital account.

Problem V

The unfinished year-end work sheet of Homer's Home Shop appears on the next page.

Required:

1. Complete the work sheet using the following adjustments information:
   a. A $725 inventory of shop supplies indicates that $1,037 of shop supplies have been used during the year.
   b. The shop equipment has depreciated $475 during the year.
   c. On December 31, wages of $388 have been earned by the one employee but are unpaid because payment is not due.

2. After completing the work sheet, prepare the year-end adjusting and closing entries.

3. Post the adjusting and closing entries to the accounts that appear in skeletonized form beginning on page 99.

4. After posting the adjusting and closing entries, prepare a post-closing trial balance.

HOMER'S HOME SHOP

Work Sheet for Year Ended December 31, 19—

ACCOUNT TITLES	UNADJUSTED TRIAL BALANCE		ADJUSTMENTS		ADJUSTED TRIAL BALANCE		INCOME STATEMENT		STATEMENT OF CHANGES IN OWNER'S EQUITY OR BALANCE SHEET	
	DR.	CR.	DR.	CR.	DR.	CR.	DR.	CR.	DR.	CR.
Cash	2,875 00									
Amounts receivable	2,000 00									
Shop supplies	1,762 00									
Shop equipment	5,125 00									
Accumulated depreciation, shop equipment		725 00								
Accounts payable		575 00								
Homer Tonely, capital		5,500 00								
Homer Tonely, withdrawals	30,000 00									
Revenue from repairs		55,785 00								
Rent expense	2,500 00									
Wages expense	18,250 00									
Miscellaneous expenses	73 00									
	62,585 00	62,585 00								
Shop supplies expense										
Depreciation expense, shop equipment										
Wages payable										

DATE		ACCOUNT TITLES AND EXPLANATION	P.R.	DEBIT	CREDIT

GENERAL LEDGER

Cash

Date		Debit	Credit	Balance
Dec.	31			2,875.00

Accounts Receivable

Date		Debit	Credit	Balance
Dec.	31			2,000.00

Shop Supplies

Date		Debit	Credit	Balance
Dec.	31			1,762.00

Shop Equipment

Date		Debit	Credit	Balance
Dec.	31			5,125.00

Accumulated Depr., Shop Equipment

Date		Debit	Credit	Balance
Dec.	31			725.00

Accounts Payable

Date		Debit	Credit	Balance
Dec.	31			575.00

Wages Payable

Date		Debit	Credit	Balance

Homer Tonely, Capital

Date		Debit	Credit	Balance
Dec.	31			5,500.00

Homer Tonely, Withdrawals

Date		Debit	Credit	Balance
Dec.	31			30,000.00

Income Summary

Date		Debit	Credit	Balance

Revenue from Repairs

Date		Debit	Credit	Balance
Dec.	31			55,785.00

Rent Expense

Date		Debit	Credit	Balance
Dec.	31			2,500.00

Wages Expense

Date		Debit	Credit	Balance
Dec.	31			18,250.00

Miscellaneous Expenses

Date		Debit	Credit	Balance
Dec.	31			73.00

Shop Supplies Expense

Date		Debit	Credit	Balance

Depr. Expense, Shop Equipment

Date		Debit	Credit	Balance

HOMER'S HOME SHOP
Post-Closing Trial Balance
December 31, 19—

Cash		
Accounts receivable		
Shop supplies		
Shop equipment		
Accumulated depreciation, shop equipment		
Accounts payable		
Wages payable		
Homer Tonely, capital		
Totals		

Problem VI

Prepare journal entries to record the following events related to Slater Company.

1. Slater Company sold 15,000 shares of common stock for $375,000.

2. In making closing entries, the net income for the year amounted to $50,000. (Close the Income Summary account.)

3. Slater Company declared $15,500 of dividends to be paid in cash to common shareholders.

4. Slater Company paid the dividends declared in (3).

GENERAL JOURNAL

DATE	ACCOUNT TITLES AND EXPLANATION	P.R.	DEBIT	CREDIT

Problem VII (This problem applies to Appendix B.)

The following statements are either true or false. Place a (T) in the parentheses before each true statement and an (F) before each false statement.

1. ( ) After the adjusting, closing, and reversing entries are posted to an account where there were end-of-period adjustments of accrued items, the account will have an opposite from normal balance.

2. ( ) Reversing entries are used only for accruals of expense items such as Salaries Expense, Tax Expense, and Interest Expense.

3. ( ) If a business records prepaid expenses with a debit to a prepaid expense account, then a reversing entry would be appropriate.

Problem VIII (This problem applies to Appendix B.)

You are given several words, phrases, or numbers to choose from in completing each of the following statements or in answering the following questions. In each case select the one that best completes the statement or answers the question and place its letter in the answer space provided.

_____ 1. The December 31, 1989, adjusting entries for Mary Swan's interior design company included accrual of $760 in secretarial salaries. This amount will be paid on January 5, as part of the normal $1,200 salary for two weeks. The bookkeeper for the company uses reversing entries where appropriate. When the secretary's salary was paid on January 10, 1990, the following entry was made.

Jan. 10   Salaries Expense 1,200
             Cash 1,200
What was the January 1, 1990, reversing entry?

  a. Salaries Payable 760
       Salaries Expense 440
         Cash 1,200
  b. Salaries Payable 440
         Salaries Expense 440
  c. Salaries Payable 760
         Salaries Expense 760
  d. Cash 1,200
         Salaries Expense 1,200
  e. The bookkeeper would not make a reversing entry for this transaction.

_____ 2. On December 31, 1989, X Company accrued salaries expense with an adjusting entry. No reversing entry was made and the payment of the salaries during January 1990 was correctly recorded. If X Company had recorded an entry on January 1, 1990, to reverse the accrual, and the subsequent payment was correctly recorded, the effect on the 1990 financial statements of using the reversing entry would have been:

  a. to increase net income and reduce liabilities.
  b. to increase 1990 expense and reduce assets.
  c. to decrease 1990 expense and increase liabilities.
  d. to decrease 1990 expense and decrease liabilities.
  e. No effect.

Problem IX (This problem applies to Appendix B.)

Based on the following end-of-period information, prepare reversing entries assuming that adjusting and closing entries have been properly recorded.

1) Depreciation on office equipment, $3,000.

2) $350 of the $1,400 Prepaid Insurance balance has expired.

3) Employees have earned salaries of $1,000 that have not been paid. They will be paid $1,750 on the next pay date.

4) The company has earned $3,050 of service fees that have not been collected or recorded.

5) The Unearned Service Fees account balance includes $1,000 that has been earned.

6) An inventory of supplies shows $250 of unused supplies. The balance of supplies on the unadjusted trial balance for the period is $900.

7) The company pays $1,200 interest on a loan each quarter. The next quarterly payment is due in two months from the end of the current period.

GENERAL JOURNAL

DATE	ACCOUNT TITLES AND EXPLANATION	P.R.	DEBIT	CREDIT

Problem X, Uno Computer Services

(This problem is a serial problem that started in Chapter 2, was continued in Chapter 3, and will be continued in Chapter 5. If you did not complete the solutions in Chapters 2 and 3, you can begin the problem at this point. However, as you continue, you may need to review some of the facts presented in the Chapters 2 and 3 segments of the problem.)

After being in business for the last three months of 1990, John Conard, the owner of Uno Computer Services, is preparing to begin the new year. In fulfilling the requirements of the problem in Chapters 2 and 3, all transactions that occurred during October, November, and December 1990, have been journalized and posted, as have been the December 31 adjusting entries. Also, financial statements for the three month period ended December 31 have been prepared.

In anticipation of closing the books, an Income Summary account (Account No. 799) has been added to the General Ledger. To complete the accounting cycle, you should journalize and post the closing entries. Also, prepare a post-closing trial balance. The general ledger accounts with their December 31, 1990, balances are as follows:

DATE		ACCOUNT TITLES AND EXPLANATION	P.R.	DEBIT	CREDIT

Cash   Account No. 111

DATE		EXPLANATION	P.R.	DEBIT	CREDIT	BALANCE
1990 Dec.	31	Balance				4 4 1 0 00

Accounts Receivable   Account No. 114

DATE		EXPLANATION	P.R.	DEBIT	CREDIT	BALANCE
1990 Dec.	31	Balance				6 7 0 00

Prepaid Insurance   Account No. 115

DATE		EXPLANATION	P.R.	DEBIT	CREDIT	BALANCE
1990 Dec.	31	Balance				1 4 6 25

Prepaid Rent   Account No. 116

DATE		EXPLANATION	P.R.	DEBIT	CREDIT	BALANCE
1990 Dec.	31	Balance				2 2 5 00

Computer Supplies   Account No. 117

DATE		EXPLANATION	P.R.	DEBIT	CREDIT	BALANCE
1990 Dec.	31	Balance				1 7 00

Office Equipment   Account No. 131

DATE		EXPLANATION	P.R.	DEBIT	CREDIT	BALANCE
1990 Dec.	31	Balance				3 4 0 00

Accumulated Depreciation, Office Equipment   Account No. 132

DATE		EXPLANATION	P.R.	DEBIT	CREDIT	BALANCE
1990 Dec.	31	Balance				2 1 25

Computer   Account No. 133

DATE		EXPLANATION	P.R.	DEBIT	CREDIT	BALANCE
1990 Dec.	31	Balance				3 0 0 0 00

Accumulated Depreciation, Computer   Account No. 134

DATE		EXPLANATION	P.R.	DEBIT	CREDIT	BALANCE
1990 Dec.	31	Balance				2 5 0 00

Accounts Payable   Account No. 211

DATE		EXPLANATION	P.R.	DEBIT	CREDIT	BALANCE
1990 Dec.	31	Balance				8 5 00

Unearned Computer Fees   Account No. 213

DATE		EXPLANATION	P.R.	DEBIT	CREDIT	BALANCE
1990 Dec.	31	Balance				4 5 0 00

Wages Payable   Account No. 215

DATE		EXPLANATION	P.R.	DEBIT	CREDIT	BALANCE
1990 Dec.	31	Balance				2 1 0 00

John Conard, Capital   Account No. 311

DATE		EXPLANATION	P.R.	DEBIT	CREDIT	BALANCE
1990 Dec.	31	Balance				8 3 4 0 00

John Conard, Withdrawals   Account No. 312

DATE		EXPLANATION	P.R.	DEBIT	CREDIT	BALANCE
1990 Dec.	31	Balance				3 1 6 0 00

Computer Services Revenue   Account No. 411

DATE		EXPLANATION	P.R.	DEBIT	CREDIT	BALANCE
1990 Dec.	31	Balance				6 8 4 0 00

Advertising Expense   Account No. 611

DATE		EXPLANATION	P.R.	DEBIT	CREDIT	BALANCE
1990 Dec.	31	Balance				3 3 0 00

Auto Expense   Account No. 612

DATE		EXPLANATION	P.R.	DEBIT	CREDIT	BALANCE
1990 Dec.	31	Balance				3 9 6 00

Computer Repair Expense

Account No. 614

DATE		EXPLANATION	P.R.	DEBIT	CREDIT	BALANCE
1990 Dec.	31	Balance				1 0 1 00

Insurance Expense

Account No. 615

DATE		EXPLANATION	P.R.	DEBIT	CREDIT	BALANCE
1990 Dec.	31	Balance				4 8 75

Hydro Expense

Account No. 616

DATE		EXPLANATION	P.R.	DEBIT	CREDIT	BALANCE
1990 Dec.	31	Balance				1 4 7 00

Computer Supplies Expense

Account No. 617

DATE		EXPLANATION	P.R.	DEBIT	CREDIT	BALANCE
1990 Dec.	31	Balance				2 1 8 00

Miscellaneous Expense

Account No. 619

DATE		EXPLANATION	P.R.	DEBIT	CREDIT	BALANCE
1990 Dec.	31	Balance				1 8 00

Rent Expense   Account No. 621

DATE		EXPLANATION	P.R.	DEBIT	CREDIT	BALANCE
1990 Dec.	31	Balance				6 7 5 00

Depreciation Expense, Office Equipment   Account No. 622

DATE		EXPLANATION	P.R.	DEBIT	CREDIT	BALANCE
1990 Dec.	31	Balance				2 1 25

Telephone Expense   Account No. 623

DATE		EXPLANATION	P.R.	DEBIT	CREDIT	BALANCE
1990 Dec.	31	Balance				3 4 3 00

Depreciation Expense, Computer   Account No. 624

DATE		EXPLANATION	P.R.	DEBIT	CREDIT	BALANCE
1990 Dec.	31	Balance				2 5 0 00

Wages Expense   Account No. 625

DATE		EXPLANATION	P.R.	DEBIT	CREDIT	BALANCE
1990 Dec.	31	Balance				1 6 8 0 00

DATE	EXPLANATION	P.R.	DEBIT	CREDIT	BALANCE

UNO COMPUTER SERVICES

Post-Closing Trial Balance

December 31, 1990

Problem I

1. T
2. F
3. T
4. F
5. F

Problem II

1. B
2. D
3. A
4. B
5. E

Problem III

Accounting cycle	3	Permanent accounts	15
Closing entries	10	Post-closing trial balance	2
Date of declaration	9	Real accounts	8 or 15
Date of payment	7	Reversing entries	16
Date of record	13	Shareholders of record	1
Deficit	6	Temporary accounts	5
Dividends Declared	4	Working papers	14
Income Summary	11	Work sheet	12
Nominal accounts	17 or 5		

Problem IV

1. the adjustments are entered in the accounts

2. debited, credited

3. (a) Is the item a debit or a credit?
   (b) On which statement does it appear?

4. credited, debited

5. first two money columns, or Unadjusted Trial Balance columns; adjustments; adjusted trial balance

6. zero

7. (a) achieve the effect of adjusting the accounts before entering the adjustments in the accounts,
   (b) sort the adjusted account balances into columns according to the statement on which they appear, and
   (c) calculate and prove the mathematical accuracy of the net income or loss.

8. contributed capital accounts, retained earnings accounts

9. zero, zero

10. temporary or nominal, revenue, expense

Problem V

HOMER'S HOME SHOP
Work Sheet for Year Ended December 31, 19—

	Unadjusted Trial Balance Dr.	Cr.	Adjustments Dr.	Cr.	Adjusted Trial Balance Dr.	Cr.	Income Statement Dr.	Cr.	Statement of Ch. in O.E. or Balance Sheet Dr.	Cr.
Cash	2,875				2,875				2,875	
Accounts receivable	2,000				2,000				2,000	
Shop supplies	1,762			(a) 1,037	725				725	
Shop equipment	5,125				5,125				5,125	
Accum. depr., shop equipment		725		(b) 475		1,200				1,200
Accounts payable		575				575				575
Homer Tonely, capital		5,500				5,500				5,500
Homer Tonely, withdrawals	30,000				30,000				30,000	
Revenue from repairs		55,785				55,785		55,785		
Rent expense	2,500				2,500		2,500			
Wages expense	18,250		(c) 388		18,638		18,638			
Miscellaneous expenses	73				73		73			
	62,585	62,585								
Shop supplies expense			(a) 1,037		1,037		1,037			
Depreciation expense, shop equipment			(b) 475		475		475			
Wages payable				(c) 388		388				388
			1,900	1,900	63,448	63,448	22,723	55,785	40,725	7,663
Net income							33,062			33,062
							55,785	55,785	40,725	40,725

Dec. 31	Shop Supplies Expense		1,037	
	Shop Supplies			1,037
31	Depr. Expense, Shop Equipment		475	
	Accumulated Depr., Shop Equipment			475
31	Wages Expense		388	
	Wages Payable			388
31	Revenue from Repairs		55,785	
	Income Summary			55,785
31	Income Summary		22,723	
	Rent Expense			2,500
	Wages Expense			18,638
	Miscellaneous Expenses			73
	Shop Supplies Expense			1,037
	Depr. Expense, Shop Equipment			475
31	Income Summary		33,062	
	Homer Tonely, Capital			33,062
31	Homer Tonely, Capital		30,000	
	Homer Tonely, Withdrawals			30,000

GENERAL LEDGER

Cash

Date		Debit	Credit	Balance
Dec.	31			2,875.00

Wages Payable

Date		Debit	Credit	Balance
Dec.	31		388.00	388.00

Accounts Receivable

Date		Debit	Credit	Balance
Dec.	31			2,000.00

Homer Tonely, Capital

Date		Debit	Credit	Balance
Dec.	31			5,500.00
	31		33,062.00	38,562.00
	31	30,000.00		8,562.00

Shop Supplies

Date		Debit	Credit	Balance
Dec.	31			1,762.00
	31		1,037.00	725.00

Homer Tonely, Withdrawals

Date		Debit	Credit	Balance
Dec.	31			30,000.00
	31		30,000.00	—0—

Shop Equipment

Date		Debit	Credit	Balance
Dec.	31			5,125.00

Income Summary

Date		Debit	Credit	Balance
Dec.	31		55,785.00	55,785.00
	31	22,723.00		33,062.00
	31	33,062.00		—0—

Accumulated Depr., Shop Equipment

Date		Debit	Credit	Balance
Dec.	31			725.00
	31		475.00	1,200.00

Revenue from Repairs

Date		Debit	Credit	Balance
Dec.	31			55,785.00
	31	55,785.00		—0—

Accounts Payable

Date		Debit	Credit	Balance
Dec.	31			575.00

Rent Expense

Date		Debit	Credit	Balance
Dec.	31			2,500.00
	31		2,500.00	—0—

GENERAL LEDGER

Wages Expense

Date		Debit	Credit	Balance
Dec.	31			18,250.00
	31	388.00		18,638.00
	31		18,638.00	–0–

Shop Supplies Expense

Date		Debit	Credit	Balance
Dec.	31	1,037.00		1,037.00
	31		1,037.00	–0–

Miscellaneous Expenses

Date		Debit	Credit	Balance
Dec.	31			73.00
	31		73.00	–0–

Depr. Expense, Shop Equipment

Date		Debit	Credit	Balance
Dec.	31	475.00		475.00
	31		475.00	–0–

HOMER'S HOME SHOP
Post-Closing Trial Balance
December 31, 19—

Cash	$ 2,875	
Accounts receivable	2,000	
Shop supplies	725	
Shop equipment	5,125	
Accumulated depreciation, shop equipment		$ 1,200
Accounts payable		575
Wages payable		388
Homer Tonely, capital		8,562
Totals	$10,725	$10,725

Problem VI

1. Cash	375,000.00	
Common Stock		375,000.00
2. Income Summary	50,000.00	
Retained Earnings		50,000.00
3. Dividends Declared	15,500.00	
Common Dividend Payable		15,500.00
4. Common Dividend Payable	15,500.00	
Cash		15,500.00

Problem VII

1. T
2. F
3. F

Problem VIII

1. C
2. E

111

Problem IX

1) No reversing entry required.

2) No reversing entry required.

3) Salaries Payable 1,000.00
    Salaries Expense 1,000.00

4) Service Fees Earned 3,050.00
    Accounts Receivable 3,050.00

5) No reversing entry required.

6) No reversing entry required.

7) Interest Payable 400.00
    Interest Expense 400.00

Problem X, Uno Computer Services

Dec. 31	Computer Services Revenue	411	6,840.00	
	Income Summary	799		6,840.00
	To close the revenue account.			
31	Income Summary	799	4,228.00	
	Advertising Expense	611		330.00
	Auto Expense	612		396.00
	Computer Repair Expense	614		101.00
	Insurance Expense	615		48.75
	Hydro Expense	616		147.00
	Computer Supplies Expense	617		218.00
	Miscellaneous Expense	619		18.00
	Rent Expense	621		675.00
	Depreciation Expense, Office Equipment	622		21.25
	Telephone Expense	623		343.00
	Depreciation Expense, Computer	624		250.00
	Wages Expense	625		1,680.00
	To close the expense accounts.			
31	Income Summary	799	2,612.00	
	John Conard, Capital	311		2,612.00
	To close the Income Summary account.			
31	John Conard, Capital	311	3,160.00	
	John Conard, Withdrawals	312		3,160.00

GENERAL LEDGER

Cash   No. 111

Date	Debit	Credit	Balance
1990 Dec. 31			4,410.00

Computer   No. 133

Date	Debit	Credit	Balance
1990 Dec. 31			3,000.00

Accounts Receivable   No. 114

Date	Debit	Credit	Balance
1990 Dec. 31			670.00

Accum. Depr., Computer   No. 134

Date	Debit	Credit	Balance
1990 Dec. 31			250.00

Prepaid Insurance   No. 115

Date	Debit	Credit	Balance
1990 Dec. 31			146.25

Accounts Payable   No. 211

Date	Debit	Credit	Balance
1990 Dec. 31			85.00

Prepaid Rent   No. 116

Date	Debit	Credit	Balance
1990 Dec. 31			225.00

Unearned Computer Fees   No. 213

Date	Debit	Credit	Balance
1990 Dec. 31			450.00

Computer Supplies   No. 117

Date	Debit	Credit	Balance
1990 Dec. 31			17.00

Wages Payable   No. 215

Date	Debit	Credit	Balance
1990 Dec. 31			210.00

Office Equipment   No. 131

Date	Debit	Credit	Balance
1990 Dec. 31			340.00

John Conard, Capital   No. 311

Date	Debit	Credit	Balance
1990 Dec. 31			8,340.00
31		2,612.00	10,952.00
31	3,160.00		7,792.00

Accum. Depr., Office Equipment   No. 132

Date	Debit	Credit	Balance
1990 Dec. 31			21.25

John Conard, Withdrawals   No. 312

Date	Debit	Credit	Balance
1990 Dec. 31			3,160.00
31		3,160.00	—0—

GENERAL LEDGER

Computer Services Revenue   No. 411

Date	Debit	Credit	Balance
1990 Dec. 31			6,840.00
31	6,840.00		–0–

Miscellaneous Expense   No. 619

Date	Debit	Credit	Balance
1990 Dec. 31			18.00
31		18.00	–0–

Advertising Expense   No. 611

Date	Debit	Credit	Balance
1990 Dec. 31			330.00
31		330.00	–0–

Rent Expense   No. 621

Date	Debit	Credit	Balance
1990 Dec. 31			675.00
31		675.00	–0–

Auto Expense   No. 612

Date	Debit	Credit	Balance
1990 Dec. 31			396.00
31		396.00	–0–

Depr. Exp., Office Equipment   No. 622

Date	Debit	Credit	Balance
1990 Dec. 31			21.25
31		21.25	–0–

Computer Repair Expense   No. 614

Date	Debit	Credit	Balance
1990 Dec. 31			101.00
31		101.00	–0–

Telephone Expense   No. 623

Date	Debit	Credit	Balance
1990 Dec. 31			343.00
31		343.00	–0–

Insurance Expense   No. 615

Date	Debit	Credit	Balance
1990 Dec. 31			48.75
31		48.75	–0–

Depr. Expense, Computer   No. 624

Date	Debit	Credit	Balance
1990 Dec. 31			250.00
31		250.00	–0–

Hydro Expense   No. 616

Date	Debit	Credit	Balance
1990 Dec. 31			147.00
31		147.00	–0–

Wages Expense   No. 625

Date	Debit	Credit	Balance
1990 Dec. 31			1,680.00
31		1,680.00	–0–

Computer Supplies Expense   No. 617

Date	Debit	Credit	Balance
1990 Dec. 31			218.00
31		218.00	–0–

Income Summary   No. 799

Date	Debit	Credit	Balance
1990 Dec. 31		6,840.00	6,840.00
31	4,228.00		2,612.00
31	2,612.00		–0–

114

UNO COMPUTER SERVICES
Post-Closing Trial Balance
December 31, 1990

Cash	$4,410.00	
Accounts receivable	670.00	
Prepaid insurance	146.25	
Prepaid rent	225.00	
Computer supplies	17.00	
Office equipment	340.00	
Accumulated depr., office equipment		$ 21.25
Computer	3,000.00	
Accumulated depr., computer		250.00
Accounts payable		85.00
Unearned computer fees		450.00
Wages payable		210.00
John Conard, capital		7,792.00
Totals	$8,808.25	$8,808.25

5 Accounting for a Merchandising Concern

After studying Chapter 5, you should be able to:

1. Analyze and record transactions that involve the purchase and resale of merchandise.

2. Explain the nature of each item entering into the calculation of cost of goods sold and gross profit from sales.

3. Prepare a work sheet and the financial statements for a merchandising business that uses a periodic inventory system and that is organized as either a corporation or a single proprietorship.

4. Prepare adjusting and closing entries for a merchandising business organized as either a corporation or a single proprietorship.

5. Define or explain the words and phrases listed in the chapter Glossary.

After studying the appendix to Chapter 5 (Appendix C), you should be able to:

6. Explain the adjusting entry approach to accounting for inventories and prepare a work sheet, adjusting entries and closing entries according to the adjusting entry approach.

7. Discuss the financial statement concepts and the qualitative characteristics accounting information should possess (Appendix D).

Topical Outline

I. Accounting for a merchandising concern differs from accounting for a service enterprise.

    A. Net income of a service organization is fees (or commissions) earned less operating expenses.

    B. Net income of a merchandising concern is sales revenue less cost of goods sold and operating expenses.

    C. Revenue from sales less cost of goods sold equals gross profit from sales—the "profit" before operating expenses are deducted.

II. Revenue from sales is:

    A. Gross sales—total cash and credit sales before any deductions—

    B. Less sales returns and allowances—the gross sales value of merchandise returned by customers and deductions from the sales price granted to customers for unsatisfactory goods—

    C. Less sales discounts—deductions from the invoice price granted to customers in return for early payment.

III. Cost of goods sold and the periodic inventory system

    A. Merchandise inventory at the end of one period is the beginning inventory of the next period.

    B. Cost of merchandise purchased includes the gross purchase price plus transportation-in, less purchases (cash) discounts and less purchases returns and allowances.

    C. Cost of goods sold is calculated as the cost of beginning inventory plus the cost of merchandise purchased less the cost of ending inventory.

    D. Inventory losses from shrinkage, spoilage, and theft are automatically included in the cost of goods sold.

IV. Classified income statement of a merchandising concern has three sections:

    A. Revenue section

    B. Cost of goods sold section

    C. Operating expenses section

V. Preparing a work sheet for a merchandising concern

    A. The titles of the accounts to be used are entered in the Account Titles column.

    B. The unadjusted account balances are entered in the Unadjusted Trial Balance columns.

    C. All necessary adjustments are entered in the Adjustments columns.

    D. The adjusted amounts are sorted to the proper financial statement columns.

    E. Cost of goods sold appears on the work sheet as follows:

        1. Beginning inventory, purchases, and transportation-in amounts appear in the Income Statement debit column.

        2. The amounts of the ending inventory, purchases returns and allowances, and purchases discounts appear in the Income Statement credit column.

    F. The formal financial statements are prepared using the information contained in the completed work sheet.

VI. Adjusting and closing entries

    A. Adjusting entries for merchandising companies include entries similar to those used in a service business.

    B. Closing entries

        1. Before closing entries are posted, the Merchandise Inventory account shows beginning-of-period inventory as a debit balance.

2. The first closing entry includes a credit to Merchandise Inventory for the amount of the beginning inventory.
3. The second closing entry includes a debit to Merchandise Inventory for the amount of the ending inventory.

VII. Financial statements in addition to the balance sheet

A. Income statement—may be designed as:

1. Classified (multiple-step) statement in which items are grouped in significant categories, or
2. Single-step statement.

B. Retained earnings statement of a corporation

1. Shows beginning retained earnings, plus net income, less dividends declared, which equals ending retained earnings.
2. May be combined with income statement.

VIII. Debit and credit memoranda

A. Used by a company to communicate with a customer or supplier.
B. Tells the customer or supplier that the amount the company expects to receive or to pay is being changed.

IX. Trade discounts

A. Deductions from list (or catalogue) price to arrive at invoice price
B. Not entered in the accounts of seller or purchaser

X. Appendix C

A. When the periodic inventory system is used, end-of-period entries to record the ending inventory and to transfer the beginning inventory to Income Summary may be done as closing entries or as adjusting entries.
B. When the adjusting entry approach is used on the work sheet, the transfer of beginning inventory and the recording of ending inventory is shown in the Adjustments columns.
C. On the work sheet, the debit and credit adjustments to Income Summary are individually extended to the Income Statement columns.
D. The adjusting entry approach and the closing entry approach result in the same amounts being reported on the financial statements.

Problem I

The following statements are either true or false. Place a (T) in the parentheses before each true statement and an (F) before each false statement.

1. ( ) Sales returns and allowances or discounts are not included in the calculation of net sales.

2. ( ) Ending inventory is subtracted from the cost of goods available for sale to determine cost of goods sold.

3. ( ) The only way to determine the current amount of inventory (assuming no shrinkage) in a periodic inventory system is to take a physical count of the merchandise on hand.

4. ( ) It is impossible to tell whether or not there were inventory losses when a periodic inventory system is used.

5. ( ) In a work sheet for a corporation, the balance of the Retained Earnings account remains the same from the Unadjusted Trial Balance—Credit column to the Retained Earnings Statement or Balance Sheet—Credit column.

6. ( ) Advance payments of income taxes are debited to an Income Taxes Expense account.

7. ( ) The net effect of putting beginning inventory, ending inventory, purchases, purchases returns and discounts, and transportation-in costs into the Income Statement columns is to put cost of goods sold into the columns.

8. ( ) The closing entry in which the Income Summary account is credited to close revenue and cost of goods sold accounts that have credit balances, also enters the ending inventory amount in the Merchandise Inventory account.

9. ( ) A debit or credit memorandum may originate with either party to a transaction, but the memorandum gets its name from the action of the selling party exclusively.

Problem II

You are given several words, phrases or numbers to choose from in completing each of the following statements or in answering the following questions. In each case select the one that best completes the statement or answers the question and place its letter in the answer space provided.

_____ 1. A method of accounting for inventories in which cost of goods sold is recorded each time a sale is made and an up-to-date record of goods on hand is maintained is called a:

    a. product inventory system.
    b. perpetual inventory system.
    c. periodic inventory system.
    d. parallel inventory system.
    e. principal inventory system.

_____ 2. Based on the following information, calculate the missing amounts.

Sales	$28,800	Cost of goods sold	?
Beginning inventory	?	Gross profit	$10,800
Purchases	18,000	Expenses	?
Ending inventory	12,600	Net income	3,600

    a. Beginning inventory, $16,200; Cost of goods sold, $12,600; Expenses, $1,800
    b. Beginning inventory, $23,400; Cost of goods sold, $10,800; Expenses, $7,200
    c. Beginning inventory, $9,000; Cost of goods sold, $14,400; Expenses, $3,600
    d. Beginning inventory, $12,600; Cost of goods sold, $18,000; Expenses, $7,200
    e. Beginning inventory, $19,800; Cost of goods sold, $25,200; Expenses, $14,400

_____ 3. What is the effect on the income statement if at the end of an accounting period the ending inventory is understated incorrectly?

    a. Cost of goods sold is overstated and net income is understated.
    b. Cost of goods sold is understated and net income is understated.
    c. Cost of goods sold is understated and net income is overstated.
    d. Cost of goods sold is overstated and net income is overstated.
    e. The errors offset each other, so there is no effect on the income statement.

_____ 4. The following information is taken from a single proprietorship's income statement. Calculate ending inventory for the business.

Sales	$165,250	Purchases returns	$ 390
Sales returns	980	Purchases discounts	1,630
Sales discounts	1,960	Transporation-in	700
Beginning inventory	16,880	Gross profit from sales	58,210
Purchases	108,380	Net income	17,360

    a. $19,840.
    b. $22,080.
    c. $21,160.
    d. $44,250.
    e. Some other amount.

_____ 5. On July 18, Double Aught Sales Company sold merchandise on credit, terms 2/10, n/30, $1,080. On July 21, Double Aught issued a $180 credit memorandum to the customer of July 18 who returned a portion of the merchandise purchased. What is the general journal entry to record the July 21 transaction?

a.	Accounts Receivable	180.00	
	Sales		180.00
b.	Sales Returns and Allowances	180.00	
	Accounts Receivable		180.00
c.	Accounts Receivable	900.00	
	Sales Returns and Allowances	180.00	
	Sales		1,080.00
d.	Sales	180.00	
	Accounts Receivable		180.00
e.	Sales Returns and Allowances	180.00	
	Sales		180.00

Problem III

Many of the important ideas and concepts discussed in Chapter 5 are reflected in the following list of key terms. Test your understanding of these terms by matching the appropriate definitions with the terms. Record the number identifying the most appropriate definition in the blank space next to each term.

_____	Cash discount	_____	Merchandise
_____	Credit memorandum	_____	Multiple-step income statement
_____	Credit period	_____	Periodic inventory system
_____	Credit terms	_____	Perpetual inventory system
_____	Debit memorandum	_____	Purchases discounts
_____	Discount period	_____	Retained earnings statement
_____	EOM	_____	Sales discounts
_____	FOB	_____	Selling expenses
_____	General and administrative expenses	_____	Single-step income statement
_____	Gross profit from sales	_____	Trade discount
_____	List price	_____	Transportation-in

1. Net sales minus cost of goods sold.

2. A method of accounting for inventories in which cost of goods sold is recorded each time a sale is made and an up-to-date record of goods on hand is maintained.

3. A deduction from a catalogue or list price that is used to determine the invoice price of goods.

4. Deductions from the invoice price granted to customers in return for early payment, i.e., cash discounts to customers.

5. A memorandum sent to notify its recipient that the business sending the memorandum has in its records debited the account of the recipient.

6. An income statement on which cost of goods sold and the expenses are subtracted in steps to get net income.

7. An abbreviation for the words "end of month" that is sometimes used in expressing the credit terms of a sales agreement.

8. The catalogue price of an item from which a trade discount, if offered, is deducted to determine the invoice or gross sales price of the item.

9. A financial statement that reports the changes in a corporation's retained earnings that occurred during an accounting period.

10. The specified amounts and timing of payments that a buyer agrees to make in return for being granted credit to purchase goods or services.

11. The agreed period of time for which credit is granted and at the end of which payment is expected.

12. Costs incurred by a business for transporting merchandise purchases to the business.

13. Deductions from the invoice price of purchased items, which are granted by suppliers in return for early payment, i.e., cash discounts from suppliers.

14. A memorandum sent to notify its recipient that the business sending the memorandum has in its records credited the account of the recipient.

15. A method of accounting for inventories in which the inventory account is brought up to date once each period, at the end of the period, by counting the units of each product on hand, multiplying the count for each product by its cost, and adding the costs of the various products.

16. The period of time during which, if payment is made, a cash discount may be deducted from the invoice price.

17. An income statement on which cost of goods sold and operating expenses are added together and subtracted in one step from net sales to get net income.

18. A deduction from the invoice price of goods that is granted if payment is made within a specified period of time.

19. The expenses of preparing and storing merchandise for sale, promoting sales, making sales, and delivering goods to customers.

20. Assets purchased and held for resale.

21. Expenses to support the management and overall operations of a business, such as central office, accounting, personnel, and credit and collections expenses.

22. The abbreviation for "free on board," which is used to denote that goods purchased are placed on board the means of transportation at a specified geographic point with all loading and transportation charges to that point to be paid by the seller.

Problem IV

Below is the Valentine Variety Store work sheet for the year ended December 31, 1990. Sort the adjusted trial balance amounts into the proper Income Statement and Balance Sheet columns and finish the work sheet. The December 31, 1990, inventory is $15,000.

VALENTINE VARIETY STORE

Work Sheet, December 31, 1990

ACCOUNT TITLES	ADJUSTED TRIAL BALANCE DR.	ADJUSTED TRIAL BALANCE CR.	INCOME STATEMENT DR.	INCOME STATEMENT CR.	STATEMENT OF CHANGES IN OWNER'S EQUITY OR BALANCE SHEET DR.	STATEMENT OF CHANGES IN OWNER'S EQUITY OR BALANCE SHEET CR.
Cash	4,000 00					
Merchandise inventory	13,000 00					
Other assets	8,000 00					
Liabilities		4,000 00				
Violet Valentine, capital		22,300 00				
Violet Valentine, withdrawals	10,000 00					
Sales		80,000 00				
Sales returns	600 00					
Purchases	48,500 00					
Purchases returns		400 00				
Purchases discounts		900 00				
Transportation-in	2,500 00					
Selling expenses	13,000 00					
General and admin. expenses	8,000 00					
	107,600 00	107,600 00				
Net income						

124

Problem V

After finishing the work sheet, use the information in its Income Statement columns to complete the following income statement.

VALENTINE VARIETY STORE

Income Statement

For the Year Ended December 31, 1990

Revenue:						
Sales						
Less: Sales returns						
Net sales						
Cost of goods sold:						
Merchandise inventory, December 31, 1989						
Purchases						
Less: Purchases returns $_____						
Purchases discounts _____						
Net purchases						
Add: Transportation-in						
Cost of goods purchased						
Goods available for sale						
Merchandise inventory, December 31, 1990						
Cost of goods sold						
Gross profit from sales						
Operating expenses:						
Selling expenses						
General and administrative expenses						
Total operating expenses						
Net income						

Problem VI

Prepare the closing entries for Valentine Variety Store. Do not give explanations, but skip a line after each entry.

DATE	ACCOUNT TITLES AND EXPLANATION	P.R.	DEBIT	CREDIT

Problem VII

Below is the Merchandise Inventory account of Valentine Variety Store as it appeared before the 1990 closing entries were posted. Note that its $13,000 debit balance shows the amount of the December 31, 1989, inventory which was posted to the account when the closing entries were made at the end of 1989. From the closing entries that were journalized in Part IV, post the appropriate amounts to the Merchandise Inventory account below.

Merchandise Inventory   Account No. 115

DATE		EXPLANATION	P.R.	DEBIT	CREDIT	BALANCE
1989 Dec.	31		G–3	13 000 00		13 000 00

Problem VIII

Complete the following statements by filling in the blanks.

1. If a company determines cost of goods sold by counting the inventory at the end of the period and subtracting the inventory from the cost of goods available for sale, the system of accounting for inventories is called

    a(n) _____.

2. Trade discounts _____ (are, are not) credited to the Purchases Discounts account.

3. After the work sheet is completed, the amount of the ending inventory is taken into the accounts by means of

    a(n) _____ entry.

4. A store received a credit memorandum from a wholesaler for unsatisfactory merchandise the store had returned

    for credit. The store should record the memorandum with a _____ (debit, credit)

    to its Purchases Returns and Allowances account and a _____ (debit, credit) to its Accounts Payable account.

5. The two common systems of accounting for merchandise inventories are the _____

    inventory system and the _____ inventory system. The _____
    inventory system is the most likely to be used in stores that sell a large volume of relatively low-priced items.

Problem IX (This problem applies to Appendix C.)

The following statements are either true or false. Place a (T) in the parentheses before each true statement and an (F) before each false statement.

1. (   ) Both the adjusting entry and closing entry approaches to accounting for merchandise inventories result in the same balances in the Income Summary account.

2. (   ) On the work sheet under the adjusting entry approach, the debit in the Merchandise Inventory account of the Adjustments column is carried directly to the Statement of Retained Earnings or Balance Sheet—Debit column.

3. (   ) If, in the Adjustments columns of a work sheet when the adjusting entry approach is used, Income Summary is debited $15,000 and credited $20,000, then the net $5,000 is carried to the Income Statement—Credit column.

Problem X (This problem applies to Appendix C.)

The trial balance that follows was taken from the ledger of Sporthaus Lindner at the end of its annual accounting period. Fritz Lindner, the owner of Sporthaus Lindner, did not make additional investments in the business during 1990.

SPORTHAUS LINDNER
Unadjusted Trial Balance
December 31, 1990

Cash	$ 1,840	
Accounts receivable	2,530	
Merchandise inventory	3,680	
Store supplies	2,070	
Accounts payable		$ 4,370
Salaries payable	....	....
Fritz Lindner, capital		5,980
Fritz Lindner, withdrawals	1,380	
Sales		14,260
Sales returns and allowances	1,150	
Purchases	5,750	
Purchases discounts		920
Transportation-in	1,150	
Salaries expense	4,370	
Rent expense	1,610	
Store supplies expense	....	....
Totals	$25,530	$25,530

Use the adjusting entry approach to account for merchandise inventories and prepare adjusting journal entries and closing journal entries for Sporthaus Lindner using the following information:

a. Ending store supplies inventory, $1,150.

b. Accrued salaries payable, $690.

c. Ending merchandise inventory, $4,830.

Problem XI (This problem applies to Appendix D.)

1. What are the basic objectives of external financial reporting?

2. Identify the qualities accounting information should possess.

3. Identify the concepts or assumptions that underlie implementation of accounting.

4. Explain the term generally accepted accounting principles (GAAP).

DATE		ACCOUNT TITLES AND EXPLANATION	P.R.	DEBIT	CREDIT

Problem XII, Uno Computer Services

(This problem is a serial problem that started in Chapter 2 and was continued in Chapters 3 and 4. If you did not complete the solutions in those chapters, you can begin the problem at this point. However, as you solve the problem in this chapter, you may need to review some of the facts presented in the Chapter 2, 3, and 4 segments of the problem.)

John Conard started Uno Computer Services on October 1, 1990. Because the business had only a few credit customers during its first three months, the Ledger included only one Accounts Receivable account. However, as business operations have expanded, John decided that the General Ledger should be expanded to contain a separate Account Receivable for each credit customer. Although each general ledger account was originally assigned a three digit number, John decided to add a fourth digit to the separate account receivable accounts. The account receivable accounts are as follows:

Account	Number
Account Receivable—AB Company	1140
Account Receivable—Ball Company	1141
Account Receivable—Call Company	1142
Account Receivable—Dog Enterprise	1143
Account Receivable—Ear Hearing	1144
Account Receivable—Farm Research	1145
Account Receivable—Goodall Limited	1146
Account Receivable—Iceman, Inc.	1147
Account Receivable—Jackets and More	1148

Ever since Uno has been in business, there have been repeated inquiries from its customers as to whether or not the company sold computer software and hardware. John Conard has analyzed the market potential and decided to carry a limited inventory of some software programs and peripheral equipment. Uno's credit terms to all of its customers who purchase merchandise on credit is 1/10, n/30.

To account for Uno's expanded operations, several additional accounts have been added to the General Ledger. They are:

Account	Number
Merchandise Inventory	118
Sales	421
Sales Returns and Allowances	422
Sales Discounts	423
Purchases	550
Purchases Returns and Allowances	551
Purchases Discounts	552
Transportation-In	553

Journalize and post the following transactions for January, February, and March 1991:

Jan. 2 Paid Ann White for four days, three days last year and one day this year, at her normal rate of $70 per day.

5 John invested an additional $3,000 in the business to purchase merchandise inventory.

6 Purchased from DataMax merchandise inventory priced at $5,750 on credit. Terms 1/10, n/30, FOB seller's warehouse.

7 Received $445 from Farm Research as final payment on its account. See transactions on November 8 (Chapter 2) and December 29 (Chapter 3).

9 Completed an $1,850 job for AB Company and billed $1,400, which is $1,850 less $450 previously received in advance. See transaction on December 9 (Chapter 3).

12 Sold merchandise on credit to Dog Enterprise for $945.

13 Paid $138 for freight charges on the merchandise purchased on January 6.

14 Received notice that Republic Bank had deducted a $9 service charge from the chequing account balance.

130

Jan. 15 Received $420 from Goodall Limited for computer services.

16 Paid DataMax for the January 6 purchase, net of the discount.

20 Dog Enterprise returned $125 of defective merchandise it had originally purchased on January 12.

21 Notified by Iceman, Inc., of acceptance of Uno's bid of $1,925 for computer services. Received a $500 advance payment.

22 Received balance due from Dog Enterprise as a result of the January 12 sale, net of the discount and the merchandise returned on January 20.

26 Returned defective merchandise to DataMax and accepted credit to apply against future purchases. Cost, less discount, was $95.

27 Sold $2,740 of merchandise on credit to Jackets and More.

28 Purchased an additional $895 of merchandise inventory on credit from DataMax, terms 1/10, n/30, FOB seller's warehouse.

29 Received a $95 credit memo from DataMax acknowledging the return of merchandise on January 26.

30 Paid hydro bill of $62 and telephone bill of $105.

30 Paid Ann White for seven days' work.

Feb. 2 Paid $675 to Town Hall Shopping Centre for an additional three months' rent.

2 Completed job for Iceman, Inc., for which they had made a partial payment in advance on January 21. Billed them for the balance due.

5 Paid DataMax for merchandise purchased on January 28, less the credit that resulted from the merchandise return on January 26, and less the discount.

9 Paid Shopper Newspaper $25 for advertisement.

10 Received amount due from AB Company as a result of the billing on January 9.

11 Completed work for Ball Company and billed them for $950.

14 Received notice that Republic Bank had deducted a $12 service charge from the chequing account balance.

14 John withdrew $650.

19 Received $520 from Ball Company in response to our February 11 billing.

20 Notified by AB Company of acceptance of Uno's bid of $2,125 for computer services. Received $600 in advance.

24 Sold merchandise, $1,285, on credit to Goodall Limited.

26 Paid telephone bill, $108, and hydro bill, $58.

27 Paid Ann White for six days' work.

27 Reimbursed Ann for business car mileage, 200 kilometres at $0.24 per km.

27 Reimbursed John for business car mileage, 300 kilometres at $0.24 per km.

Mar. 3 Received balance due from Ball Company (see transactions on February 11 and 19).

5 Completed job for AB Company and billed the balance due (see transaction on February 20).

8 Purchased $190 of computer supplies from Ajax Supply on credit.

9 Received balance due from Goodall Limited as a result of the February 24 sale.

15 Replaced damaged parts on Uno's computer. Cost was $120.

16 Notified by Jackets and More of acceptance of Uno's bid of $2,450 for computer services and received $600 in advance.

19 Paid Ajax Supply balance due. See transactions on December 11 (Chapter 3) and on March 8.

24 Completed $850 worth of service work for Ball Company and billed them.

25 Sold $1,780 worth of merchandise on credit to Dog Enterprise.

30 Sold $290 worth of merchandise on credit to Call Company.

30 Paid the hydro bill, $62, and the telephone bill, $110.

31 Paid Ann's business car mileage, 100 kilometres at $0.24 per km, and John's business car mileage, 200 kilometres at $0.24 per km.

At the end of the first quarter of 1991, John Conard is interested in knowing how Uno is doing. Therefore, you need to prepare interim financial statements. Information necessary to prepare the work sheet (which can be found at the back of this book), adjustments, and interim statements is as follows:

- a. Computer supplies ending inventory, $19.

- b. Three additional months of insurance has expired.

- c. Ann has worked four days for which she has not been paid.

- d. Ending merchandise inventory, $2,167.

- e. Three months of prepaid rent has expired.

- f. Depreciation for January through March is $250 on the computer and $21.25 on the office equipment.

Do not prepare closing entries.

DATE	ACCOUNT TITLES AND EXPLANATION	P.R.	DEBIT	CREDIT

DATE	ACCOUNT TITLES AND EXPLANATION	P.R.	DEBIT	CREDIT

DATE		ACCOUNT TITLES AND EXPLANATION	P.R.	DEBIT	CREDIT

DATE	ACCOUNT TITLES AND EXPLANATION	P.R.	DEBIT	CREDIT

DATE		ACCOUNT TITLES AND EXPLANATION	P.R.	DEBIT	CREDIT

DATE	ACCOUNT TITLES AND EXPLANATION	P.R.	DEBIT	CREDIT

Cash   Account No. 111

DATE		EXPLANATION	P.R.	DEBIT	CREDIT	BALANCE
1990 Dec.	31	Balance				4 4 1 0 00

Account Receivable—AB Company   Account No. 1140

DATE		EXPLANATION	P.R.	DEBIT	CREDIT	BALANCE

Account Receivable—Ball Company   Account No. 1141

DATE		EXPLANATION	P.R.	DEBIT	CREDIT	BALANCE

Account Receivable—Call Company   Account No. 1142

DATE		EXPLANATION	P.R.	DEBIT	CREDIT	BALANCE
1990 Dec.	31	Balance				2 2 5 00

Account Receivable—Dog Enterprise   Account No. 1143

DATE		EXPLANATION	P.R.	DEBIT	CREDIT	BALANCE

Account Receivable—Ear Hearing   Account No. 1144

DATE		EXPLANATION	P.R.	DEBIT	CREDIT	BALANCE

Account Receivable—Farm Research   Account No. 1145

DATE		EXPLANATION	P.R.	DEBIT	CREDIT	BALANCE
1990 Dec.	31	Balance				4 4 5 00

Account Receivable—Goodall Limited   Account No. 1146

DATE	EXPLANATION	P.R.	DEBIT	CREDIT	BALANCE

Account Receivable—Iceman, Inc.   Account No. 1147

DATE	EXPLANATION	P.R.	DEBIT	CREDIT	BALANCE

Account Receivable—Jackets and More   Account No. 1148

DATE	EXPLANATION	P.R.	DEBIT	CREDIT	BALANCE

Prepaid Insurance   Account No. 115

DATE		EXPLANATION	P.R.	DEBIT	CREDIT	BALANCE
1990 Dec.	31	Balance				1 4 6 25

Prepaid Rent
Account No. 116

DATE		EXPLANATION	P.R.	DEBIT	CREDIT	BALANCE
1990 Dec.	31	Balance				225 00

Computer Supplies
Account No. 117

DATE		EXPLANATION	P.R.	DEBIT	CREDIT	BALANCE
1990 Dec.	31	Balance				17 00

Office Equipment
Account No. 131

DATE		EXPLANATION	P.R.	DEBIT	CREDIT	BALANCE
1990 Dec.	31	Balance				340 00

Accumulated Depreciation, Office Equipment
Account No. 132

DATE		EXPLANATION	P.R.	DEBIT	CREDIT	BALANCE
1990 Dec.	31	Balance				21 25

Computer
Account No. 133

DATE		EXPLANATION	P.R.	DEBIT	CREDIT	BALANCE
1990 Dec.	31	Balance				3000 00

Accumulated Depreciation, Computer   Account No. 134

DATE		EXPLANATION	P.R.	DEBIT	CREDIT	BALANCE
1990 Dec.	31	Balance				250 00

Accounts Payable   Account No. 211

DATE		EXPLANATION	P.R.	DEBIT	CREDIT	BALANCE
1990 Dec.	31	Balance				85 00

Unearned Computer Fees   Account No. 213

DATE		EXPLANATION	P.R.	DEBIT	CREDIT	BALANCE
1990 Dec.	31	Balance				900 00

Wages Payable   Account No. 215

DATE		EXPLANATION	P.R.	DEBIT	CREDIT	BALANCE
1990 Dec.	31	Balance				210 00

John Conard, Capital   Account No. 311

DATE		EXPLANATION	P.R.	DEBIT	CREDIT	BALANCE
1990 Dec.	31	Balance				7792 00

John Conard, Withdrawals   Account No. 312

DATE		EXPLANATION	P.R.	DEBIT	CREDIT	BALANCE

Computer Services Revenue   Account No. 411

DATE		EXPLANATION	P.R.	DEBIT	CREDIT	BALANCE

Sales

Account No. 421

DATE		EXPLANATION	P.R.	DEBIT	CREDIT	BALANCE

Sales Returns and Allowances

Account No. 422

DATE		EXPLANATION	P.R.	DEBIT	CREDIT	BALANCE

Sales Discounts

Account No. 423

DATE		EXPLANATION	P.R.	DEBIT	CREDIT	BALANCE

Purchases

Account No. 550

DATE		EXPLANATION	P.R.	DEBIT	CREDIT	BALANCE

Purchases Returns and Allowances

Account No. 551

DATE		EXPLANATION	P.R.	DEBIT	CREDIT	BALANCE

Purchases Discounts

Account No. 552

DATE		EXPLANATION	P.R.	DEBIT	CREDIT	BALANCE

Transportation-In — Account No. 553

DATE		EXPLANATION	P.R.	DEBIT	CREDIT	BALANCE

Advertising Expense — Account No. 611

DATE		EXPLANATION	P.R.	DEBIT	CREDIT	BALANCE

Auto Expense — Account No. 612

DATE		EXPLANATION	P.R.	DEBIT	CREDIT	BALANCE

Computer Repair Expense — Account No. 614

DATE		EXPLANATION	P.R.	DEBIT	CREDIT	BALANCE

Insurance Expense — Account No. 615

DATE		EXPLANATION	P.R.	DEBIT	CREDIT	BALANCE

Hydro Expense — Account No. 616

DATE		EXPLANATION	P.R.	DEBIT	CREDIT	BALANCE

Computer Supplies Expense — Account No. 617

DATE		EXPLANATION	P.R.	DEBIT	CREDIT	BALANCE

Miscellaneous Expense — Account No. 619

DATE		EXPLANATION	P.R.	DEBIT	CREDIT	BALANCE

Rent Expense — Account No. 621

DATE		EXPLANATION	P.R.	DEBIT	CREDIT	BALANCE

Depreciation Expense, Office Equipment — Account No. 622

DATE		EXPLANATION	P.R.	DEBIT	CREDIT	BALANCE

Telephone Expense — Account No. 623

DATE		EXPLANATION	P.R.	DEBIT	CREDIT	BALANCE

Depreciation Expense, Computer — Account No. 624

DATE		EXPLANATION	P.R.	DEBIT	CREDIT	BALANCE

147

Wages Expense

DATE		EXPLANATION	P.R.	DEBIT	CREDIT	BALANCE

Income Summary

DATE		EXPLANATION	P.R.	DEBIT	CREDIT	BALANCE

UNO COMPUTER SERVICES

Statement of Changes in Owner's Equity

For Quarter Ended March 31, 1991

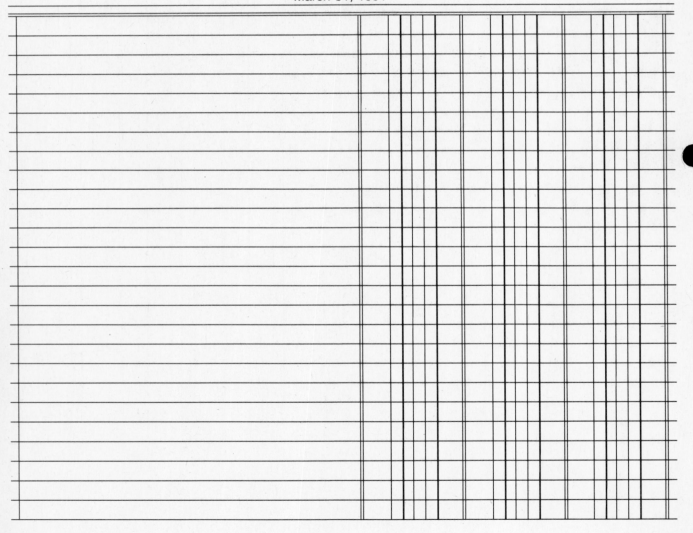

UNO COMPUTER SERVICES

Balance Sheet

March 31, 1991

Solutions for Chapter 5

Problem I

1.	F	6.	T
2.	T	7.	T
3.	F	8.	T
4.	F	9.	F
5.	T		

Problem II

1.	B
2.	D
3.	A
4.	A
5.	B

Problem III

Cash discount	18	Merchandise	20
Credit memorandum	14	Multiple-step income statement	6
Credit period	11	Periodic inventory system	15
Credit terms	10	Perpetual inventory system	2
Debit memorandum	5	Purchases discounts	13
Discount period	16	Retained earnings statement	9
EOM	7	Sales discounts	4
FOB	22	Selling expenses	19
General and administrative expenses	21	Single-step income statement	17
Gross profit from sales	1	Trade discount	3
List price	8	Transportation-in	12

Problem IV

VALENTINE VARIETY STORE
Work Sheet, December 31, 1990

	Adjusted Trial Balance		Income Statement		St. of Ch. in O.E. or Balance Sh.	
	Dr.	Cr.	Dr.	Cr.	Dr.	Cr.
Cash	4,000				4,000	
Merchandise inventory	13,000		13,000	15,000	15,000	
Other assets	8,000				8,000	
Liabilities		4,000				4,000
Violet Valentine, capital		22,300				22,300
Violet Valentine, withdrawals	10,000				10,000	
Sales		80,000		80,000		
Sales returns	600		600			
Purchases	48,500		48,500			
Purchases returns		400		400		
Purchases discounts		900		900		
Transportation-in	2,500		2,500			
Selling expenses	13,000		13,000			
General and administrative expenses	8,000		8,000			
	107,600	107,600	85,600	96,300	37,000	26,300
Net income			10,700			10,700
			96,300	96,300	37,000	37,000

151

Problem V

VALENTINE VARIETY STORE
Income Statement
For the Year Ended December 31, 1990

Revenue:			
Sales		$80,000	
Less: Sales returns		600	
Net sales			$79,400
Cost of goods sold:			
Merchandise inventory, December 31, 1989		$13,000	
Purchases	$48,500		
Less: Purchases returns	$400		
Purchases discounts	900	1,300	
Net purchases		$47,200	
Add: Transportation-in		2,500	
Cost of goods purchased		49,700	
Goods available for sale		$62,700	
Merchandise inventory, December 31, 1990		15,000	
Cost of goods sold			47,700
Gross profit from sales			$31,700
Operating expenses:			
Selling expenses		$13,000	
General and administrative expenses		8,000	
Total operating expenses			21,000
Net income			$10,700

Problem VI

Dec. 31	Income Summary	85,600.00	
	Sales Returns		600.00
	Purchases		48,500.00
	Transportation-In		2,500.00
	Selling Expenses		13,000.00
	General and Administrative Expenses		8,000.00
	Merchandise Inventory		13,000.00
31	Sales	80,000.00	
	Purchases Returns	400.00	
	Purchases Discounts	900.00	
	Merchandise Inventory	15,000.00	
	Income Summary		96,300.00
31	Income Summary	10,700.00	
	Violet Valentine, Capital		10,700.00
31	Violet Valentine, Capital	10,000.00	
	Violet Valentine, Withdrawals		10,000.00

Problem VII

DATE		EXPLANATION	P.R.	DEBIT	CREDIT	BALANCE
		Merchandise Inventory				Account No. 115
1989						
Dec.	31		G–3	13 0 0 0 00		13 0 0 0 00
1990						
Dec.	31		G–9		13 0 0 0 00	- 0 -
	31		G–9	15 0 0 0 00		15 0 0 0 00

Problem VIII

1. periodic inventory system
2. are not
3. closing
4. credit, debit
5. periodic, perpetual, periodic

Problem IX

1. T
2. T
3. F

Problem X

Adjusting Entries:

Dec. 31	Store Supplies Expense	920.00	
	Store Supplies		920.00
31	Salaries Expense	690.00	
	Salaries Payable		690.00
31	Income Summary	3,680.00	
	Merchandise Inventory		3,680.00
31	Merchandise Inventory	4,830.00	
	Income Summary		4,830.00

Closing Entries:

Dec. 31	Income Summary	15,640.00	
	Sales Returns and Allowances		1,150.00
	Purchases		5,750.00
	Transportation-In		1,150.00
	Salaries Expense		5,060.00
	Rent Expense		1,610.00
	Store Supplies Expense		920.00

Dec. 31	Sales		14,260.00	
	Purchases Discounts		920.00	
	Income Summary			15,180.00
31	Income Summary		690.00	
	Fritz Lindner, Capital			690.00
31	Fritz Lindner, Capital		1,380.00	
	Fritz Lindner, Withdrawals			1,380.00

Problem XI

1. The primary objective is to provide to decision-makers (investors and creditors) information useful in predicting the ability of an enterprise to generate future cash flows.

2. The qualities accounting information should possess are: Relevance, Reliability, Comparability and Consistency.

3. The concepts or assumptions are: Business entity, Continuing-concern, Stable unit of measure and Time-period.

4. Generally accepted accounting principles (GAAP) may be described as broad rules adopted by the accounting profession as guides in measuring, recording and reporting financial affairs and activities of a business. They consist of a number of concepts, principles and procedures.

Problem XII, Uno Computer Services

1991				
Jan. 2	Wages Payable	215	210.00	
	Wages Expense	625	70.00	
	Cash	111		280.00
	Paid Ann White for four days' work.			
5	Cash	111	3,000.00	
	John Conard, Capital	311		3,000.00
	To record owner's additional investment.			
6	Purchases	550	5,750.00	
	Accounts Payable	211		5,750.00
	Purchased merchandise on credit.			
7	Cash	111	445.00	
	Account Receivable—Farm Research	1145		445.00
	Collect customer's account.			
9	Unearned Computer Fees	213	450.00	
	Account Receivable—AB Company	1140	1,400.00	
	Computer Services Revenue	411		1,850.00
	Billed AB Company for work completed.			
12	Account Receivable—Dog Enterprise	1143	945.00	
	Sales	421		945.00
	Record sale of merchandise on credit to Dog Enterprise.			
13	Transportation-In	553	138.00	
	Cash	111		138.00
	Paid freight charges.			
14	Miscellaneous Expense	619	9.00	
	Cash	111		9.00
	Paid chequing account service charge.			

15	Cash	111	420.00	
	Computer Services Revenue	411		420.00
	Received cash from Goodall Limited for computer services.			
16	Accounts Payable	211	5,750.00	
	Cash	111		5,692.50
	Purchases Discounts	552		57.50
	Paid DataMax within discount period.			
20	Sales Returns and Allowances	422	125.00	
	Account Receivable—Dog Enterprise	1143		125.00
	Customer returned defective merchandise.			
Jan. 21	Cash	111	500.00	
	Unearned Computer Fees	213		500.00
	Received cash from Iceman, Inc., for future services.			
22	Cash	111	811.80	
	Sales Discounts	423	8.20	
	Account Receivable—Dog Enterprise	1143		820.00
	Received cash from Dog Enterprise.			
26	Accounts Payable	211	95.00	
	Purchases Returns and Allowances	551		95.00
	Returned defective merchandise to DataMax for credit.			
27	Account Receivable—Jackets and More	1148	2,740.00	
	Sales	421		2,740.00
	Sold merchandise on credit.			
28	Purchases	550	895.00	
	Accounts Payable	211		895.00
	Purchased merchandise on credit from DataMax.			
29	No entry required.			
30	Hydro Expense	616	62.00	
	Telephone Expense	623	105.00	
	Cash	111		167.00
	Paid January electric and telephone bills.			
30	Wages Expense	625	490.00	
	Cash	111		490.00
	Paid Ann White for seven days' work.			
Feb. 2	Prepaid Rent	116	675.00	
	Cash	111		675.00
	Paid three months' rent in advance.			
2	Account Receivable—Iceman, Inc.	1147	1,425.00	
	Unearned Computer Fees	213	500.00	
	Computer Services Revenue	411		1,925.00
	Completed work for Iceman, Inc.			
5	Accounts Payable	211	800.00	
	Purchases Discounts	552		8.00
	Cash	111		792.00
	Paid DataMax, less credit and discount.			
9	Advertising Expense	611	25.00	
	Cash	111		25.00
	Paid for newspaper advertisement.			

	10	Cash	111	1,400.00	
		Account Receivable—AB Company	1140		1,400.00
		Received credit customer's payment.			
	11	Account Receivable—Ball Company	1141	950.00	
		Computer Services Revenue	411		950.00
		Completed work for credit customer.			
	14	Miscellaneous Expense	619	12.00	
		Cash	111		12.00
		Chequing account service charge.			
Feb.	14	John Conard, Withdrawals	312	650.00	
		Cash	111		650.00
		Owner withdrew cash.			
	19	Cash	111	520.00	
		Account Receivable—Ball Company	1141		520.00
		Received customer's partial payment of amount due.			
	20	Cash	111	600.00	
		Unearned Computer Fees	213		600.00
		Received payment for future computer services.			
	24	Account Receivable—Goodall Limited	1146	1,285.00	
		Sales	421		1,285.00
		Sold merchandise on credit.			
	26	Telephone Expense	623	108.00	
		Hydro Expense	616	58.00	
		Cash	111		166.00
		Paid telephone and hydro bills.			
	27	Wages Expense	625	420.00	
		Cash	111		420.00
		Paid Ann White for six days' work.			
	27	Auto Expense	612	48.00	
		Cash	111		48.00
		Reimbursed Ann White for mileage.			
	27	Auto Expense	612	72.00	
		Cash	111		72.00
		Reimbursed owner for business car mileage.			
Mar.	3	Cash	111	430.00	
		Account Receivable—Ball Company	1141		430.00
		Received credit customer's payment.			
	5	Accounts Receivable—AB Company	1140	1,525.00	
		Unearned Computer Fees	213	600.00	
		Computer Services Revenue	411		2,125.00
		Billed credit customer for completed work partially paid for in advance.			
	8	Computer Supplies	117	190.00	
		Accounts Payable	211		190.00
		Purchased computer supplies from Ajax Supply on credit.			
	9	Cash	111	1,285.00	
		Account Receivable—Goodall Company	1146		1,285.00
		Received credit customer's payment.			

15	Computer Repair Expense	614	120.00	
	Cash	111		120.00
	Repaired Uno's computer.			
16	Cash	111	600.00	
	Unearned Computer Fees	213		600.00
	Received payment from Jackets and More for future computer services.			
19	Accounts Payable	211	275.00	
	Cash	111		275.00
	Paid Ajax Supply balance due.			
Mar. 24	Account Receivable—Ball Company	1141	850.00	
	Computer Services Revenue	411		850.00
	Billed credit customer for work.			
25	Account Receivable—Dog Enterprise	1143	1,780.00	
	Sales	421		1,780.00
	Sold merchandise on credit.			
30	Account Receivable—Call Company	1142	290.00	
	Sales	421		290.00
	Sold merchandise on credit.			
30	Hydro Expense	616	62.00	
	Telephone Expense	623	110.00	
	Cash	111		172.00
	Paid hydro and telephone bills.			
31	Auto Expense	612	72.00	
	Cash	111		72.00
	Reimbursed Ann White and John Conard for business car mileage.			

Adjusting entries:

31	Computer Supplies Expense	617	188.00	
	Computer Supplies	117		188.00
31	Insurance Expense	615	48.75	
	Prepaid Insurance	115		48.75
31	Wages Expense	625	280.00	
	Wages Payable	215		280.00
31	Rent Expense	621	675.00	
	Prepaid Rent	116		675.00
31	Depreciation Expense, Office Equipment	622	21.25	
	Accumulated Depreciation, Office Equipment	132		21.25
31	Depreciation Expense, Computer	624	250.00	
	Accumulated Depreciation, Computer	134		250.00

GENERAL LEDGER

Cash — No. 111

Date		Debit	Credit	Balance
1990				
Oct.	1	5,000.00		5,000.00
	2		900.00	4,100.00
	4		195.00	3,905.00
			50.00	3,855.00
	12		600.00	3,255.00
	15	500.00		3,755.00
	17		25.00	3,730.00
	19		15.00	3,715.00
	22	750.00		4,465.00
	23	250.00		4,715.00
	25		420.00	4,295.00
	30		162.00	4,133.00
	30		600.00	3,533.00
Nov.	1		36.00	3,497.00
	1		108.00	3,389.00
	4	425.00		3,814.00
	5	300.00		4,114.00
	6	1,000.00		5,114.00
	7		100.00	5,014.00
	8		350.00	4,664.00
	13		4.00	4,660.00
	15		600.00	4,060.00
	18		35.00	4,025.00
	20	500.00		4,525.00
	22		10.00	4,515.00
	22		420.00	4,095.00
	28		167.00	3,928.00
	28		650.00	3,278.00
	29		48.00	3,230.00
	29		120.00	3,110.00
Dec.	2		300.00	2,810.00
	3		76.00	2,734.00
	5	1,500.00		4,234.00
	6		280.00	3,954.00
	9	450.00		4,404.00
	13		4.00	4,400.00
	16		15.00	4,385.00
	18	495.00		4,880.00
	20		675.00	4,205.00
	29	450.00		4,655.00
	30		161.00	4,494.00
	31		12.00	4,482.00
	31		72.00	4,410.00

Cash (continued)

Date		Debit	Credit	Balance
1991				
Jan.	2		280.00	4,130.00
	5	3,000.00		7,130.00
	7	445.00		7,575.00
	13		138.00	7,437.00
	14		9.00	7,428.00
	15	420.00		7,848.00
	16		5,692.50	2,155.50
	21	500.00		2,655.50
	22	811.80		3,467.30
	30		167.00	3,300.30
	30		490.00	2,810.30
Feb.	2		675.00	2,135.30
	5		792.00	1,343.30
	9		25.00	1,318.30
	10	1,400.00		2,718.30
	14		12.00	2,706.30
	14		650.00	2,056.30
	19	520.00		2,576.30
	20	600.00		3,176.30
	26		166.00	3,010.30
	27		420.00	2,590.30
	27		48.00	2,542.30
	27		72.00	2,470.30
Mar.	3	430.00		2,900.30
	9	1,285.00		4,185.30
	15		120.00	4,065.30
	16	600.00		4,665.30
	19		275.00	4,390.30
	30		172.00	4,218.30
	31		72.00	4,146.30

Acct. Rec.—AB Company   No. 1140

Date	Debit	Credit	Balance
1990 Balance			–0–
1991 Jan. 9	1,400.00		1,400.00
Feb. 10		1,400.00	–0–
Mar. 5	1,525.00		1,525.00

Acct. Rec.—Ear Hearing   No. 1144

Date	Debit	Credit	Balance
1990 Balance			–0–

Acct. Rec.—Ball Company   No. 1141

Date	Debit	Credit	Balance
1990 Balance			–0–
1991 Feb. 11	950.00		950.00
19		520.00	430.00
Mar. 3		430.00	–0–
24	850.00		850.00

Acct. Rec.—Farm Research   No. 1145

Date	Debit	Credit	Balance
1990 Balance			445.00
1991 Jan. 7		445.00	–0–

Acct. Rec.—Call Company   No. 1142

Date	Debit	Credit	Balance
1990 Balance			225.00
1991 Mar. 30	290.00		515.00

Acct. Rec.—Goodall Limited   No. 1146

Date	Debit	Credit	Balance
1990 Balance			–0–
1991 Feb. 24	1,285.00		1,285.00
Mar. 9		1,285.00	–0–

Acct. Rec.—Dog Enterprise   No. 1143

Date	Debit	Credit	Balance
1990 Balance			–0–
1991 Jan. 12	945.00		945.00
20		125.00	820.00
22		820.00	–0–
Mar. 25	1,780.00		1,780.00

Acct. Rec.—Iceman, Inc.   No. 1147

Date	Debit	Credit	Balance
1990 Balance			–0–
1991 Feb. 12	1,425.00		1,425.00

159

Acct. Rec.—Jackets and More   No. 1148

Date	Debit	Credit	Balance
1990 Balance			–0–
1991 Jan. 27	2,740.00		2,740.00

Office Equipment   No. 131

Date	Debit	Credit	Balance
1990 Oct. 1	340.00		340.00

Prepaid Insurance   No. 115

Date	Debit	Credit	Balance
1990			
Oct. 4	195.00		195.00
Dec. 31		48.75	146.25
1991			
Mar. 31		48.75	97.50

Accum. Depr., Office Equip.   No. 132

Date	Debit	Credit	Balance
1990			
Dec. 31		21.25	21.25
1991			
Mar. 31		21.25	42.50

Prepaid Rent   No. 116

Date	Debit	Credit	Balance
1990			
Oct. 1	900.00		900.00
Dec. 31		675.00	225.00
1991			
Feb. 2	675.00		900.00
Mar. 31		675.00	225.00

Computer   No. 133

Date	Debit	Credit	Balance
1990 Oct. 1	3,000.00		3,000.00

Computer Supplies   No. 117

Date	Debit	Credit	Balance
1990			
Oct. 3	50.00		50.00
25	55.00		105.00
Nov. 7	45.00		150.00
Dec. 11	85.00		235.00
31		218.00	17.00
1991			
Mar. 8	190.00		207.00
31		188.00	19.00

Accum. Depr., Computer   No. 134

Date	Debit	Credit	Balance
1990			
Dec. 31		250.00	250.00
1991			
Mar. 31		250.00	500.00

Accounts Payable — No. 211

Date	Debit	Credit	Balance
1990			
Oct. 3		50.00	50.00
8	50.00		–0–
25		55.00	55.00
Nov. 7	55.00		–0–
Dec. 11		85.00	85.00
1991			
Jan. 6		5,750.00	5,835.00
16	5,750.00		85.00
26	95.00		(10.00)
28		895.00	885.00
Feb. 5	800.00		85.00
Mar. 8		190.00	275.00
19	275.00		–0–

John Conard, Capital — No. 311

Date	Debit	Credit	Balance
1990			
Oct. 1		8,340.00	8,340.00
Dec. 31		2,612.00	10,952.00
31	3,160.00		7,792.00
1991			
Jan. 5		3,000.00	10,792.00

Unearned Computer Fees — No. 213

Date	Debit	Credit	Balance
1990			
Dec. 9		450.00	450.00
1991			
Jan. 9	450.00		–0–
21		500.00	500.00
Feb. 2	500.00		–0–
20		600.00	600.00
Mar. 5	600.00		–0–
16		600.00	600.00

John Conard, Withdrawals — No. 312

Date	Debit	Credit	Balance
1990			
Oct. 12	600.00		600.00
30	600.00		1,200.00
Nov. 15	600.00		1,800.00
18	35.00		1,835.00
28	650.00		2,485.00
Dec. 20	675.00		3,160.00
31		3,160.00	–0–
1991			
Feb. 14	650.00		650.00

Wages Payable — No. 215

Date	Debit	Credit	Balance
1990			
Dec. 31		210.00	210.00
1991			
Jan. 2	210.00		–0–
Mar. 31		280.00	280.00

Computer Services Revenue — No. 411

Date	Debit	Credit	Balance
1990			
Oct. 5		500.00	500.00
12		750.00	1,250.00
18		1,000.00	2,250.00
23		250.00	2,500.00
24		425.00	2,925.00
28		725.00	3,650.00
Nov. 5		300.00	3,950.00
8		895.00	4,845.00
25		1,500.00	6,345.00
Dec. 18		495.00	6,840.00
31	6,840.00		–0–
1991			
Jan. 9		1,850.00	1,850.00
15		420.00	2,270.00
Feb. 2		1,925.00	4,195.00
11		950.00	5,145.00
Mar. 5		2,125.00	7,270.00

Sales No. 421

Date	Debit	Credit	Balance
1991			
Jan. 12		945.00	945.00
27		2,740.00	3,685.00
Feb. 24		1,285.00	4,970.00
Mar. 25		1,780.00	6,750.00
30		290.00	7,040.00

Purchases Discounts No. 552

Date	Debit	Credit	Balance
1991			
Jan. 16		57.50	57.50
Feb. 5		8.00	65.50

Sales Returns and Allowances No. 422

Date	Debit	Credit	Balance
1991			
Jan. 20	125.00		125.00

Transportation-In No. 553

Date	Debit	Credit	Balance
1991			
Jan. 13	138.00		138.00

Sales Discounts No. 423

Date	Debit	Credit	Balance
1991			
Jan. 26	8.20		8.20

Advertising Expense No. 611

Date	Debit	Credit	Balance
1990			
Oct. 19	15.00		15.00
Dec. 2	300.00		315.00
16	15.00		330.00
31		330.00	—0—
1991			
Feb. 9	25.00		25.00

Purchases No. 550

Date	Debit	Credit	Balance
1991			
Jan. 6	5,750.00		5,750.00
28	895.00		6,645.00

Auto Expense No. 612

Date	Debit	Credit	Balance
1990			
Nov. 1	36.00		36.00
1	108.00		144.00
29	48.00		192.00
29	120.00		312.00
Dec. 31	12.00		324.00
31	72.00		396.00
31		396.00	—0—
1991			
Feb. 27	48.00		48.00
27	72.00		120.00
Mar. 31	72.00		192.00

Purchases Returns and Allow. No. 551

Date	Debit	Credit	Balance
1991			
Jan. 26		95.00	95.00

Computer Repair Expense No. 614

Date	Debit	Credit	Balance
1990			
Oct. 17	25.00		25.00
Dec. 3	76.00		101.00
31		101.00	—0—
1991			
Mar. 15	120.00		120.00

Insurance Expense — No. 615

Date	Debit	Credit	Balance
1990			
Dec. 31	48.75		48.75
31		48.75	–0–
1991			
Mar. 31	48.75		48.75

Rent Expense — No. 621

Date	Debit	Credit	Balance
1990			
Dec. 31	675.00		675.00
31		675.00	–0–
1991			
Mar. 31	675.00		675.00

Hydro Expense — No. 616

Date	Debit	Credit	Balance
1990			
Oct. 30	47.00		47.00
Nov. 28	49.00		96.00
Dec. 30	51.00		147.00
31		147.00	–0–
1991			
Jan. 30	62.00		62.00
Feb. 26	58.00		120.00
Mar. 30	62.00		182.00

Depr. Exp., Office Equip. — No. 622

Date	Debit	Credit	Balance
1990			
Dec. 31	21.25		21.25
31		21.25	–0–
1991			
Mar. 31	21.25		21.25

Computer Supplies Expense — No. 617

Date	Debit	Credit	Balance
1990			
Dec. 31	218.00		218.00
31		218.00	–0–
1991			
Mar. 31	188.00		188.00

Telephone Expense — No. 623

Date	Debit	Credit	Balance
1990			
Oct. 30	115.00		115.00
Nov. 28	118.00		233.00
Dec. 30	110.00		343.00
31		343.00	–0–
1991			
Jan. 30	105.00		105.00
Feb. 26	108.00		213.00
Mar. 30	110.00		323.00

Miscellaneous Expense — No. 619

Date	Debit	Credit	Balance
1990			
Nov. 13	4.00		4.00
22	10.00		14.00
Dec. 13	4.00		18.00
31		18.00	–0–
1991			
Jan. 14	9.00		9.00
Feb. 14	12.00		21.00

Depr. Expense, Computer — No. 624

Date	Debit	Credit	Balance
1990			
Dec. 31	250.00		250.00
31		250.00	–0–
1991			
Mar. 31	250.00		250.00

	Wages Expense		No. 625
Date	Debit	Credit	Balance
1990			
Oct. 25	420.00		420.00
Nov. 8	350.00		770.00
22	420.00		1,190.00
Dec. 6	280.00		1,470.00
31	210.00		1,680.00
31		1,680.00	–0–
1991			
Jan. 2	70.00		70.00
Jan. 30	490.00		560.00
Feb. 27	420.00		980.00
Mar. 31	280.00		1,260.00

	Income Summary		No. 799
Date	Debit	Credit	Balance
1990			
Dec. 31		6,840.00	6,840.00
31	4,228.00		2,612.00
31		2,612.00	–0–

UNO COMPUTER SERVICES
Work Sheet for Quarter Ended March 31, 1991

Account	Unadjusted Trial Balance Debit	Unadjusted Trial Balance Credit	Adjustments Debit	Adjustments Credit	Income Statement Debit	Income Statement Credit	State. of Ch. in O.E. or Bal. Sheet Debit	State. of Ch. in O.E. or Bal. Sheet Credit
Cash	4,146.30						4,146.30	
Account receivable—AB Company	1,525.00						1,525.00	
Account receivable—Ball Company	850.00						850.00	
Account receivable—Call Company	515.00						515.00	
Account receivable—Dog Enterprises	1,780.00						1,780.00	
Account receivable—Iceman, Inc.	1,425.00						1,425.00	
Account receivable—Jackets and More	2,740.00						2,740.00	
Prepaid insurance	146.25			(b) 48.75			97.50	
Prepaid rent	900.00			(d) 675.00			225.00	
Computer supplies	207.00			(a) 188.00			19.00	
Merchandise inventory						2,167.00	2,167.00	
Office equipment	340.00						340.00	
Accumulated depreciation, office equipment		21.25		(e) 21.25				42.50
Computer	3,000.00						3,000.00	
Accumulated depreciation, computer		250.00		(f) 250.00				500.00
Accounts payable		600.00						600.00
Unearned computer fees								
Wages payable				(c) 280.00				280.00
John Conard, capital		10,792.00						10,792.00
John Conard, withdrawals	650.00						650.00	
Computer services revenue		8,120.00				8,120.00		
Sales		7,040.00				7,040.00		
Sales returns and allowances	125.00				125.00			
Sales discounts	8.20				8.20			
Purchases	6,645.00				6,645.00			
Purchases returns and allowances		95.00				95.00		
Purchases discounts		65.50				65.50		
Transportation-in	138.00				138.00			
Advertising expense	25.00				25.00			
Auto expense	192.00				192.00			
Computer repair expense	120.00				120.00			
Insurance expense			(b) 48.75		48.75			
Electric expense	182.00				182.00			
Computer supplies expense			(a) 188.00		188.00			
Miscellaneous expense	21.00				21.00			
Rent expense			(d) 675.00		675.00			
Depreciation expense, office equipment			(e) 21.25		21.25			
Telephone expense	323.00				323.00			
Depreciation expense, computer			(f) 250.00		250.00			
Wages expense	980.00		(c) 280.00		1,260.00			
	26,983.75	26,983.75	1,463.00	1,463.00	10,222.20	17,487.50	19,479.80	12,214.50
Net income					7,265.30			7,265.30
					17,487.50	17,487.50	19,479.80	19,479.80

UNO COMPUTER SERVICES
Income Statement
For Quarter Ended March 31, 1991

Revenue:			
Computer services revenue		$8,120.00	
Sales	$7,040.00		
Less: Sales returns and allowances	$125.00		
Sales discounts	8.20	133.20	
Net sales		6,906.80	
Total revenue			$15,026.80
Cost of goods sold:			
Merchandise inventory, December 31, 1990		$ —0—	
Purchases	$6,645.00		
Less: Purchases returns and allowances	$95.00		
Purchases discounts	65.50	160.50	
Net purchases	$6,484.50		
Add transportation-in	138.00		
Cost of goods purchased		6,622.50	
Goods available for sale		$6,622.50	
Merchandise inventory, December 31, 1990		2,167.00	
Cost of goods sold			4,455.50
Gross profit from sales			$10,571.30
Operating expenses:			
Advertising expense		$ 25.00	
Auto expense		192.00	
Computer repair expense		120.00	
Insurance expense		48.75	
Hydro expense		182.00	
Computer supplies expense		188.00	
Miscellaneous expense		21.00	
Rent expense		675.00	
Depreciation expense, office equipment		21.25	
Telephone expense		323.00	
Depreciation expense, computer		250.00	
Wages expense		1,260.00	
Total operating expenses			3,306.00
Net income			$ 7,265.30

UNO COMPUTER SERVICES
Statement of Changes in Owner's Equity
For Quarter Ended March 31, 1991

John Conard, capital, December 31, 1990		$ 7,792.00
Plus:		
Additional investments by owner	$3,000.00	
Net income	7,265.30	10,265.30
Total		$18,057.30
Less withdrawals by owner		650.00
John Conard, capital, March 31, 1991		$17,407.30

UNO COMPUTER SERVICES
Balance Sheet
March 31, 1991

Assets

Current assets:

Cash	$4,146.30	
Accounts receivable	8,835.00	
Prepaid insurance	97.50	
Prepaid rent	225.00	
Computer supplies	19.00	
Merchandise inventory	2,167.00	
Total current assets		$15,489.80

Plant and equipment:

Office equipment	$ 340.00		
Less accumulated depreciation	42.50	$ 297.50	
Computer	$3,000.00		
Less accumulated depreciation	500.00	2,500.00	
Total plant and equipment			2,797.50
Total assets			$18,287.30

Liabilities

Current liabilities:

Accounts payable	$ –0–	
Unearned computer fees	600.00	
Wages payable	280.00	
Total liabilities		$ 880.00

Owner's Equity

John Conard, capital	17,407.30
Total liabilities and owner's equity	$18,287.30

6

Accounting Systems

After studying Chapter 6, you should be able to:

1. Describe the type of transaction that is recorded in each journal when special journals are used and record all types of transactions in an accounting system that uses special journals.

2. Explain how a controlling account and its subsidiary ledger operate and, when special journals are used, post the amounts recorded in the journals to the General Ledger and any subsidiary ledgers.

3. Explain how to test the accuracy of the account balances in the Accounts Receivable and Accounts Payable Ledgers and prepare schedules of the accounts in each subsidiary ledger.

4. Describe how data is processed in computerized accounting systems.

5. Define or explain the words and phrases listed in the chapter Glossary.

Topical Outline

I. An accounting system

   A. Consists of the business papers, records, reports, and procedures used by a business in recording transactions and reporting their effects.

   B. Involves:

      1. Gathering transaction information into source documents.

      2. Classifying and recording the data in accounting records.

      3. Preparing timely summary reports to management and other interested parties.

II. Subsidiary ledgers

   A. Information about the amounts purchased and the amounts owed by each customer requires a separate accounts receivable account for each customer. These accounts are usually maintained in a subsidiary ledger.

   B. Each subsidiary ledger (whether it is an Accounts Receivable Ledger, an Accounts Payable Ledger, or other supplemental ledger) is represented by a controlling account in the General Ledger.

   C. A subsidiary ledger is periodically proved by totaling the balances of the accounts in the ledger and comparing the total to the controlling account's balance.

III. Special Journals

   A. Reduce writing and posting labor, by grouping similar transactions together and recording them in one place and periodically posting totals accumulated.

   B. Examples:

      1. Sales Journal—typically a single column journal in which all credit sales but no other transactions are recorded.

         a. Individual entries in the Sales Journal are posted to the accounts in the subsidiary Accounts Receivable Ledger.

         b. The column total of the Sales Journal is posted as a debit to Accounts Receivable and as a credit to Sales in the General Ledger.

      2. Cash Receipts Journal—a multicolumn journal in which all cash receipts but no other transactions are recorded.

         a. A column entitled "Other Accounts—Credit" is used to record all types of receipts that are not frequent enough to justify having separate columns. Each credit in the Other Accounts column must be posted individually.

         b. Separate credit columns for which only the totals are posted, are usually established for Accounts Receivable and Sales. A separate debit column may be used for sales discounts.

      3. Purchases Journal—all credit purchases (but no cash purchases) of merchandise are recorded in this journal. Also, separate columns may be established for frequent credit purchases such as store supplies and office supplies.

         a. If the journal does not have columns in which to enter certain types of credit purchases, those purchases must be entered in the General Journal.

         b. Credits to the accounts of particular creditors are individually posted to the subsidiary Accounts Payable Ledger.

      4. Cash Disbursements Journal—all cash payments except those made from petty cash are recorded in this journal. (A reimbursement of petty cash is, however, recorded in the Cash Disbursements Journal.)

a. A Cheque Register is a cash disbursements journal that includes a column for entering the number of each cheque.

b. An "Other Accounts—Debit" column is necessary so that the journal can accommodate all types of cash payments.

5. General Journal—must be provided even when special journals are used.

a. Allows the recording of entries which do not fit under any of the special journals.

b. Examples are:

(1) Adjusting entries.

(2) Closing entries.

(3) Other entries such as credit purchases of items other than merchandise.

IV. Other issues

A. If a company collects sales taxes from its customers, the Sales Journal usually has a separate column in which the taxes are recorded.

B. In some companies, a collection of all sales invoices serves as a Sales Journal.

C. Sales returns may be recorded in the General Journal, or a separate Sales Returns and Allowances Journal is sometimes used.

V. Computerized data processing

A. Computerized data processing systems are replacing electronic bookkeeping machine systems. These systems involve the use of a computer which is programmed to rapidly calculate and store information used in a business.

B. Some computerized systems require batch processing of accounting data and others allow online processing from a variety of input devices.

Problem I

The following statements are either true or false. Place a (T) in the parentheses before each true statement and an (F) before each false statement.

1. ( ) A Purchases Journal is used to record all purchases.

2. ( ) At month-end, the total sales recorded in the Sales Journal is debited to Accounts Receivable and credited to Sales.

3. ( ) Sales is a General Ledger account.

4. ( ) Transactions recorded in a journal do not necessarily result in equal debits and credits to General Ledger accounts.

5. ( ) If a general journal entry is used to record a charge sale, the credit of the entry must be posted twice.

Problem II

You are given several words, phrases or numbers to choose from in completing each of the following statements or in answering the following questions. In each case select the one that best completes the statement or answers the question and place its letter in the answer space provided.

_____ 1. A company that uses a Sales Journal, a Purchases Journal, a Cash Receipts Journal, a Cash Disbursements Journal, and a General Journal borrowed $1,500 from the bank in exchange for a note payable to the bank. In which journal would the transaction be recorded?

    a. Sales Journal.
    b. Purchases Journal.
    c. Cash Receipts Journal.
    d. Cash Disbursements Journal.
    e. General Journal.

_____ 2. A company that uses a Sales Journal, a Purchases Journal, a Cash Receipts Journal, a Cash Disbursements Journal, and a General Journal paid a creditor for office supplies purchased on account. In which journal would the payment transaction be recorded?

    a. Sales Journal.
    b. Purchases Journal.
    c. Cash Receipts Journal.
    d. Cash Disbursements Journal.
    e. General Journal.

_____ 3. A book of original entry that is designed and used for recording only a specified type of transaction is a:

    a. columnar journal.
    b. Cheque Register
    c. subsidiary ledger.
    d. general journal.
    e. special journal.

Problem III

Many of the important ideas and concepts discussed in Chapter 6 are reflected in the following list of key terms. Test your understanding of these terms by matching the appropriate definitions with the terms. Record the number identifying the most appropriate definition in the blank space next to each term.

_____ Accounting system		_____ Foot
_____ Accounts Payable Ledger		_____ General Ledger
_____ Accounts Receivable Ledger		_____ Online processing
_____ Batch processing		_____ Schedule of accounts payable
_____ Cheque Register		_____ Schedule of accounts receivable
_____ Columnar journal		_____ Special journal
_____ Computer program		_____ Subsidiary ledger
_____ Controlling account		_____ Time sharing
_____ Crossfoot		

1. The ledger containing the financial statement accounts of a business.

2. A book of original entry having columns, each of which is designated as the place for entering specific data about each transaction of a group of similar transactions.

3. A book of original entry that is designed and used for recording only a specified type of transaction.

4. A book of original entry for recording cash payments by cheque.

5. To add the Debit column totals of a journal, add the Credit column totals, and then compare the sums to prove that total debits equal total credits.

6. A process by which several users of a computer, each having an input-output device, can input data into a single computer and, as processing time becomes available, have their data processed and transmitted back to their output device.

7. The business papers, records, reports, and procedures used by a business in recording transactions and reporting their effects.

8. A mode of computer operation in which the program and required data are maintained in the computer so that as new data are entered, they are processed instantly.

9. A set of instructions that are entered into a computer and that specify the operations the computer is to perform.

10. A group of accounts (other than general ledger accounts) which show the details underlying the balance of a controlling account in the General Ledger.

11. A mode of computer operation in which a program and data are entered in the computer, processed, and removed from the computer before the next program and data are entered.

12. A subsidiary ledger having an account for each creditor.

13. A list of the balances of all the accounts in the Accounts Payable Ledger that is summed to show the total amount of accounts payable outstanding.

14. A list of the balances of all the accounts in the Accounts Receivable Ledger that is summed to show the total amount of accounts receivable outstanding.

15. A general ledger account the balance of which (after posting) equals the sum of the balances

of the accounts in a related subsidiary ledger, thereby proving the sum of those subsidiary account balances.

16. To add a column of numbers.

17. A subsidiary ledger having an account for each customer.

Problem IV

Complete the following by filling in the blanks.

1. When a company records sales returns with general journal entries, the credit of an entry recording such a return is posted to two different accounts. This does not cause the trial balance to be out of balance because

_____

_____.

2. Cash sales _____ (are, are not) normally recorded in the Sales Journal.

3. When multi-column special journals are used, credit purchases of store supplies or office supplies should be recorded in the _____.

4. The posting principle upon which a subsidiary ledger and its controlling account operate requires that the controlling account be debited for an amount or amounts equal to the sum of _____ to the subsidiary ledger and that the controlling account be credited for an amount or amounts equal to the sum of _____ to the subsidiary ledger.

5. Cash purchases of store supplies or office supplies should be recorded in a(n) _____
_____.

6. When a subsidiary Accounts Receivable Ledger is maintained, the equality of the debits and credits posted to the General Ledger is proved by preparing _____. At the same time the balances of the customer accounts in the Accounts Receivable Ledger are proved by preparing _____
_____.

Problem V

Below are eight transactions completed by McGuff Company on September 30 of this year. Following the transactions are the company's journals with prior September transactions recorded therein.

Requirement One: Record the eight transactions in the company's journals.

Sept. 30   Received an $808.50 cheque from Ted Clark in full payment of the September 20, $825 sales, less the $16.50 discount.
30   Received a $550 cheque from a tenant in payment of his October rent.
30   Sold merchandise to Inez Smythe on credit, Invoice No. 655, $1,675.
30   Received merchandise and an invoice dated September 28, terms 2/10, n/60 from Johnson Company, $4,000.
30   Purchased store equipment on account from Olson Company, terms n/10, EOM, $950.
30   Issued Cheque No. 525 to Kerry Meadows in payment of her $650 salary.
30   Issued Cheque No. 526 for $1,715 to Olson Company in full payment of its September 20 invoice, less a $35 discount.
30   Cash sales for the last half of the month totaled $9,450.50.

DATE	ACCOUNT TITLES AND EXPLANATION	P.R.	DEBIT	CREDIT

SALES JOURNAL   Page 8

DATE		ACCOUNT DEBITED	INVOICE NUMBER	P.R.	AMOUNT
19—					
Sept.	3	N. R. Boswell	651	√	1 875 00
	15	Inez Smythe	652	√	1 500 00
	20	Ted Clark	653	√	825 00
	24	N. R. Boswell	654	√	2 250 00

PURCHASES JOURNAL   Page 8

DATE		ACCOUNT CREDITED	DATE OF INVOICE	TERMS	P.R.	AMOUNT
19—						
Sept.	8	Johnson Company	6/9	2/10, n/60	√	3 750 00
	22	Olson Company	20/9	2/10, n/60	√	1 750 00
	24	Olson Company	22/9	2/10, n/60	√	5 625 00

CASH RECEIPTS JOURNAL

DATE	ACCOUNT CREDITED	EXPLANATION	P.R.	OTHER ACCOUNTS CREDIT	ACCOUNTS RECEIVABLE CREDIT	SALES CREDIT	SALES DISCOUNTS DEBIT	CASH DEBIT
19—								
Sept. 1	Rent Earned	Tenant's September rent	711	550 00				550 00
13	N. R. Boswell	Full payment of account	✓		1875 00		37 50	1837 50
15	Sales	Cash sales	✓			9000 00		9000 00

CASH DISBURSEMENTS JOURNAL

DATE	CH. NO.	PAYEE	ACCOUNT DEBITED	P.R.	OTHER ACCOUNTS DEBIT	ACCOUNTS PAYABLE DEBIT	PURCHASES DISCOUNT CREDIT	CASH CREDIT
19—								
Sept. 15	523	Kerry Meadows	Salaries Expense	611	650 00			650 00
16	524	Johnson Company	Johnson Company	✓		3750 00	75 00	3675 00

Requirement Two: The individual postings from the journals of McGuff Company through September 29 have been made. Complete the individual postings from the journals.

Requirement Three: Foot and crossfoot the journals and make the month-end postings.

Requirement Four: Complete the trial balance on page 182 and prove the subsidiary ledgers by preparing schedules of accounts receivable and accounts payable.

ACCOUNTS RECEIVABLE LEDGER

N. R. Boswell
2200 Falstaff Street

DATE		EXPLANATION	P.R.	DEBIT	CREDIT	BALANCE
19— Sept.	3		S–8	1875 00		1875 00
	13		R–9		1875 00	–0–
	24		S–8	2250 00		2250 00

Ted Clark
10765 Catonsville Avenue

DATE		EXPLANATION	P.R.	DEBIT	CREDIT	BALANCE
19— Sept.	20		S–8	825 00		825 00

Inez Symthe
785 Violette Circle

DATE		EXPLANATION	P.R.	DEBIT	CREDIT	BALANCE
19— Sept.	15		S–8	1500 00		1500 00

ACCOUNTS PAYABLE LEDGER

Johnson Company
118 E. Seventh Street

DATE		EXPLANATION	P.R.	DEBIT	CREDIT	BALANCE
19— Sept.	8		P–8		3750 00	3750 00
	16		D–7	3750 00		–0–

Olson Company
788 Hazelwood Avenue

DATE		EXPLANATION	P.R.	DEBIT	CREDIT	BALANCE
19— Sept.	22		P–8		1750 00	1750 00
	24		P–8		5625 00	7375 00

GENERAL LEDGER

Cash   Account No. 111

DATE	EXPLANATION	P.R.	DEBIT	CREDIT	BALANCE

Accounts Receivable   Account No. 112

DATE	EXPLANATION	P.R.	DEBIT	CREDIT	BALANCE

Store Equipment   Account No. 133

DATE	EXPLANATION	P.R.	DEBIT	CREDIT	BALANCE

Accounts Payable   Account No. 212

DATE	EXPLANATION	P.R.	DEBIT	CREDIT	BALANCE

Sales   Account No. 411

DATE	EXPLANATION	P.R.	DEBIT	CREDIT	BALANCE

Sales Discounts   Account No. 412

DATE	EXPLANATION	P.R.	DEBIT	CREDIT	BALANCE

Purchases   Account No. 511

DATE	EXPLANATION	P.R.	DEBIT	CREDIT	BALANCE

Purchases Discounts   Account No. 512

DATE		EXPLANATION	P.R.	DEBIT	CREDIT	BALANCE

Salaries Expense   Account No. 611

DATE		EXPLANATION	P.R.	DEBIT	CREDIT	BALANCE
19— Sept.	15		D–7	650 00		650 00

Rent Earned   Account No. 711

DATE		EXPLANATION	P.R.	DEBIT	CREDIT	BALANCE
19— Sept.	1		R–9		550 00	550 00

MCGUFF COMPANY
Trial Balance
September 30, 19—

Cash		
Accounts receivable		
Store equipment		
Accounts payable		
Sales		
Sales discounts		
Purchases		
Purchases discounts		
Salaries expense		
Rent earned		

MCGUFF COMPANY

Schedule of Accounts Receivable

September 30, 19—

MCGUFF COMPANY

Schedule of Accounts Payable

September 30, 19—

Problem I

1. F
2. T
3. T
4. F
5. F

Problem II

1. C
2. D
3. E

Problem III

Accounting system	7	Foot	16
Accounts Payable Ledger	12	General Ledger	1
Accounts Receivable Ledger	17	Online processing	8
Batch processing	11	Schedule of accounts payable	13
Cheque Register	4	Schedule of accounts receivable	14
Columnar journal	2	Special journal	3
Computer program	9	Subsidiary ledger	10
Controlling account	15	Time sharing	6
Crossfoot	5		

Problem IV

1. only the balance of one of the accounts, the Accounts Receivable account appears on the trial balance. The other account is a subsidiary ledger account.

2. are not

3. Purchases Journal

4. the debits posted, the credits posted

5. Cash Disbursements Journal

6. a trial balance, a schedule of accounts receivable

Problem V

Sept. 30   Store Equipment 133   950.00
            Accounts Payable—Olson Company .... 212/√   950.00

SALES JOURNAL   Page 8

DATE		ACCOUNT DEBITED	INVOICE NUMBER	P.R.	AMOUNT
19—					
Sept.	3	N. R. Boswell	651	√	1 875 00
	15	Inez Smythe	652	√	1 500 00
	20	Ted Clark	653	√	825 00
	24	N. R. Boswell	654	√	2 250 00
	30	Inez Smythe	655	√	1 675 00
	30	Accounts Receivable, Dr., Sales, Cr.			8 125 00

(112/411)

PURCHASES JOURNAL

DATE		ACCOUNT CREDITED	DATE OF INVOICE	TERMS	P.R.	AMOUNT
19—						
Sept.	8	Johnson Company	6/9	2/10, n/60	√	3 7 5 0 00
	22	Olson Company	20/9	2/10, n/60	√	1 7 5 0 00
	24	Olson Company	22/9	2/10, n/60	√	5 6 2 5 00
	30	Johnson Company	28/9	2/10, n/60	√	4 0 0 0 00
	30	Purchases, Dr., Accounts Payable, Cr.				15 1 2 5 00
						(511/212)

CASH RECEIPTS JOURNAL

DATE		ACCOUNT CREDITED	P.R.	OTHER ACCOUNTS CREDIT	ACCOUNTS RECEIVABLE CREDIT	SALES CREDIT	SALES DISCOUNTS DEBIT	CASH DEBIT
19—								
Sept.	1	Rent Earned	711	5 5 0 00				5 5 0 00
	13	N. R. Boswell	√		1 8 7 5 00		3 7 50	1 8 3 7 50
	15	Sales	√			9 0 0 0 00		9 0 0 0 00
	30	Ted Clark	√		8 2 5 00		1 6 50	8 0 8 50
	30	Rent Earned	711	5 5 0 00				5 5 0 00
	30	Sales	√			9 4 5 0 50		9 4 5 0 50
	30	Totals		1 1 0 0 00	2 7 0 0 00	18 4 5 0 50	5 4 00	22 1 9 6 50
				(√)	(112)	(411)	(412)	(111)

CASH DISBURSEMENTS JOURNAL

DATE		CH. NO.	PAYEE	ACCOUNT DEBITED	P.R.	OTHER ACCOUNTS DEBIT	ACCOUNTS PAYABLE DEBIT	PURCHASES DISCOUNTS CREDIT	CASH CREDIT
19—									
Sept.	15	523	Kerry Meadows	Salaries Expense	611	6 5 0 00			6 5 0 00
	16	524	Johnson Company	Johnson Company	√		3 7 5 0 00	7 5 00	3 6 7 5 00
	30	525	Kerry Meadows	Salaries Expense	611	6 5 0 00			6 5 0 00
	30	526	Olson Company	Olson Company	√		1 7 5 0 00	3 5 00	1 7 1 5 00
	30		Totals			1 3 0 0 00	5 5 0 0 00	1 1 0 00	6 6 9 0 00
						(√)	(212)	(512)	(111)

GENERAL LEDGER

Cash — No. 111

Date	Debit	Credit	Balance
Sept. 30	22,196.50		22,196.50
30		6,690.00	15,506.50

Sales Discounts — No. 412

Date	Debit	Credit	Balance
Sept. 30	54.00		54.00

Accounts Receivable — No. 112

Date	Debit	Credit	Balance
Sept. 30	8,125.00		8,125.00
30		2,700.00	5,425.00

Purchases — No. 511

Date	Debit	Credit	Balance
Sept. 30	15,125.00		15,125.00

Store Equipment — No. 133

Date	Debit	Credit	Balance
Sept. 30	950.00		950.00

Purchases Discounts — No. 512

Date	Debit	Credit	Balance
Sept. 30		110.00	110.00

Accounts Payable — No. 212

Date	Debit	Credit	Balance
Sept. 30		950.00	950.00
30		15,125.00	16,075.00
30	5,500.00		10,575.00

Salaries Expense — No. 611

Date	Debit	Credit	Balance
Sept. 15	650.00		650.00
30	650.00		1,300.00

Sales — No. 411

Date	Debit	Credit	Balance
Sept. 30		8,125.00	8,125.00
30		18,450.50	26,575.50

Rent Earned — No. 711

Date	Debit	Credit	Balance
Sept. 1		550.00	550.00
30		550.00	1,100.00

ACCOUNTS PAYABLE LEDGER

Johnson Company

Date	Debit	Credit	Balance
Sept. 8		3,750.00	3,750.00
16	3,750.00		–0–
30		4,000.00	4,000.00

Olson Company

Date	Debit	Credit	Balance
Sept. 22		1,750.00	1,750.00
24		5,625.00	7,375.00
30		950.00	8,325.00
30	1,750.00		6,575.00

ACCOUNTS RECEIVABLE LEDGER

N. R. Boswell

Date	Debit	Credit	Balance
Sept. 3	1,875.00		1,875.00
13		1,875.00	—0—
24	2,250.00		2,250.00

Inez Smythe

Date	Debit	Credit	Balance
Sept. 15	1,500.00		1,500.00
30	1,675.00		3,175.00

Ted Clark

Date	Debit	Credit	Balance
Sept. 20	825.00		825.00
30		825.00	—0—

MCGUFF COMPANY
Trial Balance
September 30, 19—

Cash	$15,506.50	
Accounts receivable	5,425.00	
Store equipment	950.00	
Accounts payable		$10,575.00
Sales		26,575.50
Sales discounts	54.00	
Purchases	15,125.00	
Purchases discounts		110.00
Salaries expense	1,300.00	
Rent earned		1,100.00
Totals	$38,360.50	$38,360.50

MCGUFF COMPANY
Schedule of Accounts Receivable
September 30, 19—

N. R. Boswell	$2,250.00
Inez Smythe	3,175.00
Total accounts receivable	$5,425.00

MCGUFF COMPANY
Schedule of Accounts Payable
September 30, 19—

Johnson Company	$ 4,000.00
Olson Company	6,575.00
Total accounts payable	$10,575.00

7

Internal Control and Accounting for Cash

After studying Chapter 7, you should be able to:

1. Explain why internal control procedures are needed in a large concern and state the broad principles of internal control.

2. Describe internal control procedures to protect cash received from cash sales, cash received through the mail, and cash disbursements.

3. Explain the operation of a petty cash fund and be able to journalize entries to record petty cash fund transactions.

4. Explain why the bank balance and the book balance of cash are reconciled and be able to prepare such a reconciliation.

5. Tell how recording invoices at net amounts helps gain control over cash discounts taken and be able to account for invoices recorded at net amounts.

6. Define or explain the words and phrases listed in the chapter Glossary.

After studying Appendix F at the end of Chapter 7, you should be able to:

7. Explain the use of a Voucher Register and Cheque Register and prepare entries to record and pay liabilities when these registers are used in a manual accounting system.

Topical Outline

I. Internal control procedures—designed to protect assets from fraud and theft

    A. Seven broad principles of internal control are:

        1. Responsibilities should be clearly established.
        2. Adequate records should be maintained.
        3. Assets should be insured and employees bonded.
        4. Record-keeping and custody of assets should be separated.
        5. Responsibility for related transactions should be divided.
        6. Mechanical devices should be used whenever practicable.
        7. Regular and independent reviews should be conducted.

    B. Computers and internal control:

        1. Computers provide rapid access to large quantities of information.
        2. Computers reduce processing errors.
        3. Computers allow more extensive testing of records.
        4. Computers may limit hard evidence of processing steps.
        5. Separation of duties must be maintained.

    C. Internal control for cash should include procedures for protecting:

        1. Cash receipts

            a. Cash from cash sales
            b. Cash received through the mail

        2. Cash disbursements

    D. Voucher system—used to control the incurrence and payment of obligations. With a voucher system, important business papers include:

        1. Purchase requisitions
        2. Purchase orders
        3. Invoices
        4. Receiving reports
        5. Invoice approval forms
        6. Vouchers

II. Accounting for cash

    A. Petty cash fund—used to avoid writing cheques for small amounts.

        1. Petty Cash is debited only when the fund is established or increased.
        2. Petty cash receipts are retained by the petty cashier to account for the amounts expended.
        3. When the petty cash fund is reimbursed, an entry is made to debit the expenses or other items paid for with petty cash and to credit Cash for the amount reimbursed to the petty cash fund.

    B. Cash Over and Short account—an income statement item showing the cash shortages or overages that result from making change.
    C. Reconciling the bank balance

        1. A bank reconciliation proves the accuracy of both the depositor's records and those of the bank.
        2. Items that may cause a difference between the bank statement balance and a depositor's book balance of cash:

            a. Outstanding cheques
            b. Unrecorded deposits

  c. Charges for services and uncollectible items

  d. Collections made by the bank for the depositor

  e. Errors

 3. Steps in reconciling the bank balance:

  a. Compare deposits listed on the bank statement with deposits shown in the accounting records.

  b. Determine whether other credits on bank statement (interest, etc.) have been recorded in the books.

  c. Compare canceled cheques listed on bank statement with actual cheques returned with statement.

  d. Compare previous month's outstanding cheques with canceled cheques listed on this month's bank statement.

  e. Compare canceled cheques listed on bank statement with cheques recorded in books since last reconciliation.

  f. Note any unrecorded debits shown on bank statement; e.g., cheques printing charges, NSF cheques, service charges.

  g. Prepare reconciliation.

  h. Make journal entries for any unrecorded debits or credits appearing on the bank statement.

III. Other internal control procedures

 A. Recording purchases

  1. Gross method—purchases are recorded at the invoice price without deducting cash discounts.

  2. Net method—purchases recorded at net amount of invoices (gross amount less cash discount); provides better control over purchases discounts.

IV. Recording vouchers, manual system (Appendix F)

 A. The Vouchers Payable account replaces the Accounts Payable account.

 B. Voucher Register—used to record transactions that will require payments by cheque.

  1. Replaces the Purchases Journal.

  2. Transactions are recorded in the Voucher Register after the vouchers are approved.

  3. As each voucher is paid, the cheque numbers and payment dates are entered in the payments column.

 C. Unpaid vouchers file

  1. Takes the place of a subsidiary Accounts Payable Ledger.

  2. Vouchers not paid immediately upon receipt are filed until payment is due.

  3. After month-end posting, the balance of Vouchers Payable should equal the sum of the unpaid vouchers in the unpaid vouchers file.

 D. In a voucher system, a Cheque Register replaces the Cash Disbursements Journal. The Cheque Register includes columns for Vouchers Payable, Purchase Discounts, and Cash.

 E. Purchases Returns—recorded with a general journal entry and deducted on the voucher.

Problem I

The following statements are either true or false. Place a (T) in the parentheses before each true statement and an (F) before each false statement.

1. ( ) One of the fundamental principles of internal control is that the person who has access to or is reponsible for an asset should not maintain the accounting record for that asset.

2. ( ) Procedures for controlling cash disbursements are as important as those for cash receipts.

3. ( ) When a voucher system is used, duplication of procedures among several departments is instrumental in maintaining control over cash disbursements.

4. ( ) In order to approve an invoice for payment for the purchase of assets, the accounting department of a large company should require copies of the purchase requisition, purchase order, invoice, and receiving report.

5. ( ) After the petty cash fund is established, the Petty Cash account is not debited or credited again unless the size of the fund is changed.

6. ( ) The Cash Over and Short account is usually shown on the income statement as part of miscellaneous revenues if it has a credit balance at the end of the period.

7. ( ) If 20 canceled cheques are listed on the current month's bank statement, then no less than 20 cheques could have been issued during the current month.

8. ( ) When the net method of recording invoices is used, cash discounts lost are reported as an expense in the income statement; when the gross method is used, cash discounts taken are deducted from purchases in the income statement.

Problem II

You are given several words, phrases or numbers to choose from in completing each of the following statements or in answering the following questions. In each case select the one that best completes the statement or answers the question and place its letter in the answer space provided.

_____ 1. A voucher system:

    a. permits only authorized individuals to incur obligations that will result in cash disbursements.
    b. establishes procedures for incurring such obligations and for their verification, approval, and recording.
    c. permits cheques to be issued only in payment of properly verified, approved, and recorded obligations.
    d. requires that every obligation be recorded at the time it is incurred and every purchase be treated as an independent transaction, complete in itself.
    e. does all of the above.

_____ 2. Liquidity is:

    a. the portion of a corporation's equity that represents investments in the corporation by its shareholders.
    b. cash or other assets that are reasonably expected to be realized in cash or be sold or consumed within one year or one operating cycle of the business.
    c. a characteristic of an asset indicating how easily the asset can be converted into cash or used to buy services or satisfy obligations.
    d. obligations that are due to be paid or liquidated within one year or one operating cycle of the business.
    e. economic benefits or resources without physical substance, the value of which stems from the privileges or rights that accrue to their owner.

_____ 3. A voucher is a:

    a. business paper used in summarizing a transaction and approving it for recording and payment.

    b. business form used within a business to ask the purchasing department of the business to buy needed items.

    c. document, prepared by a vendor, on which are listed the items sold, the sales prices, the customer's name, and the terms of sale.

    d. form used within a business to notify the proper persons of the receipt of goods ordered and of the quantities and condition of the goods.

    e. document on which the accounting department notes that it has performed each step in the process of checking an invoice and approving it for recording and payment.

_____ 4. Each of the following items would cause Brand X Sales Company's book balance of cash to differ from its bank statement balance.

    A. A service charge made by the bank.

    B. A cheque listed as outstanding on the previous month's reconciliation and that is still outstanding.

    C. A customer's cheque returned by the bank marked "NSF."

    D. A deposit which was mailed to the bank on the last day of November and is unrecorded on the November bank statement.

    E. A cheque paid by the bank at its correct $422 amount but recorded in error in the General Journal as $442.

    F. An unrecorded credit memorandum indicating the bank had collected a note receivable for Brand X Sales Company and deposited the proceeds in the company's account.

    G. A cheque written during November and not yet paid and returned by the bank.

Which of the above items require entries on the books of Brand X Sales Company?

    a. A, B, C, and E.
    b. A, C, E, and F.
    c. A, B, D, and F.
    d. A, B, D, E, and G.
    e. C, D, E, and F.

Problem III

Many of the important ideas and concepts discussed in Chapter 7 are reflected in the following list of key terms. Test your understanding of these terms by matching the appropriate definitions with the terms. Record the number identifying the most appropriate definition in the blank space next to each term.

_____	Bank reconciliation	_____	Invoice approval form
_____	Canceled cheques	_____	Liquid asset
_____	Cash Over and Short account	_____	Liquidity
_____	Discounts lost	_____	Net method of recording purchases
_____	Gross method of recording purchases	_____	Outstanding cheques
_____	Internal control system	_____	Purchase order
_____	Invoice	_____	Purchase requisition

	Receiving report		Voucher
_____	Reconcile	_____	Voucher Register
_____	Vendee	_____	Voucher system
_____	Vendor		

1. A form used within a business to notify the proper persons of the receipt of goods ordered and of the quantities and condition of the goods.

2. A characteristic of an asset indicating how easily the asset can be converted into other types of assets or used to buy services or satisfy obligations.

3. An expense resulting from the failure to take advantage of cash discounts on purchases.

4. Cheques that were drawn by the depositor, deducted on the depositor's records, and sent to the payees, but that have not yet reached the depositor's bank for payment and deduction.

5. The seller of goods or services.

6. A document, prepared by a vendor, on which are listed the items sold, the sales prices, the customer's name, and the terms of sale.

7. A business paper used in summarizing a transaction and approving it for recording and payment.

8. A method of recording purchases by which offered cash discounts are not deducted from the invoice price in determining the amount to be recorded.

9. An asset, such as cash, that can be easily converted into other types of assets or used to buy services or satisfy obligations.

10. Cheques that have been stamped or perforated by the bank to show they have been paid.

11. A document on which the accounting department notes that it has performed each step in the process of checking an invoice and approving it for recording and payment.

12. A business form used within a business to ask the purchasing department of the business to buy needed items.

13. An income statement account in which cash overages and cash shortages arising from making change are recorded.

14. The procedures adopted by a business to encourage adherence to prescribed managerial policies, to protect its assets from waste, fraud, and theft, and to insure accurate and reliable accounting data.

15. A set of procedures that are designed to control the incurrence of obligations and cash disbursements.

16. A business form that is sent to a vendor as a written order for the purchase of goods or services.

17. An analysis that explains the difference between the balance of a chequing account as recorded in the depositor's records and the balance as shown on the bank statement.

18. To explain or account for the difference between two amounts.

19. A method of recording purchases by which offered cash discounts are deducted from the invoice price in determining the amount to be recorded.

20. The purchaser of goods or services.

21. A book of original entry in which approved vouchers are entered.

Problem IV

Complete the following by filling in the blanks.

1. If a cashier errs while making change and gives a customer too much money back, the resulting cash shortage is recorded with a debit to an account called _____.

2. A(n) _____ form is used by the accounting department in checking and ap-

3. Cash discounts offered but not taken are _____.

4. If the size of the petty cash fund remains unchanged, the Petty Cash account _____ (is, is not) debited in the entry to replenish the petty cash fund.

5. Control of a small business is commonly gained through the direct supervision and active participation of the _____ in the affairs and activities of the business. However, as a business grows, it becomes necessary for the manager to delegate responsibilities and rely on _____ _____ rather than personal contact in controlling the affairs and activities of the business.

6. A properly designed internal control system encourages adherence to prescribed managerial policies; and it also (a) _____ _____; (b) _____ _____; and (c) _____.

7. A good system of internal control for cash requires a _____ of duties so that the people responsible for handling cash and for its custody are not the same people who _____ _____. It also requires that all cash receipts be deposited in the bank _____ and that all payments, except petty cash payments, be made by _____.

8. A bank reconciliation is prepared to account for the difference between the _____ _____ and the _____.

9. An accounting system used to control the incurrence and payment of obligations requiring the disbursement of cash is a _____.

10. A _____ is commonly used by a selling department to notify the purchasing department of items which the selling department wishes the purchasing department to purchase.

11. The business form commonly used by the purchasing department of a large company to order merchandise is called a _____.

12. Good internal control follows certain broad principles. These principles are:

    (a) Responsibilities should be clearly established, and in every situation _____ should be made responsible for each task.

    (b) Adequate records should be maintained since they provide an important means of protecting _____

    _____.

    (c) Assets should be _____ and employees _____.

    (d) Record-keeping for assets and _____ of assets should be separated.

    (e) Responsibility for related transactions should be _____ so that the work of one department or individual may act as a check on the work of others.

    (f) Mechanical devices _____ where practicable.

    (g) Regular and independent _____ of internal control procedures should be conducted.

13. After preparing a bank reconciliation, journal entries _____ (should, should not) be made to record those items listed as outstanding cheques.

Problem V

On November 5 of the current year Cullen Company drew Cheque No. 23 for $50 to establish a petty cash fund. Lon Dial, an office clerk, was appointed petty cashier.

    1. Give the cash disbursements journal entry to record the establishment of the fund.

CASH DISBURSEMENTS JOURNAL

DATE	CH. NO.	PAYEE	ACCOUNT DEBITED	P.R.	OTHER ACCOUNTS DEBIT	CASH CREDIT

After making a payment from petty cash on November 25, the petty cashier noted that there was only $2.50 cash remaining in the fund. The cashier prepared the following list of expenditures from the fund and requested that the fund be replenished.

Nov. 9	Express freight on merchandise purchased	$ 9.75
12	Miscellaneous expense to clean office	10.00
15	Office supplies	3.50
18	Delivery of merchandise to customer	8.00
23	Miscellaneous expense for collect telegram	3.25
25	Express freight on merchandise purchased	13.00

Cheque No. 97 in the amount of $47.50 was drawn to replenish the fund.

    2. In the Cash Disbursements Journal on the next page give the entry to record the cheque replenishing the petty cash fund.

CASH DISBURSEMENTS JOURNAL

DATE	CH. NO.	PAYEE	ACCOUNT DEBITED	P.R.	OTHER ACCOUNTS DEBIT	CASH CREDIT

Problem VI

Information about the following eight items is available to prepare Verde Company's December 31 bank reconciliation.

Two cheques (1) No. 453 and (2) No. 457 were outstanding on November 30. Cheque No. 457 was returned with the December bank statement but Cheque No. 453 was not. (3) Cheque No. 478, written on December 26, was not returned with the canceled cheques; and (4) Cheque No. 480 for $96 was incorrectly entered in the Cash Disbursements Journal and posted as though it were for $69. (5) A deposit placed in the bank's night depository after banking hours on November 30 appeared on the December bank statement, but (6) one placed there after hours on December 31 did not. (7) Enclosed with the December bank statement was a debit memorandum for a bank service charge and (8) a cheque received from a customer and deposited on December 27 but returned by the bank marked "Not Sufficient Funds."

1. If an item in the above lists should not appear on the December 31 bank reconciliation, ignore it. However, if an item should appear, enter its number in a set of parentheses to show where it should be added or subtracted in preparing the reconciliation.

VERDE COMPANY
Bank Reconciliation
December 31, 19—

Book balance of cash .... $X,XXX	Bank statement balance .... $X,XXX
Add:	Add:
( )	( )
( )	( )
( )	( )
Deduct:	Deduct:
( )	( )
( )	( )
( )	( )
Reconciled balance .... $X,XXX	Reconciled balance .... $X,XXX

2. Certain of the above items require entries on Verde Company's books. Place the numbers of these items within the following parentheses: (   ), (   ), (   ), (   ), (   ), (   )

Problem VII

On May 8, a company that records purchases at net amounts received a shipment of merchandise having a $3,750 invoice price. Attached to the merchandise was the invoice, which was dated May 6, terms 2/10, n/60, FOB the vendor's warehouse. The vendor, Vee Company, had prepaid the shipping charges on the goods, $125, adding the amount to the invoice and bringing its total to $3,875. The invoice was recorded and filed in error for payment on May 26. Give in general journal form the entries to record the (1) purchase, (2) discovery on May 26 of the discount lost, and (3) payment of the invoice on July 5. Do not give explanations but skip a line between entries.

DATE	ACCOUNT TITLES AND EXPLANATION	P.R.	DEBIT	CREDIT

Problem VIII

1. The ABC Company records all purchases at gross amounts. Give in general journal form the entries to record the following transactions (do not give explanations but skip a line between entries):

June 1 Received shipment of merchandise having $2,000 invoice price, terms 2/10, n/30.
June 2 Received shipment of merchandise having $500 invoice price, terms 1/10, n/30.
June 7 Paid for the merchandise that was received on June 1.
July 30 Paid for the merchandise that was received on June 2.

DATE	ACCOUNT TITLES AND EXPLANATION	P.R.	DEBIT	CREDIT

2. Show the appropriate general journal entries for the ABC Company if they had recorded purchases at net amounts (do not give explanations but skip a line between entries):

DATE	ACCOUNT TITLES AND EXPLANATION	P.R.	DEBIT	CREDIT

Problem IX

The bank statement dated September 30 for the Smith Company showed a balance of $2,876.35 which differs from the $1,879.50 book balance of cash on that date. In attempting to reconcile the difference, the accountant noted the following facts:

1. The bank recorded a service fee of $15 which was not recorded on the books of Smith Company.

2. A deposit of $500 was made on the last day of the month but was not recorded by the bank.

3. A cheque for $176 had been recorded on the Smith Company books as $167. The bank paid the correct amount.

4. A cheque was written during September but has not been processed by the bank. The amount was $422.85.

5. A cheque for $1,000 is still outstanding from August.

6. A cheque for $100 deposited by Smith Company was returned marked "Not Sufficient Funds."

7. A credit memorandum stated that the bank collected a note receivable of $200 for Smith Company and charged Smith a $2 collection fee. Smith Company had not previously recorded the collection.

Prepare, in good form, a bank reconciliation which shows the correct cash balance on September 30.

Problem X (based on Appendix F)

On the next two pages are the Cheque Register and Voucher Register of Nero Sales Company, a concern that records invoices at gross amounts. Both registers have a representation of cash disbursement transactions recorded therein. Following are six additional transactions of the company.

Required: (1) Record the transactions in the registers. (2) Crossfoot the registers and post. (3) Prepare a schedule of unpaid vouchers.

195

Feb. 21 Prepared Voucher No. 8 payable to WSID Radio Station for advertising expense, $175. Issued Cheque No. 7 in payment of the voucher.

24 Prepared Voucher No. 9 payable to Office Sales Company for the purchase of office equipment, $500, terms n/10 EOM.

25 Prepared Voucher No. 10 payable to Radion Company for the purchase of merchandise, $1,875, terms 2/10, n/60.

26 Issued Cheque No. 8 in payment of Voucher No. 7 less a 2% discount.

28 Prepared Voucher No. 11 payable to Neal Realty Company for the March rent, $500. Issued Cheque No. 9 in payment of the voucher.

28 Prepared Voucher No. 12 payable to Payroll for sales salaries, $625; and office salaries, $375. Issued Cheque No. 10 in payment of the voucher. Cashed the cheque and paid the employees.

CHEQUE REGISTER
Page 1

DATE		PAYEE	VCHR. NO.	CH. NO.	VOUCHERS PAYABLE DR.	PURCHASES DISCOUNTS CR.	CASH CR.
Feb.	1	Union Truck Company	2	1	60 00		60 00
	8	Inter-City Wholesale Company	1	2	2000 00	40 00	1960 00
	13	Alpha Supply Company	3	3	250 00		250 00
	15	Payroll	5	4	1000 00		1000 00
	17	Treadwell and Son	4	5	700 00	14 00	686 00
	18	Morning Gazette	6	6	75 00		75 00

VOUCHER REGISTER

	DATE	VCHR. NO.	PAYEE	WHEN AND HOW PAID DATE	CH. NO.	VOUCHERS PAYABLE CREDIT	PURCHASES DEBIT	TRANS-PORTA-TION-IN DEBIT	
1	Feb. 1	1	Inter-City Wholesale Co.	Feb. 8	2	2,000 00	2,000 00		1
2	1	2	Union Truck Company	1	1	60 00		60 00	2
3	5	3	Alpha Supply Company	13	3	250 00			3
4	9	4	Treadwell and Son	17	5	700 00	675 00	25 00	4
5	15	5	Payroll	15	4	1,000 00			5
6	18	6	Morning Gazette	18	6	75 00			6
7	18	7	Dale Brothers			1,250 00	1,250 00		7
8									8
9									9
10									10
11									11
12									12
13									13
14									14

VOUCHER REGISTER

	SALES SALARIES EXPENSE DEBIT	ADVER-TISING EXPENSE DEBIT	OFFICE SALARIES EXPENSE DEBIT	OTHER ACCOUNTS DEBIT ACCOUNT NAME	P.R.	AMOUNT	
1							1
2							2
3				Store Supplies		250 00	3
4							4
5	625 00		375 00				5
6		75 00					6
7							7
8							8
9							9
10							10
11							11
12							12
13							13
14							14

Cash   Account No. 111

DATE	EXPLANATION	P.R.	DEBIT	CREDIT	BALANCE

Store Supplies   Account No. 115

DATE	EXPLANATION	P.R.	DEBIT	CREDIT	BALANCE

Office Equipment   Account No. 137

DATE	EXPLANATION	P.R.	DEBIT	CREDIT	BALANCE

Vouchers Payable   Account No. 212

DATE	EXPLANATION	P.R.	DEBIT	CREDIT	BALANCE

Purchases   Account No. 511

DATE	EXPLANATION	P.R.	DEBIT	CREDIT	BALANCE

Purchases Discounts   Account No. 513

DATE	EXPLANATION	P.R.	DEBIT	CREDIT	BALANCE

Transportation-In   Account No. 514

DATE	EXPLANATION	P.R.	DEBIT	CREDIT	BALANCE

Rent Expense   Account No. 611

DATE	EXPLANATION	P.R.	DEBIT	CREDIT	BALANCE

Sales Salaries Expense   Account No. 612

DATE	EXPLANATION	P.R.	DEBIT	CREDIT	BALANCE

Advertising Expense   Account No. 613

DATE	EXPLANATION	P.R.	DEBIT	CREDIT	BALANCE

Office Salaries Expense   Account No. 652

DATE	EXPLANATION	P.R.	DEBIT	CREDIT	BALANCE

NERO SALES COMPANY
Schedule of Vouchers Payable
February 28, 19—

Voucher Number	Payee	Amount

Solutions for Chapter 7

Problem I   **Problem II**

1.	T	5.	T	1.	E
2.	T	6.	T	2.	C
3.	F	7.	F	3.	A
4.	T	8.	T	4.	B

Problem III

Bank reconciliation	17	Outstanding cheques	4
Canceled cheques	10	Purchase order	16
Cash Over and Short account	13	Purchase requisition	12
Discounts lost	3	Receiving report	1
Gross method of recording purchases	8	Reconcile	18
Internal control system	14	Vendee	20
Invoice	6	Vendor	5
Invoice approval form	11	Voucher	7
Liquid asset	9	Voucher Register	21
Liquidity	2	Voucher system	15
Net method of recording purchases	19		

Problem IV

1. Cash Over and Short

2. invoice approval

3. discounts lost

4. is not

5. owner-manager, a system of internal control

6. (a) promotes operational efficiencies; (b) protects the business assets from waste, fraud, and theft; and (c) ensures accurate and reliable accounting data

7. separation, keep the cash records, intact each day, cheque

8. book balance of cash, bank statement balance

9. voucher system

10. purchase requisition

11. purchase order

12. (a) one person; (b) assets; (c) insured, bonded; (d) custody; (e) divided; (f) should be used; (g) reviews

13. should not

Problem V

CASH DISBURSEMENTS JOURNAL

DATE		CH. NO.	PAYEE	ACCOUNT DEBITED	P.R.	OTHER ACCOUNTS DEBIT	CASH CREDIT
19—							
Nov.	5	23	Lon Dial, Petty				
			Cashier	Petty Cash		50 00	50 00

CASH DISBURSEMENTS JOURNAL

DATE		CH. NO.	PAYEE	ACCOUNT DEBITED	P.R.	OTHER ACCOUNTS DEBIT	CASH CREDIT
19—							
Nov.	25	97	Lon Dial, Petty				
			Cashier	Transportation-In		22 75	
				Misc. Gen. Exp.		13 25	
				Office Supplies		3 50	
				Delivery Expense		8 00	47 50

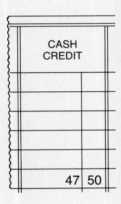

Problem VI

1. Book balance of cash .... $X,XXX   Bank statement balance .... $X,XXX
    Add: Add:
          (   )   (6)
    Deduct: Deduct:
          (4)   (1)
          (7)   (3)
          (8)   (   )

2. (4), (7), (8)

Problem VII

May	8	Purchases	3,675.00	
		Transportation-In	125.00	
		Accounts Payable—Vee Company		3,800.00
		$3,750 − ($3,750 × .02) = $3,675		
	26	Discounts Lost	75.00	
		Accounts Payable—Vee Company		75.00
July	5	Accounts Payable—Vee Company	3,875.00	
		Cash		3,875.00

Problem VIII

1.

June	1	Purchases	2,000.00	
		Accounts Payable		2,000.00
	2	Purchases	500.00	
		Accounts Payable		500.00
	7	Accounts Payable	2,000.00	
		Purchases Discounts		40.00
		Cash		1,960.00
July	30	Accounts Payable	500.00	
		Cash		500.00

2.

June	1	Purchases ($2,000 × 98%)	1,960.00	
		Accounts Payable		1,960.00
	2	Purchases ($500 × 99%)	495.00	
		Accounts Payable		495.00
	7	Accounts Payable	1,960.00	
		Cash		1,960.00
July	30	Discounts Lost	5.00	
		Accounts Payable		5.00
	30	Accounts Payable	500.00	
		Cash		500.00

Problem IX

SMITH COMPANY
Bank Reconciliation
September 30, 19—

Book balance of cash		$1,879.50	Bank statement balance	$2,876.35
Add:			Add:	
Proceeds of note less collection fee		198.00	Deposit on 9/30	500.00
		$2,077.50		$3,376.35
Deduct:			Deduct:	
NSF cheque	$100.00		Outstanding cheques:	
Service fee	15.00		August	$1,000.00	
Recording error	9.00	124.00	September	422.85	1,422.85
Reconciled balance		$1,953.50	Reconciled balance	$1,953.50

Problem X

VOUCHER REGISTER

	DATE		VCHR. NO.	PAYEE	WHEN AND HOW PAID DATE		CH. NO.	VOUCHERS PAYABLE CREDIT		PURCHASES DEBIT		TRANS- PORTA- TION-IN DEBIT		
1	Feb.	1	1	Inter-City Wholesale										1
				Company	Feb.	8	2	2,000	00	2,000	00			1
2		1	2	Union Truck Company		1	1	60	00			60	00	2
3		5	3	Alpha Supply Company		13	3	250	00					3
4		9	4	Treadwell and Son		17	5	700	00	675	00	25	00	4
5		15	5	Payroll		15	4	1,000	00					5
6		18	6	Morning Gazette		18	6	75	00					6
7		18	7	Dale Brothers		26	8	1,250	00	1,250	00			7
8		21	8	WSID Radio Station		21	7	175	00					8
9		24	9	Office Sales Company				500	00					9
10		25	10	Radion Company				1,875	00	1,875	00			10
11		28	11	Neal Realty Company		28	9	500	00					11
12		28	12	Payroll		28	10	1,000	00					12
13		28		Totals				9,385	00	5,800	00	85	00	13

VOUCHER REGISTER

	SALES SALARIES EXPENSE DEBIT		ADVER- TISING EXPENSE DEBIT		OFFICE SALARIES EXPENSE DEBIT		OTHER ACCOUNTS DEBIT ACCOUNT NAME	P.R.	AMOUNT		
1											1
2											2
3							Store Supplies		250	00	3
4											4
5	625	00			375	00					5
6			75	00							6
7											7
8			175	00							8
9							Office Equipment		500	00	9
10											10
11							Rent Expense		500	00	11
12	625	00			375	00					12
13	1,250	00	250	00	750	00			1,250	00	13

DATE		PAYEE	VCHR. NO.	CH. NO.	VOUCHERS PAYABLE DR.	PURCHASES DISCOUNTS CR.	CASH CR.
Feb.	1	Union Truck Company	2	1	60 00		60 00
	8	Inter-City Wholesale Company	1	2	2 000 00	40 00	1 960 00
	13	Alpha Supply Company	3	3	250 00		250 00
	15	Payroll	5	4	1 000 00		1 000 00
	17	Treadwell and Son	4	5	700 00	14 00	686 00
	18	Morning Gazette	6	6	75 00		75 00
	21	WSID Radio Station	8	7	175 00		175 00
	26	Dale Brothers	7	8	1 250 00	25 00	1 225 00
	28	Neal Realty Company	11	9	500 00		500 00
	28	Payroll	12	10	1 000 00		1 000 00
					7 010 00	79 00	6 931 00

GENERAL LEDGER

Cash

Date	Debit	Credit	Balance
Feb. 28		6,931.00	6,931.00

Store Supplies

Date	Debit	Credit	Balance
Feb. 5	250.00		250.00

Office Equipment

Date	Debit	Credit	Balance
Feb. 24	500.00		500.00

Transportation-In

Date	Debit	Credit	Balance
Feb. 28	85.00		85.00

Rent Expense

Date	Debit	Credit	Balance
Feb. 28	500.00		500.00

Sales Salaries Expense

Date	Debit	Credit	Balance
Feb. 28	1,250.00		1,250.00

Vouchers Payable

Date	Debit	Credit	Balance
Feb. 28		9,385.00	9,385.00
28	7,010.00		2,375.00

Advertising Expense

Date	Debit	Credit	Balance
Feb. 28	250.00		250.00

Purchases

Date	Debit	Credit	Balance
Feb. 28	5,800.00		5,800.00

Office Salaries Expense

Date	Debit	Credit	Balance
Feb. 28	750.00		750.00

Purchases Discounts

Date	Debit	Credit	Balance
Feb. 28		79.00	79.00

NERO SALES COMPANY
Schedule of Vouchers Payable
February 28, 19—

Voucher Number	Payee	Amount
9	Office Sales Company	$ 500
10	Radion Company	1,875
	Total Vouchers Payable	$2,375

8

Temporary Investments and Receivables

After studying Chapter 8, you should be able to:

1. Journalize entries to account for temporary investments; and calculate, record, and report the lower of cost or market of temporary investments in marketable equity securities.

2. Prepare entries to account for credit card sales.

3. Prepare entries to account for credit customers, including allowance method entries and direct write-off method entries to account for bad debts.

4. Calculate the interest on promissory notes and prepare entries to record the receipt of promissory notes and their payment or dishonor.

5. Calculate the discount and proceeds on discounted notes receivable and prepare entries to record the discounting of notes receivable and, if dishonoured, their dishonour.

6. Define or explain the words and phrases listed in the chapter Glossary.

TOPICAL OUTLINE

I. Temporary investments

   A. Temporary investments must be readily convertible into cash and held as a source of cash to satisfy the needs of current operations. They are classified as current assets on the balance sheet.
   B. Recorded at cost, which includes any commissions paid.
   C. Temporary investments in marketable equity securities must be reported on the balance sheet at the lower of cost or market.

II. Credit card sales

   A. Receipts from some credit card sales are deposited like cheques into a business's bank account for immediate cash credit.
   B. Receipts from other credit card sales are sent to the credit card company for payment. The business has an account receivable from the credit card company until payment is received.

III. Subsidiary Accounts Receivable Ledger

   A. Accounts Receivable account in General Ledger is controlling account for subsidiary ledger.
   B. A separate account for each customer is maintained in the Accounts Receivable Ledger.

IV. Bad debts—accounts of customers who do not pay

   A. A necessary expense associated with selling on credit.
   B. Bad debts expense should be matched with the sales that resulted in the bad debts.
   C. Methods of accounting for bad debts
      1. Allowance method—at the end of each accounting period, bad debts expense is estimated and recorded.
      2. Direct write-off method—uncollectible accounts written off directly to Bad Debts Expense. (This method mismatches revenues and expenses.)
   D. Methods of estimating bad debts expense
      1. Income statement approach—bad debts expense is calculated as a percentage of credit sales.
      2. Balance sheet approach—desired credit balance in Allowance for Doubtful Accounts is calculated:
         a. As a percentage of outstanding receivables (simplified approach).
         b. By aging of accounts receivable.
   E. Recovery of bad debts
      1. Reinstate customer's account (reverse original write-off).
      2. Record collection of reinstated account.

V. Installment accounts and notes receivable

   A. Installment account receivable—an account receivable that allows the customer to make periodic payments over several months and which usually earns interest.
   B. Note receivable—a written document promising payment and signed by the customer.
      1. Promissory notes are notes payable to the maker of the note and notes receivable to the payee.
      2. Notes receivable are generally preferred by creditors over accounts receivable.
   C. Calaculating interest

$$\text{Principle of note} \times \text{Annual rate of interest} \times \text{Time of note expressed in years} = \text{Interest}$$

D. Accounting for notes receivable

    1. Record receipt of note.
    2. Record end-of-period adjustment for accrued interest.
    3. Record receipt of note payments.
    4. If note is dishonoured, amount of note should be removed from Notes Receivable account and charged back to the account of maker.

E. Discounting notes receivable—owner endorses and delivers note to the bank for cash.

    1. Discount period—the time the bank holds the note.
    2. Bank discount—the amount of interest the bank charges during the discount period.
    3. Proceeds of the note—the maturity value of the note minus the bank discount.
    4. Contingent liability—usually the person who discounts the note is liable for payment of the note if it is dishonoured by maker.

VI. Accounting principles

A. Materiality principle—strict adherence to any accounting principle is not required if lack of adherence will not produce an error large enough to influence the judgment of financial statement readers.
B. Full disclosure principle—financial statements and their accompanying notes must disclose all information of a material nature relating to the financial position and operating results of the company for which they are prepared.

Problem I

The following statements are either true or false. Place a (T) in the parentheses before each true statement and an (F) before each false statement.

1. ( ) Temporary investments are classified as current assets on the balance sheet.

2. ( ) Investments in securities that do not mature within one year or the current operating cycle of the business can be classified as current assets on the balance sheet if they are marketable.

3. ( ) A stock quotation of $14\frac{1}{8}$ means $14.125 per share.

4. ( ) To determine the lower of cost or market of a portfolio of temporary investments in marketable equity securities, compare the individual cost of each security held with its current market value.

5. ( ) The Gain on Temporary Investments account is closed to Income Summary and reported on the income statement.

6. ( ) When the market value of temporary investments increases above cost, the resulting gain is credited to Gain on Temporary Investments.

7. ( ) If cash from credit sales is received immediately when the credit card receipts are deposited at the bank, the credit card expense is recorded at the time the sale is recorded.

8. ( ) Businesses with credit customers must maintain a separate account for each customer.

9. ( ) After all entries are posted, the sum of the balances in the Accounts Receivable Ledger should be equal to the balance of the Accounts Receivable account in the General Ledger.

10. ( ) Under the allowance method of accounting for bad debts, accounts receivable are reported on the balance sheet at the amount of cash proceeds expected from their collection.

11. ( ) At the time an adjusting entry to record estimated bad debts expense is made, the credit side of the entry is to Accounts Receivable.

12. ( ) When an account deemed uncollectible is written off against Allowance for Doubtful Accounts, the estimated realizable amount of Accounts Receivable is decreased.

13. ( ) The income statement approach to estimating bad debts is based on the idea that some percentage of credit sales will be uncollectible.

14. ( ) The balance sheet approach to estimating bad debts is based on the idea that some particular percentage of a company's credit sales will become uncollectible.

15. ( ) Aging of accounts receivable requires the examination of each account in the accounts receivable ledger.

* 16. ( ) A 90-day note, dated August 17, matures on November 16.

17. ( ) Although the direct write-off method of accounting for bad debts usually mismatches revenues and expenses, it may be allowed in cases where bad debt losses are immaterial in relation to total net sales and net income.

18. ( ) If the principal of a note exceeds the proceeds from discounting the note, the difference is debited to Interest Expense.

(* Identifies problems to be solved using the alternate method for calculation of interest calculation.)

Problem II

You are given several words, phrases or numbers to choose from in completing each of the following statements or in answering the following questions. In each case select the one that best completes the statement or answers the question and place its letter in the answer space provided.

_____ 1. On June 12, Cookie Company purchased 400 shares of Photograph Company common stock at 12⅛ plus a 1% brokerage fee as a temporary investment. What is the general journal entry to record the transaction?

    a. Temporary Investments 4,851.00
       Cash 4,851.00
    b. Cash 4,365.00
       Temporary Investments 4,365.00
    c. Temporary Investments 4,898.50
       Cash 4,898.50
    d. Cash 4,801.50
       Temporary Investments 4,801.50
    e. Temporary Investments 4,365.00
       Cash 4,365.00

_____ 2. The cost and market values of Company B's temporary investments in marketable equity securities were as follows on sequential balance sheet dates:

	Cost	Market
On December 31, 1989	$30,000	$28,000
On December 31, 1990	34,000	32,500

What general journal entry is required on December 31, 1990?

    a. Loss on Market Decline of Temporary Inv. 1,500
       Allowance to Reduce Temporary Inv. to
         Market 1,500
    b. Allowance to Reduce Temporary Inv. to Market 500
       Gain on Market Recovery of Temporary Inv. 500
    c. No entry is required.
    d. Allowance to Reduce Temporary Inv. to Market 1,500
       Loss on Market Decline of Temporary Inv. 1,500
    e. Loss of Market Decline of Temporary Inv. 3,500
       Allowance to Reduce Temporary Inv. to
         Market 3,500

_____ 3. Orion Company has decided to write off the account of Jack Irwin against the Allowance for Doubtful Accounts. The $2,100 balance in Irwin's account originated with a credit sale in July of last year. What is the general journal entry to record this write-off?

    a. Allowance for Doubtful Accounts 2,100
       Accounts Receivable—Jack Irwin 2,100
    b. Accounts Receivable 2,100
       Allowance for Doubtful Accounts 2,100
    c. Bad Debts Expense 2,100
       Allowance for Doubtful Accounts 2,100
    d. Accounts Receivable 2,100
       Accounts Receivable—Jack Irwin 2,100
    e. Bad Debts Expense 2,100
       Accounts Receivable 2,100

4. Hitech Corporation had credit sales of $3,000,000 in 1990. Before recording the December 31, 1990, adjustments, the company's Allowance for Doubtful Accounts had a credit balance of $1,400. A schedule of the December 31, 1990, accounts receivable by age is summarized as follows:

December 31, 1990 Accounts Receivable	Age of Accounts Receivable	Uncollectible Per cent Expected
$285,000	Not due	1.5
87,000	1–45 days past due	8.2
34,000	46–90 days past due	37.0
8,000	over 90 days past due	70.0

Calculate the amount that should appear on the December 31, 1990, balance sheet as allowance for doubtful accounts.

a. $28,189.
b. $ 5,600.
c. $25,314.
d. $30,989.
e. $29,589.

5. Based on the information given in problem 4, what is the general journal entry to record bad debts expense for 1990?

a. Debit Bad Debts Expense; credit Allowance for Doubtful Accounts.
b. Debit Accounts Receivable; credit Allowance for Doubtful Accounts.
c. Debit Bad Debts Expense; credit Accounts Receivable.
d. Debit Allowance for Doubtful Accounts; credit Bad Debts Expense.
e. Debit Accounts Receivable; credit Bad Debts Expense.

* 6. On June 22, Xrox Corporation accepted a $4,500, 90-day, 12% note dated June 20 from Curtis Sims. On June 30, Xrox discounted the note at the bank at 14%. What amount of interest earned (or interest expense) should Xrox Corporation record?

a. $135 interest earned.
b. $9.20 interest expense.
c. $5 interest expense.
d. $144.20 interest expense.
e. $22.50 interest expense.

* 7. What were the proceeds from discounting the note in problem 6?

a. $4,500.00
b. $4,635.00
c. $4,472.77
d. $4,490.80
e. $4,355.80

Problem III

Many of the important ideas and concepts discussed in Chapter 8 are reflected in the following list of key terms. Test your understanding of these terms by matching the appropriate definitions with the terms. Record the number identifying the most appropriate definition in the blank space next to each term.

_____ Accounts Receivable Ledger

_____ Aging of accounts receivable

_____ Allowance for doubtful accounts

_____ Allowance method of accounting for bad debts

_____ Bad debt

_____ Bank discount	_____ Materiality principle
_____ Contingent liability	_____ Maturity date of a note
_____ Controlling account	_____ Maturity value of a note
_____ Direct write-off method of accounting for bad debts	_____ Notice of protest
_____ Discount period of a note	_____ Payee of a note
_____ Discounting a note receivable	_____ Proceeds of a discounted note
_____ Dishonouring a note	_____ Protest fee
_____ Full-disclosure principle	_____ Realizable value
_____ General Ledger	_____ Temporary investments
_____ Installment accounts receivable	_____ Subsidiary ledger
_____ Lower of cost or market	_____ Short-term investments
_____ Maker of a note	

1. Selling a note receivable to a bank or other concern, usually with the provision that the seller assumes a contingent liability to pay the note if it is dishonoured.

2. One who signs a note and promises to pay it at maturity.

3. A collection of accounts other than general ledger accounts which shows the details underlying the balance of a controlling account in the General Ledger.

4. The accounting requirement that financial statements including the footnotes contain all relevant information about the operations and financial position of the entity and that the information be presented in an understandable manner.

5. An accounting procedure that (1) estimates the bad debts resulting from credit sales and reports bad debt expense during the period of the sales, and (2) reports accounts receivable in the balance sheet net of estimated uncollectibles, which is their estimated realizable value.

6. The maturity value of a note minus any interest deducted because of its being discounted before maturity.

7. A potential liability that will become an actual liability if and only if certain events occur.

8. Another name for temporary investments.

9. The fee charged for preparing and issuing a notice of protest.

10. A procedure whereby uncollectible accounts are not estimated in advance and are not charged to expense until they prove to be uncollectible.

11. Principal of the note plus any interest due on the note's maturity date.

12. Refusal of a promissory note's maker to pay the amount due upon maturity of the note.

13. The idea that the requirements of any accounting principle may be ignored if the effect on the financial statements is unimportant to financial statement readers.

14. The amount of interest charged by a bank when the bank accepts a discounted note from a customer. Also, the interest a bank deducts in advance when making a loan.

15. An uncollectible receivable.

16. Accounts receivable that allow the customer to make periodic payments over several months and which typically earn interest.

17. The expected proceeds from converting an asset into cash.

18. The one to whom a promissory note is made payable.

19. The estimated amount of accounts receivable that will be uncollectible.

20. A written statement that says a note was duly presented to the maker for payment and payment was refused.

21. The date on which a note and any interest are due and payable.

22. The number of days following the date on which a note is discounted at the bank until the maturity date of the note.

23. A process of classifying accounts receivable in terms of how long they have been outstanding for the purpose of estimating the amount of uncollectible accounts.

24. A subsidiary ledger having an account for each customer.

25. A general ledger account the balance of which is always equal to the sum of the balances in a related subsidiary ledger.

26. Investments such as government or corporate debt obligations and marketable equity securities that can be converted into cash quickly and that are held as a source of cash to satisfy the needs of current operations.

27. A method of reporting whereby the total cost of the entire portfolio of temporary investments in marketable equity securities is compared to the total market value on the date of the balance sheet and the lesser amount is reported in the balance sheet.

28. The collection of financial statement accounts of a business.

* Problem IV

On December 12, Lark Company received from Guy Hall, a customer, $300 in cash and a $1,500, 12%, 60-day note dated December 11 in granting a time extension on Hall's past-due account. On December 31, Lark Company recorded the accrued interest on the note, and Guy Hall paid the note and its interest on the following February 9. Complete the general journal entries to record these transactions.

DATE		ACCOUNT TITLES AND EXPLANATION	P.R.	DEBIT	CREDIT
Dec.	12				
		Received cash and a note in granting a time			
		extension on a past-due account.			
	31				
		To record accrued interest on a note receivable.			
Feb.	9				
		Received payment of a note and interest.			

* Problem V

On March 1 Lark Company accepted a $1,200, 12%, 60-day note dated that day from a customer, Mary Dale, in granting a time extension on the customer's past-due account. When Lark Company presented the note for payment on April 30, it was dishonored, and on December 20 Lark Company wrote off the debt as uncollectible. Present entries to record the dishonor and the write-off against the company's Allowance for Doubtful Accounts.

DATE		ACCOUNT TITLES AND EXPLANATION	P.R.	DEBIT	CREDIT
Apr.	30				
		To charge the account of Mary Dale for her			
		dishonoured $1,200, 12%, 60-day note.			
Dec.	20				
		To write off the uncollectible account of Mary Dale.			

* Problem VI

On April 2 Lark Company received from Sam Fox, a customer, a $1,000, 12%, 60-day note dated that day in granting a time extension on the customer's past-due account. Lark Company held the note until April 26 and then discounted it at its bank at 14%. The note was not protested at maturity. Complete the following entries for this note.

DATE		ACCOUNT TITLES AND EXPLANATION	P.R.	DEBIT	CREDIT
Apr.	2				
		Received a note in granting a time extension			
		on a past-due account.			
	26				
		Discounted the Sam Fox note at 14%.			

* Problem VII

On June 10 Lark Company received a $2,400, 10%, 60-day note dated that day from Ted Sack, a customer, in granting a time extension on his past-due account. The company held the note until June 16 and then discounted it at its bank at 13%. On August 10 Lark Company received notice protesting the note. It paid the bank the maturity value of the note plus a $15 protest fee. On October 8 Lark Company received a $2,495.92 cheque from Ted Sack in payment of the maturity value of his dishonoured note, the protest fee, and 10% interest on both for 60 days beyond maturity. Complete the following general journal entries to record this series of transactions.

DATE		ACCOUNT TITLES AND EXPLANATION	P.R.	DEBIT	CREDIT
June	10				
		Received a note in granting a time extension			
		on a past-due account.			
June	16				
		Discounted the Ted Sack note at 14%.			
Aug.	10				
		Paid the bank the maturity value of the			
		Ted Sack note plus a protest fee.			
Oct.	8				
		Received payment of the maturity value of the			
		Ted Sack note plus the protest fee and			
		interest on both for 60 days beyond maturity.			

Problem VIII

Marin Company uses the allowance method in accounting for bad debt losses, and over the past several years it has experienced an average loss equal to one fourth of 1% of its credit sales. During 1990 the company sold $928,000 of merchandise on credit, including a $98 credit sale to Gus Bell on March 5, 1990. The $98 had not been paid by the year's end.

1. If at the end of 1990 Marin Company, in providing for estimated bad debt losses, assumes history will repeat,

    it will provide an allowance for 1990 estimated bad debts equal to _____% of its $928,000 of 1990 charge sales; and the adjusting entry to record the allowance will appear as follows: (Complete the following entry.)

DATE		ACCOUNT TITLES AND EXPLANATION	P.R.	DEBIT	CREDIT
1990					
Dec.	31				
		To record estimated bad debts.			

2. The debit of the foregoing entry is to the expense account, _____

    _____, which is closed to the _____ account at the end of the accounting period, just as any other expense account is closed.

3. The effect of the foregoing adjusting entry on the 1990 income statement of Marin Company is to cause an estimated amount of bad debts expense to be deducted from the $928,000 of revenue from 1990 charge sales.

   This complies with the accounting principle of _____

   _____.

4. The credit of the foregoing adjusting entry is to the contra account _____

   _____.

   On the December 31, 1990, balance sheet, the balance of this contra account is subtracted from the balance

   of the _____ account to show the amount that is expected to be realized from the accounts receivable.

5. On March 31, 1991, the Accounts Receivable controlling account and the Allowance for Doubtful Accounts account of Marin Company had the following balances:

Accounts Receivable				Allowance for Doubtful Accounts	
Mar. 31	65,625			Mar. 31	4,475

   A balance sheet which was prepared on March 31, 1991, would show that Marin Company expects to collect

   $_____ of its accounts receivable.

6. On April 1, 1991, Marin Company decided the $98 account of Gus Bell (sale made on March 5 of the previous year) was uncollectible and wrote it off as a bad debt. (Complete the entry and post to the above T-accounts the portions affecting the accounts.)

DATE		ACCOUNT TITLES AND EXPLANATION	P.R.	DEBIT	CREDIT
1991					
Apr.	1				
		To write off the account of Gus Bell.			

7. If a balance sheet was prepared immediately after the entry writing off the uncollectible account of Gus Bell

   was posted, it would show that Marin Company expected to collect $_____ of

   its accounts receivable. Consequently, the write-off _____ (did, did not) affect the net balance sheet amount of accounts receivable. Likewise, the entry writing off the account did not record

   an expense because the expense was anticipated and recorded in the _____ entry made on December 31, 1990, the year of the sale.

Problem IX

Pell Company sells almost exclusively for cash, but it does make a few small charge sales, and it also occasionally has a small bad debt loss which it accounts for by the direct write-off method.

1. On the next page, give the entry made by Pell Company on February 5 to write off the $55 uncollectible account of Joan Bond (the goods were sold during the previous period.)

DATE		ACCOUNT TITLES AND EXPLANATION	P.R.	DEBIT	CREDIT
Feb.	5				

2. Writing off the foregoing bad debt directly to the Bad Debts Expense account violates the accounting principle

of _____.

However, due to the accounting principle of _____ the direct write-off is permissible in this case because the company's bad debt losses are very small in relation to its sales.

Problem X

A company that ages its accounts receivable and increases its allowance for doubtful accounts to an amount sufficient to provide for estimated bad debts had a $75 debit balance in its Allowance for Doubtful Accounts account on December 31. If on that date it estimated that $1,800 of its accounts receivable were uncollectible, it should

make a year-end adjusting entry crediting $_____ to its Allowance for Doubtful Accounts account.

Problem XI

Pierce Company allows its customers to use two credit cards: the University National Bank credit card and the Community Credit Card. Using the information given below, prepare general journal entries for Pierce Company to record the following credit card transactions:

a) University National Bank charges a 3% service fee for sales on its credit card. As a commercial customer of the bank, Pierce Company receives immediate credit when it makes its daily deposit of sales receipts.

  May 2 Sold merchandise for $525 to customers who used the University National Bank credit card.

DATE	ACCOUNT TITLES AND EXPLANATION	P.R.	DEBIT	CREDIT

b) Community Credit Card Company charges 4% of sales for use of its card. Pierce Company submits accumulated sales receipts to Community Company and is paid within thirty days.

  May 3 Sold merchandise for $675 to customers using the Community Credit Card. Submitted receipts to Community Company for payment.
  30 Received amount due from Community Credit Card Company.

DATE	ACCOUNT TITLES AND EXPLANATION	P.R.	DEBIT	CREDIT

Solutions for Chapter 8

Problem I

1. T	10. T
2. T	11. F
3. T	12. F
4. F	13. T
5. T	14. F
6. F	15. T
7. T	16. F
8. T	17. T
9. T	18. T

Problem II

1. C
2. B
3. A
4. E
5. A
6. B
7. D

Problem III

* Problem IV

Dec. 12	Cash	300.00	
	Notes Receivable	1,500.00	
	Accounts Receivable—Guy Hall		1,800.00
31	Interest Receivable ($1,500 × .12 × 20/360)	10.00	
	Interest Earned		10.00
Feb. 9	Cash	1,530.00	
	Interest Receivable		10.00
	Interest Earned		20.00
	Notes Receivable		1,500.00

* Problem V

Apr. 30	Accounts Receivable—Mary Dale	1,224.00	
	Interest Earned		24.00
	Notes Receivable		1,200.00
Dec. 20	Allowance for Doubtful Accounts	1,224.00	
	Accounts Receivable—Mary Dale		1,224.00

* Problem VI

Apr.	2	Notes Receivable	1,000.00	
		Accounts Receivable—Sam Fox		1,000.00
	26	Cash	1,005.72	
		Interest Earned		5.72
		Notes Receivable		1,000.00

($1,000 × .12 × 60/360) = $20.00
($1,020 × .14 × 36/360) = <u>14.28</u>
$ 5.72

* Problem VII

June	10	Notes Receivable	2,400.00	
		Accounts Receivable—Ted Sack		2,400.00
	16	Cash	2,392.42	
		Interest Expense	7.58	
		Notes Receivable		2,400.00

($2,400 × .10 × 60/360) = $40.00
($2,440 × .13 × 54/360) = <u>47.58</u>
$ 7.58

Aug.	10	Accounts Receivable—Ted Sack	2,455.00	
		Cash ($2,440 + $15)		2,455.00
Oct.	8	Cash	2,495.92	
		Interest Earned		40.92
		Accounts Receivable—Ted Sack		2,455.00

Problem VIII

1. one fourth of 1%, or .25%

Dec. 31	Bad Debts Expense	2,320.00	
	Allowance for Doubtful Accounts		2,320.00

2. Bad Debts Expense, Income Summary

3. matching revenues and expenses

4. Allowance for Doubtful Accounts, Accounts Receivable

5. $61,150

6.
Apr.	1	Allowance for Doubtful Accounts	98.00	
		Accounts Receivable—Gus Bell		98.00

Accounts Receivable				Allowance for Doubtful Accounts		
Mar. 31	65,625				Mar. 31	4,475
		Apr. 1	98	Apr. 1	98	

7. $61,150, did not, adjusting

Problem IX

1. Feb. 5   Bad Debts Expense 55.00

          Accounts Receivable—Joan Bond 55.00

2. matching revenues and expenses, materiality

Problem X

$1,875

Problem XI

a) May 2   Cash 509.25

          Credit Card Expense ($525 × .03) 15.75

            Sales 525.00

b) May 3   Accounts Receivable—Community Company 675.00

            Sales 675.00

       30   Cash 648.00

          Credit Card Expense ($675 × .04) 27.00

            Accounts Receivable—Community Company 675.00

9 Inventories and Cost of Goods Sold

After studying Chapter 9, you should be able to:

1. Calculate the cost of an inventory based on (a) specific invoice prices, (b) weighted-average cost, (c) FIFO, and (d) LIFO, and explain the financial statement effects of choosing one method over the others.

2. Calculate the lower-of-cost-or-market amount of an inventory.

3. Explain the effect of an inventory error on the income statements of the current and succeeding years.

4. Prepare entries to record merchandise transactions and maintain subsidiary inventory records under a perpetual inventory system.

5. Estimate an inventory by the retail method and by the gross profit method.

6. Define or explain the words and phrases listed in the chapter Glossary.

Topical Outline

I. Inventory accounting

    A. Merchandise inventory

        1. The tangible property a merchandising business holds for sale.

        2. Usually the largest current asset of a merchandising concern.

    B. Major objective in inventory accounting

        1. The proper determination of income through the process of matching appropriate costs against revenues.

        2. Means assigning costs of inventory for sale during the accounting period either to cost of goods sold or to ending inventory.

II. Periodic inventory system

    A. Cost of ending inventory is determined by:

        1. Determining quantity of each item on hand.

        2. Assigning a cost to the quantities on hand.

    B. Cost of goods sold is calculated by subtracting cost of ending inventory from goods available for sale.

    C. Four ways to assign costs

        1. Specific invoice prices

            a. Each inventory item is matched with its invoice price.

            b. This method is of practical use only with relatively high-priced items of which only a few are sold.

        2. Weighted-average cost

            a. Total cost of beginning inventory and purchases is divided by number of units to find average cost.

            b. This method tends to smooth out price fluctuations.

        3. First-in, first-out (FIFO)

            a. Costs are assigned under the assumption that the oldest goods are sold first. (This pricing method may be assumed even if physical flow of goods does not follow this pattern.)

            b. With FIFO method, inventory on the balance sheet most closely approximates current replacement cost.

        4. Last-in, first-out (LIFO)

            a. Costs are assigned under the assumption that the most recent purchases are sold first.

            b. Use of LIFO method results in better matching of current costs and revenues.

    D. Items included on an inventory

        1. All goods owned by the business and held for sale regardless of the physical location of the goods.

        2. All costs incurred in bringing an article to its existing condition and location.

III. Lower of cost or market

    A. Inventory is normally reported on the balance sheet at market value whenever market is lower than cost.

1. Market normally means replacement cost.
2. Merchandise is written down to market because the value of the merchandise to the company has declined.

B. Lower of cost or market pricing is applied either:

1. To the inventory as a whole, or
2. Separately to each product in the inventory.

C. Exceptions

1. Inventory should never be valued at more than its net realizable value (expected sales price less additional costs to sell).
2. Inventory should never be valued at less than net realizable value minus a normal profit margin.

IV. Accounting principles

A. Principle of consistency

1. Requires a persistent application of an accounting method, period after period.

B. Full-disclosure principle

1. Requires a full-disclosure of the nature of any change in accounting methods.

C. Principle of conservatism

1. When two estimates of amounts to be received or paid in the future are about equally likely, the less optimistic estimate should be used.
2. Inventory cannot be written up to market when market exceeds cost.

D. Principle of materiality

1. In pricing an inventory, incidental costs of acquiring merchandise may be treated as expenses of the period in which incurred.

V. Inventory errors

A. Periodic inventory system

1. An error in determining the end-of-period inventory will cause misstatements in cost of goods sold, gross profit, net income, current assets, and owners' equity.
2. Error will carry forward in succeeding period's cost of goods sold, gross profit, and net income.
3. Errors in cost of goods sold and net income will be offset by errors in the following period.

VI. Perpetual inventory system

A. Updates the Merchandise Inventory account after each purchase and each sale.
B. Does not use a Purchases account; cost of items purchased is debited directly to Merchandise Inventory.
C. Requires two entries to record a sale of merchandise.
D. Merchandise Inventory account serves as a controlling account to a subsidiary Merchandise Inventory Ledger, which contains a separate record for each product in stock.
E. Using LIFO, a perpetual inventory system results in different amounts of cost of goods sold and ending inventory than under a periodic inventory system.

VII. Estimated inventories

A. Retail inventory method

1. Used to estimate ending inventory on the ratios of cost of goods for sale at cost and cost of goods for sale at retail.

2. Satisfactory for interim statements, but a physical inventory should be taken at least once a year.

B. Gross profit method

1. Similar to retail method, but does not require information about retail price of beginning inventory, purchases, and markups.

2. Company must know its normal gross profit margin or rate.

Problem I

The following statements are either true or false. Place a (T) in the parentheses before each true statement and an (F) before each false statement.

1. ( ) The merchandise inventory of a business includes goods sold FOB destination if they are not yet delivered.

2. ( ) When a perpetual inventory system is used, the dollar amount of ending inventory is determined by counting the units of product on hand, multiplying the count for each product by its cost, and adding the costs for all products.

3. ( ) If prices of goods purchased remain unchanged, then all four methods of assigning costs to goods in the ending inventory would yield the same cost figures.

4. ( ) When first-in, first-out inventory pricing is used, the costs of the first items purchased are assigned to the ending inventory, and the remaining costs are assigned to goods sold.

5. ( ) If prices are rising, then using the LIFO method of pricing inventory will result in the highest net income.

6. ( ) Inventory should never be valued at more than net realizable value or less than net realizable value minus a normal profit margin.

7. ( ) Under the periodic inventory system, an error in ending inventory will carry forward and cause misstatements in the succeeding period's cost of goods sold, gross profit, and net income.

8. ( ) The perpetual inventory system uses a Purchases account to record items purchased.

9. ( ) The perpetual and periodic inventory systems never result in the same amounts of sales, cost of goods sold, and end-of-period merchandise inventory.

10. ( ) Lower of cost or market may be applied separately to each product or to the merchandise inventory as a whole.

Problem II

You are given several words, phrases or numbers to choose from in completing each of the following statements or in answering the following questions. In each case select the one that best completes the statement or answers the question and place its letter in the answer space provided.

_____ 1. Trivial Games Company's inventory consists of 80 units of product P, all of which have been damaged. The company bought the inventory for $20 per unit. Replacement cost is $22 per unit. Expected sales price is $30 per unit but this can be realized only if $7 additional cost per unit is paid. Calculate the lower of cost or market for the inventory.

  a. $1,840.
  b. $1,200.
  c. $1,760.
  d. $1,040.
  e. $1,600.

_____ 2. Magnum Company began a year and purchased merchandise as follows:

Jan. 1	Beginning inventory	40 units @ $17.00
Feb. 4	Purchased	80 units @ $16.00
May 12	Purchased	80 units @ $16.50
Aug. 9	Purchased	60 units @ $17.50
Nov. 23	Purchased	100 units @ $18.00

The company uses a periodic inventory system and the ending inventory consists of 60 units, 20 from each of the last three purchases. Determine ending inventory assuming costs are assigned on the basis of FIFO.

a. $1,040.
b. $1,000.
c. $1,069.
d. $1,080.
e. $1,022.

_____ 3. Linder Company began a year and purchased merchandise as follows:

    Jan. 1 Beginning inventory   40 units @ $17.00
    Feb. 4 Purchased   80 units @ $16.00
    May 12 Purchased   80 units @ $16.50
    Aug. 9 Purchased   60 units @ $17.50
    Nov. 23 Purchased   100 units @ $18.00

The company uses a periodic inventory system and the ending inventory consists of 60 units, 20 from each of the last three pruchases. Determine ending inventory assuming costs are assigned on the basis of LIFO.

a. $1,040.
b. $1,000.
c. $1,022.
d. $ 980.
e. $1,080.

_____ 4. Box Company began a year and purchased merchandise as follows:

    Jan. 1 Beginning inventory   40 units @ $17.00
    Feb. 4 Purchased   80 units @ $16.00
    May 12 Purchased   80 units @ $16.50
    Aug. 9 Purchased   60 units @ $17.50
    Nov. 23 Purchased   100 units @ $18.00

The company uses a periodic inventory system and the ending inventory consists of 60 units, 20 from each of the last three purchases. Determine ending inventory assuming costs are assigned on the basis of specific invoice prices.

a. $1,000.
b. $1,022.
c. $1,040.
d. $1,080.
e. $ 990.

_____ 5. Crow Company began a year and purchased merchandise as follows:

    Jan. 1 Beginning inventory   40 units @ $17.00
    Feb. 4 Purchased   80 units @ $16.00
    May 12 Purchased   80 units @ $16.50
    Aug. 9 Purchased   60 units @ $17.50
    Nov. 23 Purchased   100 units @ $18.00

The company uses a periodic inventory system and the ending inventory consists of 60 units, 20 from each of the last three purchases. Determine ending inventory assuming costs are assigned on a weighted-average basis.

a. $1,022.00.
b. $1,040.00.
c. $1,080.00.
d. $1,000.00.
e. $1,042.50.

_____ 6. Atlantis Company uses a periodic inventory system and made an error at the end of year 1 that caused its year 1 ending inventory to be understated by $5,000. What effect does this error have on the company's financial statements?

    a. Net income is understated; assets are understated.
    b. Net income is understated; assets are overstated.
    c. Net income is overstated; assets are understated.
    d. Net income is overstated; assets are overstated.
    e. Net income is overstated; assets are correctly stated.

_____ 7. Cheese Company sold $224,000 of merchandise at marked retail prices during an accounting period. The records show the following, at retail: beginning inventory = $60,000; net purchases = $214,000; additional markups = $6,000; markdowns = $5,800. At cost: beginning inventory = $40,000; net purchases = $156,000. Use the retail method to estimate the store's ending inventory at cost.

    a. $ 35,883.
    b. $ 50,200.
    c. $191,940.
    d. $ 43,260.
    e. $ 35,140.

_____ 8. Sanders Company wants to prepare interim financial statements for the first quarter of 1990. The company uses a periodic inventory system and has an average gross profit rate of 30%. Based on the following information, use the gross profit method to prepare an estimate of the March 31 inventory.

January 1, beginning inventory	$ 97,000
Purchases	214,000
Purchases returns	2,000
Transportation-In	4,000
Sales	404,000
Sales returns	5,000

    a. $ 33,700.
    b. $193,300.
    c. $119,700.
    d. $179,900.
    e. $ 26,700.

_____ 9. Assume that in addition to estimating the ending inventory by the retail method (refer to question 7), Cheese Company also took a physical inventory at marked selling prices of the inventory items which equaled $48,000. Determine the amount of the company's inventory shrinkage at cost.

    a. $12,860.
    b. $ 2,200.
    c. $ 4,740.
    d. $ 1,540.
    e. $ 2,283.

Problem III

Many of the important ideas and concepts discussed in Chapter 9 are reflected in the following list of key terms. Test your understanding of these terms by matching the appropriate definitions with the terms. Record the number identifying the most appropriate definition in the blank space next to each term.

_____	Conservatism principle	_____	Markon
_____	Consignee	_____	Markup
_____	Consignor	_____	Net realizable value
_____	Consistency principle	_____	Normal markup
_____	FIFO inventory pricing	_____	Periodic inventory system
_____	Gross profit inventory method	_____	Perpetual inventory system
_____	Interim statements	_____	Retail inventory method
_____	Inventory ticket	_____	Retail method cost ratio
_____	LIFO inventory pricing	_____	Specific invoice inventory pricing
_____	Markdown	_____	Weighted-average inventory pricing

1. The expected sales price of an item less any additional costs to sell.

2. The pricing of an inventory under the assumption that the first items received were the first items sold.

3. An inventory pricing system in which the unit prices of the beginning inventory and of each purchase are weighted by the number of units in the beginning inventory and each purchase. The total of these amounts is then divided by the total number of units available for sale to find the unit cost of the ending inventory and of the units that were sold.

4. Another name for markon.

5. The accounting requirement that a company use the same accounting methods period after period so that the financial statements of succeeding periods will be comparable.

6. An increase in the sales price of merchandise above the normal markon given the goods.

7. The ratio of goods available for sale at cost to goods available for sale at retail prices.

8. An owner of goods who ships them to another party who will then sell the goods for the owner.

9. A procedure for estimating an ending inventory in which the past gross profit rate is used to estimate cost of goods sold, which is then subtracted from the cost of goods available for sale to determine the estimated ending inventory.

10. The pricing of an inventory where the purchase invoice of each item in the ending inventory is identified and used to determine the cost assigned to the inventory.

11. A form attached to the counted items in the process of taking a physical inventory.

12. An inventory system in which cost of goods sold is recorded after each sale and the Merchandise Inventory account is updated after each purchase and each sale.

13. The pricing of an inventory under the assumption that the last items received were the first items sold.

14. A reduction in the marked selling price of merchandise.

15. The accounting principle that guides accountants to select the less optimistic estimate when two estimates of amounts to be received or paid are about equally likely.

16. An accounting system in which the Merchandise Inventory account is updated only once each accounting period, based on a physical count of the inventory.

17. A method for estimating an ending inventory based on the ratio of the amount of goods for sale at cost to the amount of goods for sale at marked selling price.

18. One who receives and holds goods owned by another party for the purpose of selling the goods for the owner.

19. Monthly or quarterly financial statements prepared in between the regular year-end statements.

20. The normal amount or percentage of cost that is added to the cost of merchandise to arrive at its selling price.

Problem IV

Complete the following by filling in the blanks.

1. Consistency in the use of an inventory costing method is particularly important if there is to be _____ _____.

2. If a running record is maintained for each inventory item of the number of units received as units are received, the number of units sold as units are sold, and the number of units remaining after each receipt or sale, the

   inventory system is called _____.

3. When a company changes its accounting procedures, the _____

   _____ principle requires that the nature of the change, justification for the

   change, and the effect of the change on _____ be disclosed in the notes accompanying the financial statements.

4. Two exceptions to the idea that market means replacement cost are:

   a. _____
      _____.

   b. _____
      _____.

5. Inventories are generally priced at cost. However, a departure from cost may be necessary for _____
   _____
   _____.

6. With a periodic inventory system, an error in taking an end-of-period inventory will cause a misstatement of

   periodic net income for _____ (one, two) accounting periods because _____
   _____
   _____.

7. When identical items are purchased during an accounting period at different costs, a problem arises as to which costs apply to the ending inventory and which apply to the goods sold. There are at least four commonly used ways of assigning costs to inventory and to goods sold. They are:

a. _____;

b. _____;

c. _____;

d. _____.

8. A major objective of accounting for inventories is the proper determination of periodic net income through the process of matching _____ and _____. The matching process consists of determining how much of the cost of the goods that were for sale during an accounting period should be deducted from the period's _____ and how much should be carried forward as _____, to be matched against a future period's revenues.

9. Although changing back and forth from one inventory costing method to another might allow management to report the incomes it would prefer, the accounting principle of _____ requires a company to use the same pricing method period after period unless it can justify the change.

10. Using _____ inventory pricing, a perpetual inventory system and a periodic inventory system may result in different amounts of _____ and _____ _____.

11. In the gross profit method of estimating an ending inventory, an average _____ _____ rate is used to determine estimated cost of goods sold, and the ending inventory is then estimated by subtracting estimated _____ from the cost of goods for sale.

12. In separating cost of goods for sale into cost of goods sold and cost of goods unsold, the procedures for assigning a cost to the ending inventory are also the means of determining _____ because whatever portion of the cost of goods available for sale is assigned to ending inventory, the remainder goes to _____.

13. Cost of an inventory item includes _____
_____
_____
_____.

14. Use of the lower-of-cost-or-market rule places an inventory on the balance sheet at a _____ figure. The argument in favor of this rule provides that any loss should be _____ in the year of the price decline.

15. When recording a sale of merchandise using a _____ (perpetual, periodic) inventory system, two journal entries must be made. One entry records the revenue received for the sale and the second entry debits the _____ account.

Problem V

A company uses a perpetual inventory system and during a year had the following beginning inventory, purchases, and sales of Product Z:

Jan. 1	Beginning Inventory	200 units @ $0.50 = $100
Mar. 15	Purchased	400 units @ 0.50 = 200
Apr. 1	Sold	300 units
June 3	Purchased	300 units @ 0.60 = 180
July 1	Sold	200 units
Oct. 8	Purchased	600 units @ 0.70 = 420
Nov. 1	Sold	500 units
Dec. 15	Purchased	500 units @ 0.80 = 400

In the spaces below show the cost that should be assigned to the ending inventory and to the goods sold under the following assumptions:

	Portions Assigned to—	
	Ending Inventory	Cost of Goods Sold
1. A first-in, first-out basis was used to price the ending inventory	$	$
2. A last-in, first-out basis was used to price the ending inventory	$	$

Problem VI

The following end-of-period information about a store's beginning inventory, purchases, markups, markdowns, and sales is available.

	At Cost	At Retail
Beginning inventory	$ 9,600	$12,000
Purchases, net	54,400	68,000
Transportation-in	1,680	
Additional markups		2,100
Markdowns		700
Sales		69,000

The above information is to be used to estimate the store's ending inventory by the retail method.

1. The store had goods for sale during the year calculated as follows:

	At Cost	At Retail
Beginning inventory	$ _____	$ _____
Purchases, net	_____	_____
Transportation-in	_____	_____
Additional markups	_____	_____
Goods for sale	_____	_____

2. The store's cost ratio was:

$ _____ / $ _____ = _____

3. Of the goods the store had for sale at market retail prices during the year, the following dollar amounts are gone because of—

Sales .... $ _____

And because of price markdowns, which in effect reduced the total goods for sale at retail .... _____

  Total sales and markdowns .... $ _____

Which left the store an estimated ending inventory at retail (goods for sale at retail less sales and markdowns) .... $ _____

4. And when the store's cost ratio is applied to this estimated ending inventory at retail, the estimated ending inventory at cost is .... $ _____

Solutions for Chapter 9

Problem I

1.	T	6.	T
2.	F	7.	T
3.	T	8.	F
4.	F	9.	F
5.	F	10.	T

Problem II

1.	E	6.	A
2.	D	7.	E
3.	B	8.	A
4.	C	9.	D
5.	A		

Problem III

Conservatism principle	15		Markon	20
Consignee	18		Markup	6
Consignor	8		Net realizable value	1
Consistency principle	5		Normal markup	4 or 20
FIFO inventory pricing	2		Periodic inventory system	16
Gross profit inventory method	9		Perpetual inventory system	12
Interim statements	19		Retail inventory method	17
Inventory ticket	11		Retail method cost ratio	7
LIFO inventory pricing	13		Specific invoice inventory pricing	10
Markdown	14		Weighted-average inventory pricing	3

Problem IV

1. comparability of the financial statements prepared period after period

2. a perpetual inventory system

3. full-disclosure, net income

4. (a) market is never more than net realizable value, (b) market is never less than net realizable value minus a normal profit margin

5. goods that have been damaged or have deteriorated and also when replacement costs for inventory items are less than the amounts paid for the items

6. two, the ending inventory of one period becomes the beginning inventory of the next

7. (a) specific invoice prices; (b) weighted-average cost; (c) first-in, first-out; (d) last-in, first-out

8. costs, revenues, revenues, merchandise inventory

9. consistency

10. last-in, first-out; cost of goods sold; ending merchandise inventory

11. gross profit, cost of goods sold

12. cost of goods sold, cost of goods sold

13. the invoice price, less the discount, plus any additional incidental costs necessary to put the item in place and in condition for sale

14. conservative, recognized

15. perpetual, cost of goods sold

Problem V

	Portions Assigned to—	
	Ending Inventory	Cost of Goods Sold
1.	$750	$550
2.	680	620

Problem VI

	At Cost	At Retail
Goods for sale:		
Beginning inventory	$ 9,600	$12,000
Purchases, net	54,400	68,000
Transportation-in	1,680	
Additional markups		2,100
Goods for sale	$65,680	$82,100
Cost ratio: $65,680/$82,100 = .80		
Sales at retail		$69,000
Markdowns		700
Total sales and markdowns		$69,700
Ending inventory at retail		
($82,100 less $69,700)		$12,400
Ending inventory at cost ($12,400 × 80%)	$ 9,920	

10 Plant and Equipment

After studying Chapter 10, you should be able to:

1. Tell what is included in the cost of a plant asset and allocate the cost of lump-sum purchases to the separate assets being purchased.

2. Describe the reasons for depreciation accounting and calculate depreciation by the straight-line and units-of-production methods.

3. Describe how depreciation is disclosed in the financial statements and explain how the original cost of a plant asset is recovered through the sale of the asset's product or service.

4. Describe the use of accelerated depreciation for financial accounting and tax purposes and calculate accelerated depreciation under *(a)* the double declining-balance method, and *(b)* the sum-of-the-years'-digits method.

5. Explain how subsidiary ledgers and related controlling accounts are used to maintain control over plant assets.

6. Define or explain the words and phrases listed in the chapter Glossary.

Topical Outline

I. Plant and equipment

   A. Includes assets that are used in the production or sale of other assets and that have an expected service life longer than one accounting period.

   B. Cost of a plant asset

      1. Includes all normal and reasonable costs incurred in getting the asset into position and in condition for intended use.

      2. Must be allocated to the accounting periods that benefit from the asset's use.

      3. Must be allocated on a fair basis such as relative appraisal values, if two or more assets are purchased for one price.

   C. Service life of a plant asset—the period of time that it will be used in producing or selling other assets or services.

   D. Salvage value of a plant asset—the net amount that will be realized when the asset is disposed of at the end of its service life. The amount to be depreciated is the asset's cost minus its salvage value.

II. Depreciation

   A. The expiration of an asset's quantity of usefulness.

   B. The cost (less expected salvage value) of the asset must be allocated as an expense to the accounting periods benefited.

   C. Typical methods of allocating depreciation

      1. Straight-line—a method that allocates an equal share of the total estimated amount a plant asset will be depreciated during its service life to each accounting period in that life.

      2. Units-of-production—a method that allocates depreciation on a plant asset based on the relation of the units of product produced by the asset during a given period to the total units the asset is expected to produce during its entire life.

   D. For assets acquired or disposed of during a year, only a partial year's depreciation should be recorded.

   E. When accelerated depreciation is used and accounting periods do not coincide with the years in an asset's life, the annual depreciation is apportioned between accounting periods on a straight-line basis. In other words, accelerated depreciation for a year is divided by twelve to get depreciation for one month.

   F. Depreciation in the financial statements

      1. The cost of plant assets and their accumulated depreciation must be shown in the statements or in related footnotes.

      2. Depreciation method must be disclosed in a balance sheet footnote or other manner.

      3. Since depreciation is a process of allocating cost, the cost (net of depreciation) is not intended to represent value.

      4. Since depreciation expense is subtracted from revenues in arriving at net income, a company recovers the original cost of its depreciable assets through the sale of its products.

III. Accelerated depreciation

   A. Depreciation for tax purposes

      1. Tax laws require that companies use double declining-balance depreciation and specify different depreciation rates for different types (or classes) of assets.

      2. Depreciation (capital cost allowance) calculated for tax purposes is the maximum amount which may be deducted for the taxation year.

IV. Control of plant assets

    A. Each plant asset should be separately identified.

    B. Periodic inventories should be taken to verify the existence and continued use of assets.

    C. Formal records of plant assets should be maintained.

        1. Controlling and subsidiary ledgers should be kept.

        2. Materiality principle may be applied for assets costing less than an established minimum amount.

Problem I

The following statements are either true or false. Place a (T) in the parentheses before each true statement and an (F) before each false statement.

1. ( ) Cost is the basis for recording the acquisition of a plant asset.

2. ( ) The cost of a plant asset constructed by a business for its own use includes depreciation on the machinery used in constructing the asset.

3. ( ) Depreciation is a process of determining the value of assets.

4. ( ) Subsidiary plant asset records are controlled by asset and accumulated depreciation accounts.

Problem II

You are given several words, phrases or numbers to choose from in completing each of the following statements or in answering the following questions. In each case select the one that best completes the statement or answers the question and place its letter in the answer space provided.

_____ 1. Flintstone Company installed a machine in its factory at a cost of $84,000 on May 1, 1990. The machine's useful life is estimated at 8 years with a $9,000 salvage value. Determine the machine's 1991 depreciation on a declining-balance basis at twice the straight-line rate.

    a. $17,500.
    b. $15,750.
    c. $15,625.
    d. $14,000.
    e. $18,750.

_____ 2. Spacely's Sprockets purchased a machine on September 1, 1990, for $400,000. The machine's useful life was estimated at six years or 500,000 units of product with a $25,000 trade-in value. During its second year, the machine produced 87,000 units of product. Assuming units-of-production depreciation, calculate the machine's second-year depreciation.

    a. $ 69,600.
    b. $108,750.
    c. $ 65,250.
    d. $116,000.
    e. $ 62,500.

_____ 3. Book value is:

    a. the carrying amount for an item in the accounting records. When applied to a plant asset, it is the cost of the asset minus its accumulated depreciation.
    b. that portion of the value of a business due to its expected ability to earn a rate of return greater than in its industry.
    c. the portion of a plant asset's cost that will be recovered at the end of its service life through a sale or as a trade-in allowance on a new asset.
    d. the expected sales price of an item less any additional costs to sell.
    e. the price of an item from which a trade discount, if offered, is deducted to determine the invoice or gross sales price of the item.

_____ 4. On January 1, 1990, a machine with a three-year life was purchased for $72,000. The machine had a salvage value of $12,000. What is the 1990 depreciation deduction for tax purposes assuming the double declining balance method?

a. $24,000.
b. $48,000.
c. $20,000.
d. $40,000.
e. $12,000.

Problem III

Many of the important ideas and concepts discussed in Chapter 10 are reflected in the following list of key terms. Test your understanding of these terms by matching the appropriate definitions with the terms. Record the number identifying the most appropriate definition in the blank space next to each term.

_____ Accelerated depreciation

_____ Book value

_____ Declining-balance depreciation

_____ Fixed asset

_____ Inadequacy

_____ Income Tax Act

_____ Land improvements

_____ Obsolescence

_____ Office Equipment Ledger

_____ Salvage value

_____ Service life

_____ Store Equipment Ledger

_____ Straight-line depreciation

_____ Sum-of-the-years'-digits depreciation

_____ Units-of-production depreciation

1. Another name for plant asset, no longer widely in use.

2. The portion of a plant asset's cost that will be recovered at the end of its service life through a sale or as a trade-in allowance on a new asset.

3. A situation in which, because of new inventions and improvements, an old plant asset can no longer produce its product on a competitive basis.

4. A depreciation method that allocates depreciation on a plant asset based on the relation of the units of product produced by the asset during a given period to the total units the asset is expected to produce during its entire life.

5. Assets that improve or increase the value or usefulness of land but which have a limited useful life and are subject to depreciation.

6. A depreciation method in which up to twice the straight-line rate of depreciation, without considering salvage value, is applied to the beginning-of-period book value of a plant asset to determine the asset's depreciation charge for the period.

7. A subsidiary ledger that contains a separate record for each item of office equipment owned.

8. A depreciation method that allocates an equal share of the total estimated amount a plant asset will be depreciated during its service life to each accounting period in that life.

9. The codification of Canadian federal tax laws.

10. A depreciation method that allocates depreciation to each year in a plant asset's life on a fractional basis. The denominator of the fractions used is the sum-of-the-years' digits in the estimated service life of the asset, and the numerators are the years' digits in reverse order.

11. The carrying amount for an item in the accounting records. When applied to a plant asset, it is the cost of the asset minus its accumulated depreciation.

12. Any depreciation method that results in greater amounts of depreciation expense in the early years of a plant asset's life and lesser amounts in later years.

13. The period of time a plant asset is used in the production and sale of other assets or services.

14. A subsidiary ledger that contains a separate record for each item of store equipment owned.

15. A situation in which a plant asset does not produce enough product to meet current needs.

Problem IV

Complete the following by filling in the blanks.

1. The estimated salvage value of a plant asset is the estimated portion of the asset's _____ that is expected to be recovered at the end of its service life.

2. There are several factors that affect the useful life of some assets. These factors include:

   a) _____;

   b) _____;

   c) _____.

3. To be classified as a plant asset, an asset must be _____

   _____;

   and it must have _____

   _____.

4. Amounts of accumulated depreciation shown on a balance sheet _____ (do, do not) represent funds accumulated to buy new assets when present assets wear out and must be discarded.

5. Recording depreciation _____ (is, is not) a process of recording the decline in the market value of a plant asset.

6. The tax advantage of accelerated depreciation is that _____

   _____.

7. Balance sheet amounts shown for plant assets may bear little relation to the market values of the plant assets

   because balance sheets show for plant assets _____
   rather than market values.

8. Recording depreciation _____ (is, is not) a process of recording the physical deterioration of a plant asset.

9. The cost of a plant asset includes _____

   _____

   _____.

10. Trucks held for sale by a dealer and land held for future expansion are not classified as plant assets because

    _____

    _____

242

11. If a company breaks even on its operations, it will eventually recover the cost of its plant assets through ___

_____.

12. The book value of a plant asset consists of the asset's cost minus its _____

_____ as reflected in the accounts.

13. Since a plant asset contributes to the production or sale of other assets for a period longer than one accounting period, if revenues and expenses are to be matched, the cost of the plant asset's quantity of usefulness must

be _____

_____

_____.

14. The amount of accumulated depreciation deducted on a balance sheet from a plant asset's cost represents

that portion of the cost that has been charged off to _____

_____ during the asset's life.

15. When a business buys a plant asset, it in effect buys a quantity of usefulness that will be consumed during the service life of the asset; and depreciation of the asset, as the phrase is used in accounting, is nothing

more than an expiration of the asset's _____

_____. Furthermore, recording depreciation on the asset is the process of

_____

_____.

Problem V

A machine was purchased for $7,000, terms 2/10, n/60, FOB vendor's factory. The invoice was paid within the discount period along with $175 of freight charges. The machine was installed on a special concrete base by the employees of the company that bought it. The concrete base and special power connections for the machine cost $575, and the wages of the employees during the period in which they installed the machine amounted to $425. The employees accidentally dropped the machine while moving it onto its special base, causing damages to the machine which cost $125 to repair. As a result of all this, the cost of the machine for accounting purposes was

$ _____.

Problem VI

A machine cost $8,000 and was estimated to have an eight-year service life and an $800 salvage value. It was further estimated that the machine would produce 40,000 units of product during its life. If the machine produced 9,000 units during its first year, the depreciation charge for the year was:

1. $ _____ calculated on a straight-line basis.

2. $ _____ calculated by the units-of-production method.

3. $ _____ calculated by the declining-balance method at twice the straight-line rate.

4. $ _____ calculated by the sum-of-the-years'-digits method.

Problem VII

In January 1990, a company purchased a heavy, general-purpose truck for $50,000. The truck is expected to last 5 years and have a salvage value of $10,000. For tax purposes, the tractor is in the 30% class of assets. Complete the table by showing the amount of depreciation to be taken each year under the two alternatives.

Year	Straight-line	CCA for Year	Undepreciated Capital Cost at End of Year
1990			
1991			
1992			
1993			
1994			

Solutions for Chapter 10

Problem I

1. T
2. T
3. F
4. T

Problem II

1. A
2. C
3. A
4. B

Problem III

Accelerated depreciation	12	Office Equipment Ledger	7
Book value	11	Salvage value	2
Declining-balance depreciation	6	Service life	13
Fixed asset	1	Store Equipment Ledger	14
Inadequacy	15	Straight-line depreciation	8
Income Tax Act	9	Sum-of-the-years'-digits depreciation	10
Land improvements	5	Units-of-production depreciation	4
Obsolescence	3		

Problem IV

1. cost

2. a) wear and tear
   b) inadequacy
   c) obsolescence

3. used in the production or sale of other assets, a useful life longer than one accounting period

4. do not

5. is not

6. it defers the payment of income taxes

7. undepreciated costs

8. is not

9. all normal and reasonable expenditures necessary to get the asset in place and ready for use

10. they are not presently being used to produce or sell other assets

11. the sale of its product

12. accumulated depreciation

13. allocated to the several accounting periods during which it will be used

14. depreciation expense

15. quantity of usefulness, allocating the cost of the asset's quantity of usefulness to the accounting periods that will benefit from its use

Problem V

(.98 × $7,000) + $175 + $575 + $425 = $8,035

Problem VI

1. ($8,000 − $800)/8 = $900

2. [($8,000 − $800)/40,000] × 9,000 = $1,620

3. $8,000 × 25% = $2,000

4. ($8,000 − $800)(8/36) = $1,600

Problem VII

Year	Straight-line	CCA for Year	Undepreciated Capital Cost at End of Year		
1990	$8,000	$15,000	$50,000 −	$15,000 =	$35,000
1991	8,000	10,500	35,000 −	10,500 =	24,500
1992	8,000	7,350	25,500 −	7,350 =	18,150
1993	8,000	5,445	18,150 −	5,445 =	12,705
1994	8,000	3,812	12,705 −	3,812 =	8,893

11 Plant and Equipment, Natural Resources, and Intangible Assets

After studying Chapter 11, you should be able to:

1. Prepare entries to record the sale or discarding of a plant asset.

2. Prepare entries to record the exchange of plant assets and the recognition of book gains and losses.

3. Make the calculations and prepare the entries to account for revisions in depreciation rates.

4. Make the calculations and prepare the entries to account for plant asset repairs and betterments.

5. Prepare entries to account for natural resources and for intangible assets, including entries to record depletion and amortization.

6. Define or explain the words and phrases listed in the chapter Glossary.

Topical Outline

I. Disposal, sale, or exchange of a plant asset

   A. Discarding a plant assset

      1. Remove cost and accumulated depreciation from accounts.

      2. Record any remaining book value as a loss on disposal.

      3. If discarded asset is damaged, record any remaining book value not recovered through insurance as a loss.

   B. Selling a plant asset

      1. Remove cost and accumulated depreciation from accounts.

      2. If proceeds greater than book value, record a gain.

      3. If proceeds less than book value, record a loss.

   C. Exchanging similar plant assets

      1. When a plant asset is exchanged for a similar plant asset, a book loss is recognized when the trade-in allowance is less than the book value of the traded asset.

      2. A book gain is recognized when the trade-in allowance exceeds the book value of the traded asset.

      3. The determination of the equivalent cash price of the asset acquired will provide guidance on the recognition of the proper gain or loss.

      4. Under the principle of materiality and when the equivalent cash price is difficult to determine, an immaterial gain or loss on the exchange may not be recognized.

II. Revising depreciation rates (an example of a change in an accounting estimate)

   A. Remaining cost to be depreciated is allocated over the remaining expected life (as revised).

   B. Depreciation expense of prior periods is not revised.

III. Ordinary and extraordinary repairs

   A. Ordinary repairs

      1. Repairs made to keep asset in normal good state of repair.

      2. Appear on income statement as expense.

   B. Extraordinary repairs

      1. Major repairs made to extend the service life beyond that originally estimated.

      2. Normally debited to the asset account and depreciated over the asset's remaining life.

IV. Betterments

   A. Modification of an existing plant asset to make it more efficient, usually by replacing part of the asset with an improved or superior part.

   B. Debited to the asset account and depreciated over the remaining service life of the asset.

V. Capital and revenue expenditures

   A. Capital expenditures

      1. Costs charged to balance sheet accounts (debited to the asset) because the expenditure is expected to benefit future periods.

      2. Examples: betterments, extraordinary repairs.

   B. Revenue expenditures

      1. Charged to the income statement of the current period.

      2. Examples: ordinary repairs, rent, salaries.

VI. Natural resources

    A. Include wasting assets such as oil reserves, timber tracts, etc.

    B. As the resources are used, their cost should be allocated to expense, known as "depletion."

    C. The total amount of cost so allocated is reported as a credit to Accumulated Depletion.

VII. Intangible assets

    A. Have no physical existence.

    B. Represent legal rights or economic relationships beneficial to owner.

    C. Are amortized or written off to expense accounts over their estimated useful lives.

    D. Examples:

        1. Patents
        2. Copyrights
        3. Leaseholds (and leasehold improvements)
        4. Goodwill
        5. Trademarks and trade names

Problem I

The following statements are either true or false. Place a (T) in the parentheses before each true statement and an (F) before each false statement.

1. ( ) The cost of extraordinary repairs which extend the service life of an asset should be debited to a Repairs Expense account.

2. ( ) The result of a betterment is a more efficient or more productive asset, but not necessarily an asset that has a longer life.

3. ( ) Natural resources appear on the balance sheet at cost less accumulated depreciation.

4. ( ) The depletion cost of any mined but unsold natural resources which are held for sale is carried forward on the balance sheet as a current asset.

5. ( ) Trademarks and organization costs are intangible assets and must be amortized over the asset's useful life (not to exceed 40 years).

6. ( ) The amortization entry for the costs of leasehold improvements involves a debit to an expense account and a credit to Leasehold Improvements.

7. ( ) Based on a given rate of return of 10%, the goodwill of a company that earns $25,000 annually of which $5,000 is above-average earnings, should be estimated at $200,000.

8. ( ) The cost of making ordinary repairs on a machine should be classified as a revenue expenditure.

9. ( ) A capital expenditure is a payment of assets that is charged immediately to expense, thus reducing the owners' equity.

10. ( ) If a cost is incurred to modify an existing plant asset for the purpose of making it more efficient or more productive, the cost is called an extraordinary repair.

11. ( ) The cost of all intangible assets must be amortized over 40 years.

Problem II

You are given several words, phrases or numbers to choose from in completing each of the following statements or in answering the following questions. In each case select the one that best completes the statement or answers the question and place its letter in the answer space provided.

_____ 1. Flintstone Company depreciated a machine that cost $21,600 on a straight-line basis for three years under the assumption it would have a five-year life and a $3,600 trade-in value. Early in the fourth year, the manager realized that the machine had three years of remaining useful life, after which it would have an estimated $2,160 trade-in value. Determine the amount of depreciation to be charged against the machine during each of the remaining years in its life.

    a. $3,240.
    b. $1,800.
    c. $2,640.
    d. $2,880.
    e. $3,888.

_____ 2. A machine that cost $40,000 and had been depreciated $30,000 was traded in on a new machine of like purpose having an estimated 20-year life and priced at $50,000. If a $13,000 trade-in allowance was received on the old machine, at what amount should the new machine be recorded in the accounts?

a. $37,000.
b. $40,000.
c. $47,000.
d. $50,000.
e. $53,000.

_____ 3. A change in a calculated amount to be reported in the financial statements that results from new information or subsequent developments and accordingly from better insight or improved judgment is a(n):

a. betterment.
b. adjusted trial balance.
c. change in an accounting estimate.
d. contra account.
e. capital expenditure.

_____ 4. Depletion is:

a. the process of periodically writing off as an expense a share of the cost of an asset, usually an intangible asset.
b. the expiration of the usefulness of equipment and the related process of allocating the cost of such assets to expense of the periods during which the assets are used.
c. the carrying amount for an item in the accounting records.
d. the amount a wasting asset is reduced through cutting, mining, or pumping.
e. a situation in which, because of new inventions and improvements, an old plant asset can no longer produce its product on a competitive basis.

_____ 5. The process of allocating the cost of a patent to expense over time:

a. is called depletion.
b. is sometimes called depreciation.
c. is usually done by the declining-balance method over 50 years.
d. is seldom limited to less than 40 years.
e. should be accomplished in 17 years or less.

_____ 6. The Romeo Company exchanged its used bottle-capping machine for a new machine. The old machine cost $14,000, and the new one had a cash price of $19,000. Romeo had taken $12,000 depreciation on the old machine and was allowed a $500 trade-in allowance. What gain or loss should be recorded on the exchange?

a. no gain or loss.
b. $ 500 gain.
c. $1,500 loss.
d. $1,500 gain.
e. $4,500 gain.

_____ 7. A machine that cost $40,000 and had been depreciated $30,000 was traded in on a new machine of like purpose having an estimated 20-year life and priced at $50,000. If a $7,000 trade-in allowance was received on the old machine, at what amount should the new machine be recorded in the accounts?

a. $40,000.
b. $47,000.
c. $50,000.
d. $53,000.
e. some other amount.

8. X-Ray Company sold for $6,000 an x-ray machine that originally cost $10,000. The accumulated depreciation on this machine was $4,000. X-Ray Company's gain (loss) on this sale is:

a. $ –0–.
b. $ 2,000.
c. $ 4,000.
d. $(6,000).
e. $10,000.

9. Cherokee Company had a bulldozer destroyed by fire. The bulldozer originally cost $16,000, but insurance paid only $14,200. Accumulated depreciation on this bulldozer was $2,000. The gain (loss) from the fire is:

a. $ –0–.
b. $ 200.
c. $ (200).
d. $(14,000).
e. $(16,000).

Problem III

Many of the important ideas and concepts discussed in Chapter 11 are reflected in the following list of key terms. Test your understanding of these terms by matching the appropriate definitions with the terms. Record the number identifying the most appropriate definition in the blank space next to each term.

_____ Amortize	_____ Lease
_____ Balance sheet expenditure	_____ Leasehold
_____ Betterment	_____ Leasehold improvements
_____ Capital expenditure	_____ Lessee
_____ Change in an accounting estimate	_____ Lessor
_____ Copyright	_____ Ordinary repairs
_____ Depletion	_____ Patent
_____ Extraordinary repairs	_____ Revenue expenditure
_____ Goodwill	_____ Trademark
_____ Income tax rules	_____ Trade name
_____ Intangible asset	

1. An exclusive right granted by the federal government to manufacture and sell a machine or mechanical device for a period of years.

2. A modification to an existing plant asset to make it more efficient, usually by replacing part of the asset with an improved or superior part.

3. That portion of the value of a business that results from the business's expected ability to earn a rate of return greater than the average in its industry.

4. An expenditure that benefits future periods because the value or asset obtained by the expenditure does not fully expire by the end of the current period.

5. Improvements to leased property made by the lessee.

6. An asset that has no physical existence but has value due to the rights resulting from its ownership and possession.

7. The individual or enterprise that has given up possession of property under the terms of a lease contract.

8. A change in a calculated amount to be reported in the financial statements that results from new information or subsequent developments and accordingly from better insight or improved judgment.

9. A unique name selected by a company for use in marketing its products or services.

10. An expenditure that benefits only the current period because the value or asset obtained by the expenditure will fully expire before the end of the current accounting period.

11. The amount a wasting asset is reduced through cutting, mining, or pumping.

12. An exclusive right granted by the federal government to publish and sell a musical, literary, or artistic work for a period of years.

13. The rights granted to a lessee under the terms of a lease contract.

14. Repairs made to keep a plant asset in its normal good operating condition.

15. A unique symbol designed by a company for use in marketing its products or services.

16. A contract that grants the right to possess and use property.

17. To periodically write off as an expense a share of the cost of an asset, usually an intangible asset.

18. Another name for capital expenditure.

19. An individual or enterprise that has been given possession of property under the terms of a lease contract.

20. Rules that govern how income for tax purposes and income taxes are to be calculated.

21. Major repairs that extend the life of a plant asset beyond the number of years originally estimated.

Problem IV

Complete the following by filling in the blanks.

1. After a plant asset is recorded in the accounts at cost, this basis is used in recording _____ on the asset and any _____ on its sale.

2. In the final analysis, goodwill is always valued at the price at which _____ _____ _____.

3. A gain or a loss on a plant asset exchange is not recognized in the accounts when the new asset is taken into the accounts at an amount equal to the _____ of the traded-in asset plus the cash given in the exchange. This amount is called the _____ of the new asset.

4. When there is a small and insignificant loss on the exchange of a plant asset, it is permissible not to record the loss under the accounting principle of _____.

5. Intangible assets should be systematically amortized or written off to expense accounts over their estimated useful lives, which in no case should exceed _____.

6. In accounting, a business is said to have _____ when its earnings rate is greater than the earnings rate normally realized in its industry.

7. In recording exchanges of similar plant assets where cash also is paid, generally accepted accounting principles require that a material _____ (gain, loss) should be recognized for accounting purposes.

Problem V

On January 8, a machine that cost $12,000 and on which $10,000 of depreciation had been recorded was traded in on a new machine of like purpose. The new machine could have been purchased without a trade-in for $14,000. Give without explnations the general journal entries to record the exchange under each of the following unrelated assumptions:

1. The old machine and $13,000 in cash were given for the new machine, and the loss is recognized.

DATE	ACCOUNT TITLES AND EXPLANATION	P.R.	DEBIT	CREDIT

2. The old machine and $13,000 in cash were given for the new machine, and the loss is not material.

DATE	ACCOUNT TITLES AND EXPLANATION	P.R.	DEBIT	CREDIT

254

3. The old machine and $10,500 in cash were given for the new machine.

DATE	ACCOUNT TITLES AND EXPLANATION	P.R.	DEBIT	CREDIT

Problem VI

On March 1, 1986, a machine was installed in a factory at a $9,000 total cost. Straight-line depreciation was recorded on each December 31 of the machine's life under the assumption it would have no salvage value at the end of a 12-year life. On February 27, 1990, the machine was destroyed by fire. On March 4 the insurance company paid $4,500 in full settlement of the fire loss claim. In the space below, give the general journal entry to record the destruction of the machine and receipt of the $4,500 from the insurance company.

DATE	ACCOUNT TITLES AND EXPLANATION	P.R.	DEBIT	CREDIT

Problem VII

Ten years ago a machine was purchased and installed at a $12,000 cost. At that time it was estimated the machine would have a 12-year life and a $600 salvage value. At the beginning of the machine's 11th year the estimated number of years remaining in its useful life was changed from two to four years and its salvage value was changed from $600 to $500.

1. Straight-line depreciation at the rate of $ _____ per year was recorded on this machine during the first ten years of its life.

2. After depreciation for its tenth year was recorded, the book value of the machine was: Cost $ _____ minus $ _____ of accumulated depreciation equals a $ _____ book value.

3. And depreciation for each of the remaining four years in the machine's life should be calculated:

$$\frac{\text{Book Value } - \text{ Salvage Value}}{\text{Remaining Useful Life}} = \text{Depreciation per Year}$$

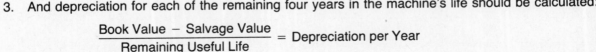

$$\$\underline{\hspace{2cm}} - \underline{\hspace{2cm}} = \$\underline{\hspace{2cm}} \text{ per Year}$$
$$\text{4 years}$$

255

Problem VIII

A machine that cost $15,500 was depreciated using straight line under the assumption that it would have a six-year life and a $1,100 salvage value. At the beginning of its sixth year, on January 1, the machine received a major overhaul that cost $4,200 and extended its life for two years beyond the six originally estimated. The overhaul did not change the machine's estimated salvage value nor increase its efficiency.

1. Give without an explanation the entry to record the overhaul.

DATE	ACCOUNT TITLES AND EXPLANATION	P.R.	DEBIT	CREDIT

2. Give the entry to record the sixth year's depreciation on the machine.

DATE	ACCOUNT TITLES AND EXPLANATION	P.R.	DEBIT	CREDIT

Problem IX

A machine that cost $25,000 was depreciated using straight line under the assumption it would have a ten-year life and no salvage value. On January 1, after four years of use, new automatic controls (not available when the machine was first purchased) that cost $7,500 and reduced operating labor by 50% were placed on the machine. The addition of the controls did not affect the machine's estimated life nor its zero salvage value.

1. Give without an explanation the entry to record the addition of the new controls.

DATE	ACCOUNT TITLES AND EXPLANATION	P.R.	DEBIT	CREDIT

2. Give the entry to record the fifth year's depreciation on the machine.

DATE	ACCOUNT TITLES AND EXPLANATION	P.R.	DEBIT	CREDIT

Problem X

A machine that cost $45,000 and has been depreciated $20,000 was traded in on a new machine that had a cash price of $35,000. After taking into account the trade-in allowance, the balance was paid in cash. Present a general journal entry to record the trade under each of the following unrelated assumptions:

(a) The trade-in allowance was $28,000.

DATE	ACCOUNT TITLES AND EXPLANATION	P.R.	DEBIT	CREDIT

(b) The trade-in allowance was $24,500, and the loss was not considered material.

DATE	ACCOUNT TITLES AND EXPLANATION	P.R.	DEBIT	CREDIT

(c) The trade-in allowance was $21,000 and the loss was considered to be material.

DATE	ACCOUNT TITLES AND EXPLANATION	P.R.	DEBIT	CREDIT

Problem XI

Farmer Company paid $208,000 plus $4,320 in closing costs for real estate. The real estate included land appraised at $64,000; land improvements appraised at $25,600; and a building appraised at $166,400. The plan is to use the building as a factory. Prepare a calculation showing the allocation of cost to the assets purchased and present the journal entry to record the purchase.

DATE	ACCOUNT TITLES AND EXPLANATION	P.R.	DEBIT	CREDIT

Solutions for Chapter 11

Problem I

1.	F	7.	F
2.	T	8.	T
3.	F	9.	F
4.	T	10.	F
5.	T	11.	F
6.	T		

Problem II

1.	D	6.	C
2.	B	7.	C
3.	C	8.	A
4.	D	9.	B
5.	E		

Problem III

Amortize	17	Lease	16
Balance sheet expenditure	18 or 4	Leasehold	13
Betterment	2	Leasehold improvements	5
Capital expenditure	4	Lessee	19
Change in an accounting estimate	8	Lessor	7
Copyright	12	Ordinary repairs	14
Depletion	11	Patent	1
Extraordinary repairs	21	Revenue expenditure	10
Goodwill	3	Trade mark	15
Income tax rules	20	Trade name	9
Intangible asset	6		

Problem IV

1. depreciation, loss or gain
2. a seller is willing to accept and a buyer is willing to pay
3. book value, cost basis
4. materiality
5. 40 years
6. goodwill
7. loss, gain

Problem V

1.	Jan. 8	Machinery	14,000.00	
		Loss on Exchange of Machinery	1,000.00	
		Accumulated Depreciation, Machinery	10,000.00	
		Machinery		12,000.00
		Cash		13,000.00
2.	Jan. 8	Machinery	15,000.00	
		Accumulated Depreciation, Machinery	10,000.00	
		Machinery		12,000.00
		Cash		13,000.00

3. Jan. 8   Machinery 14,000.00
              Accumulated Depreciation, Machinery 10,000.00
                  Machinery 12,000.00
                  Cash 10,500.00
                  Gain on Exchange of Machinery 1,500.00

Problem VI

Mar. 4   Cash 4,500.00
         Loss from Fire 1,500.00
         Accumulated Depreciation, Machinery 3,000.00
             Machinery 9,000.00

Problem VII

1. $950

2. Cost $12,000 minus $9,500 of accumulated depreciation equals a $2,500 book value.

3. $\dfrac{\$2,500 - \$500}{4 \text{ years}} = \$500 \text{ per year}$

Problem VIII

1. Jan. 9   Machinery 4,200.00
                  Cash (or Accounts Payable) 4,200.00

2. Dec. 31   Depreciation Expense, Machinery 2,200.00
                  Accumulated Depreciation, Machinery 2,200.00

Problem IX

1. Jan. 5   Machinery 7,500.00
                  Cash (or Accounts Payable) 7,500.00

2. Dec. 31   Depreciation Expense, Machinery 3,750.00
                  Accumulated Depreciation, Machinery 3,750.00

Problem X

(a)   Machinery 35,000.00
      Accumulated Depreciation, Machinery 20,000.00
          Cash ($35,000 − $28,000) 7,000.00
          Machinery 45,000.00
          Gain on Exchange of Machinery 3,000.00

(b)   Machinery 35,500.00
      Accumulated Depreciation, Machinery 20,000.00
          Cash ($35,000 − $24,500) 10,500.00
          Machinery 45,000.00

(c)   Machinery 35,000.00
      Accumulated Depreciation, Machinery 20,000.00
      Loss on Exchange of Machinery 4,000.00
          Cash ($35,000 − $21,000) 14,000.00
          Machinery 45,000.00

Problem XI

	Appraised value	Percent of total	Apportioned cost
Land	$ 64,000	25%	$ 53,080
Land improvements	25,600	10	21,232
Building	166,400	65	138,008
	$256,000	100%	$212,320

Land	53,080.00	
Land improvements	21,232.00	
Building	138,008.00	
Cash		212,320.00

12 Current and Long-Term Liabilities

After studying Chapter 12, you should be able to:

1. Explain the difference between current and long-term liabilities.

2. Explain the meaning of definite and estimated liabilities.

3. Record transactions that involve liabilities such as property taxes payable, product warranties, and short-term notes payable.

4. Explain the difference between liabilities and contingent liabilities.

5. Calculate the present value of a sum of money that will be received a number of periods in the future or will be received periodically.

6. Prepare entries to account for long-term noninterest-bearing notes payable, for installment notes payable and for capital and operating leases.

7. Define or explain the words and phrases listed in the chapter Glossary.

Topical Outline

I. Definition and classification of liabilities

    A. Liabilities—obligations resulting from past transactions that require the future payment of assets or the future performance of services.

    B. Current liabilities—debts or other obligations, the liquidation of which is expected to require the use of existing current assets or the creation of other current liabilities; they are due within one year or the current operating cycle of the business, whichever is longer.

    C. Long-term liabilities—obligations that will not require the use of existing current assets because they do not mature within one year or one operating cycle.

    D. Definite liabilities—liabilities may be indefinite with respect to:

        1. Identity of the creditor.
        2. Due date of the debt.
        3. Amount to be paid (in which case the liability is called an estimated liability).

    E. Estimated liabilities—obligations for which the amounts to be paid are uncertain but can be reasonably estimated. Examples are:

        1. Property taxes payable.
        2. Product warranty liabilities.

    F. Contingent liabilities—are not existing obligations and are not recorded as liabilities. They become obligations only if some future, uncertain event actually occurs. Examples are:

        1. Potential legal claims.
        2. Debt guaranties.

II. Short-term notes payable

    A. Examples

        1. Note given to secure a time extension on an account—provides a written promise to pay and specifies a rate of interest that will apply to the debt.
        2. Note given to secure borrowing from a bank.

            a. Loan—cash proceeds equal to the face value of the note; the note is a promise to repay the face value of the note plus interest.
            b. Discount—cash proceeds equal to the face value of the note less interest that is deducted in advance; the note is a promise to repay the face value of the note.

    B. End-of-period adjustments

        1. Accrued interest expense on outstanding notes payable should be recorded at the end of the accounting period.
        2. Interest on a discounted note must be allocated to the periods benefited.

III. Present value

    A. The concept: a dollar received in the future is worth less than a dollar received today because the dollar received today can be invested to generate a future value of one dollar plus interest.

    B. Present value tables—used instead of a formula to solve present value problems.

        1. "Present value of $1" table used for problems that involve a single payment.
        2. "Present value of $1 received periodically for a number of periods" table used for problems that involve a number of equal payments.
        3. Interest rates are normally expressed in annual amounts.

4. Discount periods can be any length of time; if less than a year, annual interest rate must be adjusted for the discount period.

IV. Exchanging a note for a plant asset

A. Two elements may or may not be stipulated in the note:

1. A dollar amount equivalent to the bargained cash price of the asset.
2. An interest factor to compensate the supplier for the use of the funds that otherwise would have been received in a cash sale.

B. Asset should be recorded at its cash price or at the present value of the note, whichever is more clearly determinable.

C. A discount on notes payable is created if the note does not have a stated interest rate or if the interest rate is unreasonably low. The discount is amortized over the life of the note.

V. Installment notes payable

A. Borrower pays back debt by making a series of periodic payments, either in the form of:

1. Equal payments, where interest and principal amounts vary, and total amount of payment stays the same, or
2. Payments that vary in total amount and consist of accrued interest to date plus equal amounts of principal.

B. Difference between notes payable and bonds

1. Usually a single creditor (e.g., a bank) is involved when a business or individual borrows by signing a note payable.
2. A bond issue generally includes a large number of bonds sold to many different lenders. Bonds may be owned by a number of people before they mature.

VI. Liabilities from leasing

A. Capital lease (or financing lease)—must meet any one of four criteria:

1. Ownership of the leased asset is transferred to the lessee at the end of the lease period.
2. The lease gives the lessee the option of purchasing the leased asset at less than fair value at some point during or at the end of the lease period.
3. The period of the lease is 75 percent or more of the estimated service life of the leased asset.
4. The present value of the minimum lease payments is 90 percent or more of the fair value of the leased asset.

B. Operating lease—any lease that does not meet any one of the preceding criteria.

C. Accounting for leases

1. Capital lease—treated as a purchase transaction. The present value of the lease payments constitutes the cost of the asset and is debited to an asset account.
2. Operating lease—annual rental payments for leased asset, as well as payments for taxes, insurance and repairs, are charged to expense.

Problem I

The following statements are either true or false. Place a (T) in the parentheses before each true statement and an (F) before each false statement.

1. (F) An example of an estimated liability is prepaid property taxes.

2. (T) Contingent liabilities are generally not recorded in the books as liabilities.

3. (T) When a borrower records the receipt of a discounted note payable, Interest Expense or Discount on Notes Payable is debited for the amount of interest deducted from the face amount of the note by the lender.

4. (T) The borrower is required to pay the lender the face amount of the note when a discounted note matures.

5. (F) The concept of present value is based on the idea that the right to receive $1 a year from now is worth more than $1 today.

6. (F) Receiving $500 on June 30 and $500 on December 31 has the same present value as receiving $1,000 on December 31.

7. (F) If a note requires quarterly payments and the borrower could obtain a 12% annual rate of interest in borrowing money, a 3% quarterly interest rate should be used to determine the present value of the note.

8. (T) A discount on a note payable is a contra liability and also represents interest that should be charged to expense during the life of the note.

9. (F) The carrying amount of a note payable decreases each year by the amount of discount on the note amortized during the year.

10. (T) If a portion of a long-term note payable comes due within 12 months, that portion must be reported on the balance sheet as a current liability.

11. (F) Depending on the terms of a lease obligation, the lease may or may not be recorded as a liability.

12. (F) Depreciation expense is recorded on a machine that was obtained under a capital lease.

13. (T) A capital lease should be recorded on the lease date at the present value of the lease payments.

Problem II

You are given several words, phrases or numbers to choose from in completing each of the following statements or in answering the following questions. In each case select the one that best completes the statement or answers the question and place its letter in the answer space provided.

_____e_____ 1. Interest charged and deducted by a bank at the time a loan is made is called a(n):

a. automatic discount.
b. sales discount.
c. capital discount.
d. amortized discount.
e. bank discount.

_*a*_ 2. During the life of a capital lease, the carrying amount of the lease is:

    a. the remaining lease liability minus the unamortized discount on the lease financing.
    b. the annual payment under a lease agreement.
    c. the remaining lease liability plus the unamortized discount on the lease financing.
    d. the original amount of the lease liability.
    e. the original amount of the lease liability minus the discount on the lease financing (the present value of the lease on the date of the lease).

_*d*_ 3. Falcon Company has entered a 14-year lease agreement on a new boat that has a fair value of $180,000 and an estimated service life of 20 years. The terms of the lease provided that Falcon Company will make equal payments of $21,750 at the end of each year of the lease, and that upon expiration of the lease the vessel must be returned to the lessor without recourse. The prevailing interest rate is 10%, and the present value of $1 received annually for 14 years, discounted at 10% is 7.3667. The lease is a(n):

    a. present value lease.
    b. capital lease.
    c. discount lease.
    d. operating lease.
    e. none of the above.

_*b*_ 4. On November 1, 1990, Profitable Company borrowed $50,000 by giving a 90-day, 12% note payable. The company has a calendar-year accounting period but prepares monthly interim financial statements. What amount should be debited to Interest Expense on January 30, 1991?

    a. $6,000.
    b. $1,500.
    c. $1,000.
    d. $ 500.
    e. $ –0–.

_*b*_ 5. Indigo Company is offered a contract whereby it will be paid $15,000 every six months for the next five years. The first payment will be received six months from today. What will the company be willing to pay for this contract if it expects a 16% annual return on the investment? [Use the appropriate present value table in the chapter in the text.]

    a. $ 49,114.50.
    b. $ 72,498.00.
    c. $100,651.50.
    d. $ 98,229.00.
    e. $ 59,890.50.

Problem III

Many of the important ideas and concepts discussed in Chapter 12 are reflected in the following list of key terms. Test your understanding of these terms by matching the appropriate definitions with the terms. Record the number identifying the most appropriate definition in the blank space next to each term.

___3___ Bank discount   ___12___ Installment notes

___10___ Capital lease   ___7___ Long-term liabilities

___2___ Carrying amount of a lease   ___1___ Operating lease

___8___ Carrying amount of a note   ___9___ Present value

___4___ Estimated liability   ___5___ Present value table

___11___ Financing lease   ___6___ Product warranty

1. A lease that does not meet any of the criteria of the CICA that would make it a capital lease.

2. The remaining lease liability minus the unamortized discount on the lease financing.

3. Interest charged and deducted by a bank at the time a loan is made.

4. An obligation that definitely exists but for which the amount to be paid is uncertain.

5. A table that shows the present values of one amount to be received at various future dates when discounted at various interest rates, or that shows the present values of a series of equal payments to be received for a varying number of periods when discounted at various interest rates.

6. A promise to a customer that obligates the seller or manufacturer for a limited period of time to pay for items such as replacement parts or repair costs if the product breaks or fails to perform.

7. Obligations that will not require the use of existing current assets in their liquidation because they do not mature within one year or one operating cycle, whichever is longer.

8. The face amount of a note minus the unamortized discount on the note.

9. The amount of money that could be currently invested at a given interest rate to accumulate a total value equal to a given amount to be received or paid at some future date(s).

10. A lease that meets any of four criteria established by the FASB, the implication of which is that the lease has essentially the same economic consequences as if the lessee had secured a loan and purchased the leased asset.

11. Another name for a capital lease.

12. Notes that require a series of payments consisting of interest plus a portion of the original amount borrowed.

Problem IV

Complete the following by filling in the blanks.

1. Use the present value tables in the text to calculate the following present values:

   a. $1 to be received 12 years hence, at 10%. $ _____0.3186_____

   b. $2,000 to be received 14 years hence, at 8%. $ _____681_____

   c. $1 to be received at the end of each year for 20 years, at 14%. $ _____6.6231_____

   d. $1,000 to be received at the end of each period for 10 periods, at 16%. $ _____4833.2_____

2. Two important examples of estimated liabilities are:

   a. _____Estimated property taxes Payable_____ , and

   b. _____Estimated warranty Liab_____.

3. If a company discounts its $2,000 note payable at the bank, the cash proceeds of the note which the company receives are (less than, equal to, more than) _____ *less than* _____ $2,000.

4. When the rate of interest on an investment is 9% compounded annually, the present value of $1,000 to be received three years hence is the amount of money that must be invested today that together with the 9% compound interest earned on the investment will equal $ _____ *1,000* _____ at the end of three years. The present value is $1,000 × _____ *0.7722* _____ = _____ *772.2* _____ .

5. When the account Discount on Notes Payable is shown on the balance sheet, does it increase or decrease the carrying amount of Notes Payable? _____ *does not decrease / increase* _____

6. Certain leases have essentially the same economic consequences as if the lessee secured a loan and purchased the leased asset. These leases are known as _____ *capital or financing lease* _____ .

7. If the interest rate changed from 5% to 8%, will the present value of $1 to be received in one year increase or decrease? _____ *decrease* _____

8. Long-term liabilities are obligations that will not require the use of _____ *current assets* _____ in their liquidation.

9. The terms of installment notes payable require one of two payment plans:

   a. _____ *Equal principal plus diff. interest* _____ ., or

   b. _____ *Equal payments that include principal & interest changing amt. of in and principal* _____ .

Problem V

A company prepares monthly financial statements and estimates property taxes based on last year's tax rate. The assessed valuation of property owned by the company is $120,000. Last year's tax levy was $0.80 per $100.

(a) Present a general journal entry to record the property tax for January.

DATE		ACCOUNT TITLES AND EXPLANATION	P.R.	DEBIT	CREDIT
1993 Jan	31	Property tax expense		80.00	
		Estimated property tax Payable			80.00
		To record property tax for the (Jan.)			

269

(b) In August, the current year's levy is determined to be $1.00. Present the general journal entry to pay the annual tax at the end of August and to record the expense for August.

DATE		ACCOUNT TITLES AND EXPLANATION	P.R.	DEBIT	CREDIT
1993 Aug	31	Property tax expense (Aug)		240.00	
		Prepaid property tax (Sep-Dec)		400.00	
	Estimated	Property tax payable		560.00	
		Cash			1,200.00
		To pay the 1993 property tax and to correct the $20 estimate error for the first seventh month.			

Problem VI

Glitz Company estimates that future costs to satisfy its product warranty obligation amount to 3% of sales. In January, the company sold merchandise for $50,000 cash and paid $1,200 to repair products returned for warranty work. Present general journal entries to record these transactions.

Jan 31   Cash   50,000.00
            Sales   50,000.00

DATE		ACCOUNT TITLES AND EXPLANATION	P.R.	DEBIT	CREDIT
1993 Jan	31	Warranty expense		1,500.00	
		Estimated warranty lia			1,500.00
		To record estimated warranty.			
		(50,000 × 0.03)			
	31	Estimated warranty lia.		1,200.00	
		Cash			1,200.00
		To record warranty work.			

Problem VII

A company with accounting periods that end each December 31 discounted its own $10,000, noninterest-bearing note at its bank for 60 days at 12% on December 16, 1990. Complete the following entries involving this note.

DATE		ACCOUNT TITLES AND EXPLANATION	P.R.	DEBIT	CREDIT
1990					
Dec.	16	Cash		9,802.74	
		Discount on Notes Payable		197.26	
		Short term - notes Payable			10,000.00
		Discounted our noninterest-bearing note for 60 days at 12%.			
	31	Interest Expense		49.31	
		Discount on Notes Payable			49.31
		To record interest expense for 1990.			
1991					
Feb.	14	Short - term Notes Payable		10,000.00	
		Cash			10,000.00
		Paid our discounted note payable.			
	14	Interest Expense		147.39	
		Discount on Notes - Payable			147.39
		To record interest expense for 1991.			

Problem VIII

Assume that on January 2, 1990, a day on which the prevailing interest rate was 12%, a company exchanged a $15,000, five-year, noninterest-bearing note payable for a machine, the cash price of which was not readily determinable.

0.5674

1. The present value of the note on the day of exchange and the amount at which the machine should be recorded is calculated:

$15,000 × _____0.5674_____ = $ ____8511____.

2. The entry to record the exchange is:

DATE		ACCOUNT TITLES AND EXPLANATION	P.R.	DEBIT	CREDIT
1990 Jan.	2	Machinery		8,511.00	
		Discount on Notes Payable		6,488.00	
		Long - term Notes Payable			15,000.00
		to exchange a 5 yr, note for a machine.			

271

3. The amount of discount to be amortized at the end of the first year in the five-year life of the note is calculated:

$ _____ 8511 _____ × 12% = $ _____ 1021.32 _____ .

4. The discount amortization entry at the end of the first year is:

DATE	ACCOUNT TITLES AND EXPLANATION	P.R.	DEBIT	CREDIT
19__ Dec 31	Interest Expense		1021.32	
	Discount on Note Payable			1021.32
	To amortize a portion			
	of the discount on a			
	note.			

5. The note should appear on the company's balance sheet at the end of its first year as follows:

Long Term Liability:				
Long-term Notes Payable			15000.00	
Less Unamortized discount				
on Notes Payable @ 12% in. rate prevailing on			5967.68	9532.32
the date of issue				
Total Long-term Notes Payable				9532.32

Problem IX

On December 31, 1990, HX Company borrowed $60,000 by signing a 14% installment note that is to be repaid with six annual payments, the first of which is due on December 31, 1991.

a. Prepare a general journal entry to record the borrowing of the money.

DATE	ACCOUNT TITLES AND EXPLANATION	P.R.	DEBIT	CREDIT
1990 Dec 31	Cash		60,000.00	
	Long-term Notes Payable			60,000.00
	To borrow money with a			
	6 yr, 14% note.			

b. Assume that the payments are to consist of accrued interest plus equal amounts of principal. Prepare general journal entries to record the first and second installment payments.

DATE			ACCOUNT TITLES AND EXPLANATION	P.R.	DEBIT	CREDIT
1991 Dec	3	1	Interest Expense		8,400.00	
			Long-term Notes Payable		10,000.00	
			Cash			18,400.00
			To pay the first installment payments.			
1992 Dec		31	Interest Expense		7000.00	
			Long-term Notes Payable		10,000.00	
			Cash			17,000.00
			To pay the second installment payments.			

c. Contrary to the assumption in (b) above, assume now that the note requires each installment payment to be $15,464. Prepare general journal entries to record the first and second installment payments. (Round all amounts to the nearest whole dollar.)

DATE			ACCOUNT TITLES AND EXPLANATION	P.R.	DEBIT	CREDIT
1991 Dec		31	Interest Expense		2,165.00	
			Long-term Notes Payable		15,464.00	
			Cash			17,629.00
			To pay the first installment payment			
1992 Dec		31	Interest Expense		6,235.00	
			Long-term Notes Payable		15,464.00	
			Cash			21,688.00
			To pay the second installment payment.			

Problem X

On December 31, 1990, Nord Company signed a 10-year lease agreement under which it promised to pay $30,000 per year in return for the use of some equipment. Assume the lease should be classified as a capital lease and an interest rate of 12% is reasonable.

  1. Prepare a general journal entry to record the lease.

5.6502

DATE			ACCOUNT TITLES AND EXPLANATION	P.R.	DEBIT	CREDIT
1990 Dec		31	Equipment		169,506.00	
			Discount on Lease Financing		130,494.00	
			Long-term Lease Lea.			300,000.00
			To buy an equipment by a long-term lease			

273

2. Prepare a general journal entry to record the first $30,000 lease payment on December 31, 1991.

DATE		ACCOUNT TITLES AND EXPLANATION	P.R.	DEBIT	CREDIT
1991 Dec	31	Long-term Lease Lia		30,000.00	
		Cash			30,000.00
		To pay the first installment lease.			

3. Prepare a general journal entry to record depreciation expense on December 31, 1991. Use straight-line depreciation and no salvage value.

DATE		ACCOUNT TITLES AND EXPLANATION	P.R.	DEBIT	CREDIT
1991 Dec	31	Depreciation Expense, equipment		16,850.60	
		accumulated depreciation, equipment			16,850.60
		To record depreciation Expense of equipment.			

4. Prepare a general journal entry to amortize the discount on lease financing for 1991.

DATE		ACCOUNT TITLES AND EXPLANATION	P.R.	DEBIT	CREDIT
1991 Dec	31	Interest Expense		20,340.72	
		Discount on Lease Financing			20,340.72
		To amortize a portion of the discount on a lease.			

Problem I

1.	F	8.	T
2.	T	9.	F
3.	T	10.	T
4.	T	11.	T
5.	F	12.	T
6.	F	13.	T
7.	T		

Problem II

1. E
2. A
3. D
4. D
5. C

Problem III

Bank discount	3	Installment notes	12
Capital lease	10	Long-term liabilities	7
Carrying amount of a lease	2	Operating lease	1
Carrying amount of a note	8	Present value	9
Estimated liability	4	Present value table	5
Financing lease	11 or 10	Product warranty	6

Problem IV

1. a. $0.3186
   b. $2,000 × 0.3405 = $681
   c. $6.6231
   d. $1,000 × 4.8332 = $4,833.20

2. a. property taxes
   b. product warranties

3. less than

4. $1,000, $1,000 × 0.7722 = $772.20

5. decrease

6. capital leases (or financing leases)

7. decrease

8. existing current assets

9. a. payments of accrued interest plus equal amounts of principal
   b. payments that are equal in total amount, consisting of changing amounts of interest and principal

Problem V

(a)

Jan. 31 Property Taxes Expense	80.00	
Estimated Property Taxes Payable		80.00

[($120,000/$100) × $0.80]/12 = $80

(b)
Aug. 31 Property Taxes Expense 240.00
        Prepaid Property Taxes (Sept.–Dec.) 400.00
        Estimated Property Taxes Payable (7 × $80) 560.00
            Cash 1,200.00
        ($120,000/$100) × $1.00 = $1,200
        ($1,200/12) × 4 = $400

Problem VI

Jan. — Cash 50,000.00
            Sales 50,000.00

     — Warranty Expense ($50,000 × .03) 1,500.00
            Estimated Warranty Liability 1,500.00

     — Estimated Warranty Liability 1,200.00
            Cash 1,200.00

Problem VII

1990
Dec. 16 Cash 9,800.00
         Discount on Notes Payable 200.00
            Notes Payable 10,000.00

     31 Interest Expense 50.00
            Discount on Notes Payable 50.00

1991
Feb. 14 Notes Payable 10,000.00
            Cash 10,000.00

     14 Interest Expense 150.00
            Discount on Notes Payable 150.00

Problem VIII

1. $15,000 × 0.5674 = $8,511

2. Jan. 2 Machinery 8,511.00
             Discount on Notes Payable 6,489.00
                Long-Term Notes Payable 15,000.00

3. $8,511 × 12% = $1,021.32

4. Dec. 31 Interest Expense 1,021.32
                Discount on Notes Payable 1,021.32

5. Long-term liabilities:
       Long-term notes payable $15,000.00
       Less unamortized discount based on the 12%
       interest rate prevailing on the date of issue 5,467.68* $9,532.32

    * $6,489.00 − $1,021.32 = $5,467.68

Problem IX

a. 1990
   Dec. 31 Cash 60,000.00
                Notes Payable   60,000,00

b. 1991
   Dec. 31 Interest Expense ($60,000 × .14) 8,400.00
            Notes Payable 10,000.00
                Cash 18,000.00

   1992
   Dec. 31 Interest Expense ($50,000 × .14) 7,000.00
            Notes Payable 10,000.00
                Cash 17,000.00

c. 1991
   Dec. 31 Interest Expense ($60,000 × .14) 8,400.00
            Notes Payable 7,064.00
                Cash 15,464.00

   1992
   Dec. 31 Interest Expense ($60,000 − $7,064) × .14 ..... 7,411.00
            Notes Payable 8,053.00
                Cash 15,464.00

Problem X

1. 1990
   Dec. 31 Equipment 169,506.00
            Discount on Lease Financing 130,494.00
                Long-Term Lease Liability 300,000.00
                ($30,000 × 5.6502 = $169,506)

2. 1991
   Dec. 31 Long-Term Lease Liability 30,000.00
                Cash 30,000.00

3. Dec. 31 Depreciation Expense, Equipment 16,950.60
                Accumulated Depr., Equipment 16,950.60
                ($169,506/10 = $16,950.60)

4.   31 Interest Expense 20,340.72
                Discount on Lease Financing 20,340.72
                ($169,506 × 12% = $20,340.72)

13 Payroll Accounting

After studying Chapter 13, you should be able to:

1. List the taxes and other items frequently withheld from employees' wages, make the calculations necessary to prepare a Payroll Register, and prepare the entry to record an accrued payroll.

2. Prepare journal entries to pay employees and explain the operation of a payroll bank account.

3. Calculate the payroll taxes levied on employers and prepare the entries to record the accrual and payment of these taxes.

4. Calculate and record employee fringe benefit costs and show the effect of these items on the total cost of employing labour.

5. Define or explain the words and phrases listed in the chapter Glossary.

Topical Outline

I. Payroll accounting—recording liabilities and cash payments to employees—also includes:

    A. Amounts withheld from employees' wages.
    B. Payroll charges levied on the employer.
    C. Employee (fringe) benefits paid by the employer.

II. The federal government provides for a number of social security programs.

    A. A federal old-age and survivors' benefits program provides retirement benefits based on contributions to the program.

        1. Funds for payment of benefits under the Canadian Pension Plan come from payroll taxes.
        2. Payroll deductions are imposed under the Canada Pension Plan on all employers and their employees.

    B. The federal unemployment insurance program.

        1. The Unemployment Insurance Commission requires deductions from employees and a tax on employers to provide funds for the federal unemployment insurance program.
        2. The federal unemployment insurance program is designed to pay unemployment compensation, to encourage the stabilization of employment, and to maintain employment offices.

III. Witholdings from employees' paycheques

    A. Federal income taxes.
    B. Unemployment Insurance.
    C. Canada Pension.
    D. Union Dues
    E. Other deductions (such as insurance premiums).

IV. Maintaining payroll records

    A. Timekeeping—compiling a record of time worked by each employee.
    B. Payroll register—summarizes and stores payroll information, such as time worked and applicable rates of pay by employee for each pay period.
    C. Payroll is recorded each pay period with a general journal entry.
    D. Payments to employees

        1. Made from a regular chequing account, or
        2. Made through a separate payroll chequing account.

    E. Individual earnings record—accumulates earnings and withholdings information for a whole year.
    F. Computerized payroll systems—commonly used by many companies to process their payrolls.

V. Payroll charges levied on employers

    A. Unemployment Insurance.
    B. Canada Pension Plan.

VI. Employee fringe benefit costs

    A. Medical insurance, life insurance, disability insurance.
    B. Retirement income plan.
    C. Vacation pay.

Problem I

The following statements are either true or false. Place a (T) in the parentheses before each true statement and an (F) before each false statement.

1. ( ) According to law, a T-4 form showing wages earned and taxes withheld must be given to each employee within one month after the year-end.

2. ( ) Federal unemployment insurance is withheld from employees' wages at the rate of 1.95%.

3. ( ) Canada Pension Plan amounts are levied equally on the employee and the employer.

4. ( ) Employee (fringe) benefit costs represent expenses to the employer in addition to the direct costs of salaries and wages.

5. ( ) Each time a payroll is recorded, a general journal entry should also be made to record the employer's unemployment insurance cost.

6. ( ) Since federal income taxes withheld from an employee's wages are expenses of the employee, not the employer, they should not be treated as liabilities of the employer.

7. ( ) Since Jon Company has very few employee accidents, the company has received a very favorable Workers' Compensation rating. As a result, Jon Company should expect to pay smaller amounts of Workers' Compensation premium than normal.

Problem II

You are given several words, phrases or numbers to choose from in completing each of the following statements or in answering the following questions. In each case select the one that best completes the statement or answers the question and place its letter in the answer space provided.

Use the following information as to earnings and deductions for the pay period ended November 15 taken from a company's payroll records for the next two questions:

Employee's Name	Earnings to End of Previous Week	Gross Pay This Week	Federal Income Taxes	Hospital Insurance Deducted
Rita Hawn	$25,700	$ 800	$155.00	$ 35.50
Dolores Hopkins	930	800	134.00	35.50
Robert Allen	49,900	1,000	193.00	42.00
Calvin Ingram	18,400	740	128.00	42.00
		$3,340	$610.00	$155.00

_____ 1. Employees' UI and CPP are withheld at an assumed 4% rate on the first $30,000 paid each employee. A general journal entry to accrue the payroll under the assumption that all of the employees work in the office should include:

    a. a debit to Accrued Payroll Payable for $3,340.
    b. a debit to UI and CPP Payable for $133.60.
    c. a debit to Payroll Expense for $133.60.
    d. a credit to Payroll Expense for $133.60.
    e. a credit to Accrued Payroll Payable for $2,441.40.

_____ 2. Assume that Canada Pension Plan applies at a rate of 2.1% on the $25,000 of eligible earnings. The general journal entry to record the employer's payroll cost resulting from the payroll should include a debit to Payroll Expense for:

   a. $ 32.34
   b. $ 49.14
   c. $ 70.14
   d. $140.28
   e. The entry does not include a debit to Payroll Expense.

_____ 3. In addition to determining and withholding income tax from each employee's wages, employers are required to:

   a. periodically deposit the withheld taxes with Revenue Canada.
   b. file a quarterly report showing the income taxes withheld.
   c. give each employee a Wage and Tax Statement for the year, Form T-4.
   d. send Revenue Canada copies of all T-4 forms given employees.
   e. All of the above.

Problem III

Many of the important ideas and concepts discussed in Chapter 13 are reflected in the following list of key terms. Test your understanding of these terms by matching the appropriate definitions with the terms. Record the number identifying the most appropriate definition in the blank space next to each term.

_____ Clock card

_____ CPP

_____ Employee's gross pay

_____ Employee's individual earnings record

_____ Employee's net pay

_____ Gross pay

_____ Income tax withholdings

_____ Payroll bank account

_____ Payroll tax

_____ Receiver General

_____ Timekeeping

_____ Unemployment insurance

_____ Wage bracket withholding table

1. Gross pay minus deductions.

2. The amount of an employee's pay before any deductions.

3. The individual authorized to receive amounts of money payable to the government.

4. Making a record of the time each employee is at his or her place of work.

5. Canada Pension Plan.

6. Income tax withholdings by employers from employee earnings.

7. A card used by an employee to record his or her time of arrival and departure to and from work.

8. A record of an employee's hours worked, gross pay, deductions, net pay, and certain personal information about the employee.

9. A special bank account into which at the end of each pay period the total amount of an employer's payroll is deposited and on which the employees' payroll cheques are drawn.

10. A charge levied by the federal government and used to pay a portion of the costs of the unemployment programs.

11. A tax levied on the amount of a payroll or on the amount of an employee's gross pay.

12. A table showing the amounts to be withheld from employees' wages at various levels of earnings.

Problem IV

Complete the following by filling in the blanks.

1. An employee who works 45 hours in one week must normally be paid his regular rate of pay for the 45 hours plus overtime premium pay at one half his regular rate for _____ of the 45 hours.

2. Funds for the payment of federal retirement benefits are raised by payroll deductions imposed under a law called the _____

_____.

3. The amount to be withheld from an employee's wages for federal income taxes is determined by (a) _____

_____

and (b) _____.

4. Weekly unemployment benefits received by workers are based on _____

_____

prior to unemployment.

5. The Canada Pension Plan Act levies a payroll tax on both covered employers and their employees. In 1989, an employer was required to withhold CPP deductions from the wages of employees at the rate of ____% of each employee's gross earnings in excess of the allowed exemption, the withholding to continue each year until the contribution exempt point is reached. In addition to the employees' CPP withholdings, an employer must also pay a CPP amount equal to the sum of the _____ withheld from the wages of all of its employees.

6. The computation of income tax withholding deductions is facilitated by the use of _____

_____ provided by Revenue Canada, Taxation.

7. Employers are required to remit the payroll deductions and withheld income taxes to the _____

_____ on or before the _____

_____ following that in which withholdings were made.

8. On or before the last day of _____ following each year, an employer must give each employee a _____. A summary of the information contained in the

_____ supported by copies of statements issued to the employees is forwarded

to the _____

_____.

9. Workers' compensation premiums are paid in total by the _____

_____

and are normally based on (a) _____

and (b) _____.

Problem V

The Payroll Register of Newman Sales for the first week of the year follows. It has the deductions and net pay of the first three employees calculated and entered.

1. Mr. Yancy's deductions are as follows:

Canada Pension Plan	$ 11.59
Unemployment Insurance	10.76
Income taxes	104.74
Medical insurance	10.00

PAYROLL REGISTER

EMPLOYEE'S NAME	CLOCK CARD NUMBER	DAILY TIME M	T	W	T	F	S	S	TOTAL HOURS	O.T. HOURS	REG. PAY RATE		REGULAR PAY		O.T. PREMIUM PAY		GROSS PAY		
Ryan Black	11	8	8	8	7	4	0	0	35		9	00	315	00			315	00	1
Jan Duncan	8	8	8	8	5	4	0	0	33		10	00	330	00			330	00	2
Walter Prince	14	8	8	7	8	4	0	0	35		11	00	385	00			385	00	3
Jack Yancy	5	8	8	8	8	8	4	0	44	4	12	00							4
																			5

Week ending January 7, 1989

DEDUCTIONS CPP		UI		INCOME TAXES		MEDICAL INSUR- ANCE		TOTAL DEDUC- TIONS		PAYMENT NET PAY		CHEQUE NUMBER	DISTRIBUTION SALES SALARIES		OFFICE SALARIES		DELIVERY SALARIES	
1	6	61	6	15	60	81	10	00	83	57	231	43						315	00
2	6	93	6	44	60	20	10	00	83	57	246	43		330	00				
3	8	08	7	51	69	33	10	00	94	92	290	08		385	00				
4																			
5																			

2. Complete the Payroll Register by totaling its columns, and give the general journal entry to record its information.

DATE	ACCOUNT TITLES AND EXPLANATION	P.R.	DEBIT	CREDIT

Newman Sales uses a special payroll bank account in paying its employees. Each payday, after the general journal entry recording the information of its Payroll Register is posted, a single cheque for the total of the employees' net pay is drawn and deposited in the payroll bank account. This transfers funds equal to the payroll total from the regular bank account to the payroll bank account. Then special payroll cheques are written on the payroll bank account and given to the employees. For the January 8 payroll, Cheque No. 845 was used to transfer funds equal to the total of the employees' net pay from the regular bank account. After this, four payroll checks beginning with payroll Cheque No. 102 were drawn and delivered to the employees.

3. Make the entry to record Cheque No. 845 in the Cheque Register below.

4. Enter the payroll cheque numbers in the Payroll Register.

CHEQUE REGISTER

DATE	CH. NO.	PAYEE	ACCOUNT DEBITED	P.R.	ACCRUED PAYROLL PAYABLE DR.	CASH CR.

5. In the space below give the general journal entry to record the payroll taxes levied on Newman Sales as a result of the payroll entered in its January 8 Payroll Register.

DATE	ACCOUNT TITLES AND EXPLANATION	P.R.	DEBIT	CREDIT

6. On the next page is the individual earnings record of Jack Yancy. Transfer from the Payroll Register on page 284 to Mr. Yancy's earnings record the payroll data for the first pay period of the year.

EMPLOYEE'S INDIVIDUAL EARNINGS RECORD

EMPLOYEE'S NAME Jack Yancey

S.I. ACCT. NO. 119-051-879

EMPLOYEE NO. 5

HOME ADDRESS 2590 Columbia Street

NOTIFY IN CASE OF EMERGENCY Mary Yancy

PHONE NUMBER 965-5698

EMPLOYED 9/1/78

DATE OF TERMINATION

REASON

DATE OF BIRTH May 20, 1943

DATE BECOMES 65 May 20, 2008

MALE (x) MARRIED (x) NUMBER OF
FEMALE ( ) SINGLE ( ) DEPENDENTS 4

PAY RATE $12.00

OCCUPATION Manager

PLACE Store and office

DATE		TIME LOST		TIME WK.		REG. PAY	O.T. PREM. PAY	GROSS PAY	CPP	UI	INCOME TAXES	MEDI-CAL INSUR-ANCE	TOTAL DEDUC-TIONS	NET PAY	CHEQUE NUMBER	CUMU-LATIVE PAY
PER. ENDS	PAID	HRS.	REASON	TOTAL	O.T. HOURS											

Solutions for Chapter 13

Problem I

1. T
2. T
3. T
4. T
5. T
6. F
7. T

Problem II

1. E
2. B
3. E

Problem III

Clock card	7	Payroll bank account	9
CPP	5	Payroll tax	11
Employee's gross pay	2	Receiver General	3
Employee's individual earnings record	8	Timekeeping	4
Employee's net pay	1	Unemployment insurance	10
Gross pay	2	Wage bracket withholding table	12
Income tax withholdings	6		

Problem IV

1. five

2. Canada Pension Plan

3. (a) the amount of his or her wages, (b) the number of his or her exemptions.

4. The average weekly wages.

5. 2.1%; amounts

6. tax withholding tables

7. Receiver General of Canada; 15th of the month

8. February; T-4 statement; T-4 statements; District Taxation Office.

9. employer (a) accident experience of the industrial classification of the business; (b) the total payroll.

Problem V

1., 2., 4., and 5.

EMPLOYEE'S NAME	CLOCK CARD NUMBER	DAILY TIME							TOTAL HOURS	O.T. HOURS	REG. PAY RATE		EARNINGS					
		M	T	W	T	F	S	S					REGULAR PAY		O.T. PREMIUM PAY		GROSS PAY	
Ryan Black	11	8	8	8	7	4	0	0	35		9	00	315	00			315	00	1
Jan Duncan	8	8	8	8	5	4	0	0	33		10	00	330	00			330	00	2
Walter Prince	14	8	8	7	8	4	0	0	35		11	00	385	00			385	00	3
Jack Yancy	5	8	8	8	8	8	4	0	44	4	12	00	528	00	24	00	552	00	4
													1,558	00	24	00	1,582	00	5

Week ending January 8, 19—

	DEDUCTIONS									PAYMENT				DISTRIBUTION					
	CPP		UI		INCOME TAXES		MEDICAL INSUR-ANCE		TOTAL DEDUC-TIONS		NET PAY		CHEQUE NUMBER	SALES SALARIES		OFFICE SALARIES		DELIVERY SALARIES	
1	6	61	6	15	60	81	10	00	83	57	231	43	102					315	00
2	6	93	6	44	60	20	10	00	83	57	246	43	103	330	00				
3	8	08	7	51	69	33	10	00	94	92	290	08	104	385	00				
4	11	59	10	76	104	74	10	00	137	09	414	91	105			552	00		
5	33	21	30	86	295	08	40	00	399	15	1,182	85		715	00	552	00	315	00

```
Jan. 7  Sales Salaries Expense ....................................... 715.00
        Office Salaries Expense ...................................... 552.00
        Delivery Salaries Expense ................................... 315.00
            Canada Pension Plan Payable ............................          33.21
            Unemployment Insurance Payable ........................          30.86
            Employees' Income Taxes Payable .......................         295.08
            Medical Insurance Payable .............................          40.00
            Accrued Payroll Payable ...............................       1,182.85
```

3.

CHEQUE REGISTER

DATE		CH. NO.	PAYEE	ACCOUNT DEBITED	P.R.	ACCRUED PAYROLL PAYABLE DR.				CASH CR.			
Jan.	9	845	Payroll Bank Account	Accrued Payroll Payable		1	1 8 2	85		1	1 8 2	85	

```
5.  Jan. 7  Payroll Taxes Expense ...................................... 76.41
            Canada Pension Plan Payable ............................          33.21
            Unemployment Insurance Payable ........................          43.20
```

6.

EMPLOYEE'S INDIVIDUAL EARNINGS RECORD

EMPLOYEE'S NAME   Jack Yancy   S.I. ACCT. NO.   119-051-879   EMPLOYEE NO.   5

HOME   NOTIFY IN CASE   PHONE
ADDRESS   2590 Columbia Street   OF EMERGENCY   Mary Yancy   NUMBER   965-5698

EMPLOYED   9/1/78   DATE OF
                          TERMINATION   REASON

DATE OF   DATE   MALE (x) MARRIED (x) NUMBER OF   PAY
BIRTH   May 20, 1943   BECOMES 65   May 20, 2008   FEMALE ( ) SINGLE ( ) DEPENDENTS   4   RATE $12.00

OCCUPATION   Manager   PLACE   Store and office

DATE		TIME LOST		TIME WK.		REG. PAY	O.T. PREM. PAY	GROSS PAY	CPP	UI	INCOME TAXES	MEDI-CAL INSUR-ANCE	TOTAL DEDUC-TIONS	NET PAY	CHEQUE NUMBER	CUMU-LATIVE PAY
PER. ENDS	PAID	HRS.	REASON	TOTAL	O.T. HOURS											
1/7	1/7			44	4	528 00	24 00	552 00	11 59	10 76	104 74	10 00	137 09	414 91	105	552 00

14 Partnership Accounting

After studying Chapter 14, you should be able to:

1. List the characteristics of a partnership and explain the importance of mutual agency and unlimited liability to a person about to become a partner.

2. Allocate partnership earnings to partners *(a)* on a stated fractional basis, *(b)* in the partners' capital ratio, and *(c)* through the use of salary and interest allowances.

3. Prepare entries for *(a)* the sale of a partnership interest, *(b)* the admission of a new partner by investment, and *(c)* the retirement of a partner by the withdrawal of partnership assets.

4. Prepare entries required in the liquidation of a partnership.

5. Define or explain the words and phrases listed in the chapter Glossary.

Topical Outline

I. Characteristics of a partnership

    A. A voluntary association.

    B. Based on a contract, which should be in writing but may be expressed orally.

    C. Limited life—death, bankruptcy, or expiration of the contract period automatically ends a partnership.

    D. Mutual agency—every partner is an agent of the partnership and can enter into and bind it to any contract within the normal scope of its business.

    E. Unlimited liability—each general partner is responsible for payment of all the debts of the partnership if the other partners are unable to pay a share.

II. Limited partnerships versus general partnerships

    A. Limited partnerships have two classes of partners

        1. General partner(s)—assumes unlimited liability for the debts of the partnership.

        2. Limited partners—have no personal liability beyond their invested amounts.

    B. In a general partnership, all partners have unlimited liability and may be called general partners.

III. Partnership accounting

    A. Owners' equity accounts

        1. Capital account for each partner.

        2. Withdrawals account for each partner.

    B. Measurement and division of earnings

        1. Salaries to partners and interest on partners' investments are not partnership expenses; they are allocations of net income.

        2. In the absence of an agreement, partnership earnings and losses are shared equally among the partners.

        3. Methods of sharing partnership earnings:

            a. On a fractional basis.

            b. Based on the ratio of capital investments.

            c. Based on salary and interest allowances with the remainder in a fixed ratio.

        4. Partners can agree to salary and interest *allowances* when distributing profits to reward unequal contribution of services or capital.

IV. Partnership financial statements

    A. Balance sheet owners' equity section may show separate capital account balance of each partner.

    B. Statement of changes in partners' equity—shows total capital balances at beginning of the period, any additional investments, net income or loss, and ending capital balances.

V. Addition or withdrawal of a partner

    A. Sale of a partnership interest requires that the old partner's capital account be transferred to the new partner's capital account.

    B. Investing in an existing partnership

        1. Partnership assets are increased.

        2. The agreement may involve a bonus to the old partners or to the new partner.

3. A bonus involves a transfer of capital account balances between the partners.
4. Goodwill may be debited and matched with credits that increase the equities of the existing partners if justified by projected future earnings.

C. Withdrawal of a partner depends on the partnership agreement.

1. Partnership assets may be revalued.
2. The agreement may result in a partner taking assets of greater or lesser value than his or her book equity.
3. The capital accounts of the partners may require adjustment to reflect the agreed-upon division of assets when a partner withdraws.

VI. Liquidations of partnerships

A. As assets are sold, gains or losses must be recorded.
B. Partnership creditors must be paid before partners.
C. If a partner's capital account is not sufficient to absorb his or her share of liquidation losses:

1. He or she must, if possible, contribute assets to the partnership to cover the deficiency.
2. Otherwise, the remaining partners' capital accounts must be charged for the capital deficiency of the defaulting partner.

Problem I

The following statements are either true or false. Place a (T) in the parentheses before each true statement and an (F) before each false statement.

1. (T) Jay and Faye are partners in the operation of an insurance agency. Business has been slow, and without consulting Faye, Jay entered into a contract with Rays Limited to purchase three satellite dishes to be sold by the partnership. Faye repudiated the contract. Rays Limited should be able to hold the partnership liable on the contract.

2. (T) Partnership accounting is exactly like that of a single proprietorship except for transactions affecting the partners' equities.

3. (T) Although a partner does not work for either a salary or interest, to be fair in the distribution of partnership earnings, it is often necessary to recognize that the earnings do include a return for services and a return on investments.

Problem II

You are given several words, phrases or numbers to choose from in completing each of the following statements or in answering the following questions. In each case select the one that best completes the statement or answers the question and place its letter in the answer space provided.

Use the following data to answer questions 1 through 5:

Reggie and Veronica began a partnership by investing $28,000 and $20,000, respectively, and during its first year the partnership earned a $42,000 net income.

_____ 1. What would be the share of each partner in the $42,000 net income if the partners failed to agree as to the method of sharing?

    a. Reggie's share, $24,500; Veronica's share, $17,500.
    b. Reggie's share, $21,400; Veronica's share, $20,600.
    c. Reggie's share, $21,000; Veronica's share, $21,000.
    d. Reggie's share, $42,000; Veronica's share, $ –0–.
    e. None of the above is correct because the partners must have an agreement as to the method of sharing.

_____ 2. What would be the share of each partner in the $42,000 net income if the partners had agreed to share in their beginning-of-year investment ratio?

    a. Reggie's share, $21,000; Veronica's share, $21,000.
    b. Reggie's share, $42,000; Veronica's share, $ –0–.
    c. Reggie's share, $21,400; Veronica's share, $20,600.
    d. Reggie's share, $24,500; Veronica's share, $17,500.
    e. Reggie's share, $20,600; Veronica's share, $21,400.

_____ 3. What would be the share of each partner in the $42,000 net income if the partners had agreed to share by giving a $16,400 per year salary allowance to Reggie and a $18,000 per year salary allowance to Veronica, plus 10% interest on their beginning-of-year investments, and the remainder equally?

    a. Reggie's share, $20,600; Veronica's share, $21,400.
    b. Reggie's share, $22,200; Veronica's share, $19,800.
    c. Reggie's share, $21,400; Veronica's share, $21,400.
    d. Reggie's share, $24,500; Veronica's share, $17,500.
    e. Reggie's share, $21,000; Veronica's share, $21,000.

294

_____d_____ 4. Assume that the partnership of Reggie and Veronica earned $28,000 rather than $42,000 and that the partners had agreed to share incomes and losses by giving salary allowances of $16,400 and $18,000 respectively, 10% interest on beginning investments, and the remainder equally. The earnings would be shared as follows:

    a. Reggie's share, $13,200; Veronica's share, $14,800.
    b. Reggie's share, $14,000; Veronica's share, $14,000.
    c. Reggie's share, $13,349; Veronica's share, $14,651.
    d. Reggie's share, $13,600; Veronica's share, $14,400.
    e. Reggie's share, $14,400; Veronica's share, $13,600.

_____a×e_____ 5. If Reggie and Veronica share incomes and losses as in question 4 above, and the partnership incurred a $7,600 loss rather than a profit, the loss would be shared as follows:

    a. Reggie's share, $(3,800); Veronica's share, $(3,800).
    b. Reggie's share, $(3,400); Veronica's share, $(4,200).
    c. Reggie's share, $(4,433); Veronica's share, $(3,167).
    d. Reggie's share, $(4,000); Veronica's share, $(3,600).
    e. Reggie's share, $(4,200); Veronica's share, $(3,400).

Problem III

Many of the important ideas and concepts discussed in Chapter 14 are reflected in the following list of key terms. Test your understanding of these terms by matching the appropriate definitions with the terms. Record the number identifying the most appropriate definition in the blank space next to each term.

_____3_____ Deficit

_____5_____ General partner

_____8_____ General partnership

_____9_____ Limited partners

_____6_____ Limited partnership

_____2×1_____ Mutual agency

_____10_____ Partnership

_____1 ×2_____ Partnership contract

_____4_____ Partnership liquidations

_____11_____ Statement of Changes in Partners' Equity

_____2_____ Unlimited liability of partners

1. A characteristic of the relationship between the partners in a partnership whereby each partner is able to bind the partnership to contracts within the apparent scope of the partnership business.

2. The agreement between partners that sets forth the terms under which the affairs of a partnership will be conducted.

3. A negative balance in an account.

4. The winding up of a partnership business by converting its assets to cash and distributing the cash to the proper parties.

5. A partner who assumes unlimited liability for the debts of the partnership.

6. A partnership that has two classes of partners, limited partners and one or more general partners.

7. The legal characteristic of a partnership that makes each general partner responsible for paying all the debts of the partnership if the other partners are unable to pay their shares.

8. A partnership in which all partners have unlimited liability for partnership debts.

9. Partners who have no personal liability for debts of the limited partnership beyond the amounts they have invested in the partnership.

10. An association by contract of two or more persons to carry on a business as co-owners for profit.

11. A financial statement that shows the total capital balances at the beginning of the period, any additional investments by the partners, the net income or loss of the period, the partners' withdrawals during the period, and the ending capital balances.

Problem IV

Complete the following by filling in the blanks.

1. Partnership accounting is exactly like that of a single proprietorship except for transactions affecting _the partner's capital equity_.

2. Four advantages of a partnership over the single proprietorship or corporation forms of organization are:

    (a) _collect more money, labor and skill by investment than single proprietorship._;

    (b) _easy to organize as compared to corporation_;

    (c) _avoid some debts and regulations which set by the Federal or provincial for the corporation to obligate_;

    (d) _There is no need to open shareholder's and director's meetings in a partnership._

3. A _____ (limited, general) partnership has two classes of partners.

4. Although a partner does not work for either a salary or interest, to be fair in the distribution of partnership earnings, it is often necessary to recognize that the earnings do include a return for _work_ and a return on _investment_.

5. Blake and Dillon are partners who have always shared incomes and losses equally. Hester has sued the partners on a partnership debt and obtained a $12,000 judgment. The partnership and Dillon have no assets; consequently, Hester is attempting to collect the entire $12,000 from Blake. Blake has sufficient assets to pay the judgment but refuses, claiming she is liable for only one half the $12,000. Hester _____ (can, cannot) collect the entire $12,000 from Blake because _Blake has a unlimited liability for the partnership and obligated to pay for other partners._

6. Since a partnership is a voluntary association, an individual _____ (can, cannot) be forced against his will to become a partner; and since a partnership is based on a contract, its life is _limited_.

7. The fact that partners cannot enter into an employer-employee contractual relation with themselves supports the contention held in law and custom that partners work for partnership _____ *earnings & return* and not for a salary. Furthermore, partners invest in a partnership for _____ *earnings* and not for interest.

8. The phrase mutual agency, when applied to a partnership, means _____ *A partner can go into a contract and act as other partners agency to deal with business within the scope of the partnership work.*

Problem V

Use the following balance sheet information to complete the work below:

PINTER, KING AND TODD
Balance Sheet
December 31, 19—

Assets		*Owners' Equities*	
Cash	$ 8,000	Martin Pinter, capital	$ 9,000
Other assets	19,000	Mike King, capital	9,000
		Harold Todd, capital	9,000
Total assets	$27,000	Total owners' equities	$27,000

1. Martin Pinter has a $9,000 equity in the partnership of Printer, King and Todd. If with the consent of his partners, he sells his equity to Lee Russell for $9,000, the entry to record the transaction is:

DATE	ACCOUNT TITLES AND EXPLANATION	P.R.	DEBIT	CREDIT
19X3 Dec 31	Martin Pinter, Capital		9000.00	
	Lee Russell, Capital			9000.00
	To record the selling of Martin capital to Lee.			

2. If rather than selling the equity for $9,000, Pinter sold it for $10,000, the entry _____ (would, would not) be the same.

Problem VI

The condensed balance sheet of Shaw, Greene, and Wilson, who have always shared incomes and losses in a 3:2:1 ratio, follows. Wilson plans to leave the partnership. Shaw and Greene plan to continue the business under a new partnership contract.

297

SHAW, GREENE, AND WILSON
Balance Sheet
December 31, 19—

Assets		*Owners' Equities*	
Cash	$10,000	Edmund Shaw, capital	$17,000
Other assets	30,000	Bernard Greene, capital	15,000
		Graham Wilson, capital	8,000
Total assets	$40,000	Total owners' equities	$40,000

1. If Wilson takes $8,000 of partnership cash in settlement for his equity, the remaining assets will total

   $___32,000___; Shaw's equity in the remaining assets will be $___17,000___; and Green's equity

   will be $___15,000___.

2. If Wilson takes $9,000 of partnership cash in settlement for his equity, the remaining assets will be

   $___31,000___; Shaw's equity in the remaining assets will be $___16,400___; and Green's equity

   will be $___14,600___.

3. If Wilson takes $7,500 of partnership cash in settlement for his equity, the remaining assets will total

   $___32,500___; Shaw's equity in these assets will be $___17,300___; and Green's equity will be

   $___15,200___.

Problem VII

Wheeler, Carson, and Young, who have operated a partnership for a number of years, sharing incomes and losses equally, are to liquidate. The assets and equities of the partnership just prior to its liquidation are shown in the T-accounts below.

Cash				Accounts Payable	
Dec. 31	9,000	Dec 31	8,000	Dec 31	9,000
Dec 31	20,000			Dec 31	9,000	Dec. 31	9,000

Other Assets				Wheeler, Capital	
Dec. 31	29,000	Dec 31	28,000	Dec 31	3,000	Dec. 31	12,000

Loss or Gain from Realization				Carson, Capital	
Dec 31	9,000		9,000	Dec 31	3,000	Dec. 31	9,000

				Young, Capital	
				Dec 31	3,000	Dec. 31	8,000

1. Make entries directly in the T-accounts to record the sale of the other assets under the assumption that the other assets are sold for $20,000.

2. Makes entries directly in the T-accounts to allocate the loss from realization to the partners.

3. Since the creditor claims take precedence over the claims of the partners, make entries in the T-accounts to pay the creditors.

4. Fill in the blanks in the following statements:

At this point in the liquidation of the partnership of Wheeler, Carson, and Young, after losses are shared and the creditors are paid, the balance of the Cash account is $ _____ 20,000 _____ and is equal to the sum of the balances of the _____ partner's capital _____ accounts. The balances of the partners' capital accounts are: Wheeler, $ _____ 9,000 _____; Carson, $ _____ 6,000 _____; and Young $ _____ 5,000 _____. Consequently, in a final distribution of cash Wheeler should receive $ _____ 9,000 _____, Carson should receive $ _____ 6,000 _____, and Young should receive $ _____ 5,000 _____.

Solutions for Chapter 14

Problem I

1. F
2. T
3. T

Problem II

1. C
2. D
3. A
4. D
5. E

Problem III

Deficit	3	Partnership	10
General partner	5	Partnership contract	2
General partnership	8	Partnership liquidations	4
Limited partners	9	Statement of Changes in Partners' Equity	11
Limited partnership	6		
Mutual agency	1	Unlimited liability of partners	7

Problem IV

1. the partners' equities

2. (a) Brings more money and skills together than a single proprietorship
   (b) Is easier to organize than a corporation
   (c) Does not have the corporation's governmental supervision or extra taxation burden
   (d) Allows partners to act freely and without the necessity of shareholders' and directors' meetings, as is required in a corporation

3. limited

4. services, investments

5. can, each partner has unlimited liability for the debts of the partnership

6. cannot, limited

7. profits or earnings, profits or earnings

8. each partner is an agent of the partnership and can bind it to contracts

Problem V

1. Dec. 31 Martin Pinter, Capital 9,000.00
                Lee Russell, Capital 9,000.00

2. would

Problem VI

1. $32,000; $17,000; $15,000.

2. $31,000; $16,400; $14,600.

3. $32,500; $17,300; $15,200.

Problem VII

1., 2., and 3.

Cash					Accounts Payable		
Dec. 31	9,000	(3)	9,000	(3)	9,000	Dec. 31	9,000
(1)	20,000						

Other Assets					Wheeler, Capital		
Dec. 31	29,000	(1)	29,000	(2)	3,000	Dec. 31	12,000

Loss or Gain from Realization					Carson, Capital		
(1)	9,000	(2)	9,000	(2)	3,000	Dec. 31	9,000

					Young, Capital		
				(2)	3,000	Dec. 31	8,000

4. Cash, $20,000, partners' capital. Partners' capital account balances: Wheeler, $9,000; Carson, $6,000; Young, $5,000. Wheeler should receive $9,000; Carson should receive $6,000; and Young should receive $5,000.

15 Organization and Operation of Corporations

After studying Chapter 15, you should be able to:

1. Explain the advantages, disadvantages, and organization of corporations, the differences in accounting for partnerships and corporations.

2. Record the issuance of no-par stock and the issuance of par value stock.

3. Record transactions involving stock subscriptions and explain the effects of subscribed stock on corporation assets and shareholders' equity.

4. Explain the differences between common and preferred stocks and allocate dividends between common and preferred stocks.

5. Describe convertible preferred stock and explain the meaning of par, redemption, book, and market values of stock.

6. Define or explain the words and phrases listed in the chapter Glossary.

Topical Outline

I. Advantages and disadvantages of the corporate form of business

   A. Advantages:

      1. Separate legal entity—a corporation, through its agents, may conduct business affairs with the same rights, duties, and responsibilities as a person.

      2. Lack of shareholders' liability.

      3. Ease of transferring ownership rights.

      4. Continuity of life—a perpetual life is possible for a successful corporation.

      5. No mutual agency—an individual, acting as a shareholder, cannot bind the corporation to contracts.

      6. Ease of capital assembly—the advantages of the corporate form make it easier for a corporation to raise large amounts of capital.

   B. Disadvantages:

      1. Increased governmental regulation.

      2. Taxation—corporate income is taxed; and when income is distributed to shareholders as dividends, it is taxed a second time.

II. Organizing, managing and accounting for a corporation

   A. Organization costs—normally debited to an asset account and amortized over a period not to exceed 40 years.

   B. Management—shareholders, board of directors and administrative officers.

   C. Accounting—shareholders' equity accounts are divided into contributed capital accounts and retained earnings accounts.

III. Common stock

   A. A corporation may issue no more stock than is authorized by its articles of incorporation or charter.

   B. Stock may be issued in exchange for cash or other assets.

   C. Par value—an arbitrary value placed on a share of stock.

   D. Premium on stock—the amount of capital contributed by shareholders above the stock's par value.

   E. No-par stock—a class of stock that does not have a par value associated with it.

   F. Subscriptions—in some instances, stock can be purchased on an installment basis.

      1. Subscriptions receivable are reported as assets.

      2. Common stock subscribed is reported in shareholders' equity.

   G. Rights of common shareholders:

      1. The right to vote in shareholders' meetings.

      2. The right to sell or otherwise dispose of their stock.

      3. The right (known as the preemptive right) of first opportunity to purchase any additional shares of common stock issued by the corporation if provided for in the articles of incorporation.

      4. The right to share pro rata with other common shareholders in any dividends distributed to common shareholders.

      5. The right to share in any assets remaining after creditors are paid if the corporation is liquidated.

IV. Preferred stock

    A. Preferred stock—so called because of preferences granted to its owners.

        1. Preference as to payment of dividends.
        2. Preference in distribution of assets in a liquidation.

    B. Cumulative or noncumulative preferred stock

        1. Cumulative—any undeclared dividends accumulate and must be paid before any dividends to common shares are paid.
        2. Noncumulative—the right to receive dividends is forfeited in any year that dividends are not declared.

    C. Participating or nonparticipating preferred stock

        1. Participating preferred stock—provides the right to share in dividends above the fixed amount or percentage which is preferred.
        2. Nonparticipating preferred stock—dividends to stock are limited to a fixed maximum amount.

V. Convertible preferred stock

    A. Initially issuing convertible preferred stock offers investors more security than common stock.
    B. The carrying amount of the converted preferred stock becomes the book value of the capital contributed for the new shares of common stock.

VI. Stock values

    A. Redemption value—the amount a corporation agrees to pay if it calls in and retires a share of its preferred stock.
    B. Market value—the amount at which a share of stock may be bought or sold.
    C. Book value—the equity represented by one share of stock in the issuing corporation's net assets as recorded in the accounts.

        1. Of common stock—total shareholders' equity (less the book value of preferred stock, if any) divided by number of common shares outstanding.
        2. Of preferred stock—redemption value (or par value if there is no redemption value) plus any cumulative dividends in arrears divided by number of preferred shares outstanding.
        3. Generally has little bearing upon liquidation value or market value.

Problem I

The following statements are either true or false. Place a (T) in the parentheses before each true statement and an (F) before each false statement.

F 1. (F) Par value generally has nothing to do with a stock's worth.

T 2. (F) Final authority in the management of corporation affairs rests with its board of directors.

3. (T) The life of a corporation may be unlimited.

4. (F) To transfer and sell his or her interest in a corporation, a shareholder must secure permission from the corporation's secretary.

5. (F) The chief executive officer of a corporation is usually elected by the shareholders at one of their annual meetings.

6. (T) The president of a corporation is responsible to its board of directors for management of the corporation's affairs.

7. (F) A premium on stock is the difference between book value and the amount at which stock is issued.

Problem II

You are given several words, phrases or numbers to choose from in completing each of the following statements or in answering the following questions. In each case select the one that best completes the statement or answers the question and place its letter in the answer space provided.

___d___ 1. The amount of capital contributed by shareholders above the stock's par value is the:

    a. contributed capital.
    b. stock dividend.
    c. redemption value.
    d. premium on stock.
    e. book value.

___a___ 2. Vector Corporation has outstanding 3,000 shares of $7, cumulative and nonparticipating preferred stock and 10,000 shares of no par value common stock. Dividends have not been paid on the preferred stock for the current and one prior year. The corporation has recently prospered, and the board of directors has voted to pay out $49,000 in dividends. If the $49,000 is paid out, how much should the preferred and common shareholders receive per share?

    a. $14.00 per share preferred, $0.70 per share common.
    b. $ 7.00 per share preferred, $2.80 per share common.
    c. $12.25 per share preferred, $1.23 per share common.
    d. $ 1.14 per share preferred, $4.56 per share common.
    e. $16.33 per share preferred, $-0- per share common.

___C___ 3. Vector Corporation has outstanding 3,000 shares of $7, noncumulative and nonparticipating preferred stock and 10,000 shares of no par value common stock. Dividends have not been paid on the preferred stock for the current and one prior year. The corporation has recently prospered, and the board of directors has voted to pay out $49,000 in dividends. If the $49,000 is paid out, how much should the preferred and common shareholders receive per share?

a. $ 1.14 per share preferred, $4.56 per share common.
b. $ 9.33 per share preferred, $2.10 per share common.
c. $ 7.00 per share preferred, $2.80 per share common.
d. $14.00 per share preferred, $0.70 per share common.
e. $12.25 per share preferred, $1.23 per share common.

___e___ 4. Participating preferred stock is:

a. preferred stock that may be exchanged for shares of its issuing corporation's common stock at the option of the shareholder.
b. preferred stock on which undeclared dividends accumulate annually until paid.
c. preferred stock for which the right to receive dividends is forfeited in any year in which dividends are not declared.
d. preferred stock which the issuing corporation, at its option, may retire by paying the shareholders the redemption value of the stock plus any dividends in arrears.
e. preferred stock that has the right to share in dividends above the fixed amount or percentage that is preferred.

___b___ 5. Stated value of no-par stock is:

a. one share's equity in the issuing corporation's net assets as recorded in the corporation's accounts.
b. an amount, (consideration received by the corporation on the issue of the shares) that is credited to the no-par stock account at the time the stock is issued.
c. the difference between the par value of stock and the amount below or above par value contributed by shareholders.
d. the market value of the stock on the date of issuance.
e. another name for redemption value.

Problem III

Many of the important ideas and concepts discussed in Chapter 15 are reflected in the following list of key terms. Test your understanding of these terms by matching the appropriate definitions with the terms. Record the number identifying the most appropriate definition in the blank space next to each term.

___10___ Book value of a share of stock

___4___ Call price of preferred stock

___2___ Callable preferred stock

___14___ Common stock

___7___ Common Stock Subscribed

___9___ Cumulative preferred stock

___18___ Dividend in arrears

___12___ Financial leverage

___17___ Noncumulative preferred stock

___5___ No-par stock

___8___ Organization costs

___20___ Par value

___15___ Participating preferred stock

___3___ Preemptive right

___11___ Preferred stock

___16___ Premium on stock

___6___ Proxy

___19___ Redemption value of preferred stock

___1___ Stated value of no-par stock

___13___ Stock subscription

1. An amount (consideration received) that is credited to the no-par stock account at the time the stock is issued.

2. Preferred stock which the issuing corporation, at its option, may retire by paying the shareholders the redemption value of the stock plus any dividends in arrears.

3. The right of common shareholders to protect their proportionate interests in a corporation by having the first opportunity to purchase additional shares of comon stock issued by the corporation.

4. Another name for redemption value.

5. A class of stock that does not have an arbitrary (par) value placed on the stock at the time the stock is first authorized.

6. A legal document that gives an agent of a shareholder the right to vote the stockholder's shares.

7. A shareholders' equity account in which a corporation records the par or stated value of unissued common stock that investors have contracted to purchase.

8. Costs of bringing a corporation into existence, such as legal fees, promoters' fees, and amounts paid to secure articles of incorporation.

9. Preferred stock that has the right to receive all preferred dividends including undeclared dividends from past years before outstanding common shares can receive any dividend.

10. The equity of one share of outstanding stock in the issuing corporation's net assets as recorded in the corporation's accounts.

11. Stock the owners of which are granted a priority status over common shareholders in one or more ways such as in the payment of dividends or in the distribution of assets upon liquidation.

12. Increasing the return to common stock as a result of paying preferred stock or creditors a given dividend or interest rate that is less than the rate earned from using the assets received by the corporation from the preferred shareholders or creditors.

13. A contractual commitment by an investor to purchase unissued shares of stock and become a shareholder.

14. Stock of a corporation that has only one class of stock, or if there is more than one class, the class that has no preferences relative to the corporation's other classes of stock.

15. Preferred stock that has the right to share in dividends above the fixed amount or percentage that is preferred.

16. The difference between the par value of stock and the amount contributed by shareholders when the amount contributed is more than par value.

17. A preferred stock for which the right to receive dividends is forfeited in any year in which dividends are not declared.

18. A dividend to cumulative preferred stock which remains upaid after the date for payment called for in the articles of incorporation.

19. The amount a corporation must pay in addition to dividends in arrears if and when it exercises its right to retire a share of callable preferred stock.

20. An arbitrary value placed on a share of stock at the time the stock is authorized.

Problem IV

1. Organization costs are classified on the balance sheet as an ___*intangible*___ _____ asset. CICA Handbook recommends that organization costs should be written off over a period not to exceed ___*40*___ years of a corporation's life.

2. When stock is issued at a price above its par value, the difference between par and the price at which the stock is issued is called a ___*premium*___.

3. Because of limited liability of shareholders, corporation laws seek to protect ___*corporation*___ ___*creditors*___, with the protection resulting from making illegal the payment of any dividends that reduce shareholders' equity below ___*stated capital*___.

4. Advantages claimed for no-par stock are: (a) Total investment by the shareholders is recorded in a ___*single*___ ___*account*___. (b) Uninformed persons buying such stock are not misled as to the stock's worth by a ___*par value*___ printed on the certificates.

5. Corporation laws require separate accounts for shareholders equity for ___*contributed capital*___ and for ___*retained earnings*___.

6. A preferred stock is so called because of the preferences granted its owners. The two most common preferences are a preference as to ___*paying dividends and any dividends in arrears in advance of common shareholders*___ and a preference ___*to allocate assets before common shareholders if the corporation is to liquidate*___.

7. In addition to its separate legal existence, other advantages of a corporation as a form of business organization are ___*lack of shareholders limited liability, shareholders do not have mutual relationship, unlimited corp life, easy collection of capital, ease of transferring ownership right*___.

8. A corporation is said to be a separate legal entity; this phrase means that in a legal sense a corporation is ___*separated from its shareholders as an legal entity and has the right as a person to direct its business*___.

Problem V

The shareholders' equity section from Sonar Corporation's balance sheet shows the following:

CAPITAL STOCK AND RETAINED EARNINGS

Preferred stock, $8, cumulative and nonparticipating, issued and outstanding 2,000 shares	$200,000	
Common stock, no par value, issued and outstanding 25,000 shares	250,000	
Total contributed capital		$450,000
Retained earnings		230,000
Total shareholders' equity		$680,000

1. If there are no dividends in arrears, the book value per share of the corporation's preferred stock is $ _100_ , and the book value per share of its common stock is $ _19.2_ .

2. If a total of two years' dividends are in arrears on the preferred stock, the book value per share of the preferred stock is $ _116_ , and the book value per share of its common stock is $ _17.92_ .

Problem VI

A corporation accepted subscriptions to 25,000 shares of its no par value common stock at $5.50 per share. The subscription contracts called for a 20% down payment with the balance in 30 days. The explanations for several entries involving this stock follow. Complete the entries.

DATE		ACCOUNT TITLES AND EXPLANATION	P.R.	DEBIT	CREDIT
Sept.	5	Common Stock Receivable		137500.00	
		Common Stock Subscribed			137500.00
		Accepted subscriptions to 25,000 shares of common stock at $5.50 per share.			
	5	Cash		27500.00	
		Common Stock Receivable			27500.00
		Received $27,500 from the common stock subscribers as down payments on their shares.			
Oct.	5	Cash		110000.00	
		Common Stock Receivable			110000.00
		Received payment in full of the balance due on the September 5 common stock subscriptions.			
	5	Common Stock Subscribed		137500.00	
		Common Stock			137500.00
		Issued the common stock of the fully paid subscribers			

Solutions for Chapter 15

Problem I

1.	T	5.	F
2.	T	6.	T
3.	T	7.	F
4.	F		

Problem II

1. D
2. A
3. C
4. E
5. B

Problem III

Book value of a share of stock	......	10
Call price of preferred stock	...	4 or 19
Callable preferred stock	....	2
Common stock	....	14
Common Stock Subscribed	....	7
Cumulative preferred stock	....	9
Dividend in arrears	....	18
Financial leverage	....	12
Noncumulative preferred stock	......	17
No-par stock	....	5
Organization costs	....	8

Par value	....	20
Participating preferred stock	....	15
Preemptive right	....	3
Preferred stock	....	11
Premium on stock	....	16
Proxy	....	6
Redemption value of preferred stock	....	19
Stated value of no-par stock	....	1
Stock subscription	....	13

Problem IV

1. intangible, forty

2. premium

3. corporation creditors, stated capital

4. (a) single account, (b) par value

5. contributed capital, retained earnings

6. the payment of dividends, in the distribution of assets if the corporation is liquidated

7. lack of shareholder liability, ease of transferring ownership rights, continuity of life, no mutual agency, and ease of capital asssembly

8. an individual body, separate and distinct from its shareholders

Problem V

1. $100, $19.20
2. $116, $17.92

Problem VI

			Debit	Credit
Sept.	5	Subscriptions Receivable, Common Stock	137,500.00	
		Common Stock Subscribed		137,500.00
	5	Cash	27,500.00	
		Subscriptions Receivable, Common Stock		27,500.00
Oct.	5	Cash	110,000.00	
		Subscriptions Receivable, Common Stock		110,000.00
	5	Common Stock Subscribed	137,500.00	
		Common Stock		137,500.00

312

16

Additional Corporate Transactions; Reporting Income and Retained Earnings; Earnings per Share

After studying Chapter 16, you should be able to:

1. Record cash dividends, stock dividends, and stock splits and explain their effects on the assets and shareholders' equity of a corporation.

2. Record purchases and sales of treasury stock and retirements of stock and describe their effects on shareholders' equity.

3. Describe restrictions and appropriations of retained earnings and the disclosure of such items in the financial statements.

4. Explain how the income effects of discontinued operations, extraordinary items, changes in accounting principles, and prior period adjustments are reported.

5. Calculate earnings per share for companies with simple capital structures and explain the difference between primary and fully diluted earnings per share.

6. Define or explain the words and phrases listed in the chapter Glossary.

Topical Outline

I. Dividends, retained earnings, and contributed capital

    A. Cash dividend—reduces in equal amounts both cash and shareholders' equity. In order to pay a cash dividend:

        1. A corporation (in most jurisdictions) must have retained earnings,

        2. A corporation must also have sufficient cash and

        3. A corporation must meet the solvency test.

    B. Generally, contributed capital may not be returned to shareholders as dividends. However, in some jurisdictions, dividends may be debited or charged to certain contributed capital accounts.

    C. Stock dividend—a distribution of a corporation's own stock to its shareholders without any consideration being received in return from the shareholders.

        1. When a common stock dividend is declared retained earnings are capitalized (debit to retained earnings and credit to stated capital).

        2. The amount of retained earnings to be capitalized is dependent on the jurisdiction, for example, market value of shares issued as a stock dividend (federal incorporation) an amount decided by the board of directors (Ontario incorporation).

II. Stock splits—involve calling in the outstanding shares of stock and replacing them with a larger number of shares.

    A. Usual purpose is to reduce the market price of the stock to facilitate trading in the stock.

    B. In recording a stock split only a memorandum entry is required.

    C. The total stated value of outstanding shares does not change, and retained earnings is not capitalized.

III. Treasury stock—a corporation's own stock that has been issued and then reacquired.

    A. When a corporation purchases its own stock, it reduces in equal amounts both its assets and its shareholders' equity.

    B. Retained earnings equal to the cost of treasury stock are restricted.

    C. Reissuing treasury stock

        1. When sold above cost, the amount received in excess of cost is credited to Contributed Capital, Treasury Stock Transactions.

        2. When sold below cost, the "loss" is debited to Contributed Capital, Treasury Stock Transactions, to the extent a balance exists in that account. Any remaining loss is debited to Retained Earnings.

    D. Retirement of stock

        1. When stock is purchased for retirement, all contributed capital amounts related to the shares being retired are removed from the accounts.

        2. If the price paid is less than the contributed capital amounts related to the purchased shares, the difference should be credited to contributed capital.

        3. If the price paid is more than the contributed capital amounts related to the purchased shares, the difference should be debited to Retained Earnings.

IV. Income and loss items not directly related to continuing operations

    A. Discontinued operations

        1. Gains or losses from operating and disposing of a discontinued business segment should be reported in a separate section of the income statement.

2. Income or loss from operating the segment is separated from the gain or loss on disposal.
3. Each gain or loss is reported net of related income tax effects.

B. Extraordinary items

1. Must be both unusual and infrequent (not typical of the normal business activities of the enterprise).
2. Reported (net of related income taxes) below discontinued operations.
3. Items that are unusual or infrequent but do not meet the *CICA Handbook* criteria for classification as extraordinary are reported in the income statement within the category of income from continuing operations.

C. Changes in accounting policy

1. Notwithstanding the consistency principle, changes in accounting principles are acceptable if justified as improvements in financial reporting.
2. Cumulative effect on prior years' incomes is reported (net of taxes) as restatement of retained earnings. Comparative statements are restated.

D. Prior period adjustments

1. Essentially limited to settlement of lawsuits arising in prior periods and one-time income tax settlement.
2. Reported in statement of retained earnings as a restatement of the beginning retained earnings balance. Comparative statements are restated.

V. Statement of changes in shareholders' equity

A. Used by some corporations instead of a statement of retained earnings.
B. The beginning and ending balances of each shareholders' equity account are reconciled by listing all changes that occurred during the year.

VI. Earnings per share—one of the most commonly reported figures in the financial press.

A. For companies with simple capital structures, it is calculated as net income (minus preferred dividend requirements, if the company has nonconvertible preferred shares outstanding) divided by the weighted-average number of common shares outstanding.
B. For companies with complex capital structures, two types of earnings per share calculations often are required:

1. Basic earnings per share.
2. Fully diluted earnings per share.

C. Generally accepted accounting principles require that earnings per share data be shown on the face of published income statements or in the notes cross-referenced to the income statement for:

1. Income from continuing operations.
2. Extraordinary items.
3. Net income.

Problem I

The following statements are either true or false. Place a (T) in the parentheses before each true statement and an (F) before each false statement.

1. (F) A stock dividend should be recorded by capitalizing retained earnings equal to the book value of the stock to be distributed.

2. (✓) In most jurisdictions, a corporation must have current net income in order to pay a cash dividend.

3. (T) Since a declared stock dividend is "payable" in stock rather than in assets, it is not a liability of its issuing corporation.

4. (T) A stock split has no effect on total shareholders' equity, the equities of the individual shareholders, or on the balances of any of the contributed capital or retained earnings accounts.

5. (F) Appropriations of retained earnings reduce total retained earnings.

6. (F) In most jurisdictions a corporation may purchase treasury stock only to the extent of its retained earnings available for dividends.

7. (T) The appropriation of retained earnings sets aside cash or funds for a special purpose.

8. (T) A cash dividend reduces a corporation's cash and its shareholders' equity, but a stock dividend does not affect either cash or total shareholders' equity.

9. (T) The cumulative effect on prior years' incomes of a change in accounting principle is reported on the statement of retained earnings.

10. (T) For companies with simple capital structures, earnings per share is calculated by dividing net income minus preferred dividends, if any, by the weighted-average number of common shares outstanding.

Problem II

You are given several words, phrases or numbers to choose from in completing each of the following statements or in answering the following questions. In each case select the one that best completes the statement or answers the question and place its letter in the answer space provided.

____C____ 1. Bartlett Company had 20,000 shares of common stock outstanding at the beginning of 1991. On April 1, the company sold 20,000 additional shares of its common stock, and on November 1 the company declared a 2 for 1 stock split. For the purpose of determining earnings per share, calculate the weighted-average number of common shares outstanding during the year.

a. 60,000.00.
b. 80,000.00.
c. 70,000.00.
d. 41,666.66.
e. 83,333.33.

2. The Poseidon Company issued $10 par value common stock for $15, with the premium being credited to Contributed Capital in Excess of Par Value, Common Stock. Later, Poseidon purchased and retired 500 shares of this stock at a cost of $17. The entry to record the retirement is as follows:

a.
Common Stock	5,000.00	
Contributed Capital in Excess of Par Value, Common Stock	2,500.00	
Retained Earnings	1,000.00	
Cash		8,500.00

b.
Common Stock	5,000.00	
Contributed Capital in Excess of Par Value, Common Stock	2,500.00	
Contributed Capital from the Retirement of Common Stock	1,000.00	
Cash		8,500.00

c.
Common Stock	5,000.00	
Contributed Capital in Excess of Par Value, Common Stock	3,500.00	
Cash		8,500.00

d.
Common Stock	5,000.00	
Contributed Capital in Excess of Par Value, Common Stock	2,500.00	
Cash		6,500.00
Contributed Capital from the Retirement of Common Stock		1,000.00

e.
Treasury Stock	8,500.00	
Cash		8,500.00

3. Captan Company purchased a depreciable asset that cost $500,000 (no salvage value) and depreciated the asset for one year based on straight-line depreciation and a five-year life. After one year, the company decided to switch from straight-line depreciation to declining-balance depreciation at twice the straight-line rate. Calculate (a) the amount of depreciation expense to be reported in the current year (year 2) and (b) the cumulative effect of the change in accounting principle.

a. (a) $200,000; (b) $120,000.
b. (a) $200,000; (b) $100,000.
c. (a) $120,000; (b) $100,000.
d. (a) $120,000; (b) $ 72,000.
e. (a) $200,000; (b) $ 60,000.

4. Earnings per share statistics that are calculated as if all dilutive securities had already been converted are called:

a. basic earnings per share.
b. secured earnings per share.
c. simple earnings per share.
d. convertible earnings per share.
e. fully diluted earnings per share.

5. The statement of changes in shareholders' equity is:

a. a financial statement that discloses the inflows and outflows of cash during the period.
b. a financial report showing the assets, liabilities, and equity of an enterprise on a specific date.

c. a financial statement showing revenues earned by a business, the expenses incurred in earning the revenues, and the resulting net income or net loss.

d. a financial statement that reconciles the beginning and ending balances of each shareholders' equity account by listing all changes that occurred during the year.

e. None of the above.

Problem III

Many of the important ideas and concepts discussed in Chapter 16 are reflected in the following list of key terms. Test your understanding of these terms by matching the appropriate definitions with the terms. Record the number identifying the most appropriate definition in the blank space next to each term.

_____8_____ Antidilutive securities

_____13_____ Appropriated retained earnings

_____2_____ Changes in accounting estimates

_____15_____ Complex capital structure

_____X_____ Dilutive securities

_____18_____ Earned surplus

_____11_____ Earnings per share

_____4_____ Extraordinary gain or loss

_____20_____ Fully diluted earnings per share

4 X 17 *not typical* Atypical gain or loss

_____3_____ Liquidating dividends

_____10_____ Basic earnings per share

_____14_____ Prior period adjustments

_____6_____ Restricted retained earnings

_____16_____ Segment of a business

_____9_____ Simple capital structure

_____1_____ Statement of changes in shareholders' equity

_____19_____ Stock dividend

_____X_____ Stock split

_____12_____ Treasury stock

1. A financial statement that reconciles the beginning and ending balances of each shareholders' equity account by listing all changes that occurred during the year.

2. Adjustments to previously made assumptions about the future such as salvage values and the length of useful lives of buildings and equipment.

3. Distributions of corporate assets to shareholders which are charged to contributed capital accounts, therefore representing amounts that had been originally contributed by the shareholders.

4. A gain or loss that is not typical of the normal activities of the business.

5. Convertible securities the assumed conversion of which would have the effect of decreasing earnings per share.

6. Retained earnings that are not available for dividends because of law or binding contract.

7. The act of a corporation to call in its stock and issue more than one new share in the place of each share previously outstanding.

8. Convertible securities the assumed conversion of which have the effect of increasing earnings per share.

9. A capital structure that does not include any rights or options to purchase common shares or any securities that are convertible into common stock.

10. Earnings per share statistics that are calculated for outstanding common stock.

11. The amount of net income (or components of income) that accrues to common shares divided by the weighted-average number of common shares outstanding.

12. Issued stock that was reacquired and is currently held by the issuing corporation.

13. Retained earnings voluntarily earmarked for a special use as a way of informing shareholders that assets from earnings equal to the appropriations are not available for dividends.

14. Items that are reported in the current statement of retained earnings as corrections to the beginning retained earnings balance.

15. A capital structure that includes outstanding rights or options to purchase common stock or securities that are convertible into common stock.

16. Operations of a company that involve a particular line of business or class of customer, providing the assets, activities, and financial results of the operations can be distinguished from other parts of the business.

17. A gain or loss that is not expected to occur again, given the operating environment of the business.

18. A synonym for retained earnings, no longer in general use.

19. A distribution by a corporation of shares of its own stock to its shareholders without any considerations being received in return and accompanied by capitalization of retained earnings.

20. Earnings per share statistics that are calculated as if all dilutive securities had already been converted.

Problem IV

Complete the following by filling in the blanks.

1. When a corporation purchases treasury stock, a portion of its retained earnings equal to the cost of the treasury stock becomes _____ restricted _____ and unavailable for _____ cash dividend _____.

2. If treasury stock is reissued at a price above cost, the amount received in excess of cost is credited to _____ Contributed capital, treasury stock transactions _____. If treasury stock is sold below cost the difference between cost and the sale price is debited to either Cntrb. Cap, Tre Stock (Tran actions) or _____ Retained earnings _____.

3. A stock dividend enables a corporation to give its shareholders some evidence of their interest in its retained earnings without reducing the corporation's _____ assets cash or other assets and total shareholders' equity _____.

4. Retained earnings are appropriated or "earmarked" as a means of informing the shareholders that _____ the appropriated Ret. Ear. are not going to _____ for declared dividends.

5. Issued stock that has been reacquired by the issuing corporation is called _treasury stock_
_____.

6. If the book value of a share of common stock before the declaration and distribution of a 20% stock dividend was $90, the declaration and distribution of the dividend changed the book value of $___75___.

7. If a corporation has sufficient retained earnings to pay a dividend, it must also have sufficient _Cash funds_ _for creditors_ before it pays that dividend.

8. Changes in accounting estimates ___are not___ (are, are not) prior period adjustments.

9. The results of discontinued operations are separated from the results of other activities on the income statement in order to _provide readers the actual financial condition of continued operations._

10. Earnings per share statistics that are calculated as if all dilutive securities had already been converted are called _fully diluted earnings per share_.

Problem V

On August 10 Mainline Corporation purchased for cash 2,000 shares of its own no par value common stock at $27 per share. On October 3 it sold 1,000 of the shares at $30 per share. Complete the entries below to record the purchase and sale of the stock.

DATE		ACCOUNT TITLES AND EXPLANATION	P.R.	DEBIT	CREDIT
Aug.	10	Treasury stock, common		54,000.00	
		Cash			14,000.00
		Purchased 2,000 shares of treasury stock.			
Oct.	3	Cash		30,000.00	
		Contributed Capital, Treasury Stock Transaction			3,000.00
		~~Common Stock~~ Treasury stock, Com.			27,000.00
		Sold 1,000 shares of treasury stock.			

320

Problem VI

The May 31 balance sheet of Eastwood Corporation carried the following shareholders' equity section:

Shareholders' Equity

Common stock, no par value, 25,000 shares authorized, 20,000 shares issued	$200,000
Retained earnings	44,000
Total contributed and retained capital	$244,000

244,000
20,000

On the balance sheet date, with the common stock selling at $12 per share, the corporation's board of directors voted a 2,000-share stock dividend distributable on June 30 to the June 20 shareholders of record. (Assume market value is capitalized).

1. In the space below give without explanations the entries to record the declaration and distribution of the dividend.

DATE		ACCOUNT TITLES AND EXPLANATION	P.R.	DEBIT	CREDIT
1993 May	31	Stock Dividends Declared		24,000.00	
		Common Stock Dividend Distributable			24,000.00
June	30	Common Stock Dividend Distributable		24,000.00	
		Common Stock			24,000.00

2. Harold Jax owned 2,000 shares of the corporation's common stock before the declaration and distribution of the stock dividend; as a result, his portion of the dividend was 200 shares.

The total book value of Jax's 2,000 shares before the dividend was $ 24,400;

the total book value of his shares after the dividend was $ 24,400; consequently,

Jax gained $ 0 in the book value of his interest in the corporation.

legal share

Problem VII

Retained earnings and shares issued and outstanding for Endel Corporation are as follows:

	Retained Earnings	Shares Issued & Outstanding
December 31, 1990	$475,000	35,000
December 31, 1991	$447,000	38,500

On April 3, 1991, the board of directors declared a $0.775 per share dividend on the outstanding stock. On August 7, while the stock was selling for $17.50 per share, the corporation declared a 10% stock dividend on the outstanding shares to be issued on November 7. Under the assumption that there were no transactions affecting retained earnings other than the ones given, determine the 1991 net income of Endel Corporation. (Assume market value of shares issued is capitalized.)

348,787.5

29,837.5
(27,375)

37,212.5

Problem VIII

Explain where each of the following items should appear in the financial statements of Odyssey Corporation.

1) The company maintains a stock investment portfolio as part of its business activities to enhance earnings. This year, for the first time in seven years, it sold stock for a gain of $2,700.

2) After depreciating equipment for three years based on an expected six-year life, the company decided this year that the value of the equipment would last five more years. As a result, the depreciation for the current year is $18,000 instead of $30,000.

1) profit 2,700   Income Statement

2) ~~Asset~~ asset
   Accumulated   Bal. Sheet
   depreciation
       18,000

Solutions for Chapter 16

Problem I

1.	F	6. T
2.	F	7. F
3.	T	8. T
4.	T	9. T
5.	F	10. T

Problem II

1. C
2. A
3. C
4. E
5. D

Problem III

Antidilutive securities	8	Basic earnings per share	10
Appropriated retained earnings	13	Prior period adjustments	14
Changes in accounting estimates	2	Restricted retained earnings	6
Complex capital structure	15	Segment of a business	16
Dilutive securities	5	Simple capital structure	9
Earned surplus	18	Statement of changes in shareholders' equity	1
Earnings per share	11		
Extraordinary gain or loss	4	Stock dividend	19
Fully diluted earnings per share	20	Stock split	7
Atypical gain or loss	4	Treasury stock	12
Liquidating dividends	3		

Problem IV

1. restricted, dividends

2. Contributed Capital, Treasury Stock Transactions; Contributed Capital, Treasury Stock Transactions; Retained Earnings

3. cash or other assets

4. assets equal in amount to the appropriation will not be paid out in dividends

5. treasury stock

6. 75

7. cash

8. are not

9. allow statement readers to better evaluate and judge the continuing operations of the business

10. fully diluted earnings per share

Problem V

Aug. 10	Treasury Stock, Common	54,000.00	
	Cash		54,000.00
Oct. 3	Cash	30,000.00	
	Treasury Stock, Common		27,000.00
	Contributed Capital, Treasury Stock Transactions		3,000.00

Problem VI

1.

May 31	Stock Dividends Declared	24,000.00	
	Common Stock Dividend Distributable		24,000.00
June 30	Common Stock Dividend Distributable	24,000.00	
	Common Stock		24,000.00

2. 200; $24,400; $24,400; $0

Problem VII

Retained earnings as of December 31, 1990		$475,000
Reductions in retained earnings due to transactions:		
Dividends declared:		
April 3, on 35,000 shares	$27,125	
Retained earnings capitalized in stock dividend	61,250	
Total reductions		88,375
Retained earnings balance before transfer of net income from Income Summary account		$386,625
Retained earnings, December 31, 1991, after transfer of net income from Income Summary account		$447,000
Deduct retained earnings balance before transfer of net income from Income Summary account		386,625
Net income		$ 60,375

Problem VIII

1) This gain is neither atypical nor infrequent, and it should be reported in the income statement as part of income from continuing operations.

2) This change from an expected useful life of six to eight years is a change in an accounting estimate. The $18,000 should be reported in the income statement as an expense in the income from continuing operations section.

17 Bonds As Liabilities and Investments

After studying Chapter 17, you should be able to:

1. Describe the various characteristics of differing bond issues and prepare entries to record bonds that are issued between interest dates.

2. Calculate the price of a bond issue that sells at a discount, and prepare entries to account for bonds issued at a discount.

3. Prepare entries to account for bonds issued at a premium.

4. Explain the purpose and operation of a bond sinking fund and prepare entries for sinking fund operations and for the retirement of bonds.

5. Describe the procedures used to account for investments in bonds.

6. Define or explain the words and phrases listed in the chapter Glossary.

Topical Outline

I. Bonds

  A. Difference between shares and bonds

    1. A share of stock represents an equity or ownership right in a corporation. (Shareholders are owners.)

    2. A bond represents a debt or liability of the corporation issuing the bond. (Bondholders are creditors.)

  B. Reasons for issuing bonds

    1. Issuance of bonds instead of shares often results in increased earnings for common shareholders.

    2. Bond interest must be paid whether or not there are earnings, but interest payments are expenses and are tax-deductible.

  C. Rights of bondholders

    1. To receive periodic interest payments.

    2. To receive the face value of the bonds when they mature.

  D. Types of bonds

    1. Serial bonds—an issue of bonds with varying maturity dates, so that the entire bond issue is repaid in installments over a period of years.

    2. Sinking fund bonds—bonds that require the issuing corporation to establish during the time the bonds are outstanding a fund that is used to retire the bonds at maturity.

    3. Registered bonds—ownership is recorded with the issuing corporation.

    4. Coupon bonds—have interest coupons that must be presented to receive interest payments.

    5. Debentures—unsecured bonds.

  E. Issuing bonds

    1. Issuing corporation usually sells bonds to an investment firm (the underwriter) which resells bonds to the public.

    2. Bond indenture—written, legal document that states the rights and obligations of the issuing company and the bondholders.

    3. A trustee (usually bank or trust company) oversees the fulfillment of contract obligation to the bondholders.

    4. Contract rate of bond interest—rate of interest applied to the par value (face amount) of bonds to determine annual cash payment to bondholders.

    5. Market rate of bond interest—interest rate that a corporation is willing to pay and investors are willing to take for use of their money to buy that corporation's bonds.

      a. Bond discount—a bond will sell for an amount less than face value if the market rate of bond interest is greater than the contract rate of bond interest.

      b. Bond premium—a bond will sell for an amount greater than face value if the market rate of bond interest is less than the contract rate of bond interest.

    6. Bonds sold between interest dates—interest that has accrued on the bonds since the previous interest payment date is customarily charged and collected from purchasers.

  F. Accounting for bonds after issuance

    1. Bond discount or bond premium must be amortized.

      a. Straight-line method—equal portion of the discount or premium is amortized each period.

      b.   Interest method—amount of discount or premium amortized changes each period.

   2.   End-of-accounting-period adjustments for accrued interest must be made.

G. Additional features of bonds

   1.   Callable bonds—may be redeemed at the issuing corporation's option, usually upon the payment of a redemption premium. (Not all bonds have this provision.)

   2.   Bond sinking fund—to provide investors with greater security, a corporation may agree to make periodic cash deposits with a sinking fund trustee. Fund is used to pay bondholders when the bonds become due.

H. Investments in bonds

   1.   Purchasers of bonds may not hold them to maturity, but may sell them to other investors.

   2.   Purchasers record bonds at cost, including any brokerage fees.

   3.   Any discount or premium on bonds held as long-term investments should be amortized using procedures similar to those for bonds payable.

   4.   A bond investment is shown as a current asset at cost (with no discount or premium amortization) only if the bonds qualify as short-term, temporary investments.

II. Mortgages

A. Bonds or notes payable are either secured or unsecured.

B. Many notes payable and bond issues are secured by a mortgage.

C. Mortgage—the legal agreement that helps protect a lender by giving the lender the right to be paid from the cash proceeds from the sale of the borrower's mortgaged assets, if the borrower fails to make payments required by a note payable or bond indenture.

D. Terms of mortgage are written in a separate legal document—a mortgage contract—which normally grants the lender (the mortgage holder) the right to foreclose if the borrower fails to pay.

Problem I

The following statements are either true or false. Place a (T) in the parentheses before each true statement and an (F) before each false statement.

1. ( ) Bondholders do not share in either management or net income of the issuing corporation.

2. ( ) Bondholders are creditors of the issuing corporation.

3. ( ) If bonds are sold at par value, the entry to record the sale has a debit to Cash and a credit to Bonds Payable.

4. ( ) Investors will be willing to pay more than par (buy at a premium) for bonds when the market rate of interest is higher than the contract rate of interest.

5. ( ) To determine the price of bonds, the present value of the future cash flows is calculated by discounting the amounts to be received in the future at the contract rate of interest.

6. ( ) If the market rate of interest is 12%, the contract rate of a bond must be set at 12%.

7. ( ) The straight-line method of amortizing bond premium allocates an equal portion of the premium to each interest period.

8. ( ) To calculate the amount of interest expense each period using the interest method, the beginning-of-period carrying amount of the bonds must be multiplied by the market rate of interest that was used to determine the proceeds from issuing the bonds.

9. ( ) When the straight-line method is used to amortize bond premium or bond discount, interest expense as a percentage of carrying amount is the same each period the bonds are outstanding.

10. ( ) Callable bonds are bonds that can be redeemed at the option of the investor.

11. ( ) Sinking fund earnings must be reported in the income statement of the issuing corporation.

Problem II

You are given several words, phrases or numbers to choose from in completing each of the following statements or in answering the following questions. In each case select the one that best completes the statement or answers the question and place its letter in the answer space provided.

_____ 1. A legal document that states the rights of the lender and the obligations of the borrower with respect to assets that are pledged as security for a bond or note payable is a:

    a. registered bond.
    b. bond certificate.
    c. bond indenture.
    d. mortgage contract.
    e. debenture.

_____ 2. How is the interest expense for each period calculated when the interest method is used to amortize bond discount?

    a. The par value of the bonds is multiplied by the contract rate of bond interest.
    b. The par value of the bonds is multiplied by the market rate of bond interest which applied to the bonds at the time the bonds were issued.
    c. The beginning-of-period carrying amount of the bonds is multiplied by the market rate of bond interest which applied to the bonds at the time the bonds were issued.

d. The beginning-of-period carrying amount of the bonds is multiplied by the contract rate of bond interest.

e. The total amount of discount at the time of issue is divided by the number of periods to maturity and added to the cash payment of interest.

_____ 3. On June 30, 1991, the DEF Corporation sold bonds with a face value of $100,000. The contract rate of bond interest was 9% with interest payments on December 31 and June 30. The bonds mature in 10 years. When the bonds were sold, the market rate of bond interest was 12%. How much money did the DEF Corporation receive when it sold the bonds? (Use the present value tables in Chapter 12 of the text and round amounts to the nearest whole dollar.)

a. $119,252.
b. $110,042.
c. $100,000.
d. $ 82,795.
e. $ 83,052.

_____ 4. What is the entry to record the payment of interest on December 31, 1991, for DEF Corporation of question 3? DEF uses the interest method of amortizing bond discount or premium.

a. Interest Expense 4,500.00
      Cash 4,500.00
b. Interest Expense 4,968.00
      Cash 4,500.00
      Discount on Bonds Payable 468.00
c. Interest Expense 6,000.00
      Cash 6,000.00
d. Interest Expense 4,500.00
      Premium on Bonds Payable 1,500.00
      Cash 6,000.00
e. Interest Expense 4,500.00
      Cash 4,230.00
      Discount on Bonds Payable 270.00

_____ 5. A callable bond is:

a. a bond that is not registered and is made payable to whoever holds the bond.
b. a bond for which the name and address of the owner are recorded with the issuing corporation.
c. an issue of bonds that mature at different points in time so that the entire bond issue is repaid gradually over a period of years.
d. a bond that requires the issuing corporation to make deposits to a separate fund of assets during the life of the bonds for the purpose of repaying the bondholders at maturity.
e. a bond that may be redeemed or repaid before its maturity date at the option of the issuing corporation.

Problem III

Many of the important ideas and concepts discussed in Chapter 17 are reflected in the following list of key terms. Test your understanding of these terms by matching the appropriate definition with the terms. Record the number identifying the most appropriate definition in the blank space next to each term.

_____ Bearer bond

_____ Bond

_____ Bond indenture

_____ Bond sinking fund

_____ Callable bond

_____ Carrying amount of bonds payable

_____ Contract rate of bond interest

_____ Convertible bond

_____ Coupon bond

_____ Debenture

_____ Discount on bonds payable

_____ Face amount of a bond

_____ Interest method of amortizing bond discount or premium

_____ Market rate for bond interest

_____ Mortgage

_____ Mortgage contract

_____ Par value of a bond

_____ Premium on bonds payable

_____ Registered bond

_____ Serial bonds

_____ Sinking fund bonds

_____ Straight-line method of amortizing bond discount or premium

1. The contract between the issuing corporation and the bondholders that states the rights and obligations of both parties.

2. The difference between the par value of a bond and the price at which it is issued when issued at a price below par.

3. The interest rate that a corporation is willing to pay and investors are willing to take for the use of their money to buy that corporation's bonds.

4. A method that calculates interest expense by multiplying the beginning-of-period carrying value of the bonds by the market rate of interest at the date of issuance and then subtracts the cash payment of interest from interest expense to determine the periodic amortization of discount or premium.

5. A legal document that states the rights of the lender and the obligations of the borrower with respect to assets that are pledged as security for a bond or note payable.

6. A bond that is not registered and is made payable to whoever holds the bond (the bearer).

7. The par value of bonds payable less any unamortized discount or plus any unamortized premium.

8. A legal agreement that helps protect a lender by giving the lender the right to be paid from the cash proceeds from the sale of specified assets that belong to the borrower.

9. The difference between the par value of a bond and the price at which it is issued when issued at a price above par.

10. Bonds that require the issuing corporation to make deposits to a separate fund of assets during the life of the bonds for the purpose of repaying the bondholders at maturity.

11. An issue of bonds that mature at different points in time so that the entire bond issue is repaid gradually over a period of years.

12. A bond that is issued with interest coupons attached to the bond certificate, so that as each interest payment date approaches, the bondholder detaches a coupon and submits it to the issuing corporation as a demand for payment.

13. A bond that may be redeemed or repaid before its maturity date at the option of the issuing corporation.

14. A rate of interest specified in the bond indenture as the rate that is applied to the par value of the bonds to determine the annual amount of cash payments to the bondholders.

15. The face amount of the bond, which is the amount the borrower agrees to repay at maturity and the amount on which interest payments are based.

16. An unsecured bond.

17. The bond's par value.

18. A method that allocates to each accounting period an equal amount of discount or premium.

19. A bond for which the name and address of the owner are recorded with the issuing corporation.

20. A long-term liability of a corporation or governmental unit, usually issued in denominations of $1,000, that requires periodic payments of interest and final payment of par value when it matures.

21. A separate pool of assets that is established by deposits from the issuing corporation of a bond issue and from earnings on investments of the assets, and which is established for the purpose of providing the cash to repay the bondholders when the bonds mature.

22. A bond that may be exchanged for shares of its issuing corporation's stock at the option of the bondholder.

Problem IV

Complete the following by filling in the blanks.

1. A bond sinking fund offers a measure of security to bondholders, since it is a fund of assets accumulated to

_____

_____.

2. Two important rights given to the owner of a bond are:

    (a) _____

    _____, and

    (b) _____

    _____.

3. A bond sinking fund would normally be shown in the section of the balance sheet entitled _____

    _____.

4. Often a corporation cannot obtain debt financing without providing security to the creditors by the issuance

    of a _____.

5. An advantage of securing capital through the sale of bonds as opposed to securing it through the sale of stock is that bondholders do not share in either _____ or _____.

6. When marketable bonds are purchased as a temporary investment, the bond investment appears on the balance sheet as a _____.

7. The rate of interest a corporation agrees to pay on a bond issue is called the _____ rate. This rate is applied to the _____ value of the bonds to determine the amount of interest that must be paid.

8. In the interest of the bondholders and as protection for the issuing corporation's financial position, a _____ may restrict the dividends a corporation may pay while its bonds are outstanding.

9. A disadvantage of securing capital through the sale of bonds is that the bondholders are _____ and must be paid whether or not there are earnings.

10. If a corporation offers to sell a bond issue on which the contract rate of interest is below the market rate, the bonds will sell at a _____; and if it offers to sell bonds on which the contract rate is above the market rate, the bonds will sell at a _____.

11. A $1,000 bond with a contract rate of bond interest at 9% would provide semiannual interest payments of $_____.

12. Bonds that may be redeemed at the issuing company's option are known as _____ bonds.

13. When a corporation sells bonds between interest dates, it collects accrued interest from the purchasers. As a result the corporation does not have to keep a record of the purchasers and the _____ on which they bought bonds, for it can pay a full period's interest to all purchasers for the period in which they bought bonds, and every purchaser receives the amount of interest he has _____ and gets back the accrued interest paid at the time of purchase.

14. The accounting procedure for dividing a discount and charging a fair share to each period in the life of the applicable bond issue is called _____ _____.

Problem V

On May 1, 1991, JJR Corporation purchased 125 $1,000, 9%, ten-year bonds dated December 31, 1990, at a price of 95 plus a $500 brokerage fee and accrued interest from LLB Co. as a short-term investment.

Make the journal entries to record the purchase of the bonds and to record the receipt of interest on June 30, 1991 (assuming interest is paid semiannually on June 30 and December 31).

DATE		ACCOUNT TITLES AND EXPLANATION	P.R.	DEBIT	CREDIT
1991 May	1	*Investment in LLB Co. Bonds*		*118850*	
		Interest Receivable		*4687.5*	
		Cash			*123832.5*
		Purchased 125 $1,000, 9%, ten-year bonds dated			
		December 31, 1990, at a price of 95 plus a $500			
		brokerage fee and accrued interest.			
June	30				
		To record receipt of interest on bonds purchased			
		May 1 from LLB Co.			

Problem VI

On December 15, 1990, Candida Corporation deposited with a trustee a bond indenture under which Candida would issue $1,000,000 of 10.2%, 20-year bonds dated December 31, 1990, and with interest payable each June 30 and December 31. The bonds were issued at par plus accrued interest on February 1, 1991.

1. Complete the 1991 entries for this bond issue.

DATE		ACCOUNT TITLES AND EXPLANATION	P.R.	DEBIT	CREDIT
1991 Feb.	1				
		Sold $1,000,000 of 10.2%, 20-year bonds at par plus one month's accrued interest.			
June	30				
		Paid the semiannual interest on the bonds.			
Dec.	31				
		Paid the semiannual interest on the bonds.			

2. Post to the T-account below the portions of the above entries that affect interest expense and then complete the statement that follows.

Interest Expense

Candida Corporation's 1991 income statement should show $_____ of interest expense and its 1992 income statement should show $_____ of interest expense.

Problem VII

On January 1, 1991, a day on which the market rate of interest for Bullock Company's bonds was 10%, Bullock Company sold bonds having a $100,000 par value, a five-year life, with interest to be paid semiannually at a 9% annual rate.

1. The buyer of these bonds received two rights: (a) the right to receive $_____ in interest at the end of each six-month interest period throughout the five-year life of the bond issue, and (b) the right to receive $_____ at the end of the bond issue's life.

334

2. To determine the present value of the rights received and to determine the price to pay for the rights, the buyer of the bonds should discount the rights at the _____% (semiannual) market rate for bond interest prevailing on the day of the purchase.

3. The calculations for determining the present value of the bond buyer's two rights, using the tables in Chapter 12 in the text are:

   Present value of $100,000 to be received _____

   periods hence, discounted at _____% per period

   ($100,000 × _____) .... $_____

   Present value of $_____ to be received

   periodically for _____ periods, discounted at

   _____% ($_____ × _____) .... _____

   Price to pay for the bonds .... $_____

4. Bullock Company's entry to record the sale of the bonds at their present value is:

DATE		ACCOUNT TITLES AND EXPLANATION	P.R.	DEBIT	CREDIT
1991 Jan.	1				
		Sold bonds at a discount.			

5. At the end of the first semiannual interest period Bullock Company calculated the number of dollars of interest to be paid its bondholders as follows:

   $_____ × _____% = $_____

6. The company then began its calculation of the amount of interest expense to be recorded for the first semiannual interest period and the amount of discount to be amortized by first determining the beginning-of-the-period carrying amount for the bonds with this calculation:

   $_____ − $_____ = $_____

7. Using the interest method, the company then calculated the amount of interest expense to be recorded at the end of the first semiannual interest period as follows:

   $_____ × _____% = $_____

8. Next, the company determined the amount of discount to be amortized with this calculation:

   $_____ − $_____ = $_____

9. After making these calculations, Bullock Company recorded the interest paid its bondholders and the discount amortized with this entry:

DATE		ACCOUNT TITLES AND EXPLANATION	P.R.	DEBIT	CREDIT
1991 June	30				
		Paid the semiannual interest on the bonds and			
		amortized a portion of the discount.			

Solutions for Chapter 17

Problem I

1. T	7. T
2. T	8. T
3. T	9. F
4. F	10. F
5. F	11. T
6. F	

Problem II

1. D
2. C
3. D
4. B
5. E

Problem III

Bearer bond	6
Bond	20
Bond indenture	1
Bond sinking fund	21
Callable bond	13
Carrying amount of bonds payable ..	7
Contract rate of bond interest	14
Convertible bond	22
Coupon bond	12
Debenture	16
Discount on bonds payable	2
Face amount of a bond ...... 17 or 15	

Interest method fo amortizing bond discount or premium	4
Market rate for bond interest	3
Mortgage	8
Mortgage contract	5
Par value of a bond	15
Premium on bonds payable	9
Registered bond	19
Serial bonds	11
Sinking fund bonds	10
Straight-line method of amortizing bond discount or premium	18

Problem IV

1. repay the bondholders at maturity

2. a) the right to receive periodic interest payments
   b) the right to receive the face amount of the bond when it matures

3. long-term investments

4. mortgage

5. management, net income

6. current asset

7. contract, par

8. bond indenture

9. creditors

10. discount, premium

11. $45

12. callable

13. dates, earned

14. amortizing a discount

Problem V

1991
May 1 Investment in LLB Co. Bonds 119,250.00
        Bond Interest Receivable 3,750.00
           Cash 123,000.00
        (125 × $1,000 × 95%) + $500 = $119,250
        $125,000 × 4.5% × 4/6 = $3,750

June 30 Cash 5,625.00
        Bond Interest Receivable 3,750.00
        Bond Interest Earned 1,875.00
        $125,000 × 4.5% = $5,625

Problem VI

1.
Feb. 1 Cash 1,008,500.00
        Interest Expense 8,500.00
        Bonds Payable 1,000,000.00
        ($1,000,000 × .102)/12 = $8,500

June 30 Interest Expense 51,000.00
        Cash 51,000.00
        ($1,000,000 × .102)/2 = $51,000

Dec. 31 Interest Expense 51,000.00
        Cash 51,000.00

2.

Interest Expense			
June 30	51,000.00	Feb. 1	8,500.00
Dec. 31	51,000.00		

$93,500, $102,000

Problem VII

1. (a) $4,500, (b) $100,000

2. 5

3. Present value of $100,000 to be received 10 periods hence,
    discounted at 5% per period ($100,000 × 0.6139) $61,390
    Present value of $4,500 to be received periodically for
    10 periods, discounted at 5% ($4,500 × 7.7217) .... 34,748 *
    Price to pay for the bonds .... $96,138 *

      * rounded to the nearest whole dollar

4. Jan. 1 Cash 96,138.00
        Discount on Bonds Payable 3,862.00
          Bonds Payable 100,000.00

5. $100,000 × 0.045 = $4,500

6. $100,000 − $3,862 = $96,138

7. $96,138 × 0.05 = $4,807 (rounded to the nearest whole dollar)

8. $4,807 − $4,500 = $307

9. June 30 Interest Expense 4,807.00
        Discount on Bonds Payable 307.00
        Cash 4,500.00

18

Statement of Changes in Financial Position (SCFP)

After studying Chapter 18, you should be able to:

1. Describe the information contained in an SCFP and classify the cash flows of a company as operating, investing, or financing activities.

2. Calculate cash inflows and outflows by inspecting the noncash account balances of a company and related information about its transactions.

3. Identify and report on the SCFP any simultaneous investing and financing transactions.

4. Prepare a working paper for a statement of changes in financial position.

5. Define or explain the words and phrases listed in the chapter Glossary.

Topical Outline

I. Content and design of the statement of changes in financial position (SCFP).

  A. Its purpose is to provide decision makers with information about a company's cash receipts and cash payments during a reporting period.

  B. The statement reconciles the beginning and ending balances of cash plus cash equivalents.

  C. A cash equivalent is a highly liquid, short-term investment that generally is readily convertible to known amounts of cash.

  D. There are three categories into which cash receipts and cash payments are classified:

    1. Cash flows from operating activities.
    2. Cash flows from investing activities.
    3. Cash flows from financing activities.

  E. Operating activities generally involve the production or purchase of merchandise and the sale of goods and services to customers. Operating activities also include administrative aspects of the business. The following items are classified as operating activities:

    1. Cash inflows such as cash receipts from customers, receipt of dividends, and receipt of interest.
    2. Cash outflows such as payments to suppliers for merchandise, to employees for wages, to creditors for interest, and to government for taxes.

  F. Investing activities basically involve the purchase or sale of long-term investments, plant assets, and other long-term productive assets. Also included are the purchase or sale of short-term investments which are not cash equivalents. Investing activities include:

    1. Cash inflows from selling productive assets (excluding merchandise), from collecting loan principal, from selling investments in debt and equity securities of other companies, and similar activities.
    2. Cash outflows for the purchase of productive assets, for the purchase of debt and equity securities of other companies, and for loans to other parties.

  G. Financing activities usually involve a company's transactions with its owners and long-term creditors. Financing activities also involve short-term cash borrowing, even if the cash is then used to buy merchandise. Financing activities include:

    1. Cash inflows from the sale of capital stock, the issuance of notes and bonds payable, and long-term and short-term borrowing.
    2. Cash outflows for dividend payments, the repayment of loans, notes, and bonds, and the purchase of treasury stock.

II. Noncash investing and financing activities

  A. Are reported as both an inflow and an outflow of cash in the appropriate sections of the SCFP.

  B. Include transactions that do not involve cash but may also include transactions that involve partial payments or receipts of cash.

  C. Examples include the conversion of debt to equity securities, the purchase of plant assets by issuing equity or debt securities, and the exchange of a noncash asset for another noncash asset.

III. Preparing an SCFP

  A. The reconciliation of net income and net cash provided (or used) by operating activities begins with the period's net income.

  B. Net income is adjusted to accomplish three purposes:

    1. To reflect the cash flow effects of increases or decreases in all noncash current asset and current liability account balances.

2. To exclude the income effects of noncash revenues and expenses.
3. To exclude from net income any gains and losses from investing and financing activities.

C. A working paper approach may be used to organize and analyze the information.

1. The working paper has four money columns.
2. Columns one and four contain the beginning and ending balances of each balance sheet account. Columns two and three are for reconciling the changes in each balance sheet account.
3. Separate sections on the working paper present *(a)* balance sheet items with debit balances; *(b)* balance sheet items with credit balances; *(c)* cash flows from operating activities, starting with net income; *(d)* cash flows from investing activities; and *(e)* cash flows from financing activities.
4. Information for sections *(c)–(e)* is developed in four steps in the Analysis of Changes columns:

   a. By adjusting net income for the changes in all noncash current asset and current liability account balances. This reconciles the changes in these accounts.
   b. By eliminating from net income the effects of all noncash revenues and expenses. This begins the reconciliation of noncurrent assets.
   c. By eliminating from net income any gains or losses from investing and financing activities. This involves the reconciliation of noncurrent assets and noncurrent liabilities and perhaps the recording of disclosures in sections *(c)–(e)*.
   d. By entering any remaining items, such as dividend payments, which are necessary to reconcile the changes in all balance sheet accounts.

Problem I

The following statements are either true or false. Place a (T) in the parentheses before each true statement and an (F) before each false statement.

1. (T) A statement of cash flows should explain the differences between the beginning and ending balances of cash and cash equivalents.

2. (T) Cash outflows to purchase items classified as cash equivalents are not shown on a statement of cash flows.

3. (F) A payment by a company in the form of a loan made to another party is an example of a financing activity.

4. (F) The Cash account of a company provides all of the information necessary to prepare a statement of cash flows.

5. (T) If a company purchases all merchandise for cash and the ending balance of Merchandise Inventory is unchanged from the beginning balance, then cost of goods sold equals the total cash payments for merchandise.

Problem II

You are given several words, phrases or numbers to choose from in completing each of the following statements or in answering the following questions. In each case select the one that best completes the statement or answers the question and place its letter in the answer space provided.

_____ e _____ 1. If a company purchases merchandise on account and there is some change in the Merchandise Inventory balance during a period, what calculations are necessary to calculate cash payments for merchandise?

   a. Purchases + Decrease (− Increase) in Merchandise Inventory.
   b. Cost of Goods Sold + Increase (− Decrease) in Merchandise Inventory.
   c. Purchases + Decrease (− Increase) in Accounts Payable.
   d. a and b.
   e. b and c.

_____ a _____ 2. Given the following T-account, determine the cash payment for interest.

Interest Payable		
7,000	12/31/89 Bal.	12,000
	Interest expense	8,000
	12/31/90 Bal.	13,000

   a. $ 7,000.
   b. $ 4,000.
   c. $ 8,000.
   d. $12,000.
   e. $20,000.

342

_d_ 3. Bat Company purchased a plant asset that cost $30,000 by borrowing $25,000 and paying the $5,000 balance in cash. What would be reported on the SCFP

    a. Cash outflow from investing activities: $5,000.
    b. Cash inflow from financing activities: $25,000.
    c. Cash outflow from investing activities: $30,000.
    d. A cash outflow from investing activities: $30,000; and a cash inflow from financing activities: $25,000.
    e. a and b only.

Problem III

Many of the important ideas and concepts discussed in Chapter 18 are reflected in the following list of key terms. Test your understanding of these terms by matching the appropriate definitions with the terms. Record the number identifying the most appropriate definition in the blank space next to each term.

_4_ Cash equivalent   _2_ Operating activities

_1_ Financing activities   _3_ Statement of changes in financial position

_5_ Investing activities

1. Transactions with the owners or long-term creditors of the business or that involve borrowing cash on a short-term basis.

2. Activities that involve the production or purchase of merchandise and the sale of goods and services to customers, including expenditures to administer the business.

3. A financial statement that reports the cash inflows and outflows for an accounting period, and that classifies those cash flows as operating activities, investing activities, and financing activities.

4. An investment that is readily convertible to a known amount of cash and that is sufficiently close to its maturity date so that its market value is relatively insensitive to interest rate changes.

5. Transactions that involve making and collecting loans or that involve purchasing and selling plant assets, other productive assets, or investments (other than cash equivalents).

Problem IV

Opposite each transaction, place an "X" in the box below the caption that best describes its disclosure category on an SCFP in the case of noncash investing and financing activities.

Transaction	Operating Activity	Investing Activity	Financing Activity	Noncash Investing & Financing Activity
1. Paid wages and salaries.	X			
2. Cash sale of used equipment.		X		
3. Received a cash dividend.	X		X	
4. Issued a long-term bond payable for cash.			X	
5. Cash sale of merchandise.	X			
6. Purchased land in exchange for common stock.				X
7. Paid a cash dividend.			X	
8. Paid interest expense.	X			
9. Purchased shares in another company for cash.		X		
10. Repaid a six-month note payable.			X	

Problem V

Analyze the information presented in each question below and determine the missing amounts.

1. Accounts receivable decreased from $25,000 at the beginning of the period to $18,000 at the end of the period. Sales revenue was $280,000. Assume all sales were on account. There were no uncollectible accounts written off during the period. How much cash was collected from customers during the period? _____ 262,000

2. Merchandise inventory increased from $90,000 at the beginning of the period to $100,000 at the end of the period. Cost of goods sold was $160,000. How much merchandise inventory was purchased during the period? _____ 170,000

3. The Accounts Payable balance decreased during the period from $30,000 to $26,000. Disregard your answer to question 2 and assume purchases of merchandise during the period totaled $120,000. How much cash was paid to merchandise suppliers during the period? _____

4. The balance of the Accumulated Depreciation account increased during the period from $200,000 to $220,000. Also, machinery originally costing $10,000 with accumulated depreciation of $8,000 was sold during the period. What was the amount of the period's depreciation expense? _____ 28,000

5. Refer back to question 1. Instead of assuming all sales revenues of $280,000 were on account, assume cash sales totaled $100,000 and credit sales totaled $180,000. How much cash was collected from customers during the period? _____

344

Problem VI

Iker Company's 1990 and 1989 balance sheets are presented below along with its 1990 income statement.

IKER COMPANY
Balance Sheet
December 31, 1990, and 1989

Assets

	1990		1989	
Cash		$ 8,000		$ 5,000
Accounts receivable		15,000		12,000
Merchandise inventory		30,000		33,000
Equipment	$40,000		$38,000	
Less accumulated depreciation	16,000	24,000	18,000	20,000
Total assets		$77,000		$70,000

Liabilities and Stockholders' Equity

	1990	1989
Accounts payable	$21,000	$17,000
Accrued liabilities	4,000	5,000
Common stock	35,000	30,000
Retained earnings	17,000	18,000
Total liabilities and stockholders' equity ...	$77,000	$70,000

IKER COMPANY
Income Statement
For Year Ended December 31, 1990

Sales		$80,000
Cost of goods sold		30,000
Gross profit on sales		$50,000
Operating expenses	$20,000	
Depreciation expense	10,000	
Loss from sale of plant assets ...	5,000	35,000
Net income		$15,000

Additional information about the company's activities in 1990 is as follows:

1. Sold used equipment costing $20,000 with accumulated depreciation of $12,000 for $3,000 cash.

2. Purchased equipment costing $22,000 by paying $17,000 cash and issuing 1,000 shares of common stock.

3. Paid cash dividends of $16,000.

Required:

a. Reconcile Iker Company's net income with its net cash flows provided (or used) by operating activities.

NI   15,000
Add

Acc Rec   (3,000)
Mer Inv   3,000
Acc Pay   (4,000)
Acc exp: liq   (1,000)
Dep. exp.   10,000
Loss from sale of plant assets   5,000
Net cash prvd by operating act.   33,000

b. Below is Iker Company's 1990 working paper for an SCFP. Complete the working paper.

IKER COMPANY
Working Paper for Statement Changes in Financial Position
For Year Ended December 31, 1990

	DECEMBER 31, 1989	ANALYSIS OF CHANGES		DECEMBER 31, 1990
		DEBIT	CREDIT	
Balance sheet—Debits:				
Cash	5 0 0 0 00			8 0 0 0 00
Accounts receivable	1 2 0 0 0 00			1 5 0 0 0 00
Merchandise inventory	3 3 0 0 0 00			3 0 0 0 0 00
Equipment	3 8 0 0 0 00			4 0 0 0 0 00
	8 8 0 0 0 00			9 3 0 0 0 00
Balance sheet—Credits:				
Accumulated depreciation	1 8 0 0 0 00			1 6 0 0 0 00
Accounts payable	1 7 0 0 0 00			2 1 0 0 0 00
Accrued liabilities	5 0 0 0 00			4 0 0 0 00
Common stock	3 0 0 0 0 00			3 5 0 0 0 00
Retained earnings	1 8 0 0 0 00			1 7 0 0 0 00
	8 8 0 0 0 00			9 3 0 0 0 00
Income statement:				
Statement of changes in financial position:				
Operating activities:				
Investing activities:				
Financing activities:				

Solutions for Chapter 18

Problem I

1. T   4. F
2. T   5. T
3. F

Problem II

1. E
2. A
3. D

Problem III

Cash equivalent	. . . .	4	Operating activities	2
Financing activities	. . . .	1	Statement of changes in financial	
Investing activities	. . . .	5	position	3

Problem IV

Transaction	Classification
1. Paid wages and salaries	Operating activity
2. Cash sale of used equipment	Investing activity
3. Received a cash dividend	Operating activity
4. Issued a long-term bond payable for cash	Financing activity
5. Cash sale of merchandise	Operating activity
6. Purchased land in exchange for common stock	Noncash investing and financing activity
7. Paid a cash dividend	Financing activity
8. Paid interest expense	Operating activity
9. Purchased shares in another company for cash	Investing activity
10. Repaid a six-month note payable	Financing activity

Problem V

1. Cash collections from customers: $280,000 + $25,000 − $18,000 = $287,000

2. Merchandise purchases: $160,000 + $100,000 − $90,000 = $170,000

3. Cash payments for merchandise: $120,000 + $30,000 − $26,000 = $124,000

4. Depreciation expense: $220,000 − $200,000 + $8,000 = $28,000

5. Cash collections from customers: $100,000 + $180,000 + $25,000 − $18,000 = $287,000

Problem VI

a.

IKER COMPANY
Reconciliation of Net Income to Net Cash
Provided by Operating Activities
For Year Ended December 31, 1990

Net income		$15,000
Adjustments:		
Less increase in accounts receivable	$ (3,000)	
Add decrease in merchandise inventory	3,000	
Add increase in accounts payable	4,000	
Less decrease in accrued liabilities	(1,000)	
Add depreciation expense	10,000	
Add loss from sale of equipment	5,000	
Total adjustments		18,000
Net cash flows provided by operating activities		$33,000

Problem VI

b.

IKER COMPANY
Working Paper for Statement of Changes in Financial Position
For Year Ended December 31, 1990

	DECEMBER 31, 1989	ANALYSIS OF CHANGES DEBIT		ANALYSIS OF CHANGES CREDIT		DECEMBER 31, 1990
Balance sheet—Debits:						
Cash	5,000	(j)	3,000			8,000
Accounts receivable	12,000	(b)	3,000			15,000
Merchandise inventory	33,000			(c)	3,000	30,000
Equipment	38,000	(h1)	22,000	(g)	20,000	40,000
	88,000					93,000
Balance sheet—Credits:						
Accumulated depreciation	18,000	(g)	12,000	(f)	10,000	16,000
Accounts payable	17,000			(d)	4,000	21,000
Accrued liabilities	5,000	(e)	1,000			4,000
Common stock	30,000			(h2)	5,000	35,000
Retained earnings	18,000	(i)	16,000	(a)	15,000	17,000
	88,000					93,000
Operating activities:						
Net income		(a)	15,000			
Increase in accounts receivable				(b)	3,000	
Decrease in merchandise inventory		(c)	3,000			
Increase in accounts payable		(d)	4,000			
Decrease in accrued liabilities				(e)	1,000	
Depreciation expense		(f)	10,000			
Loss on sale of plant assets		(g)	5,000			
Investing activities:						
Proceeds from sale of plant assets		(g)	3,000			
Purchase of plant assets				(h1)	22,000	
Financing activities:						
Issue of common stock		(h2)	5,000			
Cash dividend				(i)	16,000	
Increase in cash				(j)	3,000	
			102,000		102,000	

19 Equity Investments, Consolidations, and International Operations

After studying Chapter 19, you should be able to:

1. State the criteria for classifying equity investments as current assets or as long-term investments.

2. Describe the circumstances under which the cost method, the equity method, and consolidated financial statements are used to account for long-term stock investments.

3. Prepare entries to account for long-term equity investments according to the cost method and the equity method and to reflect lower of cost or market.

4. Prepare consolidated balance sheets and explain how to report any excess of investment cost over book value or minority interests.

5. Describe the primary problems of accounting for international operations and prepare entries to account for sales to foreign customers.

6. Define or explain the words and phrases listed in the chapter Glossary.

Topical Outline

I. Equity investments

   A. Classifying investments

      1. Marketable equity securities—shares that are marketable and are capable of reasonably prompt liquidation, are temporary investments classified as current assets.

      2. Long-term investments—shares that are not marketable or are not intended to serve as ready sources of cash are classified as noncurrent assets.

   B. Accounting for equity investments

      1. Cost method—used when the investor does not have a significant influence over the investee. The investor usually owns less than 20 percent of the investee's voting stock.

         a. Investor records entire cost of stock as a debit to the investment account.
         b. Each stock must be reported at cost with market value disclosed.
         c. A loss in value, other than a temporary decline, is reported on the income statement as a loss on investment.

      2. Equity method—used when the investor has a significant influence (usually owns 20 percent or more of the voting stock of another corporation).

         a. Investor records purchase at cost (as under the cost method).
         b. The investor corporation's share of the investee corporation's earnings is reported as an increase in the Investment account and as Earnings from Investment.

II. Parent and subsidiary corporations

   A. Consolidated financial statements—prepared when one corporation (parent) controls another corporation (subsidiary). The parent must own more than 50 percent of the subsidiary's voting stock.

      1. A work sheet is used to effect the consolidation.
      2. Duplication in items is eliminated so that they are not counted twice (e.g., parent's Investment in Subsidiary and subsidiary's equity accounts).
      3. Minority interest—the portion of the subsidiary that is not owned by the parent.
      4. Excess of investment cost over book value—created when parent pays more than book value for its share of the subsidiary. This excess should be allocated to subsidiary's assets and liabilities so that they are restated as fair values. Any remaining excess is reported as "Goodwill from consolidation."

III. Accounting for international operations

   A. Multinational businesses are those having operations in several different countries.
   B. Foreign exchange rate—the price of one currency stated in terms of another currency.
   C. Sales and purchases denominated in a foreign currency.

      1. Companies making sales (or purchases) for which they receive (or pay) foreign currency must translate the transaction amounts into domestic currency.
      2. Receivables or payables stated in terms of foreign currencies result in exchange gains or losses as the foreign exchange rates fluctuate.

   D. Consolidated statements with foreign subsidiaries—prepared using foreign exchange rates to translate the financial statements of the foreign subsidiaries into domestic currency.

Problem I

The following statements are either true or false. Place a (T) in the parentheses before each true statement and an (F) before each false statement.

1. (T) All corporate stock is listed and traded on an organized stock exchange such as the Toronto Stock Exchange.

2. (T) A stock quoted at 14⅜ means $14.375 per share.

3. (T) Receipt of a stock dividend affects the per share cost of the old shares.

4. (T) Under the cost method, when an investment in stock is sold and the proceeds net of any sales commission differ from cost, a gain or loss must be recorded.

5. (T) At acquisition, the purchase of stock is recorded at cost regardless of which method is used to account for the investment.

6. (F) When a parent company buys a subsidiary's stock, the subsidiary's (net) assets and the parent company's investment in the subsidiary are both reported on a consolidated balance sheet.

7. (F) The excess of book value over cost of a purchased subsidiary should be allocated to reduce the balance sheet valuations of any overvalued assets.

8. (✓) A credit sale by a Canadian company to a foreign customer required to make payment in Canadian dollars may result in an exchange gain or loss to the Canadian company.

Problem II

You are given several words, phrases or numbers to choose from in completing each of the following statements or in answering the following questions. In each case select the one that best completes the statement or answers the question and place its letter in the answer space provided.

_____ 1. On December 31, Inferior Company had the following shareholders' equity:

Common stock, 10,000 shares
issued and outstanding $10,000
Retained earnings 7,500
Total shareholders' equity $17,500

Superior Company purchased 7,000 of Inferior Company's outstanding shares on this date (December 31) paying $2 per share. Related to the stock purchase, what is the excess of cost over book value on the date of purchase?

a. $4,000.
b. $7,000.
c. $5,250.
d. $1,750.
e. $2,500.

_____ 2. On December 31, Inferior Company had the following shareholders' equity:

Common stock, 10,000 shares
issued and outstanding $10,000
Retained earnings 7,500
Total shareholders' equity $17,500

Superior Company purchased 7,000 of Inferior Company's outstanding shares on this date (December 31) paying $2 per share. What amount of minority interest should be reported on the consolidated balance sheet on the date of purchase?

a. $5,250.
b. $4,200.
c. $3,500.
d. $3,000.
e. $6,000.

_____ 3. On January 1, 1990, Allred Company purchased 12,000 shares of Moore Corporation's common stock at $60\frac{1}{4}$ plus a $6,000 commission. On July 1, 1990, Moore Corporation declared and paid dividends of $0.85 per share, and on December 31, 1990, it reported a net income of $156,000. Assuming Moore Corporation has 48,000 outstanding common shares, what should be the balance in the Investment in Moore Corporation account as of December 31, 1990?

a. $729,000.
b. $757,800.
c. $751,800.
d. $723,000.
e. $750,000.

_____ 4. On January 1, 1990, Allred Company purchased 12,000 shares of Moore Corporation's common stock at $60\frac{1}{4}$ plus a $6,000 commission. On July 1, 1990, Moore Corporation declared and paid dividends of $0.85 per share, and on December 31, 1990, it reported a net income of $156,000. Assuming Moore Corporation has 96,000 outstanding common shares, what should be the balance in the Investment in Moore Corporation account as of December 31, 1990?

a. $723,000.
b. $739,200.
c. $738,300.
d. $719,700.
e. $729,000.

Problem III

Many of the important ideas and concepts discussed in Chapter 19 are reflected in the following list of key terms. Test your understanding of these terms by matching the appropriate definitions with the terms. Record the number identifying the most appropriate definition in the blank space next to each term.

_____ Consolidated financial statements

_____ Cost method of accounting for stock investments

_____ Equity method of accounting for stock investments

_____ Foreign exchange rate

_____ Long-term investments

_____ Marketable equity securities

_____ Minority interest

_____ Multinational business

_____ Parent company

_____ Reporting currency

_____ Subsidiary

1. Financial statements that show the results of all operations under the parent's control, including those of any subsidiaries. Assets and liabilities of all affiliated companies are combined on a single balance sheet, revenues and expenses are combined on a single income statement, and cash flows are combined on a single statement of cash flows as though the business were in fact a single company.

2. Investments, not intended as a ready source of cash in case of need, such as bond sinking funds, land, bonds, and stocks that are not marketable or, if marketable, are not held as a temporary investment of cash available for current operations.

3. A corporation that owns a controlling interest (more than 50 percent of the voting stock is required) in another corporation.

4. The portion of a subsidiary company's stockholders' equity that is not owned by the parent corporation.

5. An accounting method whereby the investment is recorded at total cost and maintained at that amount; subsequent investee earnings and dividends do not affect the investment account.

6. An accounting method whereby the investment is recorded at total cost, and the investment account balance is subsequently increased to reflect the investor's equity in earnings of the investee, and decreased to reflect the investor's equity in dividends of the investee.

7. The price of one currency stated in terms of another currency.

8. Common and preferred stocks that are actively traded so that sales prices or bid and ask prices are currently available on a national securities exchange or in the over-the-counter market.

9. The currency in which a company presents its financial statements.

10. A corporation that is controlled by another (parent) corporation because the parent owns more than 50 percent of the subsidiary's voting stock.

11. A company that operates in a number of different countries.

Problem IV

Complete the following by filling in the blanks.

1. If a corporation acquired _____20% or more_____ of another corporation's common stock, the investor is presumed to have a significant influence over the investee corporation's operations, and the investment should be accounted for according to the ___equity method of accounting for___ ___equity Inv___.

2. When a parent company purchases an interest in a subsidiary, it may pay more than book value for its equity because:

a) _____

_____

_____

b) _____

_____

_____

c) _____

_____

_____

3. Any entries to Exchange Gain or Loss on foreign currency transactions are closed to ___Income___ ___Summary___ and included on the ___Income Statement___.

353

4. If P Corporation owns 80% of S Corporation's outstanding shares and a consolidated balance sheet for P and S is prepared, the consolidated assets will include _____ ~~100%~~ 80% _____ (80%, 100%) of S Corporation's assets.

5. When a subsidiary pays a cash dividend, the parent company records receipt of its portion with a credit to _____ Dividend Earned or Investment in subsidiary Co. _____

6. Common and preferred stocks that are actively traded so that sales prices or bid and ask prices are currently available on a national securities exchange or in the over-the-counter market are known as _____ marketable _____ equity securities

Problem V

On January 1, 1990, Large Company paid $90,000 for 36,000 of Small Company's 60,000 outstanding common shares. Small Company paid a dividend of $20,000 on November 1, 1990, and at the end of the year reported earnings of $40,000. On January 3, 1991, Large Company sold its interest in Small Company for $120,000.

[60%]

1. What method should be used in Large Company's books to account for the investment in Small Company? _____ equity method _____

2. Complete general journal entries for Large Company to record the facts presented above. Do not give explanations and skip a line between entries.

DATE		ACCOUNT TITLES AND EXPLANATION	P.R.	DEBIT	CREDIT
1990 Jan	1	Investment in Small Co. Stock		90,000.00	
		Cash			90,000.00
Nov	1	Cash		12,000.00	
		Investment in Small Co.			12,000.00
Dec	31	Investment in Small Co.		24,000.00	
		Earnings from Inv in Small Co.			24,000.00
1991 Jan	3	Cash		120,000.00	
		Invest. in Small Co.			102,000.00
		Gain on Sale of Inv Co.			18,000.00

354

Problem VI

Complete the working paper below under the assumption that Parent Company paid $95,000 for 90% of the outstanding stock of Subsidiary Company, after which it lent its subsidiary $20,000, taking a promissory note as evidence of the debt.

PARENT COMPANY AND SUBSIDIARY COMPANY
Work Sheet for Consolidated Balance Sheet
As of Date of Consolidation

	PARENT COMPANY	SUBSIDIARY COMPANY	ELIMINATIONS DR.	ELIMINATIONS CR.	CONSOLIDATED AMOUNTS
Assets					
Cash	50 000 00	20 000 00			25 000 00
Note receivable	20 000 00			(a) 20,000.00	
Investment in Subsidiary Co.	95 000 00			(b) 95,000.00	
Plant and equipment	90 000 00	73 000 00			163 000 00
Excess of cost over book value			(b) 32,000.00		32 000 00
	210 000 00	93 000 00			220 000 00
Liabilities and Equities					
Accounts payable	8 000 00	3 000 00			11 000 00
Notes payable		20 000 00	(a) 20,000.00		
Common stock	120 000 00	50 000 00	(b) 50,000.00		120 000 00
Retained earnings	82 000 00	20 000 00	(b) 20,000.00		82 000 00
Minority interest				(b) 7,000.00	7 000 00
	210 000 00	93 000 00			220 000 00

355

Solutions for Chapter 19

Problem I

1.	F	5.	T
2.	T	6.	F
3.	T	7.	T
4.	T	8.	F

Problem II

1.	D
2.	A
3.	B
4.	E

Problem III

Consolidated financial statements	...	1	Marketable equity securities	8
Cost method of accounting for stock investments	....	5	Minority interest	4
			Multinational business	11
Equity method of accounting for stock investments	....	6	Parent company	3
			Reporting currency	9
Foreign exchange rate	....	7	Subsidiary	10
Long-term investments	....	2		

Problem IV

1. 20% or more, equity method

2. a) certain of the subsidiary's assets are carried on the subsidiary's books at less than fair values
   b) certain of the subsidiary's liabilities are carried on the subsidiary's books at amounts that are greater than fair values
   c) other reasons exist that are good enough to justify paying more than the fair (market) value of its assets less liabilities

3. Income Summary, income statement

4. 100%

5. Investment in Subsidiary

6. marketable equity securities

Problem V

1. the equity method

2.

1990

Jan.	1	Investment in Small Company	90,000.00	
		Cash		90,000.00
Nov.	1	Cash	12,000.00	
		Investment in Small Company		12,000.00
Dec.	31	Investment in Small Company	24,000.00	
		Earnings from Investment in Small Company ...		24,000.00

1991

Jan.	3	Cash	120,000.00	
		Investment in Small Company		102,000.00
		Gain on Sale of Investments		18,000.00

Problem VI

PARENT COMPANY AND SUBSIDIARY COMPANY
Work Sheet for Consolidated Balance Sheet
As of Date of Consolidation

	Parent Company	Subsidiary Company	Eliminations Dr.		Eliminations Cr.		Consolidated Amounts
Assets							
Cash	5,000	20,000	....		....		25,000
Note receivable	20,000	......	....		(a)	20,000	......
Investment in Subsidiary Co.	95,000	......	....		(b)	95,000	......
Plant and equipment	90,000	73,000	....		....		163,000
Excess of cost over book value	....	......	(b)	32,000	....		32,000
	210,000	93,000					220,000
Liabilities and Equities							
Accounts payable	8,000	3,000	....		....		11,000
Note payable	....	20,000	(a)	20,000	....		......
Common stock	120,000	50,000	(b)	50,000	....		120,000
Retained earnings	82,000	20,000	(b)	20,000	....		82,000
Minority interest	....	......	....		(b)	7,000	7,000
	210,000	93,000	122,000		122,000		220,000

357

20 Analyzing Financial Statements

After studying Chapter 20, you should be able to:

1. List the three broad objectives of financial reporting by business enterprises.

2. Describe, prepare and interpret comparative financial statements and common-size comparative statements.

3. Calculate and explain the interpretation of the ratios, turnovers, and rates of return used to evaluate (a) short-term liquidity, (b) long-term risk and capital structure, and (c) operating efficiency and profitability.

4. State the limitations associated with using financial statement ratios and the sources from which standards for comparison may be obtained.

5. Define or explain the words and phrases listed in the chapter Glossary.

Topical Outline

I. Financial reporting

    A. Includes general purpose financial statements and additional financial information such as is presented in news announcements.

    B. Objectives of financial reporting—financial reporting should provide information:

        1. That is useful to present and potential investors and creditors and other users in making rational investment, credit and similar decisions.

        2. To help present and potential investors and creditors and other users in assessing the amounts, timing, and uncertainty of prospective cash flows.

        3. About the economic resources of an enterprise, the claims to those resources, and the effects of transactions, events, and circumstances that change its resources and claims to those resources.

    C. Conceptual framework—the statement of the objectives of financial reporting.

II. Comparative statements

    A. Statements with data for two or more successive accounting periods placed in columns side by side in order to better illustrate changes in the data.

    B. Trend percentages emphasize changes that have occurred from period to period and are useful in comparing data covering a number of years.

    C. Common-size comparative statements—statements in which each amount is expressed as a percentage of a base amount.

III. Analysis of short-term liquidity—the amount of working capital is not a measure of a company's ability to meet current debts or take advantage of discounts. Statistics used in the analysis include:

    A. Current ratio—current assets dividend by current liabilities.

    B. Acid-test ratio—quick assets (cash, temporary investments, accounts receivable, and notes receivable) divided by current liabilities.

    C. Accounts receivable turnover—net sales or credit sales divided by average accounts receivable.

    D. Days' sales uncollected—an indication of the speed with which a company collects its accounts; calculated by dividing accounts receivable by net credit sales and then multiplying by 365 days.

    E. Merchandise turnover—the number of times a company's average inventory is sold during an accounting period; calculated by dividing cost of goods sold by average merchandise inventory.

IV. Standards of comparison used by financial analysts

    A. Standards acquired from the analyst's own experience.

    B. Information from other competitive companies in the same industry.

    C. Published data such as that put out by Dun & Bradstreet.

    D. Information published by local and national trade associations.

    E. Rule-of-thumb standards.

V. Analysis of long-term risk and capital structure

    A. Debt and equity ratios—show the percentages of total liabilities and owners' equity supplied by creditors and by owners.

    B. Pledged plant assets to secured liabilities—measures the protection provided the secured creditors by the pledged assets.

    C. Times fixed interest charges earned—measures the security of the return to creditors; calculated by dividing income before fixed interest charges and income taxes by fixed interest charges.

VI. Analysis of operating efficiency and profitability

    A. Profit margin—measured by expressing net income as a percentage of net sales. Shows the ability to generate a net income from sales dollars.

    B. Total asset turnover—measured by dividing average total assets employed into net sales. Shows the efficiency of using assets to generate sales.

    C. Rate of return on total assets employed—measures management's performance; calculated as income before interest and income taxes divided by average total assets employed. Also measured as the product of profit margin and total asset turnover.

    D. Rate of return on common stockholders' equity—calculated as net income (minus preferred dividend requirements, if any) divided by average common stockholders' equity.

    E. Price-earnings ratio

        1. Commonly used in comparing investment opportunities.

        2. Calculated by dividing market price per share by earnings per share.

    F. Dividend yield—measured as annual cash dividends per share divided by market price per share.

Problem I

The following statements are either true or false. Place a (T) in the parentheses before each true statement and an (F) before each false statement.

1. (T) A current ratio of 2 to 1 always indicates that a company can easily meet its current debts.

2. (F) Accounts receivable turnover of 6.4 times in 1991 and 8.2 times in 1990 indicates that a company is collecting its accounts receivable more rapidly in 1991 than in 1990.

3. (F) If accounts receivable at year-end amount to $150,000, and net charge sales for the year for $1,000,000, days' sales uncollected is 15. ×4.76

4. (T) On a common-size income statement, the amount of net sales is assigned a value of 100%.

5. (F) To calculate merchandise turnover, cost of goods sold is divided by gross sales.

6. (T) The ratios and turnovers of a selected group of competitive companies normally are the best bases of comparison for analyzing financial statements.

7. (T) Return on total assets employed summarizes the two components of operating efficiency—profit margin and total asset turnover.

8. (T) Current ratio, acid-test ratio, accounts receivable turnover, and merchandise turnover are tools for evaluating short-term liquidity.

Problem II

You are given several words, phrases or numbers to choose from in completing each of the following statements or in answering the following questions. In each case select the one that best completes the statement or answers the question and place its letter in the answer space provided.

___e___ 1. To analyze long-term risk and capital structure, which of the following ratios and statistics for analysis would be used?

    a. debt ratio.
    b. equity ratio.
    c. times fixed interest charges earned.
    d. return on stockholders' equity.
    e. a, b, c, and d.

___e___ 2. During 1988, a company's sales were $360,000. In 1989 they were $334,800 and in 1990 they were $374,400. Express the sales in trend percentages, using 1988 as the base year.

    a. 1988—96%; 1989—89%; 1990—100%.
    b. 1988—100%; 1989—108%; 1990—96%.
    c. 1988—100%; 1989—100%; 1990—100%.
    d. 1988—104%; 1989—112%; 1990—100%.
    e. 1988—100%; 1989—93%; 1990—104%.

___C___ 3. Information from the 1990 income statement of Becker Company follows:

Sales	$320,000
Gross profit on sales	138,000
Operating income	32,000
Income before taxes	22,000
Net income	16,800

If the company's January 1, 1990, accounts receivable were $23,200 and its December 31, 1990, accounts receivable were $28,000, what was the company's accounts receivable turnover?

a. 7.1 times.
b. 5.4 times.
c. 12.5 times.
d. 3.9 times.
e. 10.1 times.

4. Information from the 1990 income statement of Sumner Company follows:

Sales	$300,000
Cost of goods sold:	
Merchandise inventory, January 1, 1990	$ 28,480
Purchases, net	171,040
Goods available for sale	$199,520
Merchandise inventory, December 31, 1990	19,520
Cost of goods sold	$180,000
Gross profit on sales	$120,000
Operating income	$ 34,000
Income before taxes	$ 22,400
Net income	$ 16,800

Calculate the company's merchandise turnover.

a. 7.5 times.
b. 9.2 times.
c. 12.5 times.
d. 8.3 times.
e. 17.9 times.

5. The Keyes Company had the following comparative income statements for 1990 and 1989:

	1990	1989
Net sales	$630,000	$552,000
Cost of goods sold	428,400	389,160
Gross profit from sales	$201,600	$162,840
Operating expenses	97,500	78,600
Net income	$104,100	$ 84,240

What are the cost of goods sold in common-size percentages for 1990 and 1989?

a. 110.1% in 1990; 100.0% in 1989.
b. 24.3% in 1990; 21.6% in 1989.
c. 41.2% in 1990; 46.2% in 1989.
d. 68.0% in 1990; 70.5% in 1989.
e. 147.0% in 1990; 141.8% in 1989.

Problem III

Many of the important ideas and concepts discussed in Chapter 20 are reflected in the following list of key terms. Test your understanding of these terms by matching the appropriate definition with the terms. Record the number identifying the most appropriate definition in the blank space next to each term.

__11__ Accounts receivable turnover

__19__ Acid-test ratio

__10__ Common-size comparative statements

__7__ Comparative statement

__4__ Current ratio

__12__ Days' sales uncollected

__6__ Dividend yield

__1__ Financial leverage

__20__ Financial reporting

__13__ General purpose financial statements

__17__ Merchandise turnover

__5__ Net working capital

__18__ Price-earnings ratio

__2__ Profit margin

__9__ Quick ratio

__15__ Return on common shareholders' equity

__14__ Return on total assets employed

__16__ Times fixed interest charges earned

__3__ Total asset turnover

__8__ Working capital

1. The use of debt as a source of assets in the hope of earning a return on those assets that is higher than the rate of interest paid to creditors, thereby increasing the return to shareholders.

2. A component of operating efficiency and profitability, calculated by expressing net income as a percentage of net sales.

3. A component of operating efficiency and profitability, calculated by dividing net sales by average total assets.

4. The relation of a company's current assets to its current liabilities, that is, current assets divided by current liabilities.

5. A synonym for working capital.

6. The annual amount of cash dividends paid to a share of stock divided by the market price per share; used to compare the dividend paying performance of different investment alternatives.

7. A financial statement with data for two or more successive accounting periods placed in columns side by side, sometimes with changes shown in dollar amounts and percentages.

8. Current assets minus current liabilities.

9. A synonym for acid-test ratio.

10. Comparative financial statements in which each amount is expressed as a percentage of a base amount. In the balance sheet, the amount of total assets is usually selected as the base amount and is expressed as 100%. In the income statement, net sales is usually selected as the base amount.

11. An indication of how long it takes a company to collect its accounts, calculated by dividing credit sales (or net sales) by the average accounts receivable balance.

12. The number of days of average credit sales volume that would add to the accounts receivable balance, calculated as the product of 365 times the accounts receivable balance divided by charge sales.

13. Statements published periodically, which include the income statement, balance sheet, statement of retained earnings or statement of changes in shareholders' equity, and statement of changes in financial position.

14. A summary measure of operating efficiency and management performance, calculated by expressing net income as a percentage of average total assets.

15. A measure of profitability in the use of assets provided by common stockholders, measured by expressing net income less preferred dividends as a percentage of average common stockholders' equity.

16. A measure of a company's ability to satisfy fixed interest charges, calculated as net income before interest and income taxes divided by fixed interest charges.

17. The number of times a company's average inventory is sold during an accounting period, calculated by dividing cost of goods sold by the average merchandise inventory balance.

18. A measure used to evaluate the profitability of alternative common stock investments, calculated as market price per share of common stock divided by earnings per share.

19. The relation of quick assets, such as cash, temporary investments, accounts receivable, and short-term notes receivable, to current liabilities, calculated as quick assets divided by current liabilities.

20. The process of preparing and issuing financial information about a company.

Problem IV

The sales, cost of goods sold, and gross profits from sales of the Laker Company for a five-year period are shown below:

	1990	1991	1992	1993	1994
Sales	$350,000	$385,000	$413,000	$455,000	$497,000
Cost of goods sold	250,000	280,000	305,000	345,000	375,000
Gross profit	$100,000	$105,000	$108,000	$110,000	$122,000

Laker Company's sales are expressed in trend percentages below. Express its cost of goods sold and gross profit in trend percentages in the spaces provided.

	1990	1991	1992	1993	1994
Sales	100	110	118	130	142
Cost of goods sold	100	112	122	138	150
Gross profit	100	105	108	110	122

Comment on the situation shown by the data:

Even cost of goods sold shows % trend inc. more than sales, but gross profit trend still inc.

365

Problem V

Complete the following by filling in the blanks.

1. When calculating accounts receivable turnover, the preferable sales number to use is ___*credit*___ (cash, credit, total) sales.

2. The acid-test ratio is calculated by dividing ___*quick assets*___ by ___*current lia*___ _____. This ratio is a check on ___*ability to pay debt mature near*___.

3. Merchandise turnover is calculated by dividing ___*cost of goods sold*___ _____ by ___*average merchandise Inventory*___ It is an indication of ___*no. of times merchandise sold*___.

4. A slower turnover of merchandise inventory ___*will not*___ (will, (will not)) tend to increase working capital requirements.

5. The current ratio is calculated by dividing ___*current assets*___ by ___*current lia*___. It is an indication of ___*the ease*___ with which a company can meet its current obligations.

6. The rate of return on total assets employed is calculated by dividing ___*net income*___ _____ by ___*average total assets*___ amount of assets employed during the year.

7. Times fixed interest charges earned is calculated by dividing income before deducting ___*interest*___ _____ and ___*taxes*___ by the amount of the _____ ___*interest expense*___

8. Days' sales uncollected are calculated by dividing ___*Acc Rece.*___ by ___*Charge sales*___ and multiplying the resulting quotient by ___*365*___ _____. Days' sales uncollected are an indication of ___*no. of*___ ___*volume of Acc Rec uncollected*___

9. The price-earnings ratio for a company's common stock is calculated by dividing the ___*the net p*___ ___*per sd*___ per share of the common stock by ___*earning p int per show*___

10. The rate of return on common shareholders' equity is calculated by dividing ___*net income*___ ___*dividends*___ by ___*average*___ shareholders' equity.

11. Compared to companies with an average growth rate, companies in a growth industry would be expected to have a ___*lower higher*___ (higher, lower) price-earnings ratio.

366

Problem VI

1. Following are the condensed income statements of two companies of unequal size. Examine the statement amounts and write in this space (_____ *Com. Z* _____) the name of the company that operated more efficiently. If you cannot tell from examining the statement amounts, write "cannot tell" in the blank.

COMPANIES A AND Z
Income Statements
For Year Ended December 31, 19—

	Company A	Company Z
Sales	$325,000	$265,000
Cost of goods sold	204,750	164,300
Gross profit on sales	$120,250	$100,700
Selling expenses	$ 61,750	$ 49,025
Administrative expenses	42,250	34,450
Total operating expenses	$104,000	$ 83,475
Net income	$ 16,250	$ 17,225

2. Common-size percentages are often used in comparing the statements of companies of unequal size. Below are the condensed income statements of Companies A and Z with the income statement amounts of Company A already expressed in common-size percentages. Express the income statement amounts of Company Z in common-size percentages in the spaces provided.

COMPANIES A AND Z
Income Statements
For Year Ended December 31, 19—

	Dollar Amounts		Common-Size Percentages	
	Company A	Company Z	Company A	Company Z
Sales	$325,000	$265,000	100.0	100
Cost of goods sold	204,750	164,300	63.0	62
Gross of profit on sales	$120,250	$100,700	37.0	38
Selling expenses	$ 61,750	$ 49,025	19.0	18
Administrative expenses	42,250	34,450	13.0	13
Total operating expenses	$104,000	$ 83,475	32.0	31
Net income	$ 16,250	$ 17,225	5.0	6

3. After expressing the Company Z income statement amounts in common-size percentages, examine the common-size percentages of the two companies and write in this space (_____ *Com Z* _____) the name of the company that operated more efficiently.

Solutions for Chapter 20

Problem I

1. F	5. F
2. F	6. T
3. F	7. T
4. T	8. T

Problem II

1. E
2. E
3. C
4. A
5. D

Problem III

Accounts receivable turnover	11	Merchandise turnover	17	
Acid-test ratio	19	Net working capital	5 or 8	
Common-size comparative statements	10	Price-earnings ratio	18	
Comparative statment	7	Profit margin	2	
Current ratio	4	Quick ratio	9 or 19	
Days' sales uncollected	12	Return on common shareholders' equity	15	
Dividend yield	6	Return on total assets employed	14	
Financial leverage	1	Times fixed interest charges earned	16	
Financial reporting	20	Total asset turnover	3	
General purpose financial statements	13	Working capital	8	

Problem IV

	1990	1991	1992	1993	1994
Sales	100	110	118	130	142
Cost of goods sold	100	112	122	138	150
Gross profit	100	105	108	110	122

Laker Company's sales increased each year throughout the five-year period, but its cost of goods sold increased more rapidly. This slowed the rate of increase in its gross profit.

Problem V

1. credit

2. quick assets, current liabilities, the ability to pay debts that mature in the very near future

3. cost of goods sold, average inventory, merchandising efficiency

4. will

5. current assets, current liabilities, the ease

6. net income, the average

7. income taxes, fixed interest charges, fixed interest charges

8. accounts receivable, charge sales, the number of days in a year, collection efficiency (the speed with which a company collects its accounts)

9. market price, earnings per share

10. net income less any preferred dividends, average common

11. higher

Problem VI

1. The average person cannot tell from an examination of the figures which company operated more efficiently.

2.

COMPANIES A AND Z
Income Statements
For Year Ended December 31, 19—

	Dollar Amounts		Common-Size Percentages	
	Company A	Company Z	Company A	Company Z
Sales	$325,000	$265,000	100.0	100.0
Cost of goods sold	204,750	164,300	63.0	62.0
Gross of profit on sales	$120,250	$100,700	37.0	38.0
Selling expenses	$ 61,750	$ 49,025	19.0	18.5
Administrative expenses	42,250	34,450	13.0	13.0
Total operating expenses	$104,000	$ 83,475	32.0	31.5
Net income	$ 16,250	$ 17,225	5.0	6.5

3. Company Z

21 Accounting for Manufacturing Companies

After studying Chapter 21, you should be able to:

1. Describe the basic differences in the financial statements of manufacturing companies and merchandising companies and the procedures used in a general accounting system for a manufacturing company.

2. Describe the unique accounts that manufacturing companies use, prepare a manufacturing statement, and explain its purpose and relationship to the primary financial statements.

3. Prepare a work sheet and the financial statements for a manufacturing company.

4. Prepare the adjusting and closing entries for a manufacturing company.

5. Explain the procedures for assigning costs to the different manufacturing inventories.

6. Define or explain the words and phrases listed in the chapter Glossary.

Topical Outline

I. Manufacturing accounting systems

    A. Compared with merchandising accounting systems

        1. Both depend upon the sale of one or more commodities or products for revenue.

        2. A merchandising company buys the goods it sells in the same condition in which they are sold and records the cost in the Purchases account.

        3. A manufacturing company buys raw materials which it manufactures into the finished products it sells. Then, it combines the balances of a number of material, labor, and overhead accounts to determine the cost of the goods it has manufactured for sale.

    B. Compared with a cost accounting system

        1. A general accounting system:

            a. Uses periodic physical inventories.

            b. Focuses on the determination of total cost of all goods manufactured each period.

        2. A cost accounting system:

            a. Uses perpetual inventories.

            b. Focuses on the determination of the unit cost of manufacturing a product or performing a service.

II. Manufacturing costs and accounts

    A. Elements of manufacturing costs

        1. Direct materials

            a. Direct materials—the commodities that enter into and become part of a finished product; easily traced to units of product or batches of production.

            b. Indirect materials—commodities that generally do not enter into or become a part of the finished product; materials used in the manufacturing process which are not easily traced to specific units or batches of production; accounting for as factory overhead.

            c. Raw materials—commodities usually intended for use in the production process as direct materials. Commodities purchased for use as *indirect* materials are debited to a Factory Supplies account.

        2. Direct labour

            a. Direct labour—the labour of those who work specifically on the materials being converted into finished products.

            b. Indirect labour—labour used in the manufacturing process but not applied specifically to the finished product.

        3. Factory overhead—all manufacturing costs other than direct materials and direct labour costs.

    B. Product costs and period costs

        1. Product costs—costs that are assigned to units of product; therefore, all manufacturing costs (direct materials, direct labour, and factory overhead).

        2. Period costs—costs that are assigned to expense accounts; therefore, all selling and administrative expenses not part of the manufacturing operation.

    C. Accounts unique to a manufacturing company

        1. Raw Material Purchases—debited for the cost of all raw materials.

        2. Raw Materials Inventory—debited (through a closing entry) for the cost of raw materials on hand at the end of each accounting period.

3. Goods in Process Inventory—debited (through a closing entry) for the cost of partially finished products at the end of the accounting period.
4. Finished Good Inventory—equivalent to the Merchandise Inventory account of a merchandising company; debited (through a closing entry) for the cost of the amount of finished goods on hand at the end of the accounting period.

III. Income statement of a manufacturing company—similar to that of a merchandising concern except:

A. In the cost of goods sold section "Cost of goods manufactured" replaces the "Purchases" element.
B. Finished goods inventories takes the place of merchandise inventories.

IV. Manufacturing statement

A. Contains a calculation of the cost of goods manufactured and has four sections:

1. Cost of direct materials used.
2. Cost of direct labour used.
3. Factory overhead costs incurred.
4. Allocation of total costs incurred between the change in goods in process inventory and the cost of goods manufactured.

B. Cost of goods manufactured is added (on the income statement) to the beginning-of-period finished goods inventory to determine goods available for sale.

V. Work sheet for a manufacturing company

A. Two additional columns are provided for the Manufacturing Statement.
B. Adjustments are the same as for a merchandising company.
C. The trial balance and adjustments amounts are sorted to the appropriate Manufacturing Statement, Income Statement, and Balance Sheet columns.
D. End-of-period raw materials, goods in process, and finished goods inventories are inserted in the appropriate columns.

VI. Closing entries

A. All accounts containing manufacturing costs are closed to Manufacturing Summary.
B. Manufacturing Summary is closed to Income Summary, along with other expenses.

VII. Inventory valuation—manufacturing company

A. Raw materials inventories valuation presents no problem; items are in the same form as when purchased.
B. Values of goods in process and finished goods inventories must be estimated by adding together estimates of direct materials, direct labour, and factory overhead costs applicable to each item.

Problem I

The following statements are either true or false. Place a (T) in the parentheses before each true statement and an (F) before each false statement.

1. ( ) Indirect materials are used in the manufacturing process but are not a part of the finished product.

2. ( ) An example of direct labour is the labour of someone who inspects manufactured products for quality and defects.

3. ( ) All manufacturing costs other than direct materials and direct labour costs are accounted for as factory overhead.

4. ( ) Selling and administrative expenses are factory overhead costs because they are not direct costs of manufacturing.

5. ( ) Product costs include direct material and direct labour only; factory overhead is a period cost.

6. ( ) Most of the manufacturing cost flows for a company that uses a periodic inventory system are recorded at the end of a period with adjusting and closing entries.

7. ( ) A Raw Materials Inventory account is used by a manufacturing company but not by a merchandising company.

8. ( ) The Cost of Goods Manufactured account in a manufacturing company is equivalent to a Purchases account in a merchandising company.

9. ( ) In the closing entry process of a manufacturing company, all items related to manufacturing costs are closed to Manufacturing Summary.

10. ( ) Ending raw materials and goods in process inventories are not listed on the balance sheet but are included in finished goods inventory.

Problem II

You are given several words, phrases or numbers to choose from in completing each of the following statements or in answering the following questions. In each case select the one that best completes the statement or answers the question and place its letter in the answer space provided.

_____ 1. At the beginning of a period, Tricorp Manufacturing Company had a $2,700 inventory of factory supplies. At the end of the period, it was determined that there were $900 of factory supplies remaining and that $300 of its raw materials had been used as factory supplies. The adjusting entry to record all of the factory supplies used would include:

    a. a debit to Raw Material Purchases for $300.
    b. a debit to Factory Supplies for $900.
    c. a debit to Factory Supplies Used for $1,800.
    d. a debit to Factory Supplies Used for $2,100.
    e. a credit to Factory Supplies for $900.

_____ 2. At the end of an accounting period, the debit balance in Manufacturing Summary is allocated to which account(s)?

    a. Raw Materials Inventory.
    b. Goods in Process Inventory.
    c. Income Summary.
    d. Finished Goods Inventory.
    e. a, b, and c only.

_____ 3. During a period, Tobler Company incurred $72,000 of direct labour and $27,000 of factory overhead costs. Factory overhead is assumed to be closely related to direct labour. There were 400 units of product in Goods in Process at the end of the period which included $15 of direct materials and $10 of direct labour per unit. Calculate the total cost of the ending goods in process inventory.

    a. $11,500.
    b. $20,667.
    c. $13,750.
    d. $10,000.
    e. Cannot be determined from information given.

Problem III

Many of the important ideas and concepts discussed in Chapter 21 are reflected in the following list of key terms. Test your understanding of these terms by matching the appropriate definitions with the terms. Record the number identifying the most appropriate definition in the blank space next to each term.

_____ Cost accounting system

_____ Direct labour

_____ Direct materials

_____ Factory burden

_____ Factory overhead

_____ Finished goods

_____ General accounting system for manufacturers

_____ Goods in process

_____ Indirect labour

_____ Indirect materials

_____ Manufacturing overhead

_____ Manufacturing statement

_____ Period costs

_____ Product costs

_____ Raw materials

_____ Schedule of the cost of goods manufactured

_____ Work in process

1. Costs incurred to acquire merchandise or manufacture finished goods and that, therefore, are charged to inventory accounts until the goods are sold, at which time they are reported as cost of goods sold.

2. Products that a company manufactures for sale and which have completed the manufacturing process and are ready for sale.

3. Commodities used in production and accounted for as factory overhead because they do not enter into or become a part of the finished product and, therefore, are not easily traced to specific units or batches of production.

4. An accounting system that uses perpetual inventories in accounting for manufacturing operations and that is designed to assist management's efforts to control costs.

5. A synonym for manufacturing statement.

6. Products in the process of being manufactured that have received a portion or all of their materials and have had some labour and overhead applied but that are not completed.

7. A synonym for goods in process.

8. Physical items the cost of which is easily traced to units of product or batches of production because the items enter into and become a part of a finished product.

9. A schedule that shows the costs incurred to manufacture a product or products during a period.

10. Commodities that are purchased for use in the manufacturing process as direct materials but that are sometimes used as indirect materials.

11. An accounting system that uses periodic inventories to determine the total cost of all goods manufactured during each accounting period.

12. A synonym for factory overhead or factory burden.

13. Labor the cost of which can be easily associated with and charged to units or batches of production because the labor is of those employees who work specifically on the conversion of raw materials into finished products.

14. Costs such as selling and general administrative expenses that are charged to expense in the period incurred because they are not related to the purchase of merchandise or the manufacture of finished goods.

15. The labour of superintendents, foremen, millwrights, engineers, janitors, and others that contribute to production but do not work specifically on the manufactured products; therefore, labour that cannot be easily associated with specific units of product.

16. All manufacturing costs other than for direct materials and direct labour.

17. A synonym for factory overhead or manufacturing overhead.

Problem IV

The unfinished work sheet of Karmen Corporation appears on page 378. You should assume that no adjustments are needed.

The company's year-end inventories for the year of the work sheet are: raw materials, $28,500; goods in process, $20,700; and finished goods, $25,500.

1. Since there are no adjustments, sort the trial balance amounts to the proper Manufacturing Statement, Income Statement, and Balance Sheet columns, and complete the work sheet.

2. After finishing the work sheet, use its information to complete the Manufacturing Statement on the next page and the Income Statement at the top of page 379.

KARMEN CORPORATION

Manufacturing Statement

For the Year Ended December 31, 19—

Direct materials:							
Raw materials inventory, January 1, 19—							
Raw material purchases							
Raw materials available for use							
Raw materials inventory, December 31, 19—							
Direct materials used							
Direct labour							
Factory overhead costs:							
Indirect labour							
Machinery repairs							
Factory supplies used							
Small tools written off							
Depreciation of machinery							
Total factory overhead costs							
Total manufacturing costs							
Add: Goods in process inventory, January 1, 19—							
Total goods in process during the year							
Deduct: Goods in process inventory, December 31, 19—							
Cost of goods manufactured							

KARMEN CORPORATION
Work Sheet for Year Ended December 31, 19—

ACCOUNT TITLES	UNADJUSTED TRIAL BALANCE		ADJUSTMENTS		MFG. STATEMENT		INCOME STATEMENT		STATE. OF RE OR BALANCE SHEET	
	DR.	CR.	DR.	CR.	DR.	CR.	DR.	CR.	DR.	CR.
Cash	23,100 00									
Raw materials inventory	22,200 00									
Goods in process inventory	18,600 00									
Finished goods inventory	25,800 00									
Factory supplies	600 00									
Prepaid factory insurance	900 00									
Small tools	2,400 00									
Machinery	143,100 00									
Acc. dep., machinery		20,700 00								
Accounts payable		7,800 00								
Common stock, $10 par		150,000 00								
Retained earnings		20,100 00								
Sales		289,200 00								
Raw material purchases	96,000 00									
Direct labour	55,800 00									
Indirect labour	24,900 00									
Machinery repairs	1,800 00									
Selling expenses	36,900 00									
Administrative expenses	25,200 00									
Factory supplies used	3,300 00									
Small tools written off	600 00									
Depreciation of machinery	6,600 00									
	487,800 00	487,800 00								
Cost of goods manufactured to Income Statement columns										
Net income										

KARMEN CORPORATION
Income Statement
For Year Ended December 31, 19—

Revenue:						
Sales						
Cost of goods sold:						
Finished goods inventory, January 1, 19—						
Cost of goods manufactured						
Goods available for sale						
Finished goods inventory, December 31, 19—						
Cost of goods sold						
Gross profit from sales						
Operating expenses:						
Selling expenses						
Administrative expenses						
Total operating expenses						
Net income						
Net income per common share						

3. After completing the manufacturing and income statements, prepare entries to close the company's manufacturing statement and income statement accounts.

DATE	ACCOUNT TITLES AND EXPLANATION	P.R.	DEBIT	CREDIT

DATE	ACCOUNT TITLES AND EXPLANATION	P.R.	DEBIT	CREDIT

Problem V

Karmen Corporation of Problem IV manufactures a single product. On the Study Guide date it had 1,700 units of the product in its finished goods inventory, which is valued at $15.00 per unit or a total of $25,500. (See the first page of Problem IV.) In arriving at the $15.00 per unit value, the company examined the units and estimated that each unit contained $7.50 of direct materials and that $4.50 of direct labor had been applied. The company then examined the relation between its total direct labor costs and its total overhead costs for the year (look at the manufacturing statement on page 377), and found that it had incurred $55,800 of direct labor cost and $37,200 of

overhead costs or that its overhead costs were _____% of its direct labor costs. It

then multiplied $4.50 (the direct labor cost per unit) by _____% to arrive at an estimated $3.00 per unit overhead cost. After this is added the $7.50 of estimated direct material cost plus the

$4.50 of estimated direct labor cost plus the $3.00 of estimated overhead cost to get the $_____ estimated cost per unit for its 1,700 units of finished goods.

Solutions for Chapter 21

Problem I

1. T	6. T
2. F	7. T
3. T	8. T
4. F	9. T
5. F	10. F

Problem II

1. D
2. E
3. A

Problem III

Cost accounting system	4	Indirect materials	3
Direct labour	13	Manufacturing overhead	12 or 16
Direct materials	8	Manufacturing statement	9
Factory burden	17 or 16	Period costs	14
Factory overhead	16	Product costs	1
Finished goods	2	Raw materials	10
General accounting system for manufacturers	11	Schedule of the cost of goods manufactured	5 or 9
Goods in process	6	Work in process	7 or 6
Indirect labour	15		

Problem IV

KARMEN CORPORATION
Manufacturing Statement
For Year Ended December 31, 19—

Direct materials:		
Raw materials inventory, January 1, 19—	$ 22,200	
Raw material purchases	96,000	
Raw materials available for use	$118,200	
Raw materials inventory, December 31, 19—	28,500	
Direct materials used		$ 89,700
Direct labour		55,800
Factory overhead costs:		
Indirect labour	$ 24,900	
Machinery repairs	1,800	
Factory supplies used	3,300	
Small tools written off	600	
Depreciation of machinery	6,600	
Total factory overhead costs		37,200
Total manufacturing costs		$182,700
Add goods in process inventory, January 1, 19—		18,600
Total goods in process during the year		$201,300
Deduct goods in process inventory, December 31, 19—		20,700
Cost of goods manufactured		$180,600

KARMEN CORPORATION
Work Sheet for Year Ended December 31, 19—

ACCOUNT TITLES	UNADJUSTED TRIAL BALANCE DR.	CR.	ADJUSTMENTS DR.	CR.	MFG. STATEMENT DR.	CR.	INCOME STATEMENT DR.	CR.	STATE. OF RE OR BALANCE SHEET DR.	CR.
Cash	23,100 00								23,100 00	
Raw materials inventory	22,200 00				22,200 00	28,500 00			28,500 00	
Goods in process inventory	18,600 00				18,600 00	20,700 00			20,700 00	
Finished goods inventory	25,800 00						25,800 00	25,500 00	25,500 00	
Factory supplies	600 00								600 00	
Prepaid factory insurance	900 00								900 00	
Small tools	2,400 00								2,400 00	
Machinery	143,100 00								143,100 00	
Acc. dep., machinery		20,700 00								20,700 00
Accounts payable		7,800 00								7,800 00
Common stock, $10 par		150,000 00								150,000 00
Retained earnings		20,100 00								20,100 00
Sales		289,200 00						289,200 00		
Raw material purchases	96,000 00				96,000 00					
Direct labour	55,800 00				55,800 00					
Indirect labour	24,900 00				24,900 00					
Machinery repairs	1,800 00				1,800 00					
Selling expenses	36,900 00						36,900 00			
Administrative expenses	25,200 00						25,200 00			
Factory supplies used	3,300 00				3,300 00					
Small tools written off	600 00				600 00					
Depreciation of machinery	6,600 00				6,600 00					
	487,800 00	487,800 00			229,800 00	49,200 00				
Cost of goods manufactured to Income Statement columns						180,600 00	180,600 00			
					229,800 00	229,800 00	268,500 00	314,700 00	244,800 00	198,600 00
Net income							46,200 00			46,200 00
							314,700 00	314,700 00	244,800 00	244,800 00

KARMEN CORPORATION
Income Statement
For Year Ended December 31, 19—

Revenue:
Sales $289,200
Cost of goods sold:
   Finished goods inventory, January 1, 19— . . . . $ 25,800
   Cost of goods manufactured (see Manufacturing Statement) . . . 180,600
   Goods available for sale $206,400
   Finished goods inventory, December 31, 19—   25,500
   Cost of goods sold 180,900
Gross profit from sales $108,300
Operating expenses:
   Selling expenses . . . . $ 36,900
   Administrative expenses   25,200
   Total operating expenses 62,100
Net income . . . . $ 46,200

Net income per common share $3.08

Closing entries:

Dec. 31	Manufacturing Summary	229,800.00	
	Raw Materials Inventory		22,200.00
	Goods in Process Inventory		18,600.00
	Raw Material Purchases		96,000.00
	Direct Labour		55,800.00
	Indirect Labour		24,900.00
	Machinery Repairs		1,800.00
	Factory Supplies Used		3,300.00
	Small Tools Written Off		600.00
	Depreciation of Machinery		6,600.00
31	Raw Materials Inventory	28,500.00	
	Goods in Process Inventory	20,700.00	
	Manufacturing Summary		49,200.00
31	Income Summary	268,500.00	
	Finished Goods Inventory		25,800.00
	Selling Expenses		36,900.00
	Administrative Expenses		25,200.00
	Manufacturing Summary		180,600.00
31	Finished Goods Inventory	25,500.00	
	Sales	289,200.00	
	Income Summary		314,700.00
31	Income Summary	46,200.00	
	Retained Earnings		46,200.00

Problem V

$66\frac{2}{3}$, $66\frac{2}{3}$, $15.00

22 Job Order and Process Cost Accounting Systems

After studying Chapter 22, you should be able to:

1. Explain the conditions under which job order cost accounting systems are used and prepare entries to account for the flow of costs in a job order cost system.

2. Explain how costs for individual jobs are accumulated on job cost sheets and how controlling accounts are used in job order cost systems.

3. Allocate overhead to jobs and distribute any over- or under-applied overhead.

4. Explain the conditions under which process cost systems are used, prepare entries to account for the flow of costs in such a system, and prepare a process cost summary.

5. Calculate the equivalent finished units produced during a period and explain how the concept of equivalent finished units is used in process cost accounting systems.

6. Define or explain the words and phrases listed in the chapter Glossary.

Topical Outline

I. Job order cost accounting

   A. Accumulating costs by job

     1. Costs are accumulated in terms of a job or a job lot (a special order for a customer or a quantity of identical items).

     2. A job cost sheet is maintained for each job. The job cost sheets for the jobs in process make up a subsidiary ledger called the Job Cost Ledger.

     3. The Job Cost Ledger is controlled by the Goods in Process account in the General Ledger.

   B. Accounting for materials

     1. Raw materials are requested for use on specific jobs by submitting a materials requisition to the materials storeroom keeper.

     2. The cost of raw materials listed on each materials requisition is recorded (in the Direct Materials column) on the appropriate job cost sheet.

     3. Raw materials used for overhead tasks are charged to accounts listed in the Factory Overhead Ledger.

   C. Accounting for labour

     1. Labour time tickets are used to record the labour charged to specific jobs and to overhead.

     2. The Factory Payroll account balance is transferred partially to Goods in Process (for direct labour) and partially to Factory Overhead (for indirect labour).

   D. Accounting for overhead

     1. A predetermined overhead application rate is calculated as next year's estimated overhead costs divided by next year's estimated direct labour costs (or some other variable such as estimated machine hours).

     2. Overhead is charged to specific jobs on the basis of the direct labour applied to (or perhaps machine hours used by) each job.

     3. At year-end, underapplied or overapplied overhead is allocated to goods in process, finished goods, and cost of goods sold.

II. Process cost accounting

   A. Accumulating costs by department

     1. Direct materials, direct labour, and factory overhead costs are charged to specific production departments in which units of product are processed.

     2. A separate goods in process account is used for the costs of each department.

     3. Departmental production is measured in terms of equivalent finished units.

   B. Calculating unit costs

     1. Direct materials costs incurred by a department are allocated equally to the equivalent finished units for direct materials.

     2. Direct labour costs and usually factory overhead are allocated equally to equivalent finished units for direct labour.

   C. The process cost summary is a departmental report that summarizes:

     1. The costs charged to the department.

     2. The equivalent unit processing costs of the department.

     3. The assignment of costs to the work of the department.

Problem I

The following statements are either true or false. Place a (T) in the parentheses before each true statement and an (F) before each false statement.

1. ( ) In a job cost system, inventory records are kept on a periodic basis.

2. ( ) The General Ledger accounts that keep track of the components of manufacturing costs are called controlling accounts.

3. ( ) At the beginning of an accounting period, the costs of the unfinished jobs in process will appear as a credit balance in the Goods in Process account.

4. ( ) Usually, each time a cost is added to the job cost sheets in the subsidiary ledger, this individual cost is also posted to the Goods in Process control account.

5. ( ) If a perpetual inventory system is used, a company will never take a physical count of the inventory.

6. ( ) Raw materials ledger cards, job cost sheets, and overhead cost accounts are all subsidiary ledger accounts controlled by accounts in the General Ledger.

7. ( ) A materials consumption report in a process cost system serves the same purpose as a materials requisition in a job order cost system.

8. ( ) In a process cost system, the wages of a person working full-time maintaining equipment in the mixing department would be treated as indirect labour cost.

9. ( ) Calculation of equivalent units produced is necessary only when a department using a process cost system has partially finished units in beginning or ending inventory.

10. ( ) If materials are added to a process at a different rate than labour and factory overhead are applied, separate equivalent finished units produced calculations are required for materials and for labour and overhead.

Problem II

You are given several words, phrases or numbers to choose from in completing each of the following statements or in answering the following questions. In each case select the one that best completes the statement or answers the question and place its letter in the answer space provided.

_____ 1. During a period, Department C finished and transferred 3,000 units to Department D. Of those 3,000 units, 1,000 were $\frac{1}{4}$ complete at the beginning of the period and 2,000 were started and completed during the period. During the period, 500 units were started but only $\frac{1}{2}$ completed. The number of equivalent finished units produced by Department C during the period was:

    a. 2,000 units.
    b. 2,250 units.
    c. 2,500 units.
    d. 3,000 units.
    e. 3,250 units.

_____ 2. Clapton Company has an overhead rate that is 40% of direct labour cost. The Goods in Process account has an ending balance of $87,000, which includes $45,000 of direct materials. Determine the amount of applied overhead in Goods in Process.

    a. $42,000.
    b. $30,000.
    c. $18,000.
    d. $12,000.
    e. Cannot be determined from information given.

3. Town & Country Factory established a predetermined overhead application rate based on the estimation that it would incur $120,000 of overhead during the next year and that $96,000 of direct labour will be applied to production during the year. During May, total direct labour costs totaled $8,600. What amount of overhead will be applied to Goods in Process during May?

    a. $ 6,880
    b. $10,000
    c. $10,750
    d. $12,500
    e. None of the above.

4. Assume that Merrian Company applies overhead to jobs based on a predetermined overhead application rate and that the Factory Overhead account had a credit balance of $1,400 at the end of a period. Merrian considers this balance to be material in amount. Overhead had been charged to jobs worked on during the period as follows:

Jobs still in process	$ 1,800
Jobs finished but unsold	3,600
Jobs finished and sold	6,600
Total overhead applied to jobs during the period	$12,000

    The entry to allocate any overapplied or underapplied overhead would include which of the following?

    a. Goods in Process would be debited for $1,800.
    b. Finished Goods would be debited for $420.
    c. Cost of Goods Sold would be credited for $6,600.
    d. Factory Overhead would be credited for $1,400.
    e. Goods in Process would be credited for $210.

Problem III

Many of the important ideas and concepts discussed in Chapter 22 are reflected in the following list of key terms. Test your understanding of these terms by matching the appropriate definitions with the terms. Record the number identifying the most appropriate definition in the blank space next to each term.

_____ Cost accounting system

_____ Equivalent finished units

_____ Job

_____ Job Cost Ledger

_____ Job cost sheet

_____ Job lot

_____ Job order cost system

_____ Labour time ticket

_____ Materials consumption report

_____ Materials requisition

_____ Overapplied overhead

_____ Predetermined overhead application rate

_____ Process cost system

_____ Underapplied overhead

1. A system of accounting for manufacturing costs in which costs are assembled in terms of processes or steps in manufacturing a product.

2. A subsidiary ledger that contains the job cost sheets of unfinished jobs and that is controlled by the Goods in Process account.

3. A record of how an employee's time at work was used; the record serves as the basis for charging jobs and overhead accounts for the employee's wages.

4. An accounting system based on perpetual inventory records that is designed to emphasize the determination of unit costs and the control of costs.

5. The amount by which actual overhead incurred during a period exceeds the overhead applied to production based on a predetermined application rate.

6. A document that is given to the materials storeroom keeper in exchange for raw materials and that improves control over materials and provides a basis for charging the cost of raw materials to jobs, or processing departments, or factory overhead; the document identifies the materials needed for a specific job, processing department, or purpose, and the account to which the materials cost should be charged.

7. A special production order of a unique product, often manufactured especially for and to the specifications of a customer.

8. A rate that is used to charge overhead cost to production; calculated by relating estimated overhead cost for a period to another variable such as estimated direct labour cost.

9. A measure of production with respect to direct materials or direct labour (and overhead), expressed as the number of units that could have been manufactured from start to finish during a period given the amount of direct materials or direct labour (and overhead) used during the period.

10. The amount by which overhead applied on the basis of a predetermined overhead application rate exceeds overhead actually incurred during the period.

11. A record of the costs incurred on a single job.

12. A system of accounting for manufacturing costs in which costs are assembled in terms of jobs or job lots.

13. A document that is prepared by the materials storeroom keeper as a substitute for materials requisitions and that shows the raw materials issued to each department during a cost period; provides the information necessary for journal entries that charge materials costs to the appropriate accounts.

14. A job that consists of a quantity of identical items.

Problem IV

Complete the following by filling in the blanks.

1. In a process cost system, costs are assembled by _____, with a separate Goods in Process account being used to assemble the costs of each _____.

2. When overhead is to be applied to jobs on the basis of direct labor cost, a predetermined overhead application rate is established before a cost period begins by estimating the number of dollars of _____ that will be incurred during the period, estimating the number of dollars of _____ that will be incurred during the same period, and then dividing the _____ by the _____.

3. The heart of a job order cost system is a subsidiary ledger of _____, with a separate cost sheet being used to accumulate the _____, _____ and _____ costs of each job.

4. If the year-end balance of the Factory Overhead account is a material amount, it is reasonable to dispose of it by _____ among the goods still in process, the finished goods inventory, and cost of goods sold. However, if the amount is immaterial it may be charged to _____
_____.

5. When overhead is applied to jobs on the basis of a predetermined overhead application rate, the number of dollars of overhead applied to jobs during a year will seldom be the same as the number of dollars of overhead actually incurred during the year. Consequently, if more overhead is incurred than is applied to jobs, overhead is said to be _____ (overapplied, underapplied); and if more overhead is applied to jobs than is incurred, overhead is said to be _____.

6. To gain control over direct materials in a job cost system, all raw materials purchased are placed in a materials _____ where they are kept until needed in production.

7. When a department begins and ends a cost period with partially processed units of product, its production for a cost period must be measured on the basis of _____.

8. When raw materials are needed on a job, a materials _____ is prepared and signed by a foreman or other responsible person and is given to the storeroom keeper in exchange for the raw materials.

9. The idea of an equivalent finished unit is based on the assumption that it takes the same amount of direct labour, for example, to one-fourth finish each of _____ units of product as it does to complete one unit.

10. Materials requisitions for such things as machinery lubricants, cleaning materials, and light bulbs are used to charge the costs of these indirect materials to the _____ account.

11. The materials requisitions given to the storeroom keeper in exchange for raw materials to be used on a job are sent to the accounting department where they are used to charge the cost of the raw materials to the job on the job's _____ sheet. The requisitions are also used to make entries in the Raw Materials Ledger to reduce the book record of the amount of _____ on hand, and they are the basis for the entry to charge the Goods in Process account for the cost of all the _____ used on jobs during the cost period.

12. In a job order cost accounting system, a job is a construction project, machine, or other product manufactured especially for and to the _____ of a customer. It may also be a quantity of identical items called a _____.

Problem V

During a cost period a department finished and transferred 63,000 units of product to finished goods, of which 18,000 were in process in the department one-fourth finished when the period began and 45,000 were begun and completed during the period. In addition the department had 13,500 units of product in process, two-thirds processed when the period ended. *Required:* Complete the following calculation of equivalent finished units for this department:

	Units Involved	Fraction Completed during the Period	Equivalent Units Completed
Beginning inventory units			
Units started and finished			
Ending inventory			
Equivalent finished units			

Under the assumption that the foregoing department had $54,000 of direct labour charged to it during the cost period and direct labour is added to the product of the department evenly throughout the process, complete the following calculation of the cost of an equivalent unit of direct labour in this department.

$54,000 / _____ equivalent units = $_____ per equivalent unit

After determining the cost of an equivalent unit of direct labour in this department, use this cost in completing the following calculation apportioning the $54,000 of direct labour cost between the department's inventories and its units finished:

Beginning inventory (_____ equivalent units @ $_____) . . . . $_____

Units started and finished (_____ equivalent units @ $_____) . . . .   _____

Ending inventory (_____ equivalent units @ $_____) . . . .   _____
Total direct labour charged to the department . . . . $_____54,000

Solutions for Chapter 22

Problem I

1.	F	6.	T
2.	T	7.	T
3.	F	8.	F
4.	F	9.	T
5.	F	10.	T

Problem II

1.	D
2.	D
3.	C
4.	E

Problem III

Cost accounting system	4	Materials consumption report	13
Equivalent finished units	9	Materials requisition	6
Job	7	Overapplied overhead	10
Job Cost Ledger	2	Predetermined overhead application rate	8
Job cost sheet	11	Process cost system	1
Job lot	14	Underapplied overhead	5
Job order cost system	12		
Labour time ticket	3		

Problem IV

1. departments, department

2. direct labour cost, overhead costs, overhead costs, direct labour costs

3. job cost sheets, direct materials, direct labour, factory overhead

4. apportioning it, cost of goods sold

5. underapplied, overapplied

6. storeroom

7. equivalent finished units

8. requisition

9. four

10. Factory Overhead

11. cost, raw materials, direct materials

12. specifications, job lot

Problem V

Beginning inventory units	18,000	¾	13,500
Units started and finished	45,000	all	45,000
Ending inventory	13,500	⅔	9,000
Equivalent finished units			67,500

67,500 equivalent units, $0.80 per equivalent unit

Beginning inventory (13,500 equivalent units @ $0.80) $10,800
Units started and finished (45,000 equivalent units @ $0.80) 36,000
Ending inventory (9,000 equivalent units @ $0.80) 7,200

23

Accounting for the Segments and Departments of a Business; Responsibility Accounting

After studying Chapter 23, you should be able to:

1. Describe the segmental information disclosed in the financial reports of large companies that have operations in several lines of business, and list the four basic issues faced by accountants in developing segmental information.

2. Explain why businesses are divided into subunits or departments, and explain the difference between cost centres and profit centres.

3. Describe the difference between direct and indirect expenses of departments, the bases used to allocate indirect expenses, and the procedures involved in the allocation process.

4. Prepare reports that are designed to measure the performance of a profit center, and describe the factors to be considered in eliminating an unprofitable department.

5. Explain the concept of controllable costs, and prepare reports to be used in evaluating the performance of a department manager.

6. Describe the problems associated with the allocation of joint costs between departments.

7. Define or explain the words and phrases listed in the chapter Glossary.

Topical Outline

I. Segmental reporting and departmental accounting—provide information about the parts of a business.

   A. Segmental reporting—generally refers to published information about the different industries and geographical areas in which a company does business; it is intended primarily for the use of outsiders who are interested in an overall evaluation of the business.

   B. Departmental accounting—relates to information on the subunits of a business prepared for internal managers responsible for planning and controlling the operations of the business.

II. Reporting on broad business segments

   A. Large firms operating in more than one industry must report the following information on each industrial segment:

   1. Revenues.
   2. Operating profits (before interest and taxes).
   3. Identifiable assets.
   4. Capital expenditures.
   5. Depreciation and amortization expense.

   B. Four basic issues faced by companies in developing segmental information:

   1. Identifying significant segments.
   2. Transfer pricing between segments.
   3. Measuring segmental profitability.
   4. Identifying segmental assets.

III. Departmental accounting for internal managers—characterized by two primary goals:

   A. To provide information that management can use in evaluating the profitability or cost effectiveness of each department.

   B. To assign costs and expenses to the particular managers who are responsible for controlling those costs and expenses.

IV. Departmentalizing a business

   A. Most businesses are large and complex enough to require departmentalization into subunits or departments to improve managerial efficiency.

   B. Departments may be classified as:

   1. Production departments

      a. In a manufacturing business, departments engaged directly in manufacturing operations.
      b. In a merchandising business, departments that make sales.

   2. Service departments—support the activities of production departments.

   C. Information to evaluate departments

   1. Cost centres—evaluated on the basis of their ability to control costs.
   2. Profit centres—evaluated on the basis of their ability to generate earnings.

V. Securing departmental information

   A. Separate sales accounts or sales analysis sheets may be used.
   B. Departmental expenses

1. Direct expenses are easily traced to specific departments.
2. Indirect expenses must be allocated to the departments benefiting from them.
3. The basis for allocating each expense should be a reasonable measure of the relative benefit gained by each department.
4. The total costs charged to each service department should be reallocated to production departments.

VI. Departmental contributions to overhead

A. Calculated as revenues less direct costs and expenses.
B. May be a better basis for evaluating profit centers when the allocation of indirect expenses are highly subjective.

VII. Eliminating an unprofitable department

A. Neither net income nor contributions to overhead provides the best information on which to base a decision.
B. A department should be eliminated only if its net loss exceeds its inescapable expenses.

VIII. Controllable costs and expenses

A. Costs for which a manager has the power to determine or strongly influence amounts to be expended.
B. Used to evaluate the performance of a manager.
C. Provide the basis for a system of responsibility accounting.

IX. Responsibility accounting

A. Each manager is held responsible for the costs and expenses that fall under the manager's control.
B. Performance reports compare actual costs and expenses to budgeted amounts and are used to evaluate the effectiveness of each manager.
C. A responsibility accounting system must reflect the fact that control over costs and expenses applies to several levels of management.

X. Joint costs—costs incurred to secure two or more essentially different products.

Problem I

The following statements are either true or false. Place a (T) in the parentheses before each true statement and an (F) before each false statement.

1. ( ) Controllable costs and expenses are not the same thing as direct costs and expenses.

2. ( ) The costs of service departments are direct expenses of the selling departments to which they supply services.

3. ( ) When management considers eliminating a department, management should compare the department's net income with its escapable expenses.

4. ( ) An employee's wages may be either a direct or an indirect expense.

5. ( ) The term segmental reporting usually relates to information on the subunits of a business that is prepared for the use of internal managers.

6. ( ) A responsibility accounting budget is a financial report that compares actual costs and expenses to the budgeted amounts.

7. ( ) Direct expenses do not require allocation.

8. ( ) Sales between segments are eliminated when evaluating the performance of each segment.

9. ( ) The two goals of departmental accounting are: (a) to assign costs and expenses to the particular managers who are responsible for controlling those costs and expenses and (b) to provide information that management can use in evaluating the profitability or cost effectiveness of each department.

10. ( ) Accounting departments and advertising departments are both service departments and cost centers.

Problem II

You are given several words, phrases, or numbers to choose from in completing each of the following statements or in answering the following questions. In each case select the one that best completes the statement or answers the question and place its letter in the answer space provided.

_____a_____ 1. A supervisor who works in Departments A and B spends part of his time in Department A where there are 12 employees, and part of his time in Department B where there are 6 employees. In area, Department A is half the size of Department B. Assume that the supervisor's primary task is to supervise people and that he earns $24,000 per year. How and in what amounts should the supervisor's salary be allocated between Departments A and B?

    a. $16,000 to Department A and $8,000 to Department B based on the number of employees in each department.

    b. $12,800 to Department A and $11,200 to Department B based on an average of time spent and number of employees in each department.

    c. $12,000 to Department A and $12,000 to Department B based on the number of departments supervised.

    d. $8,000 to Department A and $16,000 to Department B based on the square footage in each department.

    e. None of the above is correct.

_____ 2. Schroeder Department Store has clothing, housewares, and cosmetics departments. Net income for the departments is $7,000, $(500), and $8,500, respectively. Operating expenses for the housewares department are $9,300, of which 40% are inescapable. Should Schroeder eliminate the housewares department? Why or why not?

a. Schroeder should not eliminate the housewares department unless its net loss exceeds its inescapable expenses of $3,720.
b. Schroeder should eliminate the housewares department because it is earning a net loss of $(500).
c. Schroeder should eliminate the housewares department because its inescapable expenses exceed its escapable expenses.
d. Schroeder should not eliminate the housewares department unless its net loss exceeds its escapable expenses of $5,580.
e. None of the above.

_____ 3. Oasis Builders Company purchased a 4-story building shell and constructed 32 condominiums of different sizes and quality. Eight of the units will be luxury condos to be sold for $100,000 each, 16 will be standard 3-bedroom units for sale at $75,000 each, and 8 will be 1-bedroom units for sale at $50,000 each. The company spent $750,000 for the building and $1,250,000 for construction. Assume that the building and construction costs are to be assigned to the units as joint costs and determine the share of the costs to assign to a condomium in each price class.

	$100,000 class	$75,000 class	$50,000 class
a.	$888,889	$ 666,667	$444,444
b.	$800,000	$1,200,000	$400,000
c.	$500,000	$1,000,000	$500,000
d.	$666,667	$1,000,000	$333,333
e.	$600,000	$1,200,000	$600,000

Problem III

Many of the important ideas and concepts discussed in Chapter 23 are reflected in the following list of key terms. Test your understanding of these terms by matching the appropriate definitions with the terms. Record the number identifying the most appropriate definition in the blank space next to each term.

_____ Common expenses	_____ Inescapable expenses
_____ Controllable costs	_____ Joint cost
_____ Cost centre	_____ Performance report
_____ Departmental accounting	_____ Production departments
_____ Departmental contribution to overhead	_____ Profit centre
_____ Direct costs or expenses	_____ Responsibility accounting
_____ Direct expenses	_____ Responsibility accounting budget
_____ Escapable expenses	_____ Segmental reporting
_____ Indirect costs or expenses	_____ Service departments
_____ Indirect expenses	_____ Uncontrollable cost

1. A financial report that compares actual costs and expenses to the budgeted amounts.

2. A unit of a business that incurs costs or expenses but does not directly generate revenues; as a result, a unit the efficiency of which cannot be judged in terms of its ability to generate earnings.

3. Departments that do not manufacture products or produce revenue but that supply other departments with essential services.

4. Accounting for the "parts" or subunits of a business, especially developing subunit information for the internal use of management.

5. Expenses that are not easily associated with a specific department.

6. Providing information about the subunits of a business, especially published information about a company's operations in different industries or geographical areas.

7. Expenses that will no longer be incurred if a department is eliminated.

8. Expenses that are easily associated with and assigned to a specific department because they are incurred for the sole benefit of one department.

9. Costs or expenses that are not easily traced to a cost object such as a department; for example, costs incurred for the joint benefit of more than one department.

10. The amount by which a department's revenues exceed its direct costs and expenses.

11. A cost the amount of which a specific manager cannot control within a given period of time.

12. Those expenses of a business that benefit more than one segment of the business.

13. Accounting systems that are designed to accumulate controllable costs in timely reports to be given to each manager who is responsible for the costs, and also to be used in judging the performance of each manager.

14. A cost incurred to produce or obtain two or more essentially different products.

15. Costs or expenses that are easily traced to or associated with a cost object; for example, the cost of materials that become part of a manufactured product, or the cost of labor that is used solely in one processing department of a manufacturer, or wages expense incurred solely for the benefit of a specific department of a merchandising company.

16. Expenses that will continue even if a department is eliminated.

17. A unit of business that incurs costs and generates revenues, the efficiency of which therefore can be judged in terms of its ability to generate earnings.

18. A plan that specifies the expected costs and expenses falling under the control of a manager.

19. Subunits of a business, the operations of which involve manufacturing or selling the goods or services of the business.

20. Costs over which the manager has the power to determine or strongly influence amounts to be expended.

Problem IV

Complete the following by filling in the blanks.

1. A departmental expense allocation sheet is used to allocate _____

   expenses to all departments and also to allocate the _____ department expenses to the production departments.

2. In responsibility accounting, each manager is held responsible for the _____

   _____ that fall under the manager's control.

3. Service department expenses are in effect _____ of the selling or production departments and therefore should be allocated to these departments.

4. An examination of controllable costs may be a better way to appraise a department manager's efficiency than an evaluation of the department's net income or its contribution to overhead because _____ _____ _____ _____.

5. Direct expenses can be identified easily with specific departments; but in the calculation of departmental net incomes, _____ must be allocated on some fair basis.

6. A department's contribution to overhead is the amount its revenues _____ _____.

7. When a concern goes beyond the calculation of departmental contributions to overhead and attempts to calculate net incomes by departments, an allocation of _____ is required.

8. Unless it is continued because it brings business to other departments, an unprofitable department usually should be eliminated if its losses exceed its _____.

9. A _____ centre is a unit of the business that incurs costs but does not directly generate revenues, while a _____ centre not only incurs costs but also generates revenues.

10. Some expenses of a department may be escaped by eliminating the department, but a(n) _____ will continue even though the department is discontinued.

11. In departmental accounting two different kinds of departments are recognized. One is engaged directly in the production of a product or in making sales and is called a _____ department. The other kind is called a _____ department because these departments perform some service for the production departments.

12. Fifteen meters of Material X costing $12.00 per meter produce 5 meters of Product Y which sell for $50 per meter and 10 meters of Product Z which sell for $15 per meter. If the $180 cost of the 15 meters of Material X is allocated to Products Y and Z in the ratio of their market values, Product Y should bear $ 112.5 of the cost and Product Z should bear $ 67.5.

13. Departmental information is used by management in _____ operations, _____ performances, allocating resources, and in taking remedial actions but is generally not intended for use by outside parties.

14. The usual method for allocating a joint cost among several products is the ratio of _____

_____

_____.

15. In a system of responsibility accounting, performance reports compare _____

_____ with _____

_____.

Problem I

1.	T	6.	F
2.	F	7.	T
3.	F	8.	F
4.	T	9.	T
5.	F	10.	T

Problem II

1. A
2. A
3. D

Problem III

Common expenses	12	Inescapable expenses	16
Controllable costs	20	Joint cost	14
Cost centre	2	Performance report	1
Departmental accounting	4	Production departments	19
Departmental contribution to overhead	10	Profit centre	17
Direct costs or expenses	15	Responsibility accounting	13
Direct expenses	8	Responsibility accounting budget	18
Escapable expenses	7	Segmental reporting	6
Indirect costs or expenses	9	Service departments	3
Indirect expenses	5	Uncontrollable cost	11

Problem IV

1. indirect, service

2. costs and expenses

3. indirect expenses

4. controllable costs and expenses are under the control of the manager, and some of the factors that enter into net income and contribution to overhead are not

5. indirect expenses

6. exceed its direct costs and expenses

7. indirect expenses

8. inescapable expenses

9. cost, profit

10. inescapable expenses

11. production, service

12. Product Y, $112.50; Product Z, $67.50

13. controlling, appraising

14. the market values of the joint products at the point of separation

15. actual costs and expenses, budgeted costs and expenses

24 Cost-Volume-Profit Analysis

After studying Chapter 24, you should be able to:

1. Describe the different types of cost behaviour experienced by a typical company.

2. State the assumptions that underlie cost-volume-profit analysis and explain how these assumptions restrict the usefulness of the information obtained from the analysis.

3. Prepare and interpret a scatter diagram of past costs and sales volume.

4. Calculate a break-even point for a single product company and graphically plot its costs and revenues.

5. Describe some extensions that may be added to the basic cost-volume-profit analysis of a business's break-even point.

6. Calculate a composite sales unit for a multiproduct company and a break-even point for such a company.

7. Define or explain the words and phrases listed in the chapter Glossary.

Topical Outline

I. Cost-volume-profit analysis

   A. A means of predicting the effect of changes in costs and sales levels on the income of a business.

   B. Often called break-even analysis—because it involves the determination of the sales level at which a company neither earns a profit nor incurs a loss (the point at which it breaks even).

II. Cost behavior

   A. Fixed cost—remains unchanged in total amount over a wide range of production levels.

   B. Variable cost—total amount changes proportionately with production level changes.

   C. Semivariable cost—changes with production level changes, but not proportionately.

   D. Stair-step (step-variable) cost—remains constant over a given range of production.

III. Cost assumptions

   A. If a cost-volume-profit analysis is to be reliable, the following assumptions must be reasonably accurate:

      1. Per unit selling price must be constant.

      2. Costs classified as "variable" must, in fact, behave as variable costs.

      3. Costs classified as "fixed must, in fact, remain constant over wide changes in the level of production.

   B. These assumptions tend to provide reliable analyses because:

      1. Even if individual variable (or fixed) costs do not act in a truly variable (or fixed) manner, aggregating such costs may offset such violations of the assumption.

      2. The assumptions are intended to apply only over the relevant range of operations.

IV. Estimating cost behavior

   A. Mixed cost—a cost that includes two components, one of which is fixed and one of which is variable.

   B. Scatter diagram—a graph used to display the relationship between costs and volume in which the cost and volume for each period is shown as a point on the diagram.

   C. Estimated line of cost behavior—attempts to reflect the average relationship between total costs and sales volume.

      1. A crude means of deriving this line is the high-low method.

      2. A visual placement of the estimated line of cost behavior on a scatter diagram is often a better method.

      3. A more sophisticated method is the statistical method of least-square regression.

V. Break-even analysis

   A. Break-even point—the sales level at which a company neither earns a profit nor incurs a loss.

   B. Break-even point in units $= \dfrac{\text{Fixed costs}}{\text{Contribution margin per unit}}$

   C. Break-even point in dollars $= \dfrac{\text{Fixed costs}}{\text{Contribution rate}}$

   D. Contribution margin per unit $=$ Sales price $-$ Variable costs per unit

   E. Contribution rate $=$ Contribution margin per unit expressed as a percentage of sales price.

   F. A cost-volume-profit analysis may be shown graphically in a break-even graph.

VI. Extensions of the break-even calculation concept

A. Sales required for a desired net income

$$\text{Sales at desired income level} = \frac{\text{Fixed costs} + \text{Net income} + \text{Income taxes}}{\text{Contribution rate}}$$

B. Margin of safety

$$\text{Margin of safety} = \frac{\text{Sales} - \text{Break-even sales}}{\text{Sales}}$$

C. Income from a given sales level

$$\text{Income} = \text{Sales} - (\text{Fixed costs} + \text{Variable costs})$$

VII. Multiproduct break-even point

A. A composite unit is a hypothetical unit made up of the units of each product in their expected sales mix.

B. $$\text{Break-even point in composite units} = \frac{\text{Fixed costs}}{\text{Composite contribution margin per unit}}$$

Problem I

The following statements are either true or false. Place a (T) in the parentheses before each true statement and an (F) before each false statement.

1. (T) An example of a cost that behaves in a stair-step manner is a salesperson's compensation which consists of both a constant salary amount and a commission based on the volume of products he or she sells.

2. ( ) In cost-volume-profit analysis, the level of activity is usually measured in terms of sales volume.

3. ( ) An assumption of traditional cost-volume-profit analysis is that costs are either fixed or variable.

4. ( ) A scatter diagram allows a graphical analysis of past cost and volume relationships.

5. ( ) To find the break-even point in units, fixed costs are divided by the contribution rate.

6. ( ) A break-even chart can be completed without showing the horizontal fixed cost line.

7. ( ) In a break-even chart, the distance between the sales line and total cost line at a sales volume level to the right of the break-even point represents a loss.

8. ( ) The margin of safety is the excess of current sales over budgeted sales.

9. ( ) Cost-volume-profit analysis is not helpful for planning changes in business operations because the variables are assumed to remain constant.

10. ( ) In a multiproduct break-even analysis, a composite unit is treated as a single product.

Problem II

You are given several words, phrases or numbers to choose from in completing each of the following statements or in answering the following questions. In each case select the one that best completes the statement or answers the question and place its letter in the answer space provided.

_____ C 1. Assume that two points from the estimated line of cost behavior from a scatter diagram are as follows:

	Sales Axis	Cost Axis
First point	$42,000	$28,000
Second point	14,000	18,200

Calculate the variable cost per sales dollar (rounded to the nearest whole cent).

a. $2.86.
b. $0.01.
c. $0.35.
d. $0.82.
e. Cannot be determined from information given.

_____ 2. Functional Design Furniture Company sells a product for $79 per unit and incurs $54 of variable costs per unit sold. If the fixed costs involved in selling the product are $8,500 per month, at what sales volume will the company break even?

a. $ 8,500.
b. $34,000.
c. $ 340.
d. $26,860.
e. $18,360.

408

3. VideOasis Company has monthly fixed costs of $11,700 and a 25% contribution rate. Management has set a goal of earning a monthly after-tax income of $8,000. In order to have an $8,000 net income the company must earn a pretax income of $12,000 and pay $4,000 in taxes. What level of sales is necessary to produce the $8,000 net income?

   a. $ 78,800.
   b. $ 94,800.
   c. $ 58,800.
   d. $126,800.
   e. $ 30,800.

4. Slice Master Corp. sold 7,200 units of its product in July for $15 each. Fixed costs for the month were $43,200 and variable costs were $48,600. What is Slice Master's margin of safety in dollars for the month of July?

   a. $12,000.00
   b. $78,545.45
   c. $29,454.55
   d. $16,200.00
   e. $ –0–

Problem III

Many of the important ideas and concepts discussed in Chapter 24 are reflected in the following list of key terms. Test your understanding of these terms by matching the appropriate definition with the terms. Record the number identifying the most appropriate definition in the blank space next to each term.

_____ Break-even analysis

_____ Break-even chart

_____ Break-even graph

_____ Break-even point

_____ Contribution margin per unit

_____ Contribution rate

_____ Cost-volume-profit analysis

_____ Estimated line of cost behaviour

_____ Fixed cost

_____ High-low method

_____ Least-squares regression

_____ Margin of safety

_____ Mixed cost

_____ Relevant range of operations

_____ Sales mix

_____ Scatter diagram

_____ Semivariable cost

_____ Stair-step cost

_____ Step-variable cost

_____ Variable cost

1. A cost that can be separated into two components, one of which is fixed and one of which is variable.

2. A crude technique for deriving an estimated line of cost behavior that connects the highest and lowest costs shown on a scatter diagram with a straight line.

3. The ratio in which a company's different products are sold.

4. A synonym for cost-volume-profit analysis.

5. A cost that changes with production volume, not in the same proportion but in a curvilinear manner.

409

6. A sophisticated method of deriving an estimated line of cost behavior, the result of which is a line that best fits the actual cost and sales volume experience of a company.

7. A cost the total amount of which changes proportionately with changes in production volume.

8. The amount by which a company's current sales exceed the sales necessary to break even.

9. A method of predicting the effects of changes in costs and sales level on the income of a business.

10. The dollar amount that the sale of one unit contributes toward the recovery of fixed costs and profits.

11. A cost that remains unchanged in total amount from period to period even though production volume may vary over a wide range.

12. A graph used to display the relationship between costs and volume in which the cost and volume for each period is shown as a point on the diagram.

13. The contribution margin per unit expressed as a percentage of sales price.

14. A cost that remains constant over a range of production, then increases by a lump sum if production is expanded beyond this range, then remains constant over another range of production, and so forth.

15. A line on a scatter diagram that is intended to reflect the average relationship between costs and volume.

16. The sales level at which a company neither earns a profit nor incurs a loss.

17. The normal operating range of a business, which excludes extremely high and low levels of production that are not apt to be encountered.

18. A synonym for break-even graph.

19. A synonym for stair-step cost.

20. A graphical presentation of the revenues and total costs of a business that shows the sales volume at which the business neither earns a profit nor incurs a loss.

Problem IV

Complete the following by filling in the blanks.

1. The _____ (total, per unit) amount of a variable cost changes with production volume and in the same proportion. A typical example of a variable cost is _____.

2. A fixed cost remains _____ at all levels of production within the relevant range; however, fixed costs per unit of product produced decrease as the number of units _____. A typical example of a fixed cost is _____.

3. The _____ method of deriving an estimated line of cost behavior results in an approximation that can be described as a line that best fits the actual cost and sales volume experience of the company.

4. An obvious deficiency of the high-low method of deriving an estimated line of cost behavior is that _____

_____

_____

_____.

5. In preparing a scatter diagram of costs and volume, _____ normally is measured on the horizontal axis and _____ normally is measured on the vertical axis.

6. When lumped together, a number of variable costs that are not truly variable often tend to _____ each other and can therefore be plotted as a straight line in a cost-volume-profit analysis.

7. When the selling price per unit of product is not constant, or variable costs are not truly variable, or fixed costs are not truly fixed, the results of a cost-volume-profit analysis will not be _____.

8. Conventional cost-volume-profit analysis is based on relationships that can be expressed as straight lines. Three assumptions that underlie the analysis are:

   a. _____,

   b. _____,

   c. _____.

9. Semivariable costs vary with volume but not in the same _____.

Problem V

A company incurs $60,000 of annual fixed costs in manufacturing and selling a product that it sells for $15 per unit. The variable costs of manufacturing and selling the product are $9 per unit.

1. The contribution margin on each unit of product sold is $_____6_____.

2. The contribution rate on the product is:

   $$\frac{\text{Contribution Margin, \$} \quad 6}{\text{Selling Price per Unit, \$} \quad 15} \times 100 = \underline{\quad 40 \quad}\%$$

3. The break-even point in units is:

   $$\frac{\text{Fixed Costs, \$} \quad 60,000}{\text{Contribution Margin, \$} \quad 6} = \underline{10,000}\text{ Units}$$

4. The break-even point in dollars is:

   $$\frac{\text{Fixed Costs, \$} \quad 60,000}{\text{Contribution Rate, } \quad 40 \quad \%} = \$\underline{150,000}$$

5. Assume a 30% income tax rate, and present below the formula and the calculation of the sales volume in dollars this company must achieve to earn a $35,000 annual after-tax net income.

6. Assume a 30% income tax rate, and calculate below the after-tax income the company will earn from a $420,000 sales volume.

⑤ Dollar Sales at desired Income level = $\frac{\text{Fixed Costs + Net Income + Income Taxes}}{\text{Contribution Rate}}$

$= \frac{60,000 + 35,000 + 15,000}{40\%}$

$= \$275,000 \,/\!/$

⑥ Before Tax Income = Sales − (Fixed Costs + Variable Costs)

$= 420,000 - (60,000 + \frac{0.6 \times 420,000}{2 \times 2,000})$

$= 108,000$

Net Income = $108,000 \times 0.7 = \$75,600$

411

Solutions for Chapter 24

Problem I

1.	F	6.	T
2.	T	7.	F
3.	T	8.	F
4.	T	9.	F
5.	F	10.	T

Problem II

1. C
2. D
3. B
4. C

Problem III

Break-even analysis	4 or 9	Least-squares regression	6
Break-even chart	18 or 20	Margin of safety	8
Break-even graph	20	Mixed cost	1
Break-even point	16	Relevant range of operations	17
Contribution margin per unit	10	Sales mix	3
Contribution rate	13	Scatter diagram	12
Cost-volume-profit analysis	9	Semivariable cost	5
Estimated line of cost behavior	15	Stair-step cost	14
Fixed cost	11	Step-variable cost	19 or 14
High-low method	2	Variable cost	7

Problem IV

1. total, direct material costs

2. the same or unchanged, increases, rent or property taxes

3. least-squares regression

4. it totally ignores all of the available cost and sales volume points except the highest and the lowest

5. volume in dollars or units, cost

6. offset

7. reliable

8. a. The per unit selling price is constant.
   b. Costs classified as variable actually behave as variable costs.
   c. Costs classified as fixed actually remain unchanged over the relevant range.

9. proportion

Problem V

1. $6

2. $\dfrac{\text{Contribution Margin, \$6}}{\text{Selling Price per Unit, \$15}} = 40\%$

3. $\dfrac{\text{Fixed Costs, \$60,000}}{\text{Contribution Margin, \$6}} = 10{,}000 \text{ Units}$

4. $\dfrac{\text{Fixed Costs, \$60,000}}{\text{Contribution Rate, 40\%}} = \$150,000$

5. $\dfrac{\text{Fixed Costs, \$60,000} + \text{Net Income, \$35,000} + \text{Income Taxes, \$15,000}}{\text{Contribution Rate, 40\%}} = \$275,000$

6. Variable costs are 60% of sales.
   Before-Tax Income = Sales − [Fixed Costs + (0.6 × Sales)]
   Before-Tax Income = $420,000 − [$60,000 + (0.6 × $420,000)] = $108,000
   After-Tax Income = $108,000 × 70% = $75,600

25

The Master Budget: A Formal Plan for the Business

After studying Chapter 25, you should be able to:

1. Explain the importance of budgeting and describe the benefits that result from budgeting.

2. Describe the content of a master budget and list the sequence of steps required to prepare a master budget.

3. Prepare each budget in a master budget and explain the importance of each budget to the overall budgeting process.

4. Integrate the individual budgets into planned financial statements.

5. Define or explain the words and phrases listed in the chapter Glossary.

Topical Outline

I.   The budgeting process

   A.   Budgeting is a process of preparing a formal statement of future plans.

      1.   A master budget is a comprehensive or overall plan for the business.
      2.   Rolling budgets involve a series of revised budgets that are prepared in the practice of continuous budgeting.

   B.   Benefits from budgeting

      1.   Promotes study, research, and a focus on the future.
      2.   Provides a basis for evaluating performance.
      3.   Provides a source of motivation for employees.
      4.   Provides a means of coordinating business activities.
      5.   Provides a system of communicating plans and instructions.

   C.   Budget committee—should include representatives from the various subunits of the business that are affected by the budget.

   D.   The budget period

      1.   Normally coincides with the accounting period.
      2.   For long-range plans, may involve five to ten years in the future.

II.   The master budget typically includes:

   A.   Operating budgets

      1.   Sales budget.
      2.   For merchandising companies, a merchandise purchases budget.
      3.   For manufacturing companies:

         a.   Production budget.
         b.   Manufacturing budget.

      4.   Selling expense budget.
      5.   General and administrative expense budget.

   B.   Capital expenditures budget

   C.   Financial budgets

      1.   Budgeted statement of cash receipts and cash disbursements (called the cash budget).
      2.   Budgeted income statement.
      3.   Budgeted balance sheet.

III.   Preparing the master budget

   A.   The sales budget must be prepared first.
   B.   The remaining operating budgets are prepared next.
   C.   The capital expenditures budget is prepared next.
   D.   The budgeted statement of cash receipts and disbursements (the cash budget) is prepared next.
   E.   The budgeted income statement is prepared next.
   F.   Finally, the budgeted balance sheet is prepared.

Problem I

The following statements are either true or false. Place a (T) in the parentheses before each true statement and an (F) before each false statement.

1. ( ) Budgeting makes planning an explicit responsibility of management.

2. ( ) Because budgets use many estimates, during a performance evaluation it is better to compare actual performance results with past performance amounts, rather than with budgeted amounts.

3. ( ) As a control measure, the production department should not participate in the preparation of its own budget because it is likely that the production managers will "pad" the budgeted amounts.

4. ( ) If a company always has a budget for the next twelve months, it is using continuous budgeting.

5. ( ) The production budget is the first budget prepared by a manufacturing company.

6. ( ) The last step in the master budgeting process is to prepare a budgeted balance sheet.

7. ( ) A production budget does not include budgeted production costs.

8. ( ) A successful just-in-time inventory system depends in part upon good relations with suppliers and a sales demand that can be reasonably estimated.

9. ( ) Companies use a capital expenditures budget to ensure that they will have cash available to meet operating needs.

10. ( ) Budgets show how much money is to be received from or expended on each activity and when the receipts and expenditures are to occur.

Problem II

You are given several words, phrases or numbers to choose from in completing each of the following statements or in answering the following questions. In each case select the one that best completes the statement or answers the question and place its letter in the answer space provided.

_____ 1. Playland has budgeted sales of $34,000 during September. The store expects to begin September with an $18,700 inventory and end the month with a $16,500 inventory. Playland's cost of goods sold averages 60% of sales. Determine budgeted purchases for September.

    a. $11,400.
    b. $22,600.
    c. $30,100.
    d. $14,800.
    e. $18,200.

_____ 2. Fabricon Company manufactures a product called the Streamer. Management estimates that there will be 12,000 units of Streamer in the June 30 finished goods inventory, that 26,500 units will be sold during the third quarter, that 57,000 units will be sold during the fourth quarter, and that 24,600 will be sold during the first quarter of the next year. Management believes that the company should begin each quarter with finished goods inventory equal to 40% of the next quarter's budgeted sales. Determine the number of units to be manufactured by Fabricon during the third and fourth quarters in order to meet budgeted expectations.

    a. 37,300 third quarter; 44,040 fourth quarter.
    b. 49,300 third quarter; 66,840 fourth quarter.
    c. 38,700 third quarter; 44,040 fourth quarter.

417

d. 37,300 third quarter; 69,960 fourth quarter.
e. 61,300 third quarter; 89,640 fourth quarter.

_____ 3. High Flying Kite Company has the following sales budget:

January	$ 7,000
February	11,000
March	26,000
April	35,000

The company budgets cost of goods sold to be 60% of sales and plans to purchase enough merchandise each month to provide a beginning inventory that is 40% of budgeted cost of goods sold for the month. All purchases are on credit and 20% of the purchases in any month is paid for during the same month; another 50% is paid during the first month after purchase; and the remaining 30% is paid in the second month after purchase. Calculate the budgeted amounts of accounts payable at the end of March.

a. $14,208.
b. $19,308.
c. $17,268.
d. $24,100.
e. $17,760.

Problem III

Many of the important ideas and concepts discussed in Chapter 25 are reflected in the following list of key terms. Test your understanding of these terms by matching the appropriate definitions with the terms. Record the number identifying the most appropriate definition in the blank space next to each term.

_____ Budget

_____ Budgeted balance sheet

_____ Budgeted income statement

_____ Budgeting

_____ Capital expenditures budget

_____ Cash budget

_____ Continuous budgeting

_____ Just-in-time inventory system

_____ Manufacturing budget

_____ Master budget

_____ Merchandise purchases budget

_____ Production budget

_____ Rolling budgets

_____ Safety stock

_____ Sales budget

1. A comprehensive or overall plan for the business that typically includes budgets for sales, expenses, production, capital expenditures, cash, and also a planned income statement and balance sheet.

2. A projected balance sheet estimated to result at the end of the budget period if the activities projected in each of the related budgets actually occur.

3. A plan that states the estimated amount of goods to be sold and revenue to be derived from sales during each of the future periods covered by the budget; serves as the usual starting point in the budgeting procedure.

4. A formal statement of future plans, usually expressed in monetary terms.

5. A sequence of revised budgets that are prepared in the practice of continuous budgeting.

6. A projected income statement that draws on the estimates shown in all of the related revenue and expense budgets and shows the effects of the separate budgets on the income of the budget period.

7. A statement of the estimated costs for raw materials, direct labor, and manufacturing overhead to be incurred in producing the number of units estimated in the production budget.

8. A plan that states the number of units to be manufactured during each future period covered by the budget, based on the budgeted sales for the period and the levels of inventory necessary to support future sales.

9. A quantity of merchandise or materials, in addition to the amount necessary to satisfy budgeted sales demand, that is held as inventory to compensate for unexpected demand or delays in receipts from suppliers.

10. A plan that states the expected cash receipts and disbursements during each of the periods covered by the budget, including receipts from loans necessary to maintain an adequate cash balance and repayments of such loans.

11. A plan that states the units and/or cost of merchandise to be purchased by a merchandising company during each future period covered by the budget.

12. A plan that states the plant and equipment to be purchased during each period covered by the budget, based on the budgeted sales and manufacturing needs and the long-range plans for business expansion.

13. The process of planning future business actions and expressing those plans in a formal manner.

14. A method of keeping inventory levels at or near zero by ordering just enough merchandise (or materials) to satisfy the immediate sales demand.

15. The practice of preparing budgets for each of several future periods and revising those budgets each period, adding a new budget each time so that budgets are always available for a given number of future periods.

Problem IV

Complete the following by filling in the blanks.

1. When a budget committee returns a budget to a department for reconsideration and the department adjusts the budgeted amounts, it is especially important for all parties to agree that the budget figures are _____

_____

2. Central guidance in preparing a master budget is provided by the _____

_____, which often is made up of _____

_____

who are responsible for seeing that budget figures are realistically established and coordinated.

3. Benefits to be obtained from budgeting include:

a. _____

_____

b. _____

_____

c. _____

_____

d. _____

_____.

e. _____

_____.

4. Long-range budgets of two, three, five, and ten years should reflect the planned accomplishment of _____. These budgets are particularly important in planning for _____.

5. The first budget to be prepared in the process of developing a master budget is the _____;

the last statement or budget to be prepared in the sequence is the _____

_____.

6. The three types of budgets included in a master budget are:

a. _____.

b. _____.

c. _____.

7. The practice of revising the entire set of budgets as each monthly or quarterly budget period goes by, adding new budgets to replace those that have elapsed, thus maintaining budgets for a full year in advance, is called _____. The budgets resulting from this process are called

_____.

8. A master budget is _____

_____

9. A budget is _____

_____

10. Budgeting is the process of _____

_____

11. A company's potential need for short-term loans would be discovered in the process of preparing a

_____.

12. Planned purchases of new plant and equipment are disclosed in the _____

_____.

13. A budget that is used only by merchandising companies is the _____

_____; manufacturing companies, on the other hand, are unique in their use

of _____ and _____.

Solutions for Chapter 25

Problem I

1.	T	6.	T
2.	F	7.	T
3.	F	8.	T
4.	T	9.	F
5.	F	10.	T

Problem II

1. E
2. A
3. C

Problem III

Budget	4	Manufacturing budget	7
Budgeted balance sheet	2	Master budget	1
Budgeted income statement	6	Merchandise purchases budget	11
Budgeting	13	Production budget	8
Capital expenditures budget	12	Rolling budgets	5
Cash budget	10	Safety stock	9
Continuous budgeting	15	Sales budget	3
Just-in-time inventory system	14		

Problem IV

1. reasonable and attainable

2. budget committee, department heads or other high-level executives

3. a. Good decision-making processes based on research, study, and a focus on the future
   b. A superior basis for evaluating performance and a more effective control mechanism
   c. A means of motivating people
   d. A system of coordinating business activities
   e. A means of communicating management's plans to the organization

4. long-range objectives, major expenditures of capital to buy plant and equipment

5. sales budget, budgeted balance sheet

6. a. Operating budgets
   b. Capital expenditures budget
   c. Financial budgets

7. continuous budgeting, rolling budgets

8. a comprehensive or overall plan for the business

9. a formal statement of future plans

10. planning future business actions and expressing those plans in a formal manner

11. cash budget

12. capital expenditures budget

13. merchandise purchases budget; production budgets, manufacturing budgets

26 Flexible Budgets; Standard Costs

After studying Chapter 26, you should be able to:

1. Describe the differences between and relative advantages of fixed budgets and flexible budgets and be able to prepare a flexible budget.

2. State what standard costs represent, how they are determined, and how they are used by management to evaluate performance.

3. Calculate material, labour, and overhead variances, and state what each variance indicates about the performance of a company.

4. Explain the relevance of standard cost accounting to the management philosophy known as management by exception.

5. Prepare entries to record standard costs and to account for price and quantity variances.

6. Define or explain the words and phrases listed in the chapter Glossary.

Topical Outline

I. Fixed budgets and performance reports

   A. A fixed or static budget is based on a single estimate of sales or production volume.

   B. Comparisons between actual and budgeted amounts are presented in a performance report.

      1. Differences between actual and budgeted amounts are called variances.

      2. In a fixed budget performance report, reported variances may result from activity levels being different from budgeted amounts and also from unexpected levels of efficiency or inefficiency.

II. Flexible budgets

   A. Each type of cost is classified as a variable cost or as a fixed cost.

      1. Each variable cost is expressed as a constant amount of cost per unit of sales (or per sales dollar).

      2. Fixed costs are budgeted in terms of the total amount of each fixed cost that is expected regardless of the sales volume that may occur within the relevant range.

   B. A flexible budget performance report is designed to analyze the difference between actual performance and budgeted performance, given the actual level of operations.

III. Standard costs and variance analysis

   A. One variation of the two basic types of manufacturing systems (job order and process) is a standard cost system.

      1. Standard costs are, in effect, budgeted costs.

      2. Variances are differences between actual costs and standard costs.

   B. Material and labor variances

      1. Cost variance = quantity variance ± price variance.

      2. Quantity variance = (actual units − standard units) × standard price.

      3. Price variance = (actual price − standard price) × actual units.

   C. Overhead variances

      1. Volume variance = budgeted overhead at the actual operating level less the standard overhead charged to production.

      2. Controllable variance = overhead actually incurred less overhead budgeted at the operating level achieved.

      3. The volume and controllable variances may be combined to account for the difference between overhead actually incurred and overhead charged to production.

   D. Use of standard costs and variance analysis focuses management's attention on irregular performance and follows the principle of management by exception.

   E. Standard costs may be recorded in the accounts or used in analyses that are not entered in the accounts.

Problem I

The following statements are either true or false. Place a (T) in the parentheses before each true statement and an (F) before each false statement.

1. ( ) A fixed budget performance report compares actual costs with budgeted costs at the operating level actually achieved.

2. ( ) The classification of a cost as fixed or variable is standard for all businesses. For example, office supplies are always variable costs.

3. ( ) A flexible budget performance report bases budgeted amounts on the actual sales volume or level of activity.

4. ( ) Standard costs are determined by averaging historical costs which occur within the relevant or normal operating range of activity.

5. ( ) A variance is favourable if actual cost is below standard cost.

6. ( ) If the standard direct material cost for producing 10 units of a product is $200 and the actual direct material cost was $195 for those units, then the $5 variance must have resulted from paying a price for the material that was lower than the standard price.

7. ( ) An unfavourable volume variance indicates that plant production did not reach the expected operating level.

8. ( ) An entry to record the standard material cost in the Goods in Process account and to record an unfavourable material quantity variance would include a debit to Direct Material Quantity Variance.

9. ( ) When variances are recorded in separate variance accounts, they are closed directly to Cost of Goods Sold at the end of an accounting period if the amounts are immaterial.

Problem II

You are given several words, phrases or numbers to choose from in completing each of the following statements or in answering the following questions. In each case select the one that best completes the statement or answers the question and place its letter in the answer space provided.

_____ 1. Utopia Springs Company manufactures and sells spas. Which of the following costs is likely to be classified as fixed?

    a. Fiberglass materials used to make the spa.
    b. Installation costs.
    c. Direct labour.
    d. Depreciation on manufacturing equipment.
    e. All of the above.

_____ 2. Given the following information, calculate the actual cost of direct materials.

Standard direct materials (10 kgs. @ $4/kg.)	$40/unit
Actual direct materials used	11,340 kgs.
Direct materials cost variance	$2,400 (F)
Actual finished units manufactured	1,080

    a. $45,600.
    b. $42,960.
    c. $43,200.
    d. $40,800.
    e. $47,760.

_____ 3. Pentagonal Company's fixed budget for the first quarter of 1991 is shown below. Calculate the budgeted income from operations using a flexible budget for 28,000 units.

Sales (26,000)		$124,800
Cost of goods sold:		
Direct materials	$24,700	
Direct labour	26,000	
Depreciation	1,600	
Supervisory salaries	6,200	(58,500)
Gross profit		$ 66,300
Selling expenses:		
Sales commissions	$10,400	
Packaging expense	2,600	(13,000)
Administrative expenses:		
Administrative salaries	$ 5,200	
Insurance expense	1,300	
Office rent expense	3,900	(10,400)
Income from operations		$ 42,900

    a. $48,000.
    b. $46,200.
    c. $53,500.
    d. $47,600.
    e. $47,100.

Problem III

Many of the important ideas and concepts discussed in Chapter 26 are reflected in the following list of key terms. Test your understanding of these terms by matching the appropriate definitions with the terms. Record the number identifying the most appropriate definition in the blank space next to each term.

_____ Controllable variance   _____ Performance report

_____ Cost variance   _____ Price variance

_____ Fixed budget   _____ Quantity variance

_____ Flexible budget   _____ Standard costs

_____ Flexible budget performance report   _____ Static budget

_____ Historical costs   _____ Variable budget

_____ Management by exception   _____ Variance analysis

_____ Overhead cost variance   _____ Volume variance

1. A synonym for fixed budget.

2. A technique whereby management focuses its attention on areas in which actual costs are significantly different from standard costs and pays less attention to the cost situations in which performance is satisfactory.

3. The difference between actual cost and budgeted cost that was caused by a difference between the actual number of units used and the number of units budgeted.

4. A financial report that compares actual cost and/or revenue performance with budgeted amounts and designates the differences between them as favourable or unfavourable variances.

5. The difference between the overhead actually incurred and the overhead budgeted at the operating level achieved.

6. The difference between the amount of overhead budgeted at the actual operating level achieved during the period and the standard amount of overhead charged to production during the period.

7. A budget that is based on a single estimate of sales or production volume and that gives no consideration to the possibility that the actual sales or production volume may differ from the assumed amount.

8. The costs that should be incurred under normal conditions to produce a given product or part or to perform a particular service.

9. A difference between actual and budgeted revenue or cost caused by the actual price per unit being different from the budgeted price per unit.

10. A financial report that compares actual performance to budgeted amounts that are based on the actual sales volume or level of activity, and presents the differences between actual and budgeted amounts as variances.

11. A synonym for flexible budget.

12. The difference between the actual or incurred amount of a cost and the standard amount or, in the case of overhead, the standard amount applied to production.

13. A budget that separates variable costs from fixed costs and presents variable costs on a per unit basis so that budgeted amounts can be calculated for all levels of production within the relevant range.

14. The difference between the actual overhead incurred during a period and the standard overhead applied to production.

15. A process of examining the differences between actual revenues or costs and budgeted revenues or costs and describing the differences in terms of the amounts that resulted from factors such as price and quantity differences.

16. Dollar amounts of consideration given by the business in past transactions.

Problem IV

Complete the following by filling in the blanks.

1. Standard costs are the costs that _____ be incurred under normal conditions to produce a given product, part, or service; and they are used to judge _____ incurred when the product or service is produced. _____ are also used to identify possible problems when actual costs vary from standard.

2. A standard cost system is one based on standard or _____ costs.

3. In analyzing the total variance in a cost such as direct materials, the portion that is caused by a difference between the actual price per unit and the budgeted price per unit is called a _____.
The portion caused by a difference between the actual number of units used and the budgeted number of units to be used is called a _____.

4. A flexible budget performance report is designed to analyze _____ _____ _____, where the budgeted amounts are based on the _____ sales volume or level of activity.

5. A volume variance results when the operating level of a factory varies from the standard or _____ _____ operating level.

6. When overhead costs vary from standard, the variance may be divided into a _____ variance and a _____ variance.

7. In preparing a flexible budget each _____ cost is expressed as a constant amount of cost per unit of sales (or per sales dollar). Each _____ cost is budgeted in terms of the total amount that is expected to be incurred.

8. Preparation of a flexible budget requires that each type of cost be analyzed and classified as either _____ or _____.

9. Budgets that recognize the fact that different levels of activity should produce different amounts of cost are called _____ or _____ budgets.

10. A budget that is based on a single estimate of sales volume is called a _____ or _____ budget.

11. A variable budget is used in establishing standard overhead costs because when actual costs are known, they should be compared with the standards of the production level actually _____ and not with those of some other "hoped for" level.

12. A _____ or variable factory overhead budget is the starting point in establishing reasonable standards for overhead costs.

13. When actual costs vary from standard costs, the difference is called a _____, and may be either favourable or unfavourable. A _____ is favourable when actual costs are _____ (below, above) the standard.

14. Standard costs are established by means of accounting, engineering, personnel, and other studies made _____ (before, after) the product, part, or service is produced.

15. When management by exception is practiced, management gives its attention only to variances in which actual costs are significantly different from _____ and ignores situations in which performance is _____.

16. Control of a business is gained by _____ the actions of the people who are responsible for its revenues, costs, and expenses; and when a standard cost system is in use, control is maintained by taking appropriate actions when _____ vary from standard.

Problem V

A company purchased 940 kilos of material for $16,544 and used the material to produce 3,100 units of product. The standards for this material are 0.28 kgs. of material per unit of product at $18 per kg. Calculate the material price, quantity, and cost variances related to this situation.

Price variance:

_____ (Actual units) × _____ (Actual price)   = $_____

_____ (Actual units) × _____ (Std. price)   =   _____

Price variance _____ (favourable or unfavourable)   = $_____

Quantity variance:

_____ (Actual units) × _____ (Std. price)   = $_____

_____ (Std. units)   × _____ (Std. price)   =   _____

Quantity variance _____ (favourable or unfavourable)   = $_____

Cost variance:

_____ (Actual units) × _____ (Actual price)   = $_____

_____ (Std. units)   × _____ (Std. price)   =   _____

Cost variance _____ (favourable or unfavourable)   = $_____

Problem VI

A company operated at 82% of capacity, producing 6,560 units of product, and incurring $24,560 of overhead costs. The company was budgeted to operate at 90% of capacity, which would have produced 7,200 units of product. Budgeted overhead at 90% of capacity is $25,200, consisting of $10,800 variable cost and $14,400 fixed cost. Calculate answers to the following questions.

(a) What was the predetermined standard overhead rate (per unit of product)?

$$\frac{\text{\$_____ budgeted overhead at 90\% capacity}}{\text{_____ units of production at 90\% capacity}} \quad = \quad \$_____ \text{ per unit}$$

(b) What was the budgeted variable overhead cost per unit?

$$\frac{\text{\$_____ budgeted variable cost at 90\% capacity}}{\text{_____ units of production at 90\% capacity}} \quad = \quad \$_____ \text{ per unit}$$

(c) What amount of overhead was charged to production?

_____ units produced × _____ overhead rate   = $_____

(d) On a flexible budget, what was the budgeted amount of overhead assuming a production level of 82% of capacity of 6,560 units?

$_____ variable overhead per unit × 6,560 units   = $_____

Budgeted fixed overhead . . . .   =   _____

Total budgeted overhead at 82% of capacity . . . .   = $_____

(e) What was the volume variance?

Budgeted overhead at 82% of capacity .... = $_____

Standard overhead charged to production:

_____ std. overhead rate × 6,560 units produced .... = _____

Variance _____ (favourable or unfavourable) .... = $_____

(f) What was the controllable variance?

Actual overhead incurred .... = $_____

Overhead budgeted at operating level achieved .... = _____

Variance _____ (favourable or unfavourable) .... = $_____

Solutions for Chapter 26

Problem I

1.	F	6.	F
2.	F	7.	T
3.	T	8.	T
4.	F	9.	T
5.	T		

Problem II

1. D
2. D
3. D

Problem III

Controllable variance	. . . .	5	Performance report	. . . .	4

Controllable variance 5

Cost variance 12

Fixed budget 7

Flexible budget 13

Flexible budget performance report .. 10

Historical costs 16

Management by exception 2

Overhead cost variance 14

Performance report 4

Price variance 9

Quantity variance 3

Standard costs 8

Static budget .... 1 or 7

Variable budget .... 11 or 13

Variance analysis 15

Volume variance 6

Problem IV

1. should, the actual costs, Standard costs
2. budgeted
3. price variance, quantity variance
4. the difference between actual performance and budgeted performance, actual
5. expected or normal
6. volume, controllable
7. variable, fixed
8. fixed, variable
9. flexible, variable
10. fixed, static
11. achieved
12. flexible
13. variance, variance, below
14. before
15. standard, satisfactory
16. controlling, actual costs

Problem V

Price variance:
940 (Actual units) × $17.60 (Actual price) .... = $16,544.00
940 (Actual units) × $18.00 (Std. price) .... = 16,920.00
Price variance (favourable) .... = $ 376.00

Quantity variance:
940 (Actual units) × $18.00 (Std. price) .... = $16,920.00
868 (Std. units) × $18.00 (Std. price) .... = 15,624.00
Quantity variance (unfavourable) .... = $ 1,296.00

Cost variance:
940 (Actual units) × $17.60 (Actual price) .... = $16,544.00
868 (Std. units) × $18.00 (Std. price) .... = 15,624.00
Cost variance (unfavourable) .... = $ 920.00

Problem VI

(a) Predetermined standard overhead rate (per unit of product):

$$\frac{\$25,200 \text{ budgeted overhead at 90\% capacity}}{7,200 \text{ units of production at 90\% capacity}} = \$3.50 \text{ per unit}$$

(b) Budgeted variable overhead cost per unit:

$$\frac{\$10,800 \text{ budgeted variable cost at 90\% capacity}}{7,200 \text{ units of production at 90\% capacity}} = \$1.50 \text{ per unit}$$

(c) Amount of overhead charged to production:

6,560 units produced × $3.50 overhead rate = $22,960

(d) Budgeted amount of overhead at 82% of capacity, or 6,560 units:
$1.50 variable overhead per unit × 6,560 units .... = $ 9,840
Budgeted fixed overhead .... = 14,400
Total budgeted overhead at 82% of capacity .... = $24,240

(e) Volume variance:
Budgeted overhead at 82% of capacity .... = $24,240
Standard overhead charged to production:
    $3.50 std. overhead rate × 6,560 units produced .... = 22,960
Variance (unfavourable) .... = $ 1,280

(f) Controllable variance:
Actual overhead incurred .... = $24,560
Overhead budgeted at operating level achieved .... = 24,240
Variance (favourable) .... = $ 320

27

Capital Budgeting; Managerial Decisions

After studying Chapter 27, you should be able to:

1. Explain the importance of capital budgeting, calculate the expected payback period of an investment, and state the limitations of this method of evaluating capital investments.

2. Calculate the expected rate of return on an investment and state the assumptions on which this method of evaluating capital investments is based.

3. Describe the information obtained by using a net present value method, the procedures involved in using this method, and the problems associated with its use.

4. Explain the effects of incremental costs on decisions to accept or reject additional business and whether to make or buy a given product.

5. State the meaning of sunk costs, out-of-pocket costs, and opportunity costs, and describe the importance of each type of cost to decisions such as to scrap or rebuild defective units or to sell a product as is or process it further.

6. Define or explain the words and phrases listed in the chapter Glossary.

Topical Outline

I. Capital budgeting—planning plant asset investments

   A. Payback method of comparing investment opportunities

      1. Payback period in years $= \dfrac{\text{Cost of plant asset}}{\text{Annual net cash flow}}$

      2. This method fails to incorporate:

         a. Fluctuation in annual cash flows.
         b. Length of time revenue will continue to be earned beyond the payback period.

   B. Rate of return on average investment method

      1. Rate of return $= \dfrac{\text{After-tax net income}}{\text{Average investment}}$

      2. Calculation of average investment

         a. If net cash flows are received evenly throughout the year, average investment is the beginning book value plus any salvage value, divided by the number of years in the asset's life.
         b. If net cash flows are received at year-end, average investment is the average of the first and last year's beginning-of-year book values.

      3. This method fails to incorporate:

         a. Relative risk of alternative investments.
         b. Fluctuation in annual cash flows.

   C. Comparison of net present values

      1. All future cash flows are discounted at a rate of return deemed satisfactory by management.
      2. The cost of purchase is subtracted from the present value of future cash flows to determine net present value.
      3. A positive net present value implies a favorable investment.

II. Analysis of specific decisions

   A. Accepting additional business

      1. Incremental (or differential) costs are the relevant costs of accepting additional business.
      2. Sales from additional business should be compared to the incremental costs in deciding whether or not to accept the business.

   B. Important cost concepts

      1. Sunk costs result from past irrevocable decisions and cannot be avoided.
      2. Out-of-pocket costs require a current (or future) outlay of funds.
      3. Opportunity costs are potential benefits lost as a result of choosing an alternative course of action.

   C. Scrap or rebuild defective units

      1. Previously incurred costs to manufacture the units are sunk costs and therefore irrelevant to the decision.
      2. If rebuilding the units uses production capacity that could have otherwise been employed at some net return, that return is an opportunity cost of rebuilding.

D. Process or sell

    1. In evaluating the possibility of further processing, incremental costs and also revenue lost by not selling units as is must be subtracted from revenues from selling processed units.

    2. Past manufacturing costs are sunk costs.

E. Deciding the sales mix

    1. Production capacity should be allocated to products having the largest contribution margin.

    2. If production capacity is limited, contribution margin must be expressed in terms of the amount of return derived from the capacity available.

Problem I

The following statements are either true or false. Place a (T) in the parentheses before each true statement and an (F) before each false statement.

1. ( ) The payback period of an investment is based on estimates of net cash flow.

2. ( ) A long payback period is more desirable than a short payback period.

3. ( ) A higher expected rate of return on one investment is always preferable to a lower expected rate of return on another investment.

4. ( ) When average investment returns are used to compare capital investments, the one with the least risk, the shortest payback period, and the highest return for the longest time is usually the best.

5. ( ) Salvage value and accelerated depreciation cannot have an effect on present value analysis.

6. ( ) Some investments result in cash inflows at the end of each year and the cost recovery from depreciation is therefore assumed to occur at the end of the year. In calculating rate of return on average investment in such cases, average investment may be calculated as the average of the book values at the beginning of the first and last years of the investment.

7. ( ) When a company considers a one-time sale of additional units in a market that will not affect its normal sales activity, the sale should be accepted so long as the revenue from the sale exceeds the average cost of producing the product.

Problem II

You are given several words, phrases or numbers to choose from in completing each of the following statements or in answering the following questions. In each case select the one that best completes the statement or answers the question and place its letter in the answer space provided.

_____ 1. United Carbon Company purchased a machine for $24,000 which has an expected salvage value of $4,000 and is depreciated $4,000 each year. The company expects an after-tax net income of $4,200 from the sale of the machine's product. Assuming cash flows are received evenly throughout the year, calculate the machine's rate of return on average investment.

    a. $14,000.
    b. $12,000.
    c. 30%.
    d. 35%.
    e. 42%.

_____ 2. Motoroma Company is considering a capital investment of $240,000 which is expected to produce cash flows as follows: Year 1, $120,000; Year 2, $140,000; Year 3, $40,000. What is the net present value of the investment if the cash flows are discounted at 12%?

    a. $ 7,228.
    b. $240,180.
    c. $247,228.
    d. $ 60,000.
    e. $ 42,708.

_____ 3. Concordia Corporation has a machine that can produce 40 Zots per hour or produce 60 Pops per hour. The capacity of the machine is 2,400 hours per year. The market demand for Zots is 50,000 per year and 90,000 per year for Pops. Based on the following information, determine the most profitable sales mix for the company.

	Zots	Pops
Selling price per unit	$1.20	$1.00
Variable costs per unit	.70	.60
Contribution margin per unit	$0.50	$0.40

a. Concordia should produce 50,000 Zots and 69,000 Pops.
b. Concordia should produce 96,000 Zots only.
c. Concordia should produce 144,000 Pops only.
d. Concordia should produce 40,000 Zots and 84,000 Pops.
e. Concordia should produce 36,000 Zots and 90,000 Pops.

Problem III

Many of the important ideas and concepts discussed in Chapter 27 are reflected in the following list of key terms. Test your understanding of these terms by matching the appropriate definitions with the terms. Record the number identifying the most appropriate definition in the blank space next to each term.

_____ Capital budgeting

_____ Differential cost

_____ Incremental cost

_____ Net present value

_____ Opportunity cost

_____ Out-of-pocket cost

_____ Payback period

_____ Rate of return on average investment

_____ Sunk cost

1. A synonym for incremental cost.

2. The length of time necessary for the accumulated net cash flows from an investment to equal the original cost of the investment.

3. The benefit of one course of action that is lost or sacrificed as a result of choosing an alternative course of action.

4. A cost that requires a current outlay of funds.

5. Planning plant asset investments in a process that involves preparing cost and revenue estimates for all proposed projects, examining the merits of each, and choosing those worthy of investment.

6. A cost incurred as a consequence of a past irrevocable decision and that, therefore, cannot be avoided; hence, irrelevant to decisions affecting the future.

7. The value of an investment calculated by discounting the future cash flows from the investment at an interest rate that gives a satisfactory return on investment and then subtracting the present cost of the investment.

8. The annual after-tax income that results from using an asset divided by the average investment in the asset.

9. An additional cost that results from a particular course of action.

Problem IV

Complete the following by filling in the blanks.

1. A short payback period should not be the only factor considered in choosing between investment opportunities because the payback period ignores _____ _____ _____.

2. A short payback period is desirable in an investment because the sooner an investment is recovered the sooner the funds are _____.

3. The annual net cash flow from the sale of a machine's product includes the net income earned from the sale of the product plus the annual _____ on the machine.

4. Planning plant asset investments is called _____ _____.

5. An opportunity cost is a _____ that is lost as a result of _____ _____. Opportunity costs _____ (are, are not) entered in the accounting records.

6. An out-of-pocket cost is a cost _____ _____.

7. A sunk cost is a cost resulting from _____ _____.

8. The incremental or differential costs of accepting an additional volume of business are the _____ _____ costs.

9. In choosing between investment opportunities, an investment with a _____ net present value normally should be rejected; and in choosing between two investments that are otherwise equal, the one with the _____ positive net present value usually is the better.

10. It is impossible to say that the return on an investment is either good or bad without relating the return to _____ returns.

Problem V

A company is about to purchase a new machine that will cost $50,000, have a four-year life and no salvage value, and be depreciated on a straight-line basis. Revenues and cost recovery of depreciation are assumed to occur near the end of each year. Also assume that accounting depreciation is acceptable for tax purposes. The company expects to sell the product of the machine during each of the next four years with these annual results:

Sales		$210,000
Costs:		
Materials, labor, and overhead other than depreciation on the new machine	$115,000	
Depreciation on the new machine	12,500	
Selling and administrative expenses	65,000	192,500
Operating income		$ 17,500
Income taxes		7,000
Net income		$ 10,500

1. The investment in this machine will produce an annual net cash flow of $_____.

2. The payback period on this machine is:

$$\frac{\text{Cost of Machine, } \$_____}{\text{Annual Net Cash Flow, } \$_____} = _____ \text{ Years}$$

3. The average investment in this machine is:

$$\frac{\text{Book Value First Year, } \$_____ + \text{Book Value Last Year, } \$_____}{2} = \$_____$$

4. The rate of return on the average investment in this machine is:

$$\frac{\text{Net Income from Sales of Product, } \$_____}{\text{Average Investment, } \$_____} \times 100 = _____ \%$$

5. If the company demands a 10% compound return on capital investments, the net present value of the cash flows from this machine discounted at 10% are:

Present value of the cash flows (3.1699 × _____) .... $_____

Amount to be invested .... _____

Positive net present value .... $_____

Solutions for Chapter 27

Problem I

1. T	5. F
2. F	6. T
3. F	7. F
4. T	

Problem II

1. D
2. A
3. E

Problem III

Capital budgeting	....	5	Out-of-pocket cost	....	4
Differential cost	....	1 or 9	Payback period	....	2
Incremental cost	....	9	Rate of return on average	
Net present value	....	7	investment	....	8
Opportunity cost	....	3	Sunk cost	....	6

Problem IV

1. the length of time cash will be generated after the end of the payback period as well as fluctuations in the annual cash flows

2. available for other uses

3. depreciation

4. capital budgeting

5. potential benefit, choosing an alternative course of action, are not

6. requiring a current outlay of funds

7. a past irrevocable decision

8. additional

9. negative, higher

10. other

Problem V

1. $23,000

2. $\dfrac{\text{Cost of Machine, \$50,000}}{\text{Annual Net Cash Flow, \$23,000}} = 2.2 \text{ years}$

3. $\dfrac{\text{Book Value First Year, \$50,000} + \text{Book Value Last Year, \$12,500}}{2} = \$31,250$

4. $\dfrac{\text{Net Income from Sale of Product, \$10,500}}{\text{Average Investment, \$31,250}} \times 100 = 33.6\%$

5.
Present value of the cash flows (3.1699 × $23,000)	$72,908
Amount to be invested	50,000
Positive net present value	$22,908

28

Tax Considerations in Business Decisions

After studying Chapter 28, you should be able to:

1. Explain the meaning and importance of tax planning.

2. List the classes of income taxpayers and describe the steps an individual must go through to calculate his or her taxable income.

3. Calculate an individual's taxable income and the income tax payable.

4. Define capital assets and describe the tax treatment for capital gains on the sale of capital assets.

5. Describe the differences between calculations of taxable income and tax liability for corporations and for individuals.

6. Explain why income tax expenses shown in financial statements may differ from taxes currently payable.

7. Define or explain the terms and phrases listed in the chapter Glossary.

Topical Outline

I. Tax planning

    A. Designing business transactions to provide the minimum tax under the law is legitimate tax avoidance.

    B. Concealing legal tax liabilities is tax evasion.

    C. Tax planning should take into consideration all forms of tax, not simply income tax.

II. Income tax

    A. Is intended to accomplish a variety of social objectives.

    B. Applies to three different classes of taxpayers:

        1. Individuals.

        2. Corporations.

        3. Estates and trusts.

III. Individual income tax

    A. Typical calculation of income tax payable is:

Gross income
    Less: Deductions to arrive at net income
___

Net income
    Less: Deductions to arrive at taxable income
___

Taxable income
___

    Times: Proper federal tax rates
    Less: Nonrefundable and Dividend tax credits
___

Federal tax
    Plus: Provincial tax
___

Total income tax
___

    B. Gross income—all income from whatever source derived, unless expressly excluded from taxation by law; excluded are:

        1. Gifts.

        2. Inheritances.

        3. Scholarships (up to $500).

        4. Usually, proceeds of life insurance policies paid upon the death of the insured.

        5. Certain types of gains, e.g. on the sale of a principal residence.

    C. Deductions to arrive at net income include:

        1. Ordinary and necessary expenses of a self-employed person in carrying on a business, trade, or profession.

        2. Expenses of producing rent or royalty income.

        3. Certain alimony payments.

        4. Limited amounts of RRSP contributions.

    D. Deductions from net income

        1. Losses of other years.

        2. Capital gains deduction.

    E. Federal income tax rates

        1. Are generally progressive in nature.

        2. Are contained in Tax Rate Schedules or in simplified Tax Tables for those who qualify.

F. Tax credits may include:

   1. Credit for the elderly.
   2. Amounts for self and dependents.
   3. Premiums on Canada (Quebec) Pension and Unemployment Insurance.
   4. Medical expenses and charitable donations.

G. Special treatment of capital gains and losses

   1. As of 1988 individuals are allowed a lifetime exemption on net capital gains of $100,000.
   2. When the exemption is exceeded, 2/3 of net capital gains (3/4 after 1989) are taxable as ordinary income.

IV. Corporation income tax

A. Dividends received by a public corporation from another Canadian corporation are exempt from tax.
B. Dividends received by a private corporation from another Canadian corporation are subject to two sets of rules.
C. The capital gains deduction is not available to corporations.
D. Donations are an allowable income reduction for corporations.

V. Tax effects of business alternatives

A. Form of business organization

   1. Proprietorship or partnership income is included in the income of the proprietor or partners. (The proprietorship or partnership does not pay tax.)
   2. Corporation income is taxed at corporation rates, and any portion paid in dividends is taxed again as individual income to its stockholders.

B. Method of financing

   1. When a corporation is in need of additional financing, a tax advantage may be gained if owners supply funds through long-term loans instead of by purchasing shares.
   2. Interest on borrowed funds is a tax-deductible expense; dividends are a distribution of earnings.

VI. Financial reporting of income tax liabilities and expense

A. Financial statements for a business are prepared in accordance with generally accepted accounting principles, while tax accounting is done in accordance with tax laws. Differences may be permanent or temporary.
B. Special procedures to account for income taxes in financial statements include:

   1. Income tax expense must be calculated as the tax currently payable plus or minus the change in any future tax liability from the beginning of the year to the end of the year.
   2. The future tax liability is the estimated amount that will be due in future years, as a result of transactions that have already occurred.
   3. Depending on how far in the future the liability will be satisfied, the Future Tax Liability account balance may be reported as a long-term liability or as a current liability.

Problem I

The following statements are either true or false. Place a (T) in the parentheses before each true statement and an (F) before each false statement.

1. ( ) Interest that a taxpayer receives from ownership of a Canada Savings bond is tax-free income.

2. ( ) When the taxpayer calculates taxable income, he/she may deduct the larger of the standard deduction or itemized deductions to arrive at this figure.

3. ( ) A sole proprietorship is not a taxable entity.

4. ( ) Jeff is 10 years old and has been living with his neighbors, the Floyds, since February 1989. The Floyds provide all of Jeff's support since he does not have any income. The Floyds can claim Jeff as a dependent on their 1989 income tax return.

5. ( ) If an individual's taxable income is large enough, the 1988 federal tax rate is 29%.

6. ( ) Corporations may deduct both dividend payments to its shareholders and interest payments to its bondholders.

7. ( ) The different treatment of dividends for tax purposes and financial reporting purposes results in a permanent difference between taxable income and income before taxes.

Problem II

You are given several words, phrases or numbers to choose from in completing each of the following statements or in answering the following questions. In each case select the one that best completes the statement or answers the question and place its letter in the answer space provided.

_____ 1. For a taxpayer whose income from other sources amounts to $40,000, an additional income of $5,000 would cause the smallest increase in federal income tax liability if the $5,000 was received in the form of:

    a. salary.
    b. dividends on common stock investments.
    c. capital gains (the $100,000 exemption has not been used).
    d. interest on bonds.
    e. there is no difference in the above.

_____ 2. Lorico, a Canadian Corporation, had $25,000 income from its own operations in 1989. The company also received $1,000 of dividends from domestic corporations, none in which they have a greater than 5% ownership interest. Lorico also had a $5,000 capital gain and an $8,000 capital loss in 1989. What is Lorico's taxable income?

    a. $26,000.
    b. $31,000.
    c. $22,000.
    d. $25,000.
    e. $21,000.

3. Q, a freshman at University, received the following amounts in 1989: $25 interest on a savings account, a $4,000 salary, $250 tips from a part-time job as a waiter, a $1,000 scholarship from the University (which covered tuition and fees only), a gift from his grandmother of $500, and $100 of dividends from domestic corporations. What is Q's gross income according to federal tax laws?

   a. $5,825.
   b. $4,775.
   c. $4,250.
   d. $4,300.
   e. $4,900.

Problem III

Many of the important ideas and concepts discussed in Chapter 28 are reflected in the following list of key terms. Test your understanding of these terms by matching the appropriate definitions with the terms. Record the number identifying the most appropriate definition in the blank space next to each term.

_____ Basis   _____ Marginal tax rate

_____ Capital cost allowance   _____ Recaptured CCA

_____ Capital cost allowance rate   _____ Tax avoidance

_____ Capital gain or loss   _____ Tax credit

_____ Capital or depreciable asset   _____ Tax evasion

_____ Future income taxes payable   _____ Tax planning

_____ Gross income   _____ Taxable income

_____ Income tax act and regulations

1. Gross income minus ordinary and necessary expenses of carrying on a business, trade, or profession, or in the case of an employee, gross income minus allowable deductions and exemptions.

2. Dependent on class into which the depreciable asset falls into.

3. The difference between the proceeds from the sale of a capital asset and the basis of the asset.

4. Statutes pertaining to the taxation of income.

5. The fraudulent denial and concealment of an existing liability.

6. A unique, accelerated depreciation method prescribed in the tax law for depreciable assets used to generate revenue.

7. Any item of property which is subject to depreciation and falls into a class defined by the regulations of the tax act.

8. The difference between the income tax expense in the financial statements and the income taxes payable according to tax law, resulting from financial accounting and tax accounting timing differences with respect to expense or revenue recognition.

9. An amount realized on sale of a capital asset that falls between the book value and cost of the asset.

10. All income from whatever source derived, unless expressly excluded from taxation by law.

11. Planning the affairs of a taxpayer in such a way as to incur the smallest possible tax liability.

12. A direct, dollar for dollar, reduction in the amount of tax liability.

13. The rate that applies to the next dollar of income to be earned.

14. A legal means of preventing a tax liability from coming into existence.

15. In general, the cost of a purchased asset less any depreciation previously allowed or allowable for tax purposes.

Problem IV

Complete the following by filling in the blanks.

1. A corporation with $10,000 of capital gains in excess of capital losses in 1988 may deduct _____ of the gain and include _____ for tax purposes.

2. A business organized as a corporation must file a tax return and pay taxes on its taxable income. Also, if it pays out some of its "after-tax income" as dividends, its shareholders must report these dividends as _____ on their tax returns. Because of this, it is commonly claimed that corporation income is taxed _____.

3. All income from whatever source derived, unless expressly excluded by law, is _____ income.

4. Federal income tax rates for individuals are progressive in nature. By this is meant _____ _____.

5. Tax planners try to cause an individual's income to emerge in the form of capital gains rather than as ordinary income because _____ _____ _____.

6. A business executive _____ (will, will not) always be better off taxwise with his or her business organized as a corporation instead of a single proprietorship.

7. It is often advantageous for the owner of an incorporated business to have the business forgo the payment of dividends and to take these dividends later in the form of _____ upon the sale of the business.

8. The CICA Handbook recommends that income taxes should be allocated and reported on a concern's income statements in such a manner that any distortions resulting from _____ are removed from the statements.

9. Net income and taxable income commonly differ because net income is determined by the application of _____, while tax _____ are used in determining taxable income, and the two differ on some points.

10. A one-dollar reduction in income tax expense is commonly worth approximately a _____ reduction in any other expense.

11. To do tax planning, a taxpayer must be aware of the alternative choices available under the tax laws and select those that will result in the _____.

12. Good tax planning prevents a tax liability from _____ _____. It is legal and desirable and results in tax _____ _____.

13. The fraudulent denial and concealment of an existing tax liability is called tax _____ _____ and is illegal.

14. A business organized as a single proprietorship or a partnership is not required to pay income taxes; rather the income of such a business is taxed as _____ _____.

15. The answers to two questions are required in determining whether an item should be included or excluded from gross income for tax purposes. The questions are: _____ _____ _____.

Solutions for Chapter 28

Problem I

1. F	5. T	
2. F	6. F	
3. T	7. T	
4. F		

Problem II

1. C
2. D
3. E

Problem III

Basis	15	Marginal tax rate	13
Capital asset	7	Recaptured CCA	9
Capital cost allowance	6	Tax avoidance	14
Capital cost allowance rate	2	Tax credit	12
Capital gain or loss	3	Tax evasion	5
Future income taxes payable	8	Tax planning	11
Gross income	10	Taxable income	1
Income tax act and regulations	4		

Problem IV

1. $\frac{1}{3}$, $\frac{2}{3}$
2. ordinary income, twice.
3. taxable
4. that each additional bracket of taxable income is taxed at a higher rate.
5. capital gains are taxed at a rate that is less than that which applies to ordinary income.
6. will not
7. capital gains
8. timing differences
9. generally accepted accounting principles, laws
10. two-dollar
11. lowest possible tax
12. coming into existence, avoidance.
13. evasion
14. the individual income of the proprietor or partners
15. Is the item income? Is it expressly excluded by law?

Appendix G
Present and Future Values: An Expansion

After studying Appendix G, you should be able to:

1. Explain what is meant by the present value of a single amount and the present value of an annuity, and be able to use tables to solve problems that involve present value.

2. Explain what is meant by the future value of a single amount and the future value of an annuity, and be able to use tables to solve problems that involve future values.

Topical Outline

I. Present value of a single amount

    A. The amount that could be invested at a specific interest rate to generate a fund equal to a given amount at a definite future date.

    B. A table of present values for a single amount shows all of the present values of $1, given a variety of different interest rates and a variety of different numbers of time periods that will lapse before the $1 is received.

II. Present value of an annuity

    A. An annuity is a series of payments that are equal in amount and that are to be received or paid on a regular periodic basis.

    B. Present value of an annuity is the amount that could be invested at a specific interest rate to generate a fund that would be exhausted by a series of payments of a given amount for a given number of periods.

    C. A table of present values for an annuity shows all of the present values of different annuities where the amount of each payment is $1 but where the payments occur over different numbers of periods and a variety of different interest rates are assumed.

III. Future value of a single amount

    A. The amount that would be generated at a definite future date if a given present value were invested at a specific interest rate for a given number of periods.

    B. A table of future values of a single amount shows all of the future values of $1 invested now at a variety of different interest rates for a variety of different time periods.

IV. Future value of an annuity

    A. Future value of an annuity is the amount that would be generated at a given future time if a given series of payments were invested periodically at a given interest rate.

    B. A table of future values for an annuity shows all of the future values of different annuities where the amount of each payment is $1 but where the payments occur different numbers of periods and a variety of different interest rates are assumed.

Problem I

The following statements are either true or false. Place a (T) in the parentheses before each true statement and an (F) before each false statement.

1. ( ) In discounting, if interest is compounded semiannually, the number of periods must be expressed in terms of six-month periods.

2. ( ) One way to calculate the present value of an annuity is to calculate the present value of each payment and add them together.

3. ( ) A table for the future values of $1 can be used to solve all of the problems that can be solved using a table for the present values of $1.

4. ( ) Erlich Enterprises should be willing to invest $100,000 in an investment that will return $20,000 annually for 10 years if the company requires a 16% return on its investments. (Use the tables in your text to get your answer.)

Problem II

You are given several words, phrases or numbers to choose from in completing each of the following statements or in answering the following questions. In each case select the one that best completes the statement or answers the question and place its letter in the answer space provided. Use the tables in your text as necessary to answer the questions.

_____ 1. Ralph Norton just began a retirement plan whereby $300 is deducted from his monthly paycheck and deposited in a retirement fund which earns an annual interest rate of 12%. If Ralph continues with this plan until his retirement in four years, how much will be accumulated in the account on the date of the last deposit? (Round to the nearest whole dollar.)

     a. $ 14,400.
     b. $ 17,205.
     c. $ 18,367.
     d. $220,401.
     e. $573,477.

_____ 2. Maxwell Hammer is going to establish a fund for a future business venture. He makes an initial investment of $15,000 and plans to make semiannual contributions of $2,500 to the fund beginning in six months. The fund is expected to earn an annual interest rate of 8%, compounded semiannually. What will be the value of the fund five years hence, when Mr. Hammer plans to use the funds?

     a. $ 68,600.
     b. $ 36,706.
     c. $210,106.
     d. $ 45,015.
     e. $102,665.

_____ 3. Tricorp Investment Company is considering an investment which is expected to return $320,000, four years after the initial investment. If Tricorp demands a 14% return, what is the most Tricorp will be willing to pay for this investment?

     a. $320,000.
     b. $109,826.
     c. $189,472.
     d. $ 65,026.
     e. $275,200.

_____ 4. Tom Snap has been offered the possibility of investing $0.3756 for fourteen years, after which he will be paid $3. What annual rate of interest will Mr. Snap earn?

    a.   8.0%
    b.   10.0%
    c.   12.0%
    d.   14.0%
    e.   16.0%

Problem III

Sarah Blue has the option of receiving $1,000 per year for the next ten years, or receiving $6,000 in cash immediately, or receiving $10,000 in cash five years hence. Assuming that Ms. Blue's only goal is to maximize her wealth, and that the current interest rate is 10%, which option should she choose?

Problem IV

Complete the following by filling in the blanks. Refer to the tables in Appendix G in the text to find the answers.

1. Leila Turner expects to invest $2 at an 18% annual rate of interest and, at the end of the investment, receive

   $39.3466. Ms. Turner must wait _____ years before she receives payment.

2. Jim Ables expects to invest $1 for 37 years, after which he will receive $66.2318. Mr. Ables will earn interest

   at a rate of _____% on his investment.

3. Mr. Biter expects an immediate investment of $10.6748 to return $1 annually for 25 years, the first payment

   to be received in one year. Mr. Biter will earn interest at a rate of _____% on his investment.

Solutions for Appendix G

Problem I

1. T
2. T
3. T
4. F

Problem II

1. C
2. A
3. C
4. E

Problem III

The present value of $1,000 received annually for ten years discounted at 10% equals $6,144.60. The present value of $6,000 received now is $6,000. The present value of $10,000 to be received five years from now is $6,209. Therefore, Ms. Blue should choose to receive $10,000 five years from now.

Problem IV

1. 18. In Table G-2, where the interest rate per period = 18% and present value = 19.6733 ($39.3466/2), number of periods = 18.

2. 12. In Table G-2, where the number of periods = 37 and the future value = 66.2318, the interest rate = 12%.

3. 8. In Table G-3, where the number of periods = 25 and the present value = 10.6748, the interest rate = 8%.

Appendix H
The Accounting Problem of Changing Prices

After studying Appendix H, you should be able to:

1. Explain why conventional financial statements fail to adequately account for price changes.

2. Explain how price changes should be measured and how to construct a price index.

3. Restate historical cost/nominal dollar costs into constant purchasing power amounts and calculate purchasing power gains and losses.

4. Explain the difference between current costs and historical costs stated in constant purchasing power amounts.

5. Define or explain the words and phrases listed in the appendix Glossary.

Topical Outline

I. Conventional financial statements and price changes

    A. Balance sheet amounts are stated in nominal dollars and fail to show the effects of price changes.

    B. Expenses that are allocations of costs recorded in earlier periods are not stated in terms of current dollars.

II. Measuring the change in prices with price indexes

    A. A price index measures the weighted-average changes in the prices of a particular market basket of goods and/or services.

    B. Specific price indexes measure price changes of a narrow group of products; general price indexes measure price changes of a very broad group of products, or general purchasing power.

    C. General indexes are used to restate dollar amounts of cost paid in one period into dollars with the purchasing power of another period.

III. Historical cost/constant purchasing power accounting

    A. Uses a general price index to restate historical cost/nominal dollar statements into historical cost dollar amounts that represent current, general purchasing power.

    B. Procedures involve:

        1. Calculating general purchasing power gain or loss from owning monetary assets or owing monetary liabilities.

        2. Adjusting nonmonetary items for price changes since the items were first purchased.

    C. Does not reflect current values.

IV. Current cost accounting

    A. Uses specific price indexes and other estimates to report current costs in financial statements.

    B. Only nonmonetary items must be adjusted for specific price changes.

V. Disclosing the effects of price changes

    A. Disclosures are not required, but the CICA recommends that several items of information be disclosed.

    B. Recommended disclosures on a current cost basis include: cost of goods sold and depreciation, depletion and amortization of property plant and equipment; current and deferred amounts of income tax expense; income after reflecting these items; the amount of changes in inventories and property, plant and equipment, as well as their carrying values.

Problem I

The following statements are either true or false. Place a (T) in the parentheses before each true statement and an (F) before each false statement.

1. ( ) In conventional accounting, transactions are recorded in terms of the historical number of dollars received or paid.

2. ( ) If in 1985, the base year of a price index, a market basket of goods has a cost of $8, and in 1990, the same market basket of goods costs $9.50, the price index for 1985 is 84.2.

3. ( ) In 1987, $400 was paid to purchase items A and B when the price index for A and B was 105. In 1990, the price index for items A and B was 125. Therefore, it would take $476 to purchase items A and B in 1990.

4. ( ) Historical cost/constant purchasing power accounting uses a general price index to restate the conventional nominal dollar financial statements.

5. ( ) An investment in bonds is an example of a nonmonetary asset.

6. ( ) Monetary assets are adjusted for general price-level changes on a historical cost/constant purchasing power financial statement to reflect changes in the price level that occurred since the assets were acquired.

Problem II

You are given several words, phrases or numbers to choose from in completing each of the following statements or in answering the following questions. In each case select the one that best completes the statement or answers the question and place its letter in the answer space provided.

_____ 1. Current cost accounting:

    a. is based on the conclusion that current liquidation price is the appropriate valuation basis for financial statements.

    b. matches with current revenues the current costs to replace the resources consumed to earn the revenues.

    c. for inventories, productive capacity, cost of sales, and depreciation is required of all Canadian companies.

    d. has become the primary valuation basis for published financial statements of Canadian companies.

    e. None of the above.

_____ 2. A nonmonetary asset was purchased for $25,000 when the general price index was 125. Five years later, when the general price index was 175, the undepreciated amount that should be shown for the asset on a historical cost/constant purchasing power balance sheet is:

    a. $17,857.
    b. $25,000.
    c. $31,250.
    d. $35,000.
    e. $43,750.

_____ 3. The cost of purchasing a given market basket is as follows:

Year   Price
1990 $25.50
1991   30.00
1992   33.60
1993   36.00
Using 1991 as the base year, the price index for 1992 is:

a.   85.0
b.   89.3
c.   100.0
d.   112.0
e.   120.0

_____ 4. The price index for 1990 was 112. Prices increased 25% by 1993. The price index for 1993 is:

a.   80.
b.   100.
c.   125.
d.   137.
e.   140.

_____ 5. In preparing a historical cost/constant purchasing power balance sheet, which of the following categories must be adjusted from nominal dollar amounts to historical cost/constant purchasing power amounts?

a.   Monetary assets.
b.   Nonmonetary assets.
c.   Monetary liabilities.
d.   All assets.
e.   All liabilities and equities.

Problem III

Many of the important ideas and concepts discussed in Appendix H are reflected in the following list of key terms. Test your understanding of these terms by matching the appropriate definitions with the terms. Record the number identifying the most appropriate definition in the blank space next to each term.

_____ Current cost

_____ Current cost accounting

_____ Deflation

_____ General price-level index

_____ Historical cost/constant purchasing power accounting

_____ Historical cost/nominal dollar financial statements

_____ Inflation

_____ Monetary assets

_____ Monetary liabilities

_____ Nonmonetary assets

_____ Nonmonetary liabilities

_____ Price index

_____ Purchasing power gain or loss

_____ Specific price-level index

1. An accounting system that adjusts historical cost/nominal dollar financial statements for changes in the general purchasing power of the dollar.

2. Assets that are not claims to a fixed number of monetary units, the prices of which therefore tend to fluctuate with changes in the general price level.

3. A general increase in the prices paid for goods and services.

4. In general, the cost that would be required to acquire (or replace) an asset or service at the present time; on the income statement, the numbers of dollars that would be required, at the time the expense is incurred, to acquire the resources consumed; on the balance sheet, the amounts that would have to be paid to replace the assets or satisfy the liabilities as of the balance sheet date.

5. A measure of the changes in prices of a particular market basket of goods and/or services.

6. Conventional financial statements that disclose revenues, expenses, assets, liabilities, and owners' equity in terms of the historical monetary units exchanged at the time the transactions occurred.

7. Fixed amounts that are owed, where the number of dollars to be paid does not change regardless of changes in the general price level.

8. Obligations that are not fixed in terms of the number of monetary units needed to satisfy them, and that therefore tend to fluctuate in amount with changes in the general price level.

9. An accounting system that uses specific price-level indexes (and other means) to develop financial statements that report items such as assets and expenses in terms of the costs to acquire or replace those assets or services at the present time.

10. The gain or loss that results from holding monetary assets and/or owing monetary liabilities during a period in which the general price level changes.

11. A measure of the changing purchasing power of a dollar, spent for a very broad range of items; for example, the Consumer Price Index for All Urban Consumers.

12. Money or claims to receive a fixed amount of money, where the number of dollars to be received does not change regardless of changes in the purchasing power of the dollar.

13. An indicator of the changing purchasing power of a dollar spent for items in a category of items that includes a much narrower range of goods and services than does a general price index.

14. A general decrease in the prices paid for goods and services.

Problem IV

Complete the following by filling in the blanks.

1. If a simple average of the unit prices of several items is calculated for each of two years, a comparison of the averages will indicate the impact of the price changes on most purchasers of those items only if _____

_____.

2. Historical cost/constant dollar accounting is sometimes criticized as being an inadequate response to the problem of changing prices because it does not present _____ in financial statements.

3. The two primary alternatives to conventional accounting that make comprehensive adjustments for the effects of price changes are _____ and _____.

4. _____ represent money or claims to receive a fixed amount of money with the number of dollars to be received not changing regardless of changes in the purchasing power of the dollar.

5. If the general price index was 115 in 1988 and was 138 in 1992, it would be appropriate to say that the _____ had fallen by _____% from 1988 to 1992.

6. The basic reason why conventional financial statements fail to adequately account for inflation is _____
   _____
   _____
   _____
   _____.

7. _____ is the method of accounting that makes adjustments for specific price changes in nonmonetary assets and liabilities.

8. A _____ measures the relative costs of purchasing a given market basket of items in each of several years or time periods.

Problem V

A product that originally cost $20,000 was later sold for $30,000. At the time of sale, the cost to replace the product was $25,500. Also, the general price index rose from 92 at the time of purchase to 115 at the time of sale. Determine the gross profit from sales assuming (1) historical cost/nominal dollar financial statements; (2) historical cost/constant purchasing power accounting; and (3) current cost accounting.

	Historical Cost/ Nominal Dollar Statements	Historical Cost/ Constant Purchasing Power Accounting	Current Cost Accounting
Sales			
Cost of sales:			
Gross profit			

Problem VI

A company's Cash account showed the following activity and balances during the year:

Balance, January 1	$ 52,000
Receipts from sales	475,000
Payments of expenses	(400,000)
Payment of dividend, December 28	(50,000)
Balance, December 31	$ 77,000

Cash receipts from sales and disbursements for expenses occurred uniformly throughout the year. The general price index during the year was:

January	120
Average during the year	125
December	138

Calculate the purchasing power gain or loss from holding cash during the year.

	Historical Cost/ Nominal Dollar Amounts	Restatement Factor from Price Index	Restated to December 31	Gain or Loss
Balance, January 1	$ 52,000			
Receipts from sales	475,000			
Payments of expenses	(400,000)			
Payment of dividend	(50,000)			
Ending balance, adjusted				
Ending balance, actual	$ 77,000			
Purchasing power gain (loss)				

461

Solutions for Appendix H

Problem I

1. T
2. F
3. T
4. T
5. F
6. F

Problem II

1. B
2. D
3. D
4. E
5. B

Problem III

Current cost	4	Inflation	3
Current cost accounting	9	Monetary assets	12
Deflation	14	Monetary liabilities	7
General price-level index	11	Nonmonetary assets	2
Historical cost/constant purchasing power accounting	1	Nonmonetary liabilities	8
		Price index	5
Historical cost/nominal dollar financial statements	6	Purchasing power gain or loss	10
		Specific price-level index	13

Problem IV

1. those purchasers typically buy an equal number of units of each item

2. current values

3. historical cost/constant purchasing power accounting, current cost accounting

4. Monetary assets

5. purchasing power of the dollar, 16.7

6. that transactions are recorded in terms of the historical number of dollars paid, and these amounts are not adjusted even though subsequent changes in prices may dramatically change the value of the items purchased

7. Current cost accounting

8. price index

Problem V

	Historical Cost/ Nominal Dollar Amounts	Historical Cost/ Constant Purchasing Power Accounting	Current Cost Accounting
Sales	$30,000	$30,000	$30,000
Cost of sales:	20,000		
$20,000 × (115/92)		25,000	
			25,500
Gross profit	$10,000	$ 5,000	$ 4,500

462

Problem VI

	Historical Cost/ Nominal Dollar Amounts	Restatement Factor from Price Index	Restated to December 31	Gain or Loss
Balance, January 1	$ 52,000	138/120	$ 59,800	
Receipts from sales	475,000	138/125	524,400	
Payments of expenses	(400,000)	138/125	(441,600)	
Payment of dividend	(50,000)	138/138	(50,000)	
Ending balance, adjusted			$ 92,600	
Ending balance, actual	$ 77,000		(77,000)	
Purchasing power gain (loss)				$15,600